120 Jobs That Won't Chain You to Your Desk

The Princeton Review

120 Jobs That Won't Chain You to Your Desk

By the Staff of The Princeton Review

Random House, Inc.
New York
PrincetonReview.com

The Princeton Review, Inc.
2315 Broadway
New York, NY 10024
E-mail: bookeditor@review.com

ISBN 978-0-375-76598-8

Publisher: Robert Franek
Editor: Adrinda Kelly
Designer and Production Manager: Scott Harris
Production Editor: Christine LaRubio
Illustrator: Andrew Baker

Printed in the United States of America.

9 8 7 6 5 4 3 2 1

2008 Edition

ACKNOWLEDGMENTS

This book would not have been possible without the contributions of several members of the Book Publishing team here at The Princeton Review. Robert Franek lent his support and expertise to the development of this book; Christine LaRubio and Scott Harris transformed the raw manuscript into the book now in your hands; Suzanne Podhurst and Adam Davis merit special thanks for the valuable input they provided along the way.

I must thank Lisa Marie Rovito, Chris Maier, Maya Payne Smart, and Otilia Mirambeaux, all excellent writers whose talents helped make this book come to life. A very special thanks also goes to Andrea Kornstein, who wore many hats throughout the development of this project.

Finally there is no way you would be holding this book right now if it were not for the generous participation of the numerous folks interviewed within its pages. Although I can't name them all here, I owe each one many thanks.

—Adrinda Kelly

TABLE OF CONTENTS

INTRODUCTION

YOU FOUND THIS BOOK FOR A REASON

Sitting behind a desk was never a place at which you felt comfortable. In grade school, you were the first one out the door at recess and the last to come in when it was over. In middle school, you always chose the desk near a window and lived for gym class, art class, field trips—anything to break the monotony of sitting still in that plastic chair. In high school, you chose to curl up in an armchair to study your notes or sprawl beneath a big shady oak tree to get your reading done instead of spreading your notes across the desk in your room.

Does this sound familiar? If so (and it must, since you've picked up this book), you've spent years squirming and fidgeting behind desks—in class, at home, even at that internship you completed last summer. You've watched your parents suit up in the mornings, get in the car, and drive to an office where they spent the day behind their desks—with no gym class, art class, or free period to break up the routine. Now that you're about to graduate college and you've begun to give some serious thought to your career choices, you can't help but wonder how you'll ever survive in the real world, *behind* one of those desks. The image of cubicles with each employee working away in his or her own box for eight-plus hours a day makes you cringe. You don't know what you want to do for the rest of your life, but you do know that you'll do anything but *that*.

This book is for people like you. There are a ton of great career books out there that will tell you how to become a doctor or a lawyer, how to work your way up the corporate ladder, even how to make your mark in academia. This book is different; it is dedicated to telling you about "the road less traveled" careers, the ones you don't often hear about or perhaps never even knew existed. The careers in this book run the gamut, but together they speak to the pilgrim, the thrill seeker, or the artist in you. They show you where your vivaciousness and charm will be a professional advantage, and how you can make a living working with your hands. Whether you want to work outdoors or are simply looking for an office job that won't chain you to you desk, we made sure to include something in this book for you.

Most of the careers in this book have a less straightforward path for those looking to break in than do traditional careers. You might need to get special certifications, additional training, or more hands-on experience to enter these fields. You'll definitely need to be more assertive and take more risks—it's absolutely going to take more than a classy degree from a fancy school. To break into these professions, you'll need to put yourself out there, prove yourself, and want it more than the next person. However, the payoff is high. These careers call for people who march to the beat of their own drum.

Call them creative, alternative, nontraditional, or what have you; these careers are some of the most exciting to be had. For people who are willing to work hard to get them, they can be extremely fulfilling. Many require long hours and pay little—especially in the first few years (or even decades) within the industry. However, the rewards are those of the heart, the mind, and the creative spirit, and they pay out in huge dividends.

DESK JOBS MAKE ME YAWN

Don't get us wrong. There are many fulfilling desk jobs out there. Where do you think the writers and editors of this book were sitting when they put together these profiles? Even a fair number of the careers listed in this book require at least an occasional check-in at the office (although we promise it won't mean being chained to a desk). It's not so bad to have a desk job, as long as that suits your personality. Shows like *The Office*, movies like *Office Space*, and even books like *American Psycho* have turned the office into a taboo place at which to work. They tend to depict characters who have mundane workloads, tedious conversations, and unbearably dull coworkers who are best described by the clichés of the desk-job universe. Certainly, each job—traditional or otherwise—has its own cast of characters, and characteristics that will be more interesting than others. The desk itself is not an evil thing—it all depends on what you do there. If getting away from a desk were your only criteria for a job, you would be as happy as an air force ranger, chef, or news correspondent as you would be directing traffic or driving a bus. As you page through this book, forget the whole desk or no desk aspect for the time being and concentrate on whether you would find each profession a challenging, rewarding, and meaningful way to spend your time.

My Parents Want to Choose My Career

What defines a meaningful career in your eyes might not be what your parents have in mind for you. This conflict starts to become particularly tricky if they are helping to pay for your higher education. They may argue that because they are funding your education, they ought to have a say in how their dollars are spent. If you are pulling for a major in dance, and they picture you using your science skills for a major in chemistry, well . . . you have to make a serious choice. Having a heart-to-heart talk with your parents will help all of you gain a better understanding of each other's points of view. Talking things out with a third party might also help. If you are very serious about the dance world, your dance teacher may be able to give your parents some insight into your potential for making it on a professional level. Gather as many facts as you can. No decision should be made rashly. If you think you can make it, could handle the lifestyle, and love it enough, find a way to make that dream a reality.

Helicopter Parents: How to Deal

It's a bird! It's a plane! It's Mom and Dad, perennially hovering over your life and passive-aggressively attempting to control your every move. No matter where you go to seek refuge from your parents' anxious attention they always seem to find a way to heap their unsolicited advice or demands on you. This can be especially frustrating when it comes to choosing a major and a future career path. Students who are pursuing careers or majors that may seem risky in terms of financial outlook are particularly vulnerable to tidal waves of parental neuroses. This phenomenon may sometimes manifest itself in the form of gentle or not so gentle directives ranging from "We're not sure that being a Theater major is the best choice for you" to "If you major in Theater, we'll stop paying tuition." The helicopter school of parenting has always existed, but has recently experienced a renaissance. Why? Parents have grown accustomed to carting their children from soccer practice to capoeira lessons, academic decathlons to dance recitals; all in the name of securing a coveted position at one of the world's greatest universities and securing a great job after graduation. Needless to say, your parents' handholding habit is a hard one to break. Not to mention that with ever-increasing tuition fees, seeing Joe Jr. make the best use of his college education has become a major financial investment. Don't despair; there are some tried and true techniques for assuaging parental anxieties while happily pursuing your vocational dreams:

1. **Acknowledge that your parents have your best interests in mind.**
   Most parents are surprised by the notion that their well-intentioned comments have an adverse effect on your mental health. Before presenting any other arguments to them, make sure that you preface your statements with, "I realize that you care very much for me" or "I know that you want what's best for me." This sets a nice tone for any discussion; it'll appear that you care about being collaborative, and that you are also giving them the benefit of the doubt.

2. **Avoid getting emotional.**
   Nothing will sabotage a well-constructed speech faster than an emotional outburst. Whether this takes the form of door-slamming and stomping, tears and pleading, or silly proclamations such as "I am *too* the boss of me," any display that is driven more by pathos than logos will likely convince your parents that you are, in fact, too young and immature to make decisions for yourself. The more well prepared you are to present your argument, the less likely you are to lose your cool.

3. **Stick with just the facts.**
   Because parents are most often concerned about the practicality of your choices, take the initiative by presenting them with facts and figures that support your point. For example, if you plan to pursue a career in broadcasting, check your college career center's website for any statistics about graduating students or alumni in that major.

If there are several students who are employed in broadcasting, cite those examples. Visit trade websites and print out information on internship opportunities and entry-level positions. If your parents aren't aware of the ins and outs of a particular profession, such literature can help keep doubts and concerns at bay. Remember to choose facts that don't backfire on you! Salary range information can be particularly alarming, as most entry-level positions in nearly *any* industry aren't terribly impressive.

4. **Offer them a roadmap.**
Sure, you don't know *exactly* what you'll be doing in a month, let alone two semesters from now. But by committing some goals to paper you'll be able to show your parents that you have considered the various options available to you, and how your future goals build on immediate goals, eventually bringing you to a satisfying outcome. This exercise of setting short and long-term goals is positive both for you and the well-intentioned parental units who love and worry about you.

5. **Invite them to participate.**
If your parents find themselves worrying excessively about the ramifications of your choices, invite them to join you during a visit to your college career center. Nearly every career counselor is open to family appointments, and this gesture will show them that you not only appreciate their input, you welcome their active participation in your life. Career counselors can be particularly helpful at mediating parent/caretaker/student disputes about career choices, especially when it comes to generating alternative options that will satisfy all parties.

I Just Graduated—Now What?

It's perfectly fine (in fact, it is absolutely normal) not to know what you want to do with your life at this moment in time. You have just spent several intense years in the world of academia—which is a pretty surreal place all its own. Now you're thrown from that frying pan and into the fires of the real world. It might have you wanting to scream, "Hey, somebody, *help* me!"

Go ahead and scream if you want. It might feel good. We can all but guarantee that the majority of working people—even those who now adore their careers—felt a wave of helplessness wash over them around graduation time. (And it doesn't help that everyone wants to know what your plans are for the future.)

You have a few options. First, you can take a break to think it over. This is an attractive short-term option. In many cases, however, while it may sound like a good idea at the outset, it can end up backfiring when you slide deeper into uncertainty at the sight of all of your friends moving into the next phases of their lives while you sit at home with the Xbox. Instead, consider applying for jobs. Lots of jobs. Naturally, your chances of getting interviews increases with the number of jobs to which you apply. So what if you're not sure of what you want to do. You never know where you'll find something that will give you a major clue. It might happen while you're reading a job description on an online job board or during an interview for a job you didn't think would interest you.

I Hate My Desk Job and Want to Start Over. Is It Too Late?

No way. It's never too late to change careers. Before you tackle the major life overhaul that often comes with a career change, however, consider why you're unhappy in your current job. Your situation can be likened to the dilemma of a freshman who wants to transfer colleges halfway through his or her first year. Is that student unhappy with the school or having a tough time with college life in general? In your case, is it the career or the specific job that's got you on the hunt? Is there a related career that might interest you? Perhaps you're bored, burned out, or uninspired by the monotony of a job you've been in for several years. A new job at a different company might do the trick. A long vacation might even go a long way toward reinvigorating you. Or if the problem is that your present employer doesn't offer room for growth, maybe another employer will. It's important to look close to home before you leap into the unknown.

There are many people who spend the day staring out the windows of their offices (if they even have windows, or offices for that matter) wishing they could ditch the desk and do something more active, exciting, or meaningful. Will the reality live up to the fantasy? We know someone who worked as a magazine editor who thought she wanted a new life. She left her job and tried many new things. She enrolled in baking school and worked at a bakery. After that, she worked at a children's adventure camp, did research for a university, and wrote travel articles for a website. She even looked into a class in hotel management. A year later, none of these avenues had sparked her interest for the long-term in the way she had imagined they might. She realized she had been a capable editor who had been stuck at a company that wasn't a good fit for her. She updated her resume, started a new job search, and returned to publishing. It turns out she needed a breather and a new job with new challenges—not a full-blown career makeover.

Could this be you? It is easy to romanticize other careers, especially when you've convinced yourself that the grass is greener—that is, until you get to the other side and find out every job in every field has its own troubles. Some companies allow employees to arrange a one-time period of unpaid extended time off. If you can afford it, this time away could help you reflect and regroup. Even if you don't have that luxury, start talking to friends about what they do and what they see you doing. Some surprisingly interesting observations may emerge from people you know well—and even from those who don't know you as well. Scour books like this one and go online to learn about other careers. Set out on some informational interviews to learn about career paths that might suit you better than your current one.

Obviously, a career change needs to be a meaningful one. The new career—even if it means starting over at the bottom of the totem pole—has to strike an inner chord that your present one can't. If you've tried to fill in that void with hobbies and other changes to no avail, your career could be the culprit.

There's no need to quit your job outright to forge a new path for yourself. In the wake of your decision, you can start actively investigating new career options and redesigning your resume to make yourself marketable in another field. Whether you enroll in continuing education courses, participate in weekend workshops, attend career revamp lectures, enroll in school part-time, or take the plunge and apply to grad school, the options for transferring your current experience to another field come in all forms, and require time, energy, and financial commitments. Once you're serious about making a move, you may want to consider meeting with a career counselor. They don't come cheap, but these professionals are highly skilled at reshaping a resume and giving it a new spin to help you land work in a new field. They may also have some good advice on ways to vamp up your experience and how to put your best foot forward during the interview process.

So You' re Ready to Choose a (New) Career . . .

What's most important in choosing a career is not whether it's a desk job or career on the go, but whether it's a good fit for you. You'll have to know yourself and know your options to make a good match between the two. This book aims to help you expand your options by presenting a more unusual set of career choices from which you might choose. When the time comes to make a decision, you'll have a more informed idea of what you would like to do day-to-day—at a desk or otherwise.

Ideally, you will have the chance to experience different types of careers—whether through internships, volunteer work, or extracurricular activities—before you make that initial commitment. A part-time job, a day spent job shadowing, or just an informational interview can all help you get a quick glimpse into the day-to-day life of potential long-term jobs that might appeal to you. This is so important that we've devoted a large piece of each of the career profiles in this book to divulging that very information. Before we get ahead of ourselves, let's spend some time talking about how you should go about figuring out what you might like to do in the first place.

Four Things You Should Know About Choosing a Career

A career can sprout from almost anything: a hobby, an interest, a talent, or a conviction. Ask 50 people how they knew what they wanted to do for a living and you'll get 50 different answers. There's no magic formula for choosing a career path. On the upside, that leaves your own personal path open to all possibilities. Anything that makes you who you are could be a component of your future career choice. On the downside, it can be overwhelming to have to determine what you want to do out of thousands of choices. Even after you decide on a career path, it can be frustrating to figure out how to reach that goal. Before you let the whole process throw you into a panic, you should understand the following:

- **If you don't know what you want to do, start with what you do know: You.**
  That's easy enough, right? Nobody knows better than you what your current interests, skills, values, and personal style are—all of which are the makings of a choice about the work you might like to pursue. When you start thinking about a career to pursue there's no better place to begin.

- **There is no wrong career choice if you're truly passionate about it.**
  It's important not to become paralyzed by fear and self-doubt when it comes to finding a career that will make you happy. It's easy to have thoughts like, "I'm not good enough to do that," "I don't have any connections in that field that could get me in," or "My friends and family will think it's a silly choice." You are good enough, you can meet people and go places and gain experience that will help you get your foot in the door, and there's nothing silly about a particular career you find attractive. There have been plenty of parents who told their kids they couldn't make a living playing sports or doing magic tricks or that they weren't in a position to make it to Broadway or on the big screen. Likewise, there have been plenty of children who bravely (and respectfully) proved their parents wrong. Don't let anyone talk you into or out of a career.

- **A single career can provide many different ways of getting your foot in the door.**
  Deciding on a career can sometimes be easier than actually figuring out a way to break in. Take heart—some people shoot straight into a career, while others take the long way around. If there is a career that speaks to you, you can find a way to make it happen one way or another.

- **Just because you settle on a career doesn't mean you can't change your mind later and try another one (or two or three . . .).**
  Gone are the days of taking the first job that comes your way, working like a dog for 35 years in the same place of employment, and retiring at 65 with a pension. The website JobBankUSA.com reports that most Americans switch careers three times during their lives. According to the website of the career counseling firm Career Transitions, "studies show the average working American will have three to five careers and between 10 to 12 jobs during his or her lifetime." Apparently it depends on whom you ask, but the consensus is that your first career is highly unlikely to be your last. As more people shuffle around to find career choices that best suit them at different stages of their lives, the more open employers will be considering career changers on their lists of qualified job applicants.

If you love it now, you might love it for a lifetime (or a long time)

Everything that is important to you right now is a potential clue to what might satisfy you for years to come. That said, while it's important to think about the big picture, it's equally important not to obsess over it. Some people have known all their lives that they wanted to be in show business or on the police force or working with animals. If you didn't have those kinds of childhood intuitions, however, don't sweat it. Instead of worrying about what you want to do for the next 10, 20, or 30 years, think only about what you want to do *now*. Start by answering the following questions:

What Are Your Interests?

- **What do you love to do?** Think about what you enjoyed most in school as well as after school and on the weekends. What do you love to do on vacation? If you could do only one thing for the rest of your life, what would it be? Answering these question will help you identify your passions.

- **What do you know a lot about?** Are you a military history buff? Do you know the names of all the major fashion designers, or the difference between a film noir and a roman a clef? Consider your top areas of expertise, even if they seem to have no apparent connection to a future career.

- **What would you like to learn more about?** If you could take a class or workshop on anything, what would it be? Are there certain TV channels or shows that get you going?

- **What can you see yourself doing day to day (no matter how outrageous or far-fetched)?** This is dream-job territory. In this early phase of career exploration, don't get fenced in by thoughts about practicality. Any way you'd like to spend your day is fair game.

What Are Your Skills?

- **What do you excel at?** Start with school subjects, sports, and hobbies. Then take it from there. You might be good at problem-solving, communication, or diplomacy during an argument between friends. Do you have a knack for digging up facts, helping someone get through tough times, relating to young children, following directions to build a model, or taking amazing photos? Each skill or talent that you possess can be applied to a specific career.

- **What would you like to be even better at?** You can probably think of several things that you'd like to excel in if you had the time or opportunity—such as horseback riding or becoming fluent in Spanish. Is there something you've never tried but you think you might like if you had the chance? Designing clothing, decorating a home, doing stunts for movies, or leading a group on a hike? Even something you've never tried before in your life can lead you toward a career calling.

What Are Your Values?

- **What do you believe in?** This can be anything, from the principles of your religious faith to the U.S. Constitution to animal rights. If you believe that laughter heals or that music is the key to leading a richer life, these count too.

- **What do you value most?** Time with family? A good meal? A day out in nature? Freedom of speech? A career that makes you happy will probably encompass some of your core values.

What Are Your Personal Style?

- **Are you energized by other people or are you happiest working on your own to get the job done?** Do you love the spotlight group dynamics can provide or do you gravitate more toward one-on-one interaction?

- **Do you prefer to be challenged physically or not so much?** Some of the jobs in this book have a very physical aspect to them—a real on-the-job perk for the right person.

- **Are you a fan of spontaneity or do you prefer structure and a set schedule?** Be honest! If you love to have the week planned out so you know what to expect and can control any unwelcome surprises, this is the time to admit it. If you can't commit to anything more than 24 hours in advance because you love the thrill of flying by the seat of your pants, own up to it. One preference is no better than the other, but knowing where you stand will help you seek out a career that can better accommodate your style.

- **Do you take direction well or do you excel when you are left to your own devices?** You probably learned this one early on. Remember paint-by-numbers and Simon Sez? You either love to follow the rules or you love to break them and make up your own as you go along. Luckily, there are careers out there for both types.

- **Would you call yourself a risk taker or do you crave stability?** Some careers, especially those with an entrepreneurial bent, do not come with a steady paycheck. One month you might rake in the greenbacks, while the next you're scraping to find your next meal. It can be a tough existence if you're not the type who is willing to eat a can of soup every night until business picks up again.

In searching for answers to these questions you'll be many steps ahead of those who jump into a career choice without making sure it fits in with who they already are. A realistic assessment of what makes you tick will put you on your way.

WEIGHING YOUR OPTIONS

Choosing a career can feel like sitting down in a restaurant and being handed a menu full of strange dishes you've never tried before. Everything looks the same. How can you pick something that you'll like from a list of things you're never tried? In career terms, how can you know what you'd like to do or what you'll be good at if you've never had the chance to try it out? What if you make a wrong choice? Fortunately, choosing a career doesn't have to feel as if you were jumping off a cliff. Just as you can figure out something to order from the menu by looking at the ingredients you normally like, you can choose a career that has elements of your interests, skills, values, and personal style.

Undoubtedly, a whole slew of careers will seem alluring in one way or another. There's no wrong choice, so don't get caught up in thinking that you only have one chance to get it right. Choose wisely, but rest assured: Life in the world of work spans decades. Like returning to a new favorite restaurant to try something else, you can choose again and again.

THE STRAIGHT AND NARROW PATH CAN LEAD TO STRAIGHT AND NARROW PLACES

You may have grown up taking a lot of flak for not sticking to the straight and narrow path, for questioning the directions adults gave you, or for straying from traditional rules and ideals because the nontraditional simply interested you more. Now that you're grown, you don't have to take flak from anyone. You're calling the shots. And while the straight and narrow path is good for some, a wide-open field with endless options is much better for others. It might be time to embrace your inner renegade.

Creative types are born creative, but they must also be feisty. Making it in a creative career requires not only talent and ability, but also a fearless determination to make a living doing what you love. When we stipulate *creative*, we don't just mean artists and writers and musicians. Entrepreneurial careers—there are a number of them in this book—require creativity on another level. They combine an ambition to be self-employed and the ability to endure financial highs and lows with the creative knack for problem solving and making things happen. In addition, plenty of jobs in this book call for an adventurous spirit. This sometimes comes in the form of physical daring; other times, pure curiosity and a willingness to try new things will do.

If you happen to be creative or entrepreneurial or adventuresome, you're cheating yourself out of some rich life experiences by passing up careers in that vein so you can cling to a job that's safe and predictable. Pioneers in life should be pioneers in their job search, too. To be avant-garde your whole life, then turn around and opt for the orthodox when it comes to finding a job just doesn't make much sense. It could be a recipe for a confused career path that starts off on the wrong foot. It bears repeating: Stay true to yourself, even if it means forgoing the straight and narrow.

What's So Great About the Proverbial Road Less Traveled?

You've read it before. Those oft-quoted words penned in 1920 by Robert Frost in his poem *The Road Not Taken*:

> I shall be telling this with a sigh
> Somewhere ages and ages hence
> Two roads diverged in a wood, and I—
> I took the one less traveled by,
> And that has made all the difference.

This book is filled with career equivalents of the road less traveled. The challenge of that journey presents itself in these 120 professions—from comic book writer to crisis negotiator—for those who choose to accept it. But why bother?

There are many benefits to going against the grain when you are choosing your livelihood. First, the level of self-awareness it takes merely to decide to carve an atypical career path will serve you well in other areas of life. Knowing what moves you, where your convictions lie, and what your skills are can serve you in other areas of life—not just professionally. You'll come back to it when you assess a potential lifelong partner or when you think about where you want to live. Second, while it might take longer to land your dream job, you will love what you do and find it deeply rewarding. Third, in the process of chasing your dream, you'll strengthen your patience, stamina, tenacity, and resilience.

Forging your own path takes guts. People do it because they believe it's worth doing it. When they have a bad day, they still love the career they've chosen. When people ask them what they do, they light up. When they think about what's next, they see a world full of possibility because they know they can find their way. If they ever get let go from a job, or their company goes out of business, or they start to loose their minds, they know how to market themselves and find something else that will get them going all over again.

How to Be a Trailblazer

Two men set out from the bottom of a mountain to find their way to the top. One left with a detailed map of the trails, the other chose only a compass and a machete to cut the overgrown brush from his path. Several days later, the man with the compass and machete reached the peak. The other man was sitting there having a comfortable lunch in the sun. "Looks like I found the way a bit faster," he said, taking a bite of his sandwich. The man with the machete did not respond. He was looking at the man's map that was atop a nearby rock. A light breeze lifted a corner, caused it to stir, and suddenly carried it away on a gust, over the edge of the mountain. "Yes, you did," he finally said. "But I'll know how to find my way back down."

There is much to be said for blazing your own trail. Here are some ways to get started (machete notwithstanding).

- Experience life.

- Be open to meeting new people and learning from their experiences.

- Try everything that comes your way—from Ethiopian food to mah-jongg to skydiving.

- Get involved in activities about which you're passionate and work toward leadership positions in them if you are still in school.

- Be proactive about your happiness and well-roundedness.

- If something doesn't pan out, don't let it be for lack of effort.

- Pursue internships or part-time jobs in fields that jump out at you. Pick up a few books on related subjects. Talk to people who love their jobs or have careers you admire. Ask them how they came to be where they are today.

- Be flexible. If you give a career path everything you've got and still see yourself elsewhere, give yourself the freedom to cut those ties and move on to the next adventure.

- Don't listen to the naysayers. Ever.

Debunking the Myths

Many of the careers in this book are surrounded by a certain mystique. They require strength of self, a call to adventure, and a creative flair. With mystique and mystery, however, come myths. We've taken a moment to address the four most common misconceptions regarding the jobs in this book.

Myth 1: You don't need a college degree in this field; it's real-world experience that counts.
Reality: In many fields, though not all of them, college degrees count a great deal. You can rest assured that degrees never hurt. While real-world experience is important for someone starting out in *any* field, a college or even trade school/junior college degree will give you a solid foundation for sniffing out the best real-world opportunities possible and knowing what to do with them once you find them. A college degree will not only equip you with important knowledge in a number of subjects, but also help you further define yourself and your interests and give you an idea of where and how to best apply them. It might sound like a cliché that your time in college will help shape you as an adult, but it's true. Even if your top-choice career doesn't require a college degree, if things don't pan out you'll have something to fall back on. Career paths aside, you will meet very few (if any) people in life who regret their decision to attend college. You are much more likely to meet those who wish they had made it a priority. Yes, you may be able to enter a

field on real-world experience alone, but your chances of rising to the top levels of *any* career are greatly increased when you are carrying with you that impressive achievement of graduating from college.

Myth 2: I can find a job where I will never need to be at a desk.

Reality: Most jobs involve at least a small fraction of time spent at a desk. That could mean once a day, once a week, or even less frequently, but few jobs come with zero administrative tasks that require you to show up at an office. Even an acrobat, adventure guide, or sports referee might have to come in at the end of the week to fill out a timesheet or sit down with a manager every few months for a performance review. They might also be required to attend regular staff meetings to receive updates or put in classroom time learning new techniques they can apply to their work in the field.

Myth 3: Choosing a nontraditional career means resigning to be one of those broke-but-happy people.

Reality: Is that such a bad thing? There are loads of starving artists who would rather live frugally for the rest of their lives than put down their paintbrushes and find an office job with a steady paycheck. Which is not to say that you need to starve to have a job that you love, only that creative jobs do traditionally pay less than your standard suit-and-tie gig. We agree that it's not fair. There is no fair-and-square way to put a price on skills and talent and determine which types of work are more worthy of the big bucks than others. Part of the reason nontraditional jobs often pay less is that people would line up down the block for a chance at one of these coveted positions simply because they are passionate about the work itself. If you saw *The Devil Wears Prada* you'll recall the many staff members of *Runway* magazine who constantly reminded Andy of how many other girls would kill for her job. Yet she doesn't make enough money to adhere to the high style office dress code (never mind the long hours and incessant, often ludicrous, demands her boss makes). That's the cruel side of some creative professions. You'll work your butt off to get in, you'll slave over menial tasks for long hours to earn a paltry paycheck, and you'll wonder why you put up with it. At the end of the day, however, you go home with the knowledge that despite the rocky beginnings, you're on the right path and deep down you love what you do. Broke but happy? Yes—at least for a while. Investing some sweat equity in most fields results in moving up the ranks and eventually earning better wages. If your main goal in life is to be as rich as a duke, this may not be the book for you. We salute you anyway for knowing yourself well and wish you the best in that rather focused pursuit.

Myth 4: Creative jobs are pretty easy because a lot of the day is spent goofing around and having fun.

Reality: There is a huge misconception about creative careers being a walk in the park simply because they are famous for having some really fun moments. Choosing one of the careers in this book definitely isn't about taking the easy route (as you'll soon find out). These are full-time jobs that require at least as much work as a job built around crunching numbers and writing reports—possibly more. In many cases, those careers that sound the most glamorous—actor, fashion designer, and independent filmmaker—often require the most discipline, the longest hours, and a heavy dose of grunt work before the fun even begins. You may have a blast in the career you eventually choose—and you should—but it's unlikely to be easy. Would you even want it to be? Everybody knows: When you start at the bottom, you appreciate the top.

HOW TO USE THIS BOOK

There's a saying that goes, "It's better to be busy than bored." The one thing these jobs are not is boring. Whether you're into working with your hands, exchanging air kisses with the fabulous people, flirting with danger, or suffering from wanderlust, there's something in this book for you. Our goal in selecting the jobs profiled in this book was to offer a *representation* of the kinds of careers available to people of a certain bent. It aims to reveal the breadth of options available to you—no career guide can cover every job in the world, and this one doesn't even come close. We looked online, thumbed through other career guides, talked to career counselors, and heard from students about the qualities job seekers look for in careers when they choose to go off the beaten path. We used this information as a starting point to come up with a list of careers that reflected those qualities. For every job in the book, there's five we couldn't include—for that reason, you should use it as a starting point for thinking about embarking on that road less traveled to help point you in the right direction for further research and exploration. All of the jobs in this book are guaranteed to get your blood pumping. Some of them just might be more fun than you ever thought possible.

THE JOB CATEGORIES

To help match your cravings with the best choice from the career menu, we've divided the jobs in this book into seven categories by chapter, in the following order:

Mobile Office
Schmoozing
Travel
Roll Up Your Sleeves
The Great Outdoors
Living on the Edge
Artistic Talent

The chapters are arranged on a continuum from the (somewhat) more traditional to the truly unique. Within each chapter, the jobs are listed alphabetically.

What follows is an overview of the kinds of jobs you'll find in each category, the personalities they tend to attract, and what you need to get started.

Mobile Office Jobs

- **Generally speaking:** Largely project-based, these jobs require people to take their office with them.

- **Great for:** People who are self-motivated, have a lot of initiative, and don't mind putting in time at the office occasionally.

- **Essential equipment:** Laptop and cell phone.

Schmoozing Jobs

- **Generally speaking:** These jobs require you to put in some serious face time and network to close the deal and/or and get the sale.

- **Great for:** "People" persons, people who love meeting new people and like to be on the scene.

- **Essential equipment:** Charm, salesmanship, and thick skin.

Travel Jobs

- **Generally speaking:** These jobs involve a lot of travel, sometimes to exotic locations.

- **Great for:** People with a get up and go attitude.

- **Essential equipment:** A passport and an ability to quickly and successfully adjust to unfamiliar people and situations.

Roll Up Your Sleeves Jobs

- **Generally speaking:** These jobs require you to roll up your sleeves and work with your hands.

- **Great for:** People who like to have something to show for their work at the end of the day.

- **Essential equipment:** Your tools of trade.

The Great Outdoors

- **Generally speaking:** These jobs involve working outside and/or with animals.

- **Great for:** Outdoorsy types.

- **Essential equipment:** A pair of comfortable jeans and a willingness to get dirty.

Living on the Edge Jobs

- **Generally speaking:** These jobs involve an element of risk (usually bodily).

- **Great for:** Thrill seekers who crave adrenaline rushes on a daily basis.

- **Essential equipment:** Fearless attitude.

Artistic Talent

- **Generally speaking:** These jobs require a special creative talent.

- **Great for:** Artistic people who are into the performing arts.

- **Essential equipment:** Inspiration and endurance.

Each chapter lists career profiles for some of the most popular as well as best-kept-secret professions in today's job market—120 in all. These profiles cover the gamut of jobs known for lots of time spent away from a big, burly desk. Together, as unique and varied as they are, they represent just a sample of what's out there. It's up to you to find the perfect one for you. To get you started, each profile explores

- **A (Relatively) Typical Day in the Life:** This section paints a picture of what the job is like day to day. If you like what you see, read on.

- **An Extreme Day in the Life:** An insider working in this career gives you the scoop on an extreme day on the job. Depending on the profile, this professional might relive their most frustrating moment or their most triumphant—from a wedding photographer who chased a wedding band–toting hound that ran off in the middle of the ceremony to a coach whose key player won a tournament because of his encouragement.

- **Prepare for Success:** Before you can get your feet wet in these careers, you're going to need to make yourself appealing to prospective employers. In this section you'll find out exactly what kind of education and preparation you'll need, along with which talent and skills will boost your resume to the top of the pile. You will find out whether you should you do two internships, find a mentor, choose a college with a co-op program, or get a summer job in a related industry.

- **Getting Your Foot in the Door:** Even once you've got the skills, degree, and/or experience, breaking into the industry can be a bear of a challenge. When it comes to exciting jobs like these, competition is usually fierce. Here, we list our best tips for finding an in and going for it.

- **Biggest Challenges and Best Perks:** Every job in this book comes with challenges and perks. Is it difficult to get an entry-level job? (Is there even such a thing?) Are the hours long? Does it involve a lot of driving in a car away from home? Is it difficult to progress within the industry? The career's testing moments of truth are revealed here. Just to balance things out, we talk about those fun extras that make even a terrific opportunity all the more worthwhile, from industry parties to world travel to lots of time off to a casual dress code.

In addition, don't miss the great information listed in each profile's sidebar.

- **Desk Time**—An icon indicating how much desk time you will have in that occupation:

 = none

 = a quarter

 = half

 = more than half.

While some jobs may have a significant portion of desk time, they will also have (in order to be included in the book) a sizable portion of time away from the desk and out of the office.

- **Are You Interested In?**—Related interests in school and otherwise that would make sense for you to check out this profession

- **Related College Majors**—Majors that might lead to this kind of job

- **Salary**—Average entry-level salary, 5-year salary, and 10- to 15-year salary reported for each profession. When that information is not available, average median salary for the field is reported.

- **Jargon**—Learn the lingo that will have you sounding like a pro.

- **For More Information:** Related websites and/or organizations for this career to get you started on further research.

When it's time to hunker down to find a job, our appendices should come in handy for your search.

- **Appendix I:** Crash Course in Networking. Whether you call it networking or schmoozing, it's one of the most essential, practical, and effective tools in the current workplace. Learn it, use it, and be glad that you did. There's nothing wrong with making meaningful connections with people who might someday be happy to give your career a quick boost in the right direction.

- **Appendix II:** Resumes/Portfolios for Creative People. How does a resume for a set designer differ from one for a stockbroker? Creative jobs call for creative people. Employers begin the get-to-know-you process with their first glance at an applicant's resume; therefore, you'll need to make a strong and lasting impression. Here we let you know how to distinguish yourself on paper and beyond.

- **Appendix III:** Power Jargon: Every industry and every job has its own lingo—the faster you can learn how to talk the talk, the easier it'll be to get your foot in the door. Learning how to "sound like a pro" should be part of your job-search preparation. Here's a primer on what it takes to learn the language of success.

The information in this book came from a variety of sources, including government publications, published reports, industry self-reporting statistics, professional associations, telephone interviews, and Internet resources. They should all be used as guidelines; specific statistics and experiences will vary on a case-by-case basis. What might seem overwhelming at the moment will seem much less so when you're armed with the valuable career insights and information to be found between these pages. Here's to finding a career that you love. If it won't chain you to your desk—all the better!

THE JOBS

MOBILE OFFICE

ANTIQUES/ART/RARE BOOKS/VINTAGE ITEMS DEALER

A (Relatively Typical) Day in the Life

Sure—rummaging through your grandma's attic for buried treasures can be fun, but knowing what her cast-offs are worth, how to market them, and where to sell them at a great price are the makings of a full-time career.

An antiques dealer is a skilled salesperson of items now rare and unavailable in your standard retail stores. Same goes for people who sell art, vintage clothing and collectibles, or rare books. Antiques dealers may specialize in certain items, from furniture to rugs, jewelry, dishes, clothing, or toys, and some may focus on certain eras or styles. Most, however, are generalists who are interested in an assortment of pieces with varying history, aesthetic, and value.

Antiques dealers must possess expert knowledge about the pieces they sell. Clients want to know where items came from, how they were made, what they were used for, and why the price tag is what it is. A dealer needs to know everything, as pieces with a known history often garner a better price. Above all, dealers need to understand their client's needs and wants and what goods will most satisfy them.

Dealers are busy individuals, acquiring inventory, selling pieces they have, researching items, and managing a business, as many are self-employed. They also develop relationships with restorers, financiers, and auctioneers. This stream of talent is the reason it is difficult to become and remain an antiques dealer. What's more, dealers must invest a bundle in building up their inventory. This comes with a high degree of risk. Dealers assess the value of each piece before they buy, and then try to sell it at a profitable mark-up as quickly as possible. In a town with many antiques shops, competition can be stiff. Shopkeepers must be savvy with merchandise, offer great customer serv-

An Extreme Day in the Life

Many antiques dealers, like Sheila Britz, owner of Antiques 202 in New York City, need to travel to track down merchandise. In addition to frequenting antiques shows nationwide, Sheila travels to Europe several times a year. Her buying trips are made up of extreme days, one after another, like on this recent shopping excursion in Paris: "It starts when the flight is late taking off. You get there having to meet someone and start shopping immediately so you don't waste any time. It is too early to check into your hotel room so you have to find a ladies room somewhere to freshen up. You rush to meet the first dealer, but in Europe, dealers rarely honor their appointments. You've made an appointment to see a piece but then they are late or they don't show at all. So you jump back in the car and move on to the next dealer across the city and the next. You end up waiting around a lot and calling people trying to find out if they are going to show up. Many times you're very hungry because in Europe they do not serve food continually. And you feel thrown off by the time difference. Eventually, you do meet with a dealer and then you have to decide if you want to buy the piece. Can you get it at a good price? Will you be able to sell it at a profit that makes it worth taking it back? It's a lot of pressure but I love the treasure hunt. I keep going because I know I will find that fabulous piece at a great price that is going to be perfect in the store. The biggest thing I've learned is that not everything I love is going to sell. You have to really investigate each piece and the market for it. You can't do it all on personal taste."

Antiques dealers must possess expert knowledge about the pieces they sell.

ice, and do their best to make their store and everything in it stand out from the rest.

An antiques dealer spends long hours inspecting pieces, visiting other dealers' stores, reviewing documentation, and researching. Keen attention to detail pays off when determining the value of a piece (the toughest part of being a dealer) as worth can waiver with the slightest detail. An antiques dealer must trust her assessment of a piece's value, and puts her reputation on the line with every buy.

Prepare for Success

A college degree in history, art history, fine arts, furniture design, business, or marketing makes a solid foundation for someone interested in pursuing this career. Dealers need to be historians, art aficionados, and good business people. Finding an internship at an antiques market, auction house, appraiser, or other related business will help you develop specialized industry know-how. Work on honing interpersonal and research skills. Trying your hand at picking up a few pieces and selling them for a profit on eBay.com will help you test your eye without an enormous investment upfront.

Getting Your Foot in the Door

Many aspiring antiques dealers learn the business as assistants for established professionals. They may handle correspondence, do research, schedule appointments, do light bookkeeping, and help tend shop. Many eventually get involved with client contact and assist in valuation decisions. Long hours and low pay are balanced by plenty of responsibility and the chance for insider training.

Biggest Challenges and Best Perks

When the economy takes a downturn, antiques buyers keep a tighter grip on their pocketbooks just like everybody else—which can mean an unexpected and long-lasting dip in projected sales. A large client base of regular buyers will ensure a self-supporting antiques business. Choosing a good location and creating a strong retail presence within the community can help a store flourish and become an antiques destination. A knowledgeable dealer who is able to track down even the most unusual requests will stand out. This can be a challenging but highly gratifying field. The joys of being surrounded daily with items of financial and historical value seem to buoy many people through the long hours, the erratic and often low profit margins, and the difficulty in establishing oneself as an independent dealer.

Professional Profile
Avg. starting salary: $19,800
Avg. salary after 5 years: $28,900
Avg. salary 10 to 15 years: $52,400

Jargon
Antique Generally used to define valuable items more than 100 years old

Vintage Generally used to define items less than 100 years old but more than 10 years old

Are you Interested In?
Antiques, art, history

Related College Majors
History, art history, fine arts, furniture design, business, marketing

For More Information
Art Dealer's Association of America Inc:
www.artdealers.org

National Antique and Art Dealers Association of America:
www.naadaa.org

Sotheby's:
www.sothebys.com

AUDIO/VIDEO TECHNICIAN

A (RELATIVELY) TYPICAL DAY IN THE LIFE

An audio/visual technician is qualified to work on a variety of different projects, ranging from editing songs for a major entertainer and working as a sound engineer in a studio session to working directly for a corporation as their in-house network conference specialist. Audio/video technicians handle and troubleshoot all manner of audiovisual equipment and may be responsible for setting up meetings, conferences, parties, and any other scenario in which sound and video will be used. Another aspect of the job is actual editing and production of raw footage for music, movies, commercials, and everything in between.

A typical day in this profession involves a lot of time with delicate equipment, so alertness and attention to detail are key. You could start the day traveling to a huge, rented studio to work with an artist on songs for a new CD, or by turning on your home computer to upload footage that you need to edit before a deadline. Still others might start their day off by heading to a large hotel or auditorium to oversee and fine tune the audio and visual aspects of a board meeting or a sold out concert. Later on in the day, you might meet with the team responsible for filming a particular event and talk about how things will be shot and what your role will be in the shooting and editing process. From there, the day could go on for hours. Whatever specialization you've chosen within the audio/visual technician profession, one thing is for sure: You'll constantly be under a deadline.

An Extreme Day in the Life

Taylor Rivelli began working with sound before graduating high school. He interned with a studio straight out of high school and then went on to earn a degree in audio engineering and production. He now owns Taylormade Sounds LLC and Hotbox Studios, and alternates between creating and producing beats, editing audio content for clients, and performing as a guitarist with a live hip hop band, Dujeous. Taylor started out by being called into studios during production sessions to work as the engineer/audio technician for projects. He soon realized that the high demand for quality sound engineering would make opening his own business a good idea. He sees a shift in the profession right now: "Traditionally, you would strictly edit music. There's a shift toward requiring more from a technician/engineer creatively today. A lot of times, people come in with a lot of music and a short deadline and expect something good enough to get on the radio or on a mix tape, and they want you to add that special edge to it." Extreme days in his line of work usually come around the deadline of a large project. Due to the sophistication of today's audio technology, clients often expect audio technicians to work magic with content that might, frankly, be lacking in appeal to begin with. Taylor recounts how, "When working with some artists, you're hired to record music and edit it. You can end up spending valuable time dealing with the [demands] of the artist and even writing part of a song, when this isn't your job." Taylor's not complaining though, because while he feels that, "Many people work as audio technicians to get into the field in order to learn how to do work on their own creative projects and support themselves while doing it." He's made that leap himself and now supports himself with his own audio engineering work.

Many people get into the field learn how to do work on their own creative projects and support themselves while doing it.

Prepare for Success

You don't need a college degree to become an audio/video technician, but some jobs may require a degree in lieu of a lot of experience. If you are in college, consider a major in visual arts, audio or video engineering, or production. Many technical institutes also offer short training programs towards degrees and certifications in the field. Whether you decide to take classes or not, once you've decided what area of the job interests you, take the time to familiarize yourself with the audio or video equipment and computer programs you'll be using on the job. Another good idea is to research job descriptions for positions you'd like to hold to make sure you're working toward the required skills.

Getting Your Foot in the Door

Many production companies and electronics stores will hire an audio/video technician with little experience as long as you're willing to work for a little less at first and make an effort to learn on the job. Start out by getting experience in student or community theatre productions, completing an internship with a studio or on a movie set, or interning with companies that hire in-house technicians to prepare and maintain the audio/video equipment for their organization. Since many of these positions are short term, take on a variety of them; once you've built up your experience, it will be easier to get well-paying jobs on the strength of your own resume, and leave you room to be selective.

Biggest Challenges and Best Perks

One of the best perks of this career choice is being able to work independently; whether you work for an electronics company installing equipment, or for a company as their in-house technician, you spend your time either traveling to residences/companies to perform maintenance and installation, or you work on different assignments every day throughout the office, setting up and troubleshooting equipment in-house. Another perk, depending on the branch you go into, is location. Audio/video technicians on movie and music assignments get to travel with the production team. The biggest challenge of this job is being on other people's schedules a lot of the time. Successful technicians are reliable and responsible, since you may be the only expert in your field working on a particular project or at a company. If you work on your own, managing your time well is even more essential: It's hard to keep a client if you miss deadlines!

Professional Profile
Avg. starting salary: $36,000

Avg. salary after 5 years: $42,000

Avg. salary 10 to 15 years: $49,000

Jargon
Sound Mixer The member of a production crew responsible for recording all sound on set

Boom Operator The sound engineer's assistant, responsible for operating the mikes

Are you Interested In?
Music, video, computers, technology

Related College Majors
Visual arts, audio or video engineering, sound production

For More Information
Society of Broadcast Engineers:
www.sbe.org

National Association of Broadcasters:
www.nab.org

InfoComm International:
www.infocomm.org

CATERER

A (Relatively Typical) Day in the Life

A caterer works closely with clients to design, prepare, and serve menus for events, including weddings, charity balls, holiday brunches, office lunches, and any other occasion at which people gather and consume food. A caterer must understand how dishes work together; have strong interpersonal, and particularly listening, skills; and possess the ability to manage a cooking and serving staff. More than 70 percent of all catering services are owner-operated, so many caterers must also have sharp business acumen. Most people are drawn to the industry because of their love of cooking or preparing elegant meals for special events. In their first few years in catering, many people find that talent only gets you so far—you can have dozens of clients, great reviews, and the best products, and still end up losing money.

Management and organizational skills are critical for those caterers who wish to keep their business concerns solvent. Caterers spend considerable amounts of time developing their menus, unique styles, and business plans, and are responsible for overseeing every aspect of the business. While some catering services do employ hundreds of full- and part-time staff, the vast majority have fewer than six full-time employees and hire temporary staff on an as-needed basis. Business is driven by season, and the caterer that finds him-or-herself sleepless during the wedding months may be yawning with boredom in October. A caterer may have three to five meetings with prospective clients to work out the details of an event. The caterer provides menus; the clients choose their favorite dishes and work with the caterer to assemble a meal in which each dish complements the rest. Successful caterers are able to guide people to decisions that will benefit the event.

Prepare for Success

There are no educational requirements for becoming a caterer, though many people choose to attend a culinary academy to learn the basics of certain schools of cooking. Other caterers attend restaurant management school or at least take course work that addresses some of the concerns of the business, such as finance, management, and

An Extreme Day in the Life

A lot of future four-star chefs turn to catering to earn some money while they put themselves through school. Holly Moore, now at the French Culinary Institute, is one of those people. She found catering to be a high-energy endeavor: "An 'extreme day' for me is usually a two-day block. The day before a large party is always hectic because there are many things you can't prepare until the day before because they'll lose their flavor/color/consistency. Then, the actual day of the event is equally as crazy, because you have set it all up and make sure everything is working correctly. You have to stay on your toes and be creative, because at any event, there is going to be something you didn't plan for and you have to make it work. I once worked on *Queer Eye for the Straight Guy*, doing a surprise wedding, and I was making mini-wedding cakes for the reception. I had to prepare most of the cakes in our small office kitchen in NYC, then get them all sent to the wedding site in NJ. At the site, I had to teach the groomsmen how to make the cakes themselves, so they could do it on camera. Between them and the Fab Five, I think we went through three gallons of icing—it was everywhere!"

At any event, there is going to be something you didn't plan for and you have to make it work.

organization. Those caterers who do not attend any special schools should have some type of professional food preparation experience; cooking food for large numbers of people in a limited time frame is a crucial (and not necessarily intuitive) skill. Caterers also have to be certified for sanitary cooking conditions and safe equipment. Most boards of health offer two- or three-day courses in health laws for prospective caterers and restaurants.

GETTING YOUR FOOT IN THE DOOR

Caterers are chefs of a sort, and the vast network of restaurateurs and culinary professionals is always a good one in which to roam; many caterers introduce their services to local restaurant owners to persuade the owners to recommend them to clients who need catering services. Caterers typically excel by making sure that their name and contact information is available in all of the right circles, especially during the holidays and summer months. Since a lot of caterers are chosen based on word-of-mouth recommendations, especially on the party circuit, every job has the potential to lead to another, and a satisfied client is usually more than happy to pass along their favorite caterer's info.

BIGGEST CHALLENGES AND BEST PERKS

In the early years, caterers develop their identities, define menus, and network. Earnings are generally low and the hours are long and strenuous. Fewer than half of the people who start out as caterers remain after two years in the profession. The majority go out of business in fewer than eighteen months because of their failure to manage costs or establish a positive reputation. Caterers who have lasted five years in the business often attempt to expand during these years. However, overexposure, lack of centralized quality control, and rising costs can make expansion a mixed blessing at best.

The hours are long, but once caterers have established areas of responsibility for each of their full-time employees and have learned how to delegate authority, satisfaction is high, and the earnings have typically become livable. Caterers who last ten years have a reliable client base, so earnings are consistent and strong, and many long-term caterers will choose to sell their businesses to newer entrants in the field or long-term partners.

PROFESSIONAL PROFILE
Avg. starting salary: $40,200
Avg. salary after 5 years: $48,600
Avg. salary 10 to 15 years: $55,600

JARGON
Mobile Caterer Someone who serves food directly from a vehicle or handcart equipped with food preparation equipment

ARE YOU INTERESTED IN?
Cooking

RELATED COLLEGE MAJORS
Culinary arts, restaurant management

FOR MORE INFORMATION
The Culinary Institute of America: www.ciachef.edu
Mobile Industrial Caterers Association: www.mobilecaterers.com

CELEBRITY PHOTOGRAPHER (PAPARAZZI)

A (Relatively) Typical Day in the Life

A member of the paparazzi is a celebrity photographer. The job has elements of journalism, photography, and sleuthing. It is not for the faint of heart or those lacking patience, persistence, and tenacity. While some celebrities are gracious about being photographed, many have developed a distaste for the paparazzi that makes this career suffer from bad publicity. Photographers who have acted unprofessionally cast a dark shadow on the whole field. Though the public often sides with celebrities who claim that the paparazzi invade their privacy and cross too many lines, these are often the same people who devour the celebrity-photo-laden tabloids while standing in line at the supermarket.

Those who do get into this line of work must have a thick skin and a belief in what they do for a living. (If they can do it for a living; many simply do it on the side.) A typical day might involve driving around to notable celebrity hangouts hoping for a sighting. Some paparazzi even have informants who let them know when and where to get a good shot. Others are able to befriend celebs and get insider invitations to events. When they spot a subject, they must act quickly and fearlessly. Just a moment's hesitation can be costly. When they've got the image, they must know when and where to send it to get the biggest price before another photographer beats them to it with a similar image.

Not all paparazzi shots are candid. On the red carpet, a celebrity is there to smile and be photographed. Many paparazzi consider their jobs to be just another part of the show business machine. There's an obvious, reciprocal

An Extreme Day in the Life

An art photographer based in New York City who began selling candid celebrity photos for extra cash, Melissa L. found herself in the world of the paparazzi by accident. She says that living in a fashionable downtown neighborhood, she ended up spying the rich and famous periodically when she was out shooting her own work. Realizing she could support her art in this way, she made more and more efforts to get a good celebrity shot. "One day I was at Bryant Park, waiting for a musician to show up who was doing a promotion there. I had to jockey for a spot among other photographers while we waited and waited for her to arrive. We were all trying to guess where we could get the best angle and the longer we waited the more irritated we were getting. Her limo finally pulled up. I was reaching in my camera bag for an extra lens when I lost my balance and slipped from the ledge I had been standing on. By the time I got back up and had my camera ready, she had already walked past us and into a little VIP tent that was set up for her party. Security wouldn't let us anywhere near it and I had lost my opportunity. I could have waited for her to come out another hour later, but I was so mad and frustrated that I headed home. Back in my neighborhood, I decided to get a latte in my favorite coffee shop to cheer myself up. I walked in and had to look twice. A certain actress from *Friends* was ordering a coffee at the counter. I grabbed my camera and got the shot! It was incredible. I was able to sell it a few days later and that totally redeemed the day."

The thrill—and payoff—of an amazing shot can be addictive.

relationship between stars and the press: They need each other to make money.

Prepare for Success

Many paparazzi didn't plan on this career, but if they are good at it and are making money, they tend to stick with it. Being a fast and sharp-shooting photographer is key. You'll need some good photography equipment, an eye for the shot, a nose for adventure, and pure guts. The more you practice getting fast shots of moving targets, the better you'll be. When you're not out shooting or trying to track someone down, spend some time scanning through a pile of the latest Hollywood gossip rags. It pays to know where the "it" list lives and vacations, where they've been spotted and with whom, and whom they're dating.

Getting Your Foot in the Door

You can make connections with an agency by submitting amazing shots they haven't already seen. Your work speaks for itself, and if you're good you'll be paid. You'll soon discover what they want most, so figure out how to get it. The thrill—and payoff—of an amazing shot can be addictive for the rookie paparazzo.

Biggest Challenges and Best Perks

Much of this career revolves around being the first and the best. It's not easy to be the first on the scene if a celeb gets in a fender bender or leaves her hotel room to frolic on a Caribbean beach in a bikini. Being the first to shoot it and/or having the best shot is the constant challenge. The press may receive many submissions, but they only need one good photo. As a result, a "hurry up and wait" aspect characterizes this profession—you might rush to a nightclub on a tip only to wait hours for a certain someone to emerge. Nights, weekends, and holidays are all fair game. If a celeb can be photographed, your personal life will have to wait.

On the upside, being in the right place at the right time with the right lens just might earn you some nice cash. A generic headshot might sell to an agency for $100, but through the years the shot can be used again and again, earning a commission each time. A more unusual shot might earn a few thousand dollars when it is published for the first and only time. This career's high profit potential and unpredictability (not to mention regular brushes with celebrity!) are some of its best perks.

PROFESSIONAL PROFILE
Avg salary: Varies considerably, depending on the photos

JARGON
Finder A viewing device on a camera that shows the subject area who will be recorded on the film

ARE YOU INTERESTED IN?
Photography, celebrity

RELATED COLLEGE MAJORS
Photography

FOR MORE INFORMATION
American Society of Media Photographers:
www.asmp.org

Professional Photographers of America:
www.ppa.com

CELEBRITY PERSONAL ASSISTANT

A (Relatively) Typical Day in the Life

Most celebrities have two jobs: their chosen career as an actor, model, singer, and so on, and their job of just being a famous personality. These two obligations leave them little time to attend to the everyday tasks: stocking the fridge, making dinner reservations, shopping for gifts, picking up the dry cleaning, and walking the dog. That's where a personal assistant comes in. This is the job for people who admire the lifestyles of the rich and famous.

A personal assistant needs to be ready for anything. Their day may be filled with setting up the client's calendar, scheduling appointments, getting clothes ready for engagements, ordering lunch, responding to fan mail, or running errands. Then there are the unexpected duties that come with the job: flagging down cabs to chase after clients who leave cell phones and purses behind or screening calls from agents, lawyers, accountants, shrinks, ex-wives, ex-husbands, children, and even parents. Assistants live on the inside of a celebrity's life—for better or worse. They may help them get dressed, hand them tissues when they cry, or sneak out of the room when they start fighting with a spouse. The career can be intense! Others, however, enjoy getting up close and personal. Personal assistants do grunt work and gopher chores, but can usually overlook that aspect of the job out of great admiration for their bosses. More than a mere job, an assistant builds a complex relationship. They have access to the client's most personal details, including house/car keys, alarm codes, and bank accounts. Assistants need to protect their clients' privacy and act in their best interests.

Prepare for Success

Personal assistants live where famous people live, namely New York City and Los Angeles. The more marketable the skills you bring to the table—financial, culinary, administrative—the better. You'll need to be savvy

---

An Extreme Day in the Life

Assistants who don't happen to live in Los Angeles or New York may work as à la carte personal assistants. Instead of attending to the needs of just one person, these assistants help an ever-changing roster of clients. Dallas-based On the Run, Inc. provides personal errand services for a wide-range of clients: doctors, lawyers, CEOs, and any celebs who are passing through Dallas. Owner Robert Granado says typical client requests include grocery shopping, shoe repairs, coordinating auto maintenance, pet walking/sitting, and paying bills. Then, there are the not-so-typical requests: "One of the perks of providing errand services to wealthy families and celebrities is the exposure to their amazing lifestyles. We may drive a $100,000 sports car one day and deliver gourmet food to their private jet the next. Just some of the things we have been asked to do are: deliver 60 frozen turkeys to individuals as holiday corporate gifts; pick up bull semen that had been flown in for reproductive purposes; pick up a pregnant client's house key from the delivery room to go let her dogs out; transport wedding cakes; decorate/deliver items to hotel suites to accommodate celebrity requests; purchase items for royal families while they are in town; pick up gourmet hot dogs for a celebrity and then turn around to go get him antacids!"

Assistants live on the inside of a celebrity's life—for better or worse.

around town, and know where to get the best cashmere or cannoli and how to get it in a hurry. During the interview process, be able to articulate why you want this job, why you'd be good at it, and why you'll stay. Assistants should be able to take direction and not take things too personally if someone throws a tantrum. Be a great listener, consistent, punctual, reliable, trustworthy, and discreet. Celebrities are looking for someone who is self-sufficient, has sound judgment, can work quickly under pressure, and will represent them in a professional manner. Because assistants may need to socialize or do some cajoling, wallflowers need not apply. But neither should diva types who may steal attention from the star who is running the show.

GETTING YOUR FOOT IN THE DOOR

Although there are agencies that specialize in placing personal assistants, jobs are usually filled through word-of-mouth referrals. Connecting with people who celebrities work with—agents, managers, lawyers, and so on—is another good way to get your foot in the door. Expect a nerve-racking interview that involves a fact-to-face meeting with the celebrity, in addition to one or two personal staff members. They want to make sure the two of you will click. They may ask questions about home and personal management or about who you know in the industry. Be yourself. Your personality is as important as any experience. Most assistants have little or no job training before they're thrust into the fire. It's learn as you go, and you better learn fast. A memory like a steel trap and a mind for details are crucial. It's the assistant's job to keep everything in order, make sure all needs are met, and complete each task perfectly every time.

BIGGEST CHALLENGES AND BEST PERKS

When you work for a celeb, everything revolves around them. Make no mistake, it's a subservient gig that requires extreme intimacy with the client, many who are as eccentric and high-maintenance as it gets. There is a high turnover rate among assistants who get fed up with canceling their own plans to fulfill extravagant, last-minute requests at all hours of the day and night. Not everyone is comfortable having someone else—especially someone so well-known and successful—be completely dependent on them for the simplest and most minute matters.

On the contrary, celebrity personal assistants can look forward to a daily dose of the good life. Free travel, great parties, and the opportunity to rub elbows with the rich and famous are all great perks. Other extras range from hand-me-down designer duds, concert and sports tickets, laptops and cell phones, and expensive gifts (or re-gifts, but who's complaining?). Most assistants are drawn to the job by the glamour of celebrity, not the size of the paycheck.

PROFESSIONAL PROFILE
Avg. starting salary: $33,924
Avg. salary after 5 years: : $36,596
Avg. salary 10 to 15 years: $38,883

JARGON
BevHills Beverly Hills
Ink To sign a contract
Praiser Publicist

ARE YOU INTERESTED IN?
Celebrity lifestyles

RELATED COLLEGE MAJORS
Public relations, communications, business administration

FOR MORE INFORMATION
Association of Celebrity Assistants—
Los Angeles:
www.celebrityassistants.org

Celebrity Personal Assistants, Inc:
www.celebritypersonalassistants.com

Personal Assistant Pro:
www.personalassistantpro.com

EBAY BUSINESS OWNER

A (Relatively) Typical Day in the Life

Those who have experienced the natural high of finding unwanted things around the house and earning money by selling them on eBay.com can understand why thousands have chosen this website as the foundation for their full-time careers. While it's fun to buy items on eBay, it's even sweeter to sell things off and watch your bank account balance rise in the process. Few sales jobs offer such captivated buyers: eBay's global marketplace attracts 200 million shoppers and counting.

eBay uses the power of the Internet to fulfill an American dream—working for oneself and amassing a fortune reflective of the work one puts in. There are two main types of eBay business owners. There are those who work from a home office, listing and selling merchandise from any number of sources. In addition to personal castoffs, they go to auctions, estate sales, thrift shops, garage sales, outlet stores, and department store sales racks for new or used finds that will turn a profit on eBay. Or they might order new wholesale merchandise in bulk and resell the items individually on eBay. The other type of eBay business owner mainly sells other people's loot then takes a cut of the profits. These eBay middlemen, also known as trading assistants, often have a brick-and-mortar retail store-front where people bring in items that they want to sell but don't have the time or know-how to list.

For the scout-and-sell eBayer, the average workday is divided between finding merchandise, photographing it, writing listing descriptions, shipping sold items, and leaving feedback for buyers. A trading assistant with a drop-off store has the added time commitment of meeting, communicating, and paying clients, and maintaining a retail store. Both types need to be savvy in attracting online buyers to their listings, pricing items competitively, and fig-uring out the most economical and efficient shipping methods for items sold. An ability to recognize what has resale value and, even more important, what doesn't, is essential. eBay sellers should choose a specialized niche and become experts on their merchandise; this goes a long way in building a base of repeat customers.

An Extreme Day in the Life

Aaron Price started selling on eBay to earn enough to pay his rent. He is now the owner of eflord-ables, an eBay drop-off store in Washington, DC, and has three employees and a warehouse. During the six-year history of his business, he has specialized in a number of merchandise categories, includ-ing liquidating business inventory, musical instruments, consumer electronics, automobiles, and sporting goods. He sells items for individuals, but recently a large part of his business has been sell-ing excess and damaged goods from retailers and manufacturers, with a focus on Harley Davidson motorcycle parts. "Everything comes in by freight so we have palettes of merchandise that need to be broken down piece by piece. When you have merchandise like this coming in at the same time that you have things going out, that's when it gets extreme." Aaron says it takes smarts to know which items will reap top dollar. "I go after fanatical markets. When people get off work, what do they like to go home and spend their money on? That's what I look for."

Watching as your auction is bid up to a frenzy before time runs out is like watching the last minutes of a good horse race.

Prepare for Success

There are few requirements to start selling things on eBay. Sellers need to be 18 years old, have an e-mail and bank account, and a credit card. Beyond that, let the free enterprise begin! eBay makes it incredibly easy to sell often and sell much. (They take a cut of every listing, so they want to help each sale along.) The website contains pages upon pages for sellers—both novice and advanced—along with a community of chatty sellers ready to speak from experience. Through the eBay University program, sellers can learn the biz through online courses and weekend workshops in cities across the United States. Sellers willing to fork over a modest monthly fee (starting at $15.95) can create an eBay custom storefront for all listings, gain access to marketing tools and traffic reports, and utilize toll-free phone support. Most traditional jobs don't offer as much training as this website does.

Getting Your Foot in the Door

Even those new to eBay soon realize just how addictive it really is. For your first sell, start small; work your way up to bigger, more profitable items. (And be sure to buy a few items to learn the business from both sides.) You'll quickly learn how to list an item, what sells best, pricing, and how to give and receive feedback for each transaction. Building positive feedback is important because that is how potential buyers know they can trust you. Make use of eBay's seller resources and you'll be on your way to a career that can be as big as you're willing to make it.

Biggest Challenges and Best Perks

Knowing your merchandise and what it's worth is a constant challenge for eBay sellers. There is great variance and no guarantees. A Minnie Mouse costume will sell better two weeks before Halloween than it will two weeks after, but many items are shrouded in mystery in terms of how high they will go. The nuance of writing a compelling listing to evoke and intrigue buyers is an art. Certain product categories are overcrowded while others remain underrepresented. Dealing with non-paying bidders is a hassle that wastes sellers' time and money. On the upside, watching as your auction is bid up to a frenzy before time runs out is like watching the last minutes of a good horse race. As you refresh your computer screen, you can see people from across the country, possibly the world, all competing to win your item as the price creeps higher and higher. It's exhilarating. When buyers leave positive feedback, it feels good knowing you were the source of providing them something they're excited to own.

ENTREPRENEUR

A (Relatively) Typical Day in the Life

Why report to a boss when you can be your own? Well, for one thing, you'll get a steady paycheck, normal hours, and when the roof falls in on your office space it's someone else's problem. Still not dissuaded from becoming an entrepreneur? Good for you. It's not an endeavor for the faint of heart.

Entrepreneurs take all their money, time, and energy and generally put it into an idea, a company, or possibly several companies. They risk everything (sometimes including their own minds) to get their ideas off the ground, keep the ideas afloat, and attempt to make a living in the process. It's the American dream. Success is sweet, when it happens, but failure is common and many walk away heartbroken and flat broke.

Let's focus on the positives: Successful entrepreneurs have a strong mind for business. They've also had a great deal of experience, done extensive research, and are motivated to the point of being unstoppable. They see the average 70- to 80-hour workweek as a welcome challenge. Detail-oriented and passionate about their chosen areas of expertise, they spend countless hours focused on their ideas and how to bring their businesses to fruition.

Their days are spent promoting, marketing, and networking to get the word out about what they are doing. They've established business models and are the head honchos for seeing it through. An entrepreneur's job is never done. The to-do list is a constant work in progress. One of the most important things entrepreneurs can do is believe in their own businesses. Serious problems can crop up when the person flying the plane no longer believes in air travel.

The good news is that business owners who find that magic formula have the satisfaction of a job well done. When their hard works pays off, they have themselves to thank for it. It's a high-pressure job that consumes anyone who tries. More than three-fifths of new businesses fail within 18 months of opening their doors and not for lack of trying. If you open up a great deli and as soon as you have a sizable customer base, a Subway sandwich shop opens across the street and out-prices you it could mean your deli's demise. That said, entrepreneurship continues to attract thousands of people each year who long to be their own bosses, run a company, and be the sole keepers of the profits, assuming there are profits to be had.

An Extreme Day in the Life

Darrell Whitelaw, 25, is married, has a baby, and loves the freedom of owning his own companies: Factory Production and Merch Girls, which specialize in merchandising and clothing production. (They make the t-shirts some of your favorite bands sell, among other things.) Darrell says he loves his job but admits that the entire profession is one extreme day after another: "Owning your business is the most rewarding and punishing profession of them all. In any given day, you can expect to work 18 hours, deal with nightmares from customers and employees, face bills you can't pay, and have any number of things go wrong. However, you can also expect to be able to say 'I feel like catching the 2:00 P.M. matinee of Superman Returns' or 'Hey, 10 days in New York City sounds great this month.' But you learn to be a master electrician, a certified Apple repair specialist, and a carpenter out of necessity and survival. As hard as it is, it's also very rewarding. It's the ultimate test of your character."

Owning a business is like having a child: As long as it's still alive, it will always be your pride and joy.

Prepare for Success

Seek out and use every available resource. Many nonprofit organizations exist to help small businesses establish themselves. The community you live in may also have a set of resources for local entrepreneurs. Once you have a business plan in place and working, be ready to reorganize, rethink, and expand. A financially viable company with a good track record should be able to secure long-term financing relationships that will enable growth. You may need to hire a staff and deal with managerial issues. Oddly, highly successful entrepreneurs often have the option of selling out while the going's good. Many who do immediately miss the business and start over with a new idea.

Getting Your Foot in the Door

Do your homework. A good idea with no research to back it up isn't good at all. A college major in business is a good start or at least some business classes. An MBA is even better. Experience in the business world is also valuable. Unfortunately, entrepreneurship is learned partly on the job, a costly training period that sends many new businesses down the tubes during the first two years. Many put heart, soul, and most of their waking hours into their business ventures. However, experience, connections, reputation, and some good luck are all factors. Those who weather the first few years learn a great deal about how to run a business. Few strike it rich; most earn just enough to get by.

Biggest Challenges and Best Perks

Owning a business is like having a child: It's the first thing you think about when you get up in the morning, the last thing you think about when you fall asleep, and, as long as it's still alive, it will always be your pride and joy. Your real life and business life become difficult to separate, financially, mentally, emotionally, and time-wise. Disappointment and frustration reign for the budding entrepreneur. Shaking off the desire to throw in the towel and constantly find new and better solutions for success is key. Darrell Whitelaw says, "The sacrifice of your free time and weekends is worth it when you can just up and leave to sit on the beach and watch the surf crash in, with nobody to answer to but yourself." Making your own hours, calling the shots, and working hard to create your own success are some of entrepreneurs' favorite perks. They also get some pretty decent write-offs when tax time rolls around.

Professional Profile
Avg. salary: Varies

Jargon
Venture capital A term used to describe the financing of start-up and early stage businesses as well as businesses in turnaround situations. Venture capital investments generally are higher risk investments but offer the potential for above-average returns.

Are you Interested In?
Entrepreneurship

Related College Majors
Business management, marketing

For More Information
Center for International Private Enterprise:
www.cipe.org

CEO Club:
www.ceoclubs.com

Committee of 200:
www.c200.0rg

EVENT PLANNER

A (Relatively) Typical Day in the Life

Event planners are called upon to organize all sorts of gatherings, from weddings to office holiday parties, and family reunions to trade shows. Once the client has handed the event over to you, your days may be filled with a variety of different tasks: choosing flowers, contracting security coverage, collaborating with caterers, and even testing smoke machines. Organizational and follow-through skills are key since every detail is ultimately your responsibility. No client wants to hear that the chairs and tables won't be arriving on time—after all, that's what they've hired you for.

A typical day involves a lot of telephone and travel time. A good calendar is a must, since you'll probably be running from one appointment, site, or store to another. Even before you make it to the office, you might have to take a trip to the early-opening flower districts or call a vendor across the country. At your office, you might review your schedule for the day, check on orders that should be coming in for a party that night, and confirm meetings and phone

An Extreme Day in the Life

Jennifer Outler is an events manager for *Time* magazine. Jennifer got her first event planning experience while she was working in advertising at *Essence* magazine: "With *Essence* being such a small company, I would help out with events and was eventually promoted to the division that worked on the *Essence* Awards and *Essence* Music Festival." Jennifer recalls an extreme moment on the job that occurred while she was planning one of these high-profile events: "I remember the mistakes. The mistakes prepare you for the worst so we must be thankful for them, as hard as they are on the ego. At the *Essence* Awards in LA one year, I signed off on the use of a logo from one of our sponsors and it turned out to be the wrong logo. Unfortunately, I wasn't made aware of this until the event was in progress and the sign, with the incorrect logo, was up (just to be clear, this was a huge sign at the Kodak theater in LA where sponsors, talent, and the public could see). The president of the company noticed the error and my boss wanted to know who signed off on this. It was me. It was an oversight, but in business, as in events, oversights can lead to misspent marketing dollars and a misrepresentation of a brand. I remember that experience every time I want to skim over a document or rush [to] read something. I also learned about accountability that day; I was too naive to lie about the mistake and I am grateful for that. Owning up to the mistake eased the pressure on everyone else and allowed me to deal with the problem and move on. People are a lot more understanding of your mistakes when you own up to them and try to make them right." Jennifer's advice for students interested in this career is to "volunteer at a few events. That way you learn on someone else's dime and see the reality of what it takes to conceptualize, plan, and execute an event. Most think that it's ultra sexy and just perks everywhere. While it can be that way, there are also a lot of late nights, lonely travel, and management of egos. Volunteering or interning will give you a realistic idea of what your lifestyle would be like. After that, a lot of it is who you know, so make those connections and don't be afraid to talk to people."

To keep a strong client base, you have to go to parties and events . . . even when it's been a long week.

calls scheduled throughout the day. After that, you are out and about: sitting down with a new client to make sure you've fully grasped what they have in mind for their event, checking out the spaces where you may hold upcoming parties or meetings, or actually attending one of the events you've spent so much time planning to make sure everything goes smoothly.

PREPARE FOR SUCCESS

You don't necessarily need a college degree to become a successful event planner, but many colleges offer two to four year programs in event planning or management. There are also domestic and international organizations that offer certifications in different areas of event planning. Many corporations look for these certifications on an event planner's resume to help in their screening process. Be mindful of the details because clients will be confident in your competency if you show you have an energetic and outgoing personality and a polished appearance.

GETTING YOUR FOOT IN THE DOOR

If you want to get a feel for the profession, then it's a good idea for you to intern or assist at an event planning firm or boutique. If you succeed at this temporary position, you can either become employed with a company or build up the contacts and know-how to start your own business. Volunteering for event planning at a local club, charity, or institution is another great way to build up your portfolio. Event planning is client-based and dictated, so get the word out to your friends, acquaintances, and family that you're taking on your own clients. Someone you already know, rather than a stranger, is more likely to hire you when you're starting out, so pull out your contact list and start calling around. Landing one great client and having everything run smoothly is the best advertisement.

BIGGEST CHALLENGES AND BEST PERKS

One of the biggest challenges of this profession may be the need to be on other people's schedules at all times. You have to juggle several deadlines without dropping the ball all while appearing pulled together and unflappable to your clients so they don't panic. Making time for much-needed networking is another challenge: to keep a strong client base, you have to go to parties and events . . . even when it's been a long week. However, the thrill of attending a well-organized event that you planned from start to finish is one of the biggest perks of this profession. The job involves juggling a lot of details and loose ends while keeping the client's creative vision and budget in mind; seeing it all come together in a finished product provides a huge sense of accomplishment. The constant variety of activities and settings is another perk; each assignment calls for a new location and set of tasks.

PROFESSIONAL PROFILE
Avg. starting salary: $45,000

Avg. salary after 5 years: : $51,000

Avg. salary 10 to 15 years: $64,000

JARGON

BO (banquet order) A document that lists the food items on the menu for all the meals at a particular event

Fam trip Familiarization tour of a facility or location to determine its suitability for a function

MOD Manager on duty

ARE YOU INTERESTED IN?
Catering, hosting

RELATED COLLEGE MAJORS
Event planning, event management, marketing, accounting, sales

FOR MORE INFORMATION
International Special Events Society:
www.ises.com

Convention Industry Council:
www.conventionindustry.org

Association of Destination Management Executives:
www.adme.org

FILM CRITIC

A (Relatively) Typical Day in the Life

The first prerequisite to becoming a movie critic is that you have to absolutely love to watch movies. When things get hectic you might be watching three in a day. We're not just talking about *Casablanca* and *The Godfather* and *Wedding Crashers*; we're also talking about the sorts of movies that make you wonder if the art of film has finally died. When you slip into the theater, don't expect to have a bucket of popcorn in one hand and a 32-ounce soda in the other. This is, after all, your job. Your hands will be busy holding a notebook and a pen. After you watch a movie, it's your job to assess its success in clean and engaging prose. You probably won't have a lot of time to sit around and think about it. After all, most film critics work for newspapers, magazines, and websites that are published once a week, sometimes daily. There's no compromising with deadlines.

The second prerequisite is that you must be in possession of a writing style that's analytic, yet zesty and inviting. Film critics write for a wide audience, from the haughtiest movie snobs to the average Joes who are just trying to make plans for Friday night. A strong knowledge of film, past and present, can help because it allows you to discuss the latest release in the context of other films—films that your readers might recognize. Film critics also devote time in each review to giving a plot synopsis of the film (hence the "no on popcorn but yes on notebook" rule). When all is said and done, critics often bestow the movie with a rating—four stars, thumbs up, that sort of thing.

Can it be a lot of work? Yeah. It can take some effort—to get and do the job. However, if you have a soft spot for movies and a way with the pen, you might not find a more enjoyable way to earn your rent money.

Prepare for Success

If you're in college and it's not too late, run to the registrar's office and enroll yourself in a film studies and English (or journalism) double major. Or at least find some time before graduation to take a class or two that gives you exposure to important films and a chance to polish your writing skills. The importance of strong writing skills cannot be emphasized enough. You might be able to recite every Coen Brothers film forward and backward, but if

An Extreme Day in the Life

Sara Michelle Fetters is senior editor for theatrical releases at Moviefreak.com, a film review site that receives 75,000 to 100,000 hits a day. As senior editor, she oversees a small staff of writers, edits their reviews, and, of course, sees and reviews a ton of movies herself. She also conducts interviews with people in the film industry. She says that her "scariest day" on the job was when she was supposed to interview one of those people. "[I] was going to an advance screening of Glory Road. Jerry Bruckheimer was introducing the picture that night and I was to meet him afterward. For some reason, talking with this guy really made me sweat. Granted, he's probably one of the five or so most powerful men in all of Hollywood, so I guess that made sense."

She continues, "Of course, wouldn't you know it, I was scheduled to interview him the next day and he got called out before my time came around. After sweating and fussing furiously over the thing, the darn interview never even happened. Talk about getting all worked up for nothing!"

Watching movies, talking about them, writing about them, letting them enrapture, enrage, and enliven you is really ... fulfilling.

you can't manage a few lively and insightful paragraphs explaining why *The Big Lebowski* is such a gem, then you're going to have trouble finding yourself a job. The best thing to do, then, is to begin writing film reviews for your school newspaper, small regional newspapers, and independent weeklies (if your town has any). Your pay will be small, if you get paid at all, but it doesn't matter. Do whatever you can to get some practice and to begin building a portfolio of published work that you can show to employers when you hit the job market. Oh, and watch a whole bunch of movies.

GETTING YOUR FOOT IN THE DOOR

If you love sci-fi movies, there's no reason why you shouldn't try to land some gigs reviewing sci-fi flicks. Early on in your career, don't be too stingy about what you want to review. Present yourself as a jack-of-all-trades, as eager to sit down with *Shrek* as with *Snakes on a Plane*. If you're working as a freelancer—as many aspiring film critics will have to do in the early days—try your hand at a variety of mediums. In other words, create the most diverse portfolio you can. Then when that magazine or website or daily newspaper that you totally want to work for announces an opening, you'll have clips to demonstrate that you're right for the job.

BIGGEST CHALLENGES AND BEST PERKS

You might think that writing about movies day in and day out would be a breeze, but when writer's block or exhaustion or general movie malaise sets in it's not always fun. Film festivals can also take their toll. No doubt they're fun, and full of great films, but trying to catch as many movies as possible, conduct interviews, sit in on press conferences, and take notes on every single thing you see can lead to a wearying day. Weary day or not, the deadlines loom. As Moviefreak.com's Sara Michelle Fetter says, "Looking at the clock ticking ominously forward when you have two columns and five reviews to write before Thursday's late-night deadline is rather depressing." She adds, "Watching movies, talking about them, writing about them, letting them enrapture, enrage, and enliven you is really one of the most fulfilling parts of my entire life. Sometimes it's a pain, sure, but if doing it wasn't sometimes trying how would you ever know you loved it so darn much?"

PROFESSIONAL PROFILE
Avg. salary: $20,000 to $60,000 per year.

Varies considerably based on whether reviewer is working part time and/or as a freelancer.

JARGON
Roman à clef A film that uses thinly veiled fictional surrogates for real people

Formalism Academic term for a film that calls attention to its artificiality

ARE YOU INTERESTED IN?
Movies, writing

RELATED COLLEGE MAJORS
Film studies, English, journalism

FOR MORE INFORMATION
Broadcast Film Critics Association: www.bfca.org

Los Angeles Film Critics Association: www.lafca.net

The Online Film Critic Society: http://ofcs.rottentomatoes.com

FORENSIC SCIENTIST

A (Relatively) Typical Day in the Life

Forensic scientists are involved in the search for and examination of physical evidence—gunshot residue, fingerprints, blood and tissue remnants, forged signatures, and any other clues that can be pieced together to help solve a crime. A day at the "office" could be spent in a morgue, at a crime scene, in a laboratory, or in the courtroom, where you may testify as an expert witness and explain your evaluation of the evidence and the techniques you used to reach your conclusions.

There are several career paths within the field of forensic science. Using chemicals, special instruments, and reenactment, a criminalist identifies evidence that can link a suspect to the crime scene; this may include isolating blood at a crime scene that doesn't match the victim, for example. Forensic dentists (odontologists) are generally called to crime scenes to assist with the investigation, and to give expert testimony in both criminal and civil cases. One of the most popularized fields of forensic science is forensic pathology—think of those autopsy room scenes in *Law & Order*. Forensic pathologists investigate the circumstances of death and are relied upon to determine the cause of death—natural, accidental, homicide, and so on. In addition to investigating violent death, pathologists also look for clues in sudden, unexpected deaths of healthy individuals and deaths that could have been the result of malpractice or negligence.

While it's not a career for the fainthearted, there's certainly not a lot of monotony in this field. When a forensic scientist is brought onto a case or project, they are being asked to solve a puzzle, and their unique training will give them the clearest view of the pieces needed to put it together.

An Extreme Day in the Life

Dr. Frederick Bieber has been an associate professor of pathology with Harvard Medical School's Brigham and Women's Hospital for more than 25 years, and he constructs a typical busy day at his job: "An extreme day for me would begin with final preparation for a lecture to our medical students on a topic such as wounding patterns from gunshots or edged weapons. After my lectures, I'd typically discuss details of the lecture with students, then head to the hospital to finalize lab results on genetic tests. This activity would face interruptions by my trips to the autopsy room to supervise a postmortem examination. Somewhere in the day, I'd meet with law enforcement or attorneys to discuss individual investigations or trial testimony, and I might also e-mail or talk with colleagues with whom I'm working on a manuscript to submit to a medical or scientific journal. If I'm lucky, I'd be able to sit still for 10 minutes to have a quick bite to eat with a colleague."

Dr. Bieber adds: "[I also field many calls] from all over the world about topics relating to science, law and medicine, including calls about how to tell whether twins are identical or not, and the best antivenom for a bite by the black mamba snake. This all makes for exhausting days, but each one is different and I can count on interesting conversation with my brilliant colleagues and students. I feel fortunate to have found a way to combine my academic and scholarly interests in genetics and pathology with law, medicine, and ethics. It's been a wonderful experience and provides a great substrate to teach and encourage students."

> When a forensic scientist is brought onto a case or project, they are being asked to solve a puzzle.

PREPARE FOR SUCCESS

Forensic scientists don't deal in dime-store whodunnits; they undergo intense training to prepare for both the scientific and psychological aspects of the work. All areas of forensic science require a strong problem-solving capacity, good speaking skills, natural curiosity, and excellent note-taking skills. All members of the field must hold at least a bachelor's degree, and most jobs require a master's or doctoral degree. Many concentrations call for the scientist to hold a medical degree and undergo training in scene and evidence investigation. This may entail an apprenticeship or residency following medical school graduation, proceeded by a one- or two-year fellowship. Ideally, coursework should include microscopy, statistics, chemistry, and biology. It also should be noted that indiscretions and even excessive traffic violations can prevent you from getting through the application process—so you'll need to make sure you maintain a clean record.

GETTING YOUR FOOT IN THE DOOR

Forensic science is no paper route; dedication to your training and education is the best way to show commitment to your career. The forensic residencies and fellowships that accompany any medical training will offer a natural course into the forensic field, but some labs offer trainee positions that do not require previous experience in the field. Most scientists start out as lab technicians in one of the natural sciences and parlay this experience into a position in the field of forensics.

BIGGEST CHALLENGES AND BEST PERKS

The extensive training process means you'll receive a gradual immersion into the sometimes harsh (and gross!) world of forensic science. Entry-level forensic scientists seldom go to crime scenes, finding their most frequent contact with law enforcement officials as they document the transfer of evidence and lab results from technicians to investigators, which provides a bird's-eye view of the law and a chance to see their work's impact. Most hands-on dirty work won't come until years down the line, by which point most people are chomping at the bit to take on cases of their own or focus on a specialty such as DNA evidence or crime scene investigation.

Advances in the field can come at an alarming rate, meaning you must keep constantly up-to-date on new methods and technologies, even long after you've left any sort of formal training. Sharing results logged throughout years of handling evidence and cases is vital to scientists across the world, and scientists are constantly challenged to improve on established techniques and to develop new disciplines. Forensic science is a relatively new field, and there are plenty of opportunities for scientists to leave their mark on the profession.

PROFESSIONAL PROFILE
Avg. starting salary: $30,000

Avg. salary after 5 years: : $55,000

Avg. salary 10 to 15 years: $65,000

JARGON
Ballistics The science that deals with the motion, behavior, and effects of projectiles, especially bullets

Dactylography The study of fingerprints as a method of identification

ARE YOU INTERESTED IN?
Crime-solving, chemistry, computers, puzzles

RELATED COLLEGE MAJORS
Forensic psychology, forensic science, criminal justice, criminology

FOR MORE INFORMATION
American Academy of Forensic Sciences:
www.aafs,org

American College of Forensic Examiners:
www.acfei.com

IMAGE CONSULTANT

A (Relatively) Typical Day in the Life

The image consulting industry gained popularity with the onslaught of television makeover shows that hire experts to hone regular everyday people into polished masterpieces. Many professionals, from stylists and makeup artists to speech therapists and etiquette instructors, work under the image consultant banner. The common thread is chipping away at the bad manners, dowdy wardrobe, bumbling speech, and other attributes that prevent the world from seeing a person's better self.

As an image consultant you might specialize in one area such as communication skills and whip clients into shape with diction, body language, and conflict resolution training. You might concentrate on physical appearance and give clients lessons on makeup application, wardrobe selection, and grooming. Or you could run a full-service consultancy that assesses and refines clients' images from head to toe and from work to play. Regardless of the path you take, no two days will be alike as you run around booking plastic surgery appointments, holding mock interviews, lecturing on table manners, and offering flirting pointers.

You better know your stuff. Discriminating customers can spot a phony from a mile away so image consultants must always bring their A-game. They have to look good, speak well, dress impeccably, and move gracefully to earn the trust of coveted clients. You must, in short, look the part. Once you've developed a client base, you must continue to offer valuable services as their needs change because of the success of your early efforts. The awkward bachelor whose

An Extreme Day in the Life

Just six years after launching her image consulting business out of a studio apartment in Boston, Samantha von Sperling is a sought after consultant with a global client list that runs the gamut from soccer moms and executives to socialites and royalty. She's appeared in *The Wall Street Journal*, *Details* magazine, *New York Daily News*, and more. She warns aspiring image consultants that success stories like hers are few and far between and that most do not yield a full-time income. "There are a handful of people who are very successful in this field and I'm happy to count myself among them. It didn't happen by accident either. I worked and worked and worked. And I still work hard. I'm almost never at my desk. These days I'm at the point that when I sit down to do some paperwork or filing I don't have a clue anymore. My mobile device is my office. Here's the downside: I work morning, noon, and night. I work seven days a week and I am on call from my clients all the time. I have clients worldwide and deal with multiple time zones from Hong Kong to Paris. It requires one to really like building relationships with people. If you don't like people, this is not the job for you. You deal with everybody's personalities, complexes, and inner turmoil. Whatever's going on in your client's life you are at the forefront of it. Nobody just says, 'I need a suit.' There's always an underlying reason. There's a reason that a 40-year-old asks you to teach him how to use a knife and fork. Something else has occurred in that person's life. In the process of providing the solution to the problem you deal with the whole person's issues."

Whatever's going on in your client's life, you are at the forefront of it. Nobody just says, 'I need a suit.'

pad you redecorated may now need some dancing and etiquette lessons for his upcoming wedding. Lucky for you, there's always room for improvement.

Prepare for Success

A wide array of life and professional experiences can prepare you well for this field. The trick is to build on your strengths. If you've come from humble circumstances and have a knack for fashion on a budget, don't position yourself as a high-end stylist. Instead, sell style consultations and closet clean-outs to soccer moms and other middle market clients. Similarly, if you're well-traveled and fluent in several languages you may be an international business etiquette trainer in disguise. Many image consultants fail because they haven't identified a clear market for their products or offer services they aren't qualified to give. Irreparable reputation damage can occur when dissatisfied customers tell the world how incompetent they think you are. You can also bolster your expertise by earning credentials, joining trade groups, and writing articles. Check out the websites of successful image consultants and study their accomplishments.

Getting Your Foot in the Door

There's really no substitute for hustle in this field where building up a well-paying clientele is an exercise in ingenuity. If you're in a hot image consulting market such as New York or Los Angeles, there is great demand for your services, but also extraordinary competition for the work. In less chic markets, you may find that there are too few potential customers to support your practice or that the marketing and advertising costs of finding the clients you want may be too high. In the early days, you'll need to knock on doors and write your own press releases just to let people know you exist.

Biggest Challenges and Best Perks

As an image consultant, you are subject to all the emotions and turmoil that come along with major life changes. You're an artist, but your canvas can talk back, resist recommendations, and insist on doing things in his or her own way to disastrous effect. Therefore, image consulting is a field that requires extreme patience, sensitivity, and determination. If change were easy, what would they need you for anyway?

On the upside, the independence of image consulting is a major draw for talented people who loathe the routine and bureaucracy of corporate work. Instead of sitting around waiting for a supervisor to recognize your extraordinary talents, you can build a business around the strengths you recognize in yourself. What's more you can see clients transformed before your eyes. Their lives, appearance, outlook, demeanor, and confidence can all be made over under your capable tutelage. It is a tremendous feeling to have a positive impact on someone's life and see the whole person emerge triumphantly.

Professional Profile
Salaries for image consultants vary widely depending on the area in which they work and how successful they are in building up a client base.

Avg. starting salary: $22,744

Avg. salary after 5 years: : $56,862

Avg. salary 10 to 15 years: $75,816

Jargon
Capsule wardrobe A wardrobe of basic clothing pieces that an image consultant will help you construct; covers casual, professional, and evening looks

Are you Interested In?
Personal style, etiquette, body language, fashion

Related College Majors
Communications, fashion design, human behavioral psychology

For More Information
Association of Image Consultants International:
www.aici.org

Flair Consulting:
www.flairconsulting.com

INTERIOR DESIGNER

A (Relatively) Typical Day in the Life

An interior designer is responsible for the interior design, decoration, and functionality of a client's space, whether the space is commercial, industrial, or residential. Interior designers work closely with architects and clients to determine the structure of a space, the needs of the occupants, and the style that best suits both. The position is a combination of engineer and artist, and it takes a unique type of mind to handle both of those concepts well. Interior designers have to be good with more than color, fabric, and furniture; interior designers must know materials, have budgeting skills, communicate well, and oversee the ordering, installation, and maintenance of all objects that define a space. They also have to know about electrical capacity, safety, and construction. Interior designers have to be able to work with contractors and clients alike, planning and implementing all aesthetic and functional decisions, usually within a fixed budget. Interior designers are hired for their expertise in a variety of styles and approaches, not merely their own personal vision. Therefore, they have to be willing to put their clients' tastes first. This requirement can be frustrating at first for many who enter the profession. Interior

An Extreme Day in the Life

Marsha Blum is an interior designer based in Denver, Colorado. Some of her most extreme moments involved just building up enough courage to pursue interior design as a career: "As a teenager in the 60s, I didn't have a clue as to what I should major in. I came up with sociology as a major since it seemed serious." After several semesters, Marsha realized that she needed to reconsider her direction. "During my sophomore year I had taken one interior design class. The fact that I couldn't stay awake past midnight studying for a sociology test, but could pull an all-nighter for my design project was a giant clue for me." This epiphany led Marsha to transfer to Pratt Institute in New York: "During my three years at Pratt, I had held many part-time jobs (working in a furniture store in Chinatown, for a solo furniture designer, a multi-disciplinary firm in Manhattan, and a firm that both designed and manufactured display items) and they taught me so much; I feel that the design schools that integrate internships into their programs are doing their students a great service." For Marsha, "the profession is a little like being a hairdresser; you need to listen to your client and interpret what they are saying. As an interior designer, I really enjoy the fact that I have great diversity in the tasks that are required of me. A large part is creative work, which is gratifying, but there is also a lot of organizational work and paperwork that wasn't taught when I went to school. Many people think that being a designer is just having good taste, but there are many aspects that are quite technical." Marsha warns, "Having to depend on other people to do the various parts of the work necessary to complete the projects can be distressing. When these people don't follow through, the client always looks to the designer, and the situations can be very stressful." She offers this advice to aspiring interior designers: "A strong portfolio is a must. Having good references from internships is a great bonus as well. A well-organized page that is both informative and graphically pleasing will make a good first impression. After all, the people reading these resumes are usually designers themselves."

"Interior designers have to be willing to put their clients' tastes first.

designers are often asked to begin their planning before construction of a space is finished; this means that they must be good at scheduling and comfortable reading blueprints. This element of the job comes as a surprise to many new interior designers, who expect to have less of an administrative and technical role and more of a role in influencing the overall feel and appearance of a space. This ability to balance the practical with the aesthetic is crucial to being a successful interior designer.

PREPARE FOR SUCCESS

The academic and professional requirements for most areas of design are fairly general, with the emphasis on portfolio development and professional experience. Interior design, however, has nationally standardized requirements. Interior designers must have a bachelor's degree. Employers look favorably upon those who have studied engineering, design, and art. Those who want more specific study complete interior design programs. Interior designers must also be familiar with federal, state, and local interior design codes (involving such issues as capacity, flammability, and stress levels). To be federally licensed, prospective interior designers must pass the qualification exam given by the National Council for Interior Design. Professional organizations are significant in this field, and many interior designers find it helpful to join one or more of them.

GETTING YOUR FOOT IN THE DOOR

Two years into the profession, many aspiring interior designers are working as interns or assistants, as entry into the field is competitive. A number of students make connections through relationships their schools have with major employers. During these first two years, many act as assistants, learning budgeting, competitive pricing, and client communication skills. Salaries are low or nonexistent in these early years, hours are long, and satisfaction may be low. About 20 percent of potential interior designers leave the profession within the first three years.

BIGGEST CHALLENGES AND BEST PERKS

This profession allows designers to apply their creativity and expansive technical knowledge to their work. Expertise in both realms is paramount to success and this, unfortunately, takes time to acquire. Frequently, designers can find themselves at odds with their clients and it takes deft communication skills and diplomacy to work through creative differences. That said, interior designers do get to explore their creative vision and have fun of shopping on someone else's dime.

PROFESSIONAL PROFILE
Avg. starting salary: $21,200
Avg. salary after 5 years: $39,100
Avg. salary 10 to 15 years: $69,640

JARGON
Shabby chic A design style that purposely uses old, worn items.
Murphy bed A bed that folds down from the wall.

ARE YOU INTERESTED IN?
Design, art, architecture

RELATED COLLEGE MAJORS
Interior design, architecture, art history, graphic art, industrial design

FOR MORE INFORMATION
American Society of Interior Designers:
www.asid.org
Foundation for Interior Design Education Research:
www.fider.org
International Interior Design Association:
www.iida.org

JOURNALIST

A (Relatively) Typical Day in the Life

There are many types of journalists, from local beat newspaper reporters to foreign correspondents, magazine feature writers to freelance book reviewers, and so on. It is difficult to pin down the daily routine of an average journalist. Journalists interview sources and review records to assemble, collect, and report information and explore the implications of the facts. Journalism informs, educates, and chastises: Never underestimate the power a journalist holds. Think back to the Watergate scandal, when Robert Woodward and Carl Bernstein, two reporters for *The Washington Post*, discovered and published information that led to the resignation of Richard Nixon.

Professionals must be able to report quickly and accurately. Time pressure is one of the most distinguishing features of this job. Journalists must maintain a point of view while remaining objective about their subjects, which can be difficult; even colleagues sometimes get too involved in the stories. Interpersonal skills, excellent writing skills, and a reporter's instinct (the ability to accurately assess the significance of obscure and incomplete information) are essential to success.

The uncertainty of the daily routine makes it difficult to incorporate family, hobbies, and any regularly scheduled plans; but those who detest the predictability of nine-to-five jobs are attracted to journalism because no day is

An Extreme Day in the Life

As a journalist for the *Hyde Park Herald*, the oldest community newspaper in Chicago, Kiratiana Freelon says her days on the job were intense from the very beginning: "I was doing the education beat so we covered the Chicago public schools a lot. When I came in they had a very controversial plan to close underperforming schools and reopen them as charters mainly in lower-income and minority neighborhoods. This plan was affecting a lot of schools in Hyde Park. My second week on the job I had to cover a Chicago public school board meeting. There was a huge protest—300 people—parents, kids, and community members chanting slogans for and against the plan." For Kiratiana, this was an apt introduction to what life as a journalist would entail. "The good thing about the education beat is that people get passionate about kids. Going to the board meeting gave me the opportunity to meet people who were advocates for education in my community. It was a great way to build rapport with the movers and shakers whom I would be calling on for info. I found that I had to work hard to find a healthy balance between being out in the field and actually coming back to my desk to write the story. The pressure to meet deadlines is intense. If you don't get your articles done you put the whole production schedule behind." Kiratiana has this advice for aspiring journalists: "If you want a long-term career in journalism don't be adverse from starting from the bottom. If you want to start off with a decent salary right out of college get involved with national journalism associations like the Society of Professional Journalists. Go to their national conferences to take advantage of networking opportunities and to attend job fairs. It's about getting in front of the right people. Complete as many internships as you possible can during the summer. In journalism, even if you have great education and a great degree it all comes down to experience." Kiratiana is also the author of a self-published travel guide to Paris.

No day is a carbon copy of the previous one.

a carbon copy of the previous one. Long hours and chronic deadline pressure can be significantly negative factors. When an editor calls you in on a breaking story, you have to be prepared to drop everything; when you're on deadline, you can get crazed trying to write a complicated story in half the time you would normally need.

Prepare for Success

Most journalists hold a bachelor's degree in journalism, communications, English, or political science. More than a few distinguished careers have begun at the school newspaper or at a neighborhood magazine or newspaper. Many journalists come to the profession later in life after gaining expertise and connections in other professions. Journalism jobs are highly competitive: Credentials and experience must be accompanied by gumption and hard work. Excellent writing skills are a must, as are computer word-processing skills. Brush up on proofreading skills before applying for any job. Foreign language skills may be necessary for people who report on the international scene. Persistence, initiative, stamina, and the desire to tell real stories about real events are critical to the survival of the budding journalist. The best journalists have a knack for putting contemporary events into historical perspective.

Getting Your Foot in the Door

Many aspiring reporters begin their careers by pitching story ideas to local newspapers and magazines on a piecemeal basis. Writers who can show clippings from school newspapers or other publications—no matter how minor—begin with an advantage if the prose is good. Aspiring writers may have to survive repeated rejections before a story idea is finally accepted for publication, and the income stream from freelance journalism is so unpredictable that many take more regular-paying jobs. Most aspire to a salaried job at a local newspaper during these scrambling years. As at all levels of this profession, satisfaction is high despite low income.

Biggest Challenges and Best Perks

Journalism is a tough, transient industry where rejection is customary, especially when first embarking on your career. Jobs will likely be sporadic and pay low in the beginning but many journalists think the risks are well worth it. The job is imbued with an unpredictable nature, which frequently brings excitement and adventure. Not a single day is routine. A variety of stories allow you to interact many different people and communities. Deadlines and challenging articles can make for stressful scenarios but ultimately nothing is more thrilling than seeing your name in print and knowing you are reaching an audience.

PROFESSIONAL PROFILE
Avg. starting salary: $28,100
Avg. salary after 5 years: : $44,600
Avg. salary 10 to 15 years: $69,300

JARGON
Shield laws Laws that protect a journalist's right to keep their sources confidential

Dingbat Typographical device used for ornamentation

Kill To remove or delete copy

ARE YOU INTERESTED IN?
Writing, reporting, media

RELATED COLLEGE MAJORS
Journalism, communications, English, creative writing

FOR MORE INFORMATION
American Society of Journalists and Authors:
www.asja.org

The Newspaper Guild:
www.newsguild.org/

Society of Professional Journalists:
www.spj.org

MEDIATOR

A (Relatively) Typical Day in the Life

Being a professional mediator is all about conflict resolution, and so the job demands a person with excellent reasoning, problem-solving, and peace-making abilities. When two parties have a dispute and wish to avoid the legal intricacies of litigation, they may call in a mediator to facilitate an equitable solution. While lawyers and attorneys are sometimes regarded with suspicion, mediators are more often attributed with qualities of wisdom, trustworthiness, and neutrality. Unlike lawyers and judges, who evaluate, assess, and decide for others, mediators help participating parties evaluate, assess, and decide for themselves. Parties wishing to avoid the delays, high costs, publicity, and ill will brought on by litigation look to mediators as a more peaceful, inexpensive, and expedient alternative.

The mediator's job is to listen, sort through differences between the two parties involved in a dispute, and find common ground upon which to ascertain a solution. A good mediator is honest, neutral, and encouraging; listens well; and has excellent communication skills. Helping two parties arrive at a mutually agreeable solution also takes a fair amount of creativity. Mediation is considered a form of Alternative Dispute Resolution (ADR). Although ADR sounds like a terrible syndrome, it is, in fact, a more Zen-like approach to conflict resolution, with mediators as the master practitioners. Corporations, government agencies, community organizations, schools, neighborhoods, and even families will turn to mediators when they seek mutually acceptable answers to their problems. Examples of conflicts they work to resolve include labor/management issues, health care disputes, environmental/public policy issues, and international conflicts.

An Extreme Day in the Life

As a mediator, every day on the job is extreme. This is definitely not a job for people who are afraid of conflict and confrontation. The mediator we spoke with is the Director for School Programs at a Conflict Resolution Center in California, and appreciates how successful conflict resolution techniques can help create a safer school environment: "I schedule student, staff, and/or parent training at school sites on how to communicate effectively to solve problems. I contract with individual trainers who have the necessary skills and meet with school administrators with plans to create and maintain a safe school environment for all. My organization can provide neutral third-party assistance when necessary, assist with mediations at school sites, and facilitate staff and/or parent meetings, particularly if there are differences." While the best days on the job are those that end with mutually agreeable solutions on the table, every day brings its own challenges and rewards: "It's fun and satisfying to work with students, staff, and parents. They all appreciate acquiring the skills to communicate more effectively. Greatest challenge for me was getting it all done in the time allotted. There are 23 school districts with over 120 schools in the county, so there's far more work to be done."

Helping two parties arrive at a mutually agreeable solution also takes a fair amount of creativity.

Prepare for Success

The educational background of a professional mediator varies widely. A fair number in the field hold law degrees, while others may not even hold a bachelor's degree. Most important is an education in mediation, whether taken as part of an undergraduate degree or as individual training courses. University degrees in public policy, law, and related fields also provide helpful backgrounds. While few states require licenses or certification to practice mediation, most individuals in the profession have completed training and pledged to abide by certain ethical standards.

Getting Your Foot in the Door

Most people come to this profession after working in another field. Lawyers, religious leaders, social workers, counselors, and educators are often called on to mediate. Judges and magistrates also play the role of mediator. Strong mediators have many possible professions open to them, including that of diplomat and politician.

In the business realm, mediation has long been used as a source for conflict resolution. Since 1887, the American government has promoted arbitration and mediation for contractual disputes involving commerce. Today, increasing numbers of colleges and universities offer degrees in dispute resolution and conflict management. Students who combine a business/law background with conflict management expertise can expect to be highly marketable in this field.

Biggest Challenges and Best Perks

The biggest challenge, of course, is the act of mediation itself. The pressure to come up with a solution that both parties can agree on is intense. In addition, being the person thrown into the middle of a dispute can be an uncomfortable position, to say the least.

One of the biggest perks of being a professional mediator is the ability to set your own hours. A dispute may arise at any time, but unless there is a pending deadline, mediators tend to work eight-hour days. In addition, mediators have the potential to make a genuine difference in the lives of the disputing parties. As a mediator's experience increases, they are called upon to help resolve larger disputes. Some of the more experienced mediators travel extensively to help resolve disputes anywhere in the world. Highly competent mediators may be called upon to handle high-profile cases ranging from corporate disputes to international peacekeeping missions.

PROFESSIONAL PROFILE
Avg. starting salary: N/A

Avg. salary 5 years: N/A

Avg. salary 10 to 15 years: N/A

JARGON
Active listening The process of seeking to understand another person's point of view without judgment

"I"-message A technique for expressing your feelings assertively, without evaluating or blaming others

MLATNA Most Likely Alternative To a Negotiated Agreement

FOR MORE INFORMATION
Association of Family and Conciliation Courts:
www.afccnet.org

Association for Conflict Resolution:
www.acrnet.org

Southern California Mediation Association:
www.scmediation.org

MYSTERY SHOPPER

A (Relatively) Typical Day in the Life

An entire industry of anonymous product evaluators (AKA mystery shoppers) has cropped up across the globe. Market research firms, merchandising companies, private investigation firms, and training organizations all hire investigators to go shopping and then write about their experiences. Mystery shoppers poke around retail stores judging customer service, wait times, ease of product return, and item quality. They can also be found in banks, restaurants, and anywhere else the public frequents for goods and services.

Before setting foot in the store, the mystery shopping company briefs shoppers on what they need to keep an eye out for and assess. They may provide a script for questions to ask, complaints to have, or things to purchase. Then the shoppers get to work, executing the plan. The mystery part comes in because they have to gather information subtly and appear to be a normal customer. So no notebooks are allowed and shoppers must make mental notes as they evaluate sales techniques, product knowledge, store cleanliness, and employee integrity. Later they'll need to complete a questionnaire giving specific, detailed feedback on their experiences, such as how long sales associates took to greet them.

Ultimately, the post-shopping information they provide is aggregated with other mystery shopper's experiences to help client companies improve their employee training and customer service.

An Extreme Day in the Life

Deborah Abrams Kaplan has always been a stickler for customer service, but she generally kept her evaluations to herself until a friend got her hip to the undercover world of mystery shopping. Now she sips lattes, dines in chic restaurants, sees movies, and gets her oil changed on mystery shopping companies' tabs. "The best one was a movie theater gig. Once a month, I got reimbursed to see whatever movie I wanted. I also had to go to the café and the snack stand with a certain allowance and got $10 in addition. Afterward I had to fill out a form about the customer service and list what trailers were shown. It's a cheap date. It takes about 20 to 40 minutes to complete the paperwork. Filling out the form is a huge drag. Every form is different and the requirements for each shop is different."

The mother of two small children mystery shops on a part-time basis, but has signed up with about 20 customer evaluation companies to keep up a steady stream of assignments that help defray the cost of household or entertainment expenses. For example, Deborah takes the two family cars in for oil changes every three months and gets reimbursed for the expense. "Preparation is important. You're not supposed to walk in there with a notebook. You have to know what you need to get, remember it and come back and enter the information on their website. Sometimes you'll need to fax in or scan in receipts, usually within 24 hours or there's a clause where you won't get paid. It is important to meet the deadline and do a good job. Some of the companies rank your work and let you know what your scores are. They may ban you from doing further assignments."

> No notebooks are allowed and shoppers must make mental notes as they evaluate sales techniques, product knowledge, store cleanliness, and employee integrity.

Prepare for Success

The best way to prepare for mystery shopping opportunities is to conduct Internet research. The website of the Mystery Shopping Providers Association is a great place to find reputable secret shopping companies and a database of available jobs. You do not need to spend a dime to enter this field so beware of scams that require you to pay to become a mystery shopper. Also watch out for online ruses that ask aspiring secret shoppers to deposit a check, keep a portion as their mystery shopping fee, and then wire the rest to another recipient. In this scam, the check is bad and the poor shopper loses the transferred funds and the wire transfer fee. A Federal Trade Commission consumer alert urges consumers to be skeptical of mystery shopping companies that advertise in newspapers' help wanted sections or by e-mail, guarantee jobs, charge a fee for shopping opportunities, or sell directories of mystery shopping companies.

Getting Your Foot in the Door

Hundreds of mystery shopping opportunities are available online and you'll boost your chances of finding great gigs if you apply to several customer evaluations firms and mystery shopping schedulers. If your application is accepted, the hiring company will teach you everything that you need to know to do a great job. Don't be frustrated if you don't hear back from anyone right away. The number of mystery shopping opportunities varies widely depending upon the number of stores in your area and the popularity of mystery shopping. The MSPA offers a certification program for mystery shoppers that is not required by most companies, but could set you apart in a competitive market.

Biggest Challenges and Best Perks

Very few people are savvy and industrious enough to earn a full-time living mystery shopping so don't expect to get rich if this is your main income source. Mystery shoppers are independent contractors and must be selective in the assignments they accept or else the time and hassle involved in the shopping trip and evaluation may outweigh any benefits. A mystery shopper could even potentially lose money if the money you spend on gas exceeds the fee you earn from the shopping trip or if you don't complete the evaluation form in the contracted time period and the company doesn't pay you.

Even though the average pay of $10 to $20 per shopping trip may not be much to write home about, many mystery shoppers say other perks like free meals and merchandise discounts make the job worthwhile. Plus, mystery shoppers enjoy the emotional payoff of helping to improve the service sector and hopefully spare others bad shopping experiences.

Professional Profile
Avg. salary: $10 to $20 per shopping trip, plus lots of free perks

Jargon
U&A (Usability and Attitude Surveys) Attempt to measure the ease of use and effectiveness of a product or service and the attitudes of a target group of consumers toward the product or service

Are you Interested In?
Shopping, customer service

Related College Majors
Operations management, marketing

For More Information
Mystery Shopping Providers Association:
www.mysteryshop.org

The Secret Shopper Company:
www.secretshoppercompany.com

Reality Check Mystery Shoppers:
www.rcmysteryshopper.com

OUTSIDE SALES REPRESENTATIVE

A (Relatively) Typical Day in the Life

Opportunities for sales representatives have progressed beyond selling vacuums door-to-door or making cold calls about life insurance. Granted, there are still old-fashioned traveling salesmen toting cases of kitchen knives from place to place, but the modern sales representative uses technology to their every advantage in their day-to-day lives. Pitches, presentations, and contracts are e-mailed, faxed, or shipped halfway across the world via next-day delivery. Although a lot of the personal interaction that used to drive the business
world has been replaced by electronic means of communication, there's still nothing that can drive a sale like face time with your prospective client. An outside sales representative can still expect to spend a lot of time on the phone making arrangements to meet with one prospective client while pitching to another. Most outside sales representatives cover a geographical area, and depending on the company this could be as small as one city or as large as a few states. Either way, the miles start to add up as you travel to maintain client relationships or sign new deals. Because clients are bound to be as busy as you are, days can be long, and you have to be prepared with an agenda for each client you meet. To foster the best relationship with your customer, you also have to be well-versed in every product your company offers. This means staying on top of new developments, procedures, and even new hires if they're going to be interacting with your client. Unless you're lucky enough to work for a corporation that dominates the market, you're also going to have to spend time staying on top of what the competition is up to—and this can involve some creative maneuvering.

An Extreme Day in the Life

Michael Parnes, account executive for Equifax Corp., one of three credit bureaus in the United States, says that the biggest motivation for him to enter sales was the "earnings potential." He didn't intend to take this path, however. "I was a district operations manager for over 20 years. I chose not to sell for 16 of those years." Being an outside sales rep means having a lot of independence in how you structure your days and the leads you choose to follow. To keep up-to-date on current trends and prospective clients, Michael "look(s) at business news in the paper and on the Internet" as part of his daily routine. The biggest challenge he faces in maintaining and attracting new clients is "price pressure from competition. Technology is changing the product and pricing landscape so rapidly that what you believe to be a core competency or cutting edge solution could become outdated within weeks." Landing a big account is a memorable moment for any sales rep, and one such triumph stands out for Michael. He "proposed a $1 million+ deal that was accepted by a company in which they would have been the first to purchase a particular system. That was a big win." However, there are no guarantees in life or sales. "The company was sold four days before the deal was signed and the deal was dead." The biggest piece of advice Michael offers to anyone interested in getting into sales is to remember that "'No' is just another word. People will listen to you as long as you are prepared to hold a conversation with them."

> 'No' is just another word. People will listen to you as long as you are prepared to hold a conversation with them.

Prepare for Success

An undergraduate degree is almost always required, although a specialized degree in sales isn't necessary. It's more important to further educate yourself by reading industry and business publications and developing your public speaking and presentation skills. Offer your services to the school newspaper selling advertising space and classified ads to get some experience to add to your resume. Jobs in inside sales departments (telemarketing, for example) tend to be extremely flexible with school schedules and can be a great way to build your confidence and sales persona. Often outside sales reps have so little time to spend in the office taking care of paperwork, that they really need help with the clerical side of things. That's where interns come in handy. Remember, in a job interview you're selling yourself to your prospective employer, so if you have a specific company or industry you want to work in, do your homework and be prepared to discuss specifics.

Getting Your Foot in the Door

If you're willing to work for low—or even no—wages, the door might open a little wider for you. Be prepared to start out in an entry-level position, as an intern, an administrative assistant, or a call center representative. This will help you understand the company and its services before you try to move up. Most companies have their own styles of selling, and actually prefer to catch you while you're still green. The Internet is brimming with advertisements for salespeople, and they attract countless job seekers. The key to getting noticed is persistence—send a resume, find someone already in the business to call in a recommendation, and follow up on your application. If you appear willing to work as hard on the job as you did to get the job, chances are they might put more thought into how you'd fit with the company than they will for other applicants.

Biggest Challenges and Best Perks

It's not hard to get an entry-level sales job, but once you are ready to take on the role of an actual outside sales representative, the competition between job hunters becomes more fierce. Landing the job isn't always the hardest part, however; the competition for clients between companies can be fierce. Whatever it is you're selling, the biggest perk of the job remains the same—winning the hard-to-get account (not to mention the financial reward that comes from doing so). Some sales representatives are paid only based on the customers and accounts they bring in; it can be difficult to grow accustomed to putting in the hours and not being guaranteed a paycheck.

PROFESSIONAL PROFILE

Avg. salary: $30,423 plus bonuses and commission

Avg. salary after 5 years: : $64,809 plus bonuses and commission

Avg. salary 10 to 15 years: $101,162 plus bonuses and commission

JARGON

Close A statement that ends the sales pitch and asks the customer to purchase the product

ARE YOU INTERESTED IN?

Sales, business

RELATED COLLEGE MAJORS

Liberal arts, business, economics, technology

FOR MORE INFORMATION

Health Industries Representative Association:
www.hira.org

Manufacturer's Agents National Association:
www.manaonline.org

North American Industrial Representatives Association:
www.nira.org

PRIVATE TUTOR

A (Relatively) Typical Day in the Life

At The Princeton Review, we like to think we know a little something about helping young people navigate the complex transition from high school to college. Each year a new group of young people takes the standardized exams, fills out the applications, and writes the essays before sending the package off with bated breath in hopes of getting in to the college of their dreams. Year after year, as competition to impress college admissions boards continues to build, so to does the role of the private tutor.

It has always been the job of the private tutor to prepare young people—especially teenagers—to excel at school and on standardized tests, but where there was once the assumption that the only students being tutored were those falling behind, today, the drive for perfection among many successful students has blown the tutoring market wide open. As you'd probably expect, the typical day for a tutor—assuming it's a weekday while school is in session—begins sometime after three. Don't let the name fool you, tutors are teachers. They may not be state certified—although that's not a safe assumption—but make no mistake about it, what goes on in those private sessions is teaching. The only difference is that the tutor-to-student ratio allows the student to receive more focused attention to their individual problems, resulting in a better chance of overcoming them.

An Extreme Day in the Life

Jacqueline Byrne is a private tutor working in New Jersey who specializes in getting kids ready for college in one of two ways: test preparation and college application essay editing and development. While editing essays seems natural to her—she got her start more than two decades ago working behind the scenes editing essays for a college counselor—Jacqueline's still a little surprised by how well she's taken to tutoring students who are trying to improve their standardized test scores. The trick, it seems, is in finding some way to make what can be some pretty dry material fresh for both the tutor and the student. "Motivating kids to do their best is the real challenge and reward of this career. The SAT and ACT get boring after a while, but if you love the students then teaching them to prepare for [those] tests is a pleasure." After working out of her home for six years, Jacqueline turned the satisfaction she gets from teaching into a bankable business. She's one of the founders of Ivy Educational Services and author of a test preparation guide designed to help improve students' verbal scores on the SAT. How does her approach differ from some of her colleagues? "I believe in teaching the academic material and then strategies, but many tutors just teach the tricks." Jacqui believes that it's her job "to find a way to teach them the material." It's in the ability to reach kids who may have seemed unreachable, whether through bumping up their test scores, or improving their level of reading comprehension that Jacqui finds her daily motivation. "I love my students, and I will not give up on them. [They] make me happy every day."

The drive for perfection among many successful students has blown the tutoring market wide open.

PREPARE FOR SUCCESS

While nothing's written in stone regarding what you have to do to become a private tutor, one thing's for sure: You have to know your stuff. If you're going to teach for the SAT, for instance, you're going to be expected to be capable of getting an 800 for whichever section you plan on teaching. Clearly, a prerequisite for test prep tutoring would be a history of testing well yourself. From there, most parents are going to want to know your educational background before they let you anywhere near their kids (let alone pay you for your services). At the very least, an undergraduate degree is going to be a must have. Also, if it'd be helpful if your degree were in the field in which you're claiming to specialize—just a suggestion. A lot of tutors are current or former teachers.

GETTING YOUR FOOT IN THE DOOR

Depending on your aspirations, it may not be that difficult to get your foot in the door. Tutoring and test preparation is a huge growth industry, and if you're qualified it probably won't be that tough to get a position at a tutoring agency. Agencies pay fairly well, but they have a tendency to require that you sign an agreement stating that you will not compete with the agency. The downside of this, of course, is that it eliminates—while you're working at the agency and for a time thereafter—your ability to work independently, and freelance work is where your potential earning power increases exponentially.

BIGGEST CHALLENGES AND BEST PERKS

Tutoring is not easy work. Regardless of their student's grade point average, a private tutor comes into a young person's life during a pretty tense time. Whether they're struggling to get by, or just looking for a small improvement on their test scores, they and their parents have come to you with a certain amount of concern and hope. Their concern stems from a fear of failure (in all its forms), and they hope that you can work your magic and help the student succeed. It can be a pretty intense situation. There will be high, even impossible expectations, and it's your job to keep everybody focused on reality and the task at hand. While balancing parents' expectations with students' abilities can be hard work, it can also be very lucrative. The money's nothing compared with the feeling you get from helping a young person through what can be an immensely stressful period of their life.

PROFESSIONAL PROFILE
Avg. salary: $30 per hour, at agency; varies

Avg. salary: $80 per hour, private; varies

JARGON
Differentiated instruction A method of customized instruction, for example, different teaching methods for students with learning disabilities

LD Learning disability

ARE YOU INTERESTED IN?
Education

RELATED COLLEGE MAJORS
No specific major required, although a B.A. or B.S. degree or higher is essential

FOR MORE INFORMATION
National Tutoring Association: www.ntatutor.org

The Princeton Review: www.PrincetonReview.com

PRODUCER (FILM, TV, MUSIC)

A (RELATIVELY) TYPICAL DAY IN THE LIFE

Producers are essentially project managers for the movies, TV shows, or music pieces on which they are working. Every detail from start to finish is within the scope of your responsibility; while you should delegate, you should also be ready to be intimately familiar and involved with every aspect of the project. This is a real hands-on job with erratic, often long hours, and requires you to wear several hats.

Producers need to meet with the heads of the television shows and movies on which they are working. This meeting usually includes the director, who naturally handles the creative direction of the project, and the writers. You'll spend a lot of time hashing out details with the heads of the project from other areas, such as hiring, figuring out whether or not an important part of the set has been procured, finding out what actor is having trouble with the project or might need coaching, and tying up any other loose ends. Afterward, you might spend time watching the filming and taking note of what shots need better props. You might also spend a few hours making phone calls to pull in additional funding and ensure that project deadlines are met. You might meet with a bunch of extras later in the day and reconvene with the project leaders to figure out what needs to happen overnight to keep the show going. Over the course of the day you could spend hours checking information, speaking to financial backers and distributors, hiring or firing actors and other key personnel, and generally paving the way for the show or movie to be finished successfully within budget and on time. The day could end as late as the next morning, especially when there is a deadline looming.

PREPARE FOR SUCCESS

For a job as a producer, it's a good idea to get a college degree in some area of the visual arts. A handful of colleges and universities now offer degrees in arts management; this proves useful—both in providing experiences and

An Extreme Day in the Life

Hardy Spire sees all the events leading up to his current position as senior producer for the *CBS News Early Show* as having a consistent theme. He says, "I've always had an interest in working in television. From the childhood idea of life as a TV weatherman to my college internship, it was the common denominator of everything that interested me the most." In his current position, he "supervise[s] a staff of seven producers and associate producers responsible for coverage of breaking news and feature stories for the network's daily national morning news broadcast," so he is definitely familiar with extreme days on the job. The show's early airtime means an extremely early call time in the mornings; as producer, he is responsible for getting everything leading up to the broadcast ready, whether he delegates or does it himself. Spire's advice to anyone who wants to become a producer is simple: "Be willing to take any job in the area that interests you, no matter how low on the totem poll. First jobs never last for very long, and you can't get the job you want until you figure out a way to get in the door. Also, don't count on any of those contacts you made as an intern to pay off unless you use them immediately after your internship is over."

This job requires huge reserves of diplomacy, tact, and firmness.

offering network opportunities—to aspiring film producers. It takes a lot of work to become head producer, so be willing to pay your dues for several years by taking on low-paying grunt work in different areas of production to learn the ropes. Many producers start out as assistant producers—often a gopher position—on various projects, where they shadow higher-level producers and do all the odd jobs for a project. If your interest is specific to a certain type of project, you can start by volunteering on sets and interning during summers or for a semester.

GETTING YOUR FOOT IN THE DOOR

Since this is a job that covers so many areas of media, contacts can be invaluable in getting jobs and keeping clients. If you are equipped with the right skills and talents, a sufficient supply of drive, and an enviable Rolodex, you are well on your way. Be proactive about meeting people in the industry and keep in touch with your contacts to make sure they think of you when new projects come up. At the beginning of your career, it is definitely a mistake to turn down projects, even if they aren't in your area of interest. Future clients will look at your past work as a measure of your talent, so take any projects that come your way so that you can learn the ropes and build some solid experience for your resume. Short-term positions in every other aspect of a movie or TV project will only help you learn more about a producer's job, so look for entry level assignments in writing, casting, and any other related job.

BIGGEST CHALLENGES AND BEST PERKS

The biggest challenge in the job of a producer is staying on top of all the details involved with bringing a project to fruition. The job can call for exhausting hours for days on end, and it's challenging to stay fresh and innovative under these conditions. Many producers find the biggest challenge to be negotiating the artistic vision of the client and the reality of budget and time constraints. The job requires huge reserves of diplomacy, tact, and firmness.

The job of a producer is different every day and this variety is one of the biggest perks of the profession. You will meet people in many different areas of media over the course of a project, and you will most likely travel with the set. There are often opportunities to take long breaks between projects, during which you can relax, work on hobbies, or even get started on a pet project of your own for the future.

PROFESSIONAL PROFILE
Avg. starting salary: $20,000
Avg. salary after 5 years: $50,000
Avg. salary 10 to 15 years: $100,000

JARGON

Attached Denotes that the interest and/or commitment of an actor to a project has been secured for the purpose of attracting the interest of a network

Beat sheet An abbreviated outline of a story, or blueprint for a script, with brief descriptions of each scene

Blind commitment A deal made by a network or studio with a producer, writer, or actor to develop new projects following the success of a current project

ARE YOU INTERESTED IN?
Media and entertainment

RELATED COLLEGE MAJORS
Visual arts, audio or video engineering, sound production, arts management

FOR MORE INFORMATION
Producers Guild of America:
www.producersguild.org

National Association of Television Program Executives:
www.natpe.org

PRODUCT TESTER

A (Relatively) Typical Day in the Life

If you've ever worked on a computer, called a friend on a cell phone, worn a t-shirt, or eaten processed food, you've most likely benefited from the work of product testers. These are the people who spend hours trying to beat a video game to make sure that all the wrinkles have been ironed out before it hits the market. They might be responsible for breaking in a pair of shoes to make sure the soles won't crack after five wears. They are also the people who work in laboratories testing everything from a product's light sensitivity to its temperature threshold. Product testers decide whether the manufactured goods we spend our money on are actually up to snuff—in terms of safety, functionality, and enjoyment.

Sound like fun? It can be. But be aware that "product testing" can mean many different things. In many cases, a product tester works for a particular manufacturer and uses whatever tools are available to locate defects in the goods being made. (They sometimes do inspection work as well, making sure that the products meet regulatory standards.) Product testers may see an item in its early and middle stages of development, and just before its release to the public; they often have the chance to be involved—in a very fundamental way—in the step-by-step manufacturing of the things we use in our everyday lives. At other times, however, product testers are assigned to one point

An Extreme Day in the Life

Darien Patrick Buchanan is a software quality assurance analyst who works as an independent consultant. According to Darien, "software quality assurance in the information age will always have many interesting moments." One particularly nightmarish project involved developing an interface for a financial institution's product and sales teams that was capable of real-time updating:

"When you work for a financial company, every dollar and penny has to be accounted for. A mistake could cost millions. One of the programmers felt she could accomplish this great feat alone, and the nightmare began. She was the only person that understood her code, and when deadlines were missed, she was forced to stay at the bank and work around the clock until all issues had been resolved. Every time a fix was ready we had to be ready to test, which meant my boss and I worked around the clock as well. I typically slept under my cubicle or in empty conference rooms, showering in a nearby hotel next to the office complex. After about two weeks, the overzealous programmer cracked and escaped to Puerto Rico. She returned after about a week, sanity intact. The project was completed soon after, leading to an increase of millions in revenue monthly. The project was a success, but it was quite an experience."

Darien offers this advice to aspiring product testers interested in working with software: "This is not a job that should be taken lightly. The business expects you to ensure the functionality of its products, which means you are essentially responsible for ensuring quality. The stress can be immense. Long hours are standard, and weekends are inevitable. You will rarely get praise for your efforts, but if something goes wrong, you are the first one they look for. If you want to move ahead, you have to work incredibly hard to stay current with technology, testing methodologies, and automated methods of testing."

The better you know your products, the better tester you'll be.

in the production process—say, examining the hemlines of jeans as they roll down the assembly line. Working conditions and pay vary according to employer, but significantly higher salaries apply if you're planning to enter product testing/development in the tech fields or as a scientific analyst.

Prepare for Success:

What sort of product testing are you interested in? Knowing this will help you determine what you'll need to accomplish before stepping into the job. For many standard positions in a factory or plant, a solid high-school education will do the trick; whatever other training you need, you'll get on the job. However, product testers are increasingly sought by manufacturers/developers in specialized fields ranging from computer software to car parts, and to be an effective tester in these areas, you'll need to know your stuff. A summer job is a great way to land the hands-on experience that employers will prize. And if computer software is your thing, take all the technology courses your schedule can fit; anything that lets you get your virtual hands dirty with the latest computer programs. The better you know your products, the better tester you'll be.

Getting Your Foot in the Door:

Internships are the best means of entry to professional product testing, especially if you're looking to break into a specialized field. If product testing (and, perhaps, product fixing) at Microsoft is your goal, take advantage of your "free" summers to put in some hours at a local technology firm. The same goes for general product testing. The networks and contacts you establish as an intern will give you a leg up when it's time to find that full-time job. When scanning want ads for product testing positions, be sure to read the fine print. The "product testing" umbrella covers many "jobs" that entail very short-term work (frequently in the form of surveys) in exchange for premiums or gift certificates. And while a free electronic handheld thesaurus is a cool toy, it doesn't exactly pay the bills at the end of the month.

Biggest Challenges and Best Perks:

Each particular job will come with its own challenges. But across the board, you'll need to be the kind of person who is meticulous, persistent, and detail-oriented. This can lead to fatigue, frustration, and plenty of eye-crossing. But this profession also offers the opportunity to be creative. This is especially true for product testers in high-tech industries who not only locate problems, but diagnose them and propose solutions. This means that sharp, imaginative minds that can examine a problem from a range of perspectives are well appreciated. You'll play an important role in making the world we live in a better—or, at least, more functional—place.

PROFESSIONAL PROFILE
Avg. salary: $10–$16/hr
(manufacturing)

Avg. salary: $48,238 (tech fields)

JARGON
Alpha Test In-house testing of products during pre-production to find and eliminate the most obvious design defects or deficiencies.

Gap Analysis The difference between projected outcomes and desired outcomes.

Needs Statement Summary of consumer needs and wants

ARE YOU INTERESTED IN?
Gadgets, tinkering, computers

RELATED COLLEGE MAJORS
Chemistry, physics, engineering, computer science, marketing

FOR MORE INFORMATION
American Society For Quality Control:
www.asq.org

Consumer Reports:
www.consumerreports.org

PROPERTY MANAGER

A (Relatively) Typical Day in the Life

Property managers take care of any residential or commercial property from both a physical and a tenant-relations standpoint. They maintain and upgrade facilities while acting as liaisons between property owners and tenants. In many cases, property managers are responsible for attracting tenants to the properties. Since most property managers are in charge of a number of properties at any time, the job can involve frantic work, unusual hours, and extremely difficult schedule coordination. It takes strong communications skills, strong organizational skills, and a flair for numbers to handle this demanding position. Property managers have the most client contact when disasters occur, such as flooded basements, heating systems that break down, or even burglaries. This can be daunting for individuals who don't perform well in crisis situations. The best property managers are proactive rather than reactive. If they anticipate potential problems and prevent them, then they don't have to deal with as many problems. When things do fall apart, managers must respond quickly and decisively. More mundane tasks, such as collecting rent and coordinating garbage removal, cannot suffer because of unanticipated events. Many property managers feel that the best feature of the profession is the chance to work with a variety of people on a number of different tasks. They never know what their day is going to look like. While property managers spend a lot of their time dealing with paperwork and talking on the telephone, the problems with which they deal vary greatly from day to day, giving most property managers a sense of creative challenge that keeps the job fresh.

An Extreme Day in the Life

Andre Kelly Sr. has worked in the real estate agent industry for the past 20 years. He recalls many extreme days working as a property manager for Holly Park Apartments in New Orleans: "Doing evictions is definitely one of the negatives of this job. One of my worst was this lady who happened to be in a situation where she was extremely low-income and only had to pay $3 of rent per month [the federal government subsidized the rest]. I approached her several times about the rent. Three months pass and now she owes rent plus late fees. I approach her again and she becomes agitated. I bring her into my office and said since you are not going to pay I have to evict you. She reaches into her dress and takes out a wad of money and throws it at me. I threw her out of my office. The next day I filed an eviction at court. The tenant shows up in court and we present our sides. The judge gives her 48 hours to pay rent—the lady still doesn't pay. I had a court order so I called the court to request assistance evicting her. The sheriff comes with four or five cars. They eventually have to handcuff her and forcibly remove her from the property." That's not all he had to go through. He adds, "I've had to deal with bomb threats, suicide attempts, courts, lawyers, police; as a property manager, you have to wear many hats." Mr. Kelly offers this advice to those considering this profession: "Make sure you have a tough skin. This is not a job for the weak or meek. But most of the tenants are good people, and every time you give someone a key, you get to see their face light up."

It takes strong communications skills, strong organizational skills, and a flair for numbers to handle this demanding position.

PREPARE FOR SUCCESS

Most major employers ask that property managers have a bachelor's degree, although no formal requirements are inherent to the field. Coursework that proves helpful to candidates includes real estate, organizational behavior, mathematics, accounting, finance, logic, psychology, and public relations. Property managers who are responsible for recruiting new tenants might benefit from marketing courses as well. After being hired, many people attend brief weekend or three-day training programs, sponsored by the hiring company, that acquaint them with the concerns and obligations of the property manager.

GETTING YOUR FOOT IN THE DOOR

Individuals who wish to become property managers in the public sector—in subsidized federal housing, for example—must be certified, although certification carries weight in the private sector as well. Professional organizations such as the Institute of Real Estate Management or the National Organization of Home Builders administer these exams. Since they are well versed in the ins and outs of real estate, many property managers become commercial real estate agents. Only a few property managers with finance experience move into property development, particularly on a local level. Some of them become specialists in building maintenance and repair, using their industry connections to get regular work.

BIGGEST CHALLENGES AND BEST PERKS

Client contact is immediate in this business, and responsibilities run high right away. Five years into the profession, property managers may manage one large complex of buildings or a number of small properties. The hours and salaries increase, but responsibility for tenant satisfaction and the smooth maintenance of the property still rest with the manager. Many people switch employers halfway through their careers, looking for the right balance between challenge and salary. Individuals who been property managers for ten years have developed a system to keep track of maintenance issues, financial obligations, and tenant happiness. A number of them begin to manage groups of less experienced property managers. Contacts made during the first five years (along with invaluable practical experience) come in handy as emergencies are dealt with swiftly and efficiently.

PROFESSIONAL PROFILE
Avg. starting salary: $25,470
Avg. salary after 5 years: : $36,880
Avg. salary 10 to 15 years: $56,000

JARGON
Section 8 A housing program designed to increase the housing choices available to very low-income households by making privately owned rental housing affordable to them through rent subsidies.

ARE YOU INTERESTED IN?
Real estate, customer service

RELATED COLLEGE MAJORS
Real estate, organizational behavior, accounting, business management, marketing

FOR MORE INFORMATION
Century 21:
www.century21.com
Institute of Real Estate Management:
www.irem.org

REAL ESTATE DEVELOPER

A (RELATIVELY TYPICAL) DAY IN THE LIFE

Developers find undeveloped property and build on it or convert it for optimal use. A typical day moves at a frenzied pace—to get a deal together, developers need to quickly coordinate the financial, production, and sales elements. Few properties are developed without tenants already lined up to move in post-construction. This places an added burden on the developer, who must give the tenants a reliable date on which they can move in.

Developers' responsibilities depend on which of three areas they call their specialty: finance, construction, or recruitment. Developers involved in the finance end are busiest at the initial stages of projects, when they research and negotiate the terms of new deals. They work with banks, government agencies, and financial consultants, calculating the feasibility of projects, reviewing sites, and planning for contingencies. Financial developers oversee all payments, rates of production, and negotiations with banks during and after the development of a site.

Construction liaisons work with construction managers and local agencies to act as a "policeman" for the job, ensuring the structure meets local building codes, all necessary permits are obtained, and production moves along on schedule. Developers who supervise construction can often be caught between the financial developer and the general contractor, and the policy of not killing the middleman is sometimes a difficult one to enforce.

A recruiter puts together statistics, models, and plans for the site and then sells rental space to tenants. Construction delays, labor holdups, or permit problems are not considered valid excuses for delays of occupancy, and many clients insist on penalties for missing the date of completion. Successful recruiters rely to a large extent on their expertise in construction scheduling.

An Extreme Day in the Life

Richard Brand has been a real estate developer since 1979, and has the added bonus/threat of a law degree. His days are full of permits and follow-up phone calls, but he's managed a very successful lifelong career and currently owns multiple properties across the country. In the business for 27 years, he's constantly reminded exactly how hectic things can get: "We're putting a wrought-iron deck across the back of a very valuable brownstone that we rent out, and we need the Landmark Preservation Commission's approval because it's a landmark building. I was told it would take three weeks to get the approval and in the meantime I've got an extremely expensive duplex that rents out for $7000-8000 a month just sitting empty, which I can't rent until I get this approval. Three weeks came and went, and we called the Commission. They wouldn't even answer the phone, so three weeks dragged onto six weeks, and we had to call someone who was a supervisor, who determined that the approval had been granted and told us we'd be getting paperwork in a couple of days. That was 12 days ago. This is a typical frustration, when you need other people to do their job and they don't always do it was expeditiously as they promised. You're often dealing with a bureaucratic agency that has no incentive to act quickly, since the money's not coming out of their pocket. So what should only take a couple of days ends up taking 7-8 weeks. You're basically in someone else's hands, and you're waiting for something to happen over which you have no control. There are times when you have to be in twelve places at one time, which is virtually impossible."

To do this, one must have expertise, access to capital, and a strong stomach for taking risks.

While some thrive on the fast pace of developing, the pressure gets to others. The ultimate goal for most people in development is to work on their own projects. To do this, one must have expertise, access to capital, and a strong stomach for taking risks.

Prepare for Success

The aspiring developer needs an academic background with an emphasis on real estate, finance, managerial skills, psychology, or accounting; an understanding of basic engineering and construction principles is also helpful. Many developers work for a few years and then return to school for an MBA—the degree of choice. Work experience in real estate or finance is important. Some employers require new employees to have real estate licenses or accounting accreditations prior to starting work. As people in the industry pursue specializations, accreditations like the CPA and CFA become more important.

Getting Your Foot in the Door

When it comes to finding an "in" into the development world, experience is valuable, and most employers recognize this fact. Most developers start out as assistants to senior developers, putting in long hours doing anything and everything the boss needs. Aggressive opportunity seeking and long hours of careful work mark the people who advance beyond this stage. Unlike many other fields in which applicants are exposed to the entire process, and then slotted to their specific skill set, employees are hired for a specialization within a development company and immersed in the details of the occupation right away.

Biggest Challenges and Best Perks

There can be big payoffs, but real estate development is definitely a no pain, no gain profession. Deals are very risky—they seem to earn either a continuing 18–22 percent return or a 35–44 percent loss—and sometimes this uncertainty can lead to the development of ulcers instead of property. A staggering 18 percent of developers per year leave their jobs within their first five years. Most aspiring developers have to travel to be able to work on a variety of projects, or they risk facing long periods of time during which their expertise is of little or no use.

However, the upsides are money, money, and money. Even though a developer's profit is subject to the caprice of many independent variables, the market should remain at its current level for the next few years, and the developer's role is secure for the foreseeable future. Developers dream of working on their own projects, and many spend their free time socializing with financial, construction, and property management contacts.

Professional Profile
Avg. salary: $62,000 (Varies considerably depending on commission structure)

Jargon
Built to suit Developing real estate to suit the client's needs

Perc Test A test to determine the absorption rate of soil for a septic drain field; required in order toobtain the permits necessary to build a house.

Variance A written authorization from an agency permitting construction

Are you Interested In?
Construction, architecture

Related College Majors
Real Estate, construction management, finance, accounting, civil engineering

For More Information
American Institute of Architect New York Chapter:
www.aiaonline.org

Associated Landscape Contractors of America:
www.acla.org

Institute of Real Estate Management:
www.irem.com

SMALL BUSINESS OWNER

A (Relatively) Typical Day in the Life

The small business owner is the backbone of the U.S. economy. About 99 percent of all employers are small business owners. Small business owners work out of garages, small stores on main streets, and huge corporate offices. Before you begin selling t-shirts in Times Square or offering oranges in Orlando, you need a business plan. It includes a description of your product or services, how you are going to finance your business (loans, investors, and so on), deadlines for your business, and the ultimate goal. As a small business owner, you need to be aware of the six M's.

Mission: You have to know exactly what your services will do for your clients.

Market: You have to know who your clients are and how you can reach them.

Message: Your mission has to be clear.

Media: What is the best way to get your message out into the world?

Method: You know what to do, with whom, with what, when, and how to do it. You're in control of your business.

Management: This is your way of operating your business so that your clients are completely satisfied.

An Extreme Day in the Life

Scott Ruprecht is the president of Sportfishing Worldwide, a company that escorts corporate clients on customized fishing adventures to the top freshwater and saltwater destinations in the world. A long-time recreational fly-fisher, Scott still can't believe how lucky he is to be earning money doing something he loves. Some of his most extreme moments involved the challenges of just getting started: "I graduated with a degree in accounting and went to work for one of the Big 6 accounting firms. I was at the firm for a year before I got canned. I remember sitting there getting fired thinking this is awesome: I get to get out of accounting. It was only then that I thought, 'Oh crap, I just lost my job.'" But for Scott, this turned out to be an incredible motivator: "I was 23 with no money and no ideas, but I always wanted to have my own company. I set a date two years out for starting my own business and spent the time brainstorming and reading up on different things. By September 1998 I had written a business plan and was off and running." Things weren't easy at first. "The only time the phone rang the first year it was my family. I tried every marketing strategy, from direct mail, to web, to brochures and fax broadcasts. I saw the light for one month in August 2001 when the phone was ringing all the time. Then September 11 happened. This was devastating for a small business that was a specialized travel company. I learned that no matter what business you're in, business happens in cycles and you milk it when it's good and weather the storm when it's bad." Today, Scott reaps the benefits of toughing it out: "I flew to Alaska three weeks ago with ten clients from Fresno. I look around at my 'office' on the side of a stream with silver salmon swimming around and brown bears all over. I get a pull on my fly rod and I look up—eight of my clients have bites. I felt so lucky to be doing what I do." Scott offers this advice to dreamers looking to strike out on their own: "Don't be afraid to roll the dice a little bit. Just take the chance. The hardest part is starting—once you're in it you will gain confidence and if you work hard everything will come together."

There's just no substitute for being your own boss.

An ideal small business owner knows how to make plans; solve problems; and hire, train, motivate, and lead employees. Being a small business owner is risky; it is probably one of the riskiest careers you can choose. However, with a lot of hard work—and we mean a lot—a dash of determination, and plenty of luck, the rewards of starting your own business can be excellent.

PREPARE FOR SUCCESS

While it may be helpful to have a college business degree when starting your own business, it is not necessary. In fact, many small business owners don't have a college degree at all. Instead they rely on a great idea, and a passion to see it come to fruition—this is a profession that rewards hard work and dedication. The most important aspect of starting a small business is planning. Many companies offer help with preparing a business plan, from seminars to online courses to professional editing services. Background/experience in budgeting, forecasting, marketing, and persuasive presentation skills is also helpful.

GETTING YOUR FOOT IN THE DOOR

Do your research. You'll need an expert knowledge of the industry you're trying to break into to get started. The key to getting your business of the ground is building relationships with the right people, and successful marketing of your products and/or services. You'll need to get to know various people in their industry or community and use these relationships to drive your business. (For example, a hairstylist interested in opening his own salon should spend time developing a loyal own client base before venturing out on his own.) In addition, come up with a great marketing plan. Check out what the competition is doing and do it better, or look outside of your industry to come up with a unique angle for promoting your business.

BIGGEST CHALLENGES AND BEST PERKS

Starting your own business is not easy. Some statistics show that small businesses will not see a significant profit for two years. In addition, the hours are long. Self-employed contract workers may work long hours under tight deadlines, while store owners may spend anywhere from 80 to 120 hours or more a week maintaining their businesses. Then there are the local and federal regulations—break one and you just might find yourself out of business in no time. If you've got the will, determination, and the means to make it work, there's just no substitute for being your own boss.

PROFESSIONAL PROFILE
Avg. starting salary: $20,000
Avg. salary 5 years: $65,000
Avg. salary 10 to 15 years: $97,500

JARGON
Franchising License granted by a company to an individual or group to market its products or services in a specific territory; can potentially be very lucrative for the licensee

ARE YOU INTERESTED IN?
Entrepreneurship

RELATED COLLEGE MAJORS
Business administration, marketing

FOR MORE INFORMATION
National Small Business Association:
www.nsba.biz

Small Business Administration:
www.sba.gov

Small Business Help Center, Inc.:
www.helpbizowners.com

SPORTS ANNOUNCER

A (Relatively) Typical Day in the Life

Did you ever dream of a life in sports as a kid? Maybe you did your own play-by-play: Game seven; bottom of the ninth; two outs; the count is full; and you've got runners at first and third. You're pitching to yourself; you've given the ball just a little bit of air; gripping the bat, you watch it go up and come back down; down into the zone; you hold your breath and swing. Whiff! The ball drops safely to the ground. Err—was the count really full? Maybe a life playing sports for a living is going to have to remain a dream, but there are other options.

While a life in the competitive field of sports broadcasting is hardly a sure thing, becoming a sports announcer may be a far more plausible goal if you're a sports fanatic who, shall we say, may have called for one too many do-overs in your time. Sports announcers work primarily in radio and television, and, as any casual sports fan would know, their job is to work play-by-play and colorful commentary of sporting events for fans who are not in attendance. The day doesn't necessarily begin with the first pitch, nor end with the last out. You need something to say on the air after all, and when was the last time you watched or listened to a game where the announcer only did play-by-play? They recite stats, standings, and recount anecdotes; to this end, research and interviews are a major part of almost any broadcaster's workday.

An Extreme Day in the Life

"In what other profession can you really do this? To combine your love of sports with making a living at it?" This is how Ted Patterson views his long and successful career as a radio and television sports announcer. Ted has been in the profession for more than 40 years, starting out early as a free-lancer "stringing" for AP and CBS, where he'd go into the locker room after games to get interviews and then send down the tapes to the network before he could get home—around 12:00 or 1:00 A.M.— just to start all over again at 4:30 A.M. He remembers that in those days, it was almost a relief when the team went on the road! Ted feels that he's had a crazy day recently, with his coverage of the Professional Senior Golf tournament, the Orioles playing at home, and the Ravens getting ready for the upcoming games. He's up at 4:30 A.M to do the early morning sportscast, spends the remainder of the day doing interviews with golf professionals and members of the Baltimore Ravens, and then spends some time at the ballpark interviewing Orioles until 8:00 or 9:00 P.M. "I idolized these sports announcers as a kid and to then sit next to the dugout and interview [the players] is amazing." He's been able to interview greats such as Ted Williams, Muhammad Ali, Joe Lewis, Jessie Owens, and Jack Dempsey. How's that for a great sports story?

Regardless of the depth of your education and experience, it will all be meaningless if you lack basic love of the game.

PREPARE FOR SUCCESS

The first thing you're going to need is a love and knowledge of the sport—or sports—you wish to cover. Regardless of the depth of your education and experience, it will all be meaningless if you lack basic love of the game. That being said, a career in sports broadcasting, as with any competitive field, will typically require that you have the proper training and educational background. A bachelor's degree in journalism, preferably broadcast journalism or some other related field, will be essential for the majority of people looking to enter the field.

GETTING YOUR FOOT IN THE DOOR

If you've got a degree and some experience, it may not be that difficult for you to find work in one of the smaller markets doing commentary at local high school or minor league events. Of course, that may depend on your willingness to relocate for a low-paying, no-profile job broadcasting high school football games for a single watt radio station in a town you've never heard of. It won't be glamorous, but it's not supposed to be. This will be your time to really work on harnessing your skills and putting an audition tape together. These are the jobs that will allow you to get a lot of experience and, with any luck, act as the springboard that will help you land a much more competitive position in the future.

BIGGEST CHALLENGES AND BEST PERKS

One of the toughest realities for aspiring sports broadcasters who got degrees and are paying their dues in a small market, is turning on a national broadcast and hearing the voice of a former player doing announcing work. It's difficult enough to get work in the field without having to compete against retired athletes who are not satisfied to stay out of the game now that their playing career is over. Who ever said it was going to be easy to get a career in sports anyway? It's tough for a reason. It's really fun. You get to, or rather, it is your *job* to go to games, to interview players, and to do professionally what you've probably been pretending to do all your life—call games. If that's not a perk, we don't what is.

PROFESSIONAL PROFILE
Avg. salary: $43,646

Varies depending on size of market, ranging from $10,608 in the smallest to $106,200 in the largest markets.

JARGON
Aspirin tablet In baseball, term used by sports announcers to describe a fastball that's so effective it looks tiny and nearly impossible to hit

ARE YOU INTERESTED IN?
Sports, writing, public speaking

RELATED COLLEGE MAJORS
Journalism, broadcast journalism, communications, rhetoric, digital communications and media/multimedia, radio and television broadcasting

FOR MORE INFORMATION
American Sportscasters Association: www.americansportscastersonline.com

Victory Sports Network: www.victorysportsnetwork.com

National Association of Sports Public Address Announcers: www.naspaa.net

VOICE-OVER ARTIST

A (Relatively) Typical Day in the Life

Voice actors do the off-screen voices you hear in commercials, trailers, and animations—and don't forget that automated robot from directory assistance, that funny talking doll that all the kids wanted last Christmas, or that book-on-tape you listened to in college instead of reading the actual text. Anywhere a voice is needed, there's an actor who is ready to fill in. Voice-over artists can even be movie or TV stars—think John Forsythe in *Charlie's Angels*.

For most actors in the field, voice acting has all of the benefits of regular acting work without the hassle of the makeup, costumes, and lighting. Once you've broken into the business and are getting called for readings, a day at the office can mean 30 minutes in a sound studio. Virtually every day brings brand new material—a car dealer spot to be aired in Georgia, a surly New Yorker voice for a radio promo, or a friendly animated handyman reminding warehouse employees to lift with their knees. Though many voice actors develop a signature persona to market, the particular aspects of the job and the character change from day to day.

In most cases, actors don't see the script for the reading until they arrive at the studio; they have to be prepared for anything. Competition can be fierce, but even the smallest local network station needs a promo, so opportunity

An Extreme Day in the Life

Chuck Patterson is a man of many voices, and his clients pay to put those voices in people's heads. Having worked as a voice-over artist for more than 12 years, Chuck's days are filled with scripts and microphones coming at him from every direction. One year, as the stores were scrambling to get the holiday shoppers, he had a particularly interesting afternoon: "I was attempting to make a 9:00 A.M. session to do an 'After-Christmas Sale' radio spot. I arrived at 8:57 A.M., charmed the client, recorded a version they liked in three or four takes, and hit the door to make my 10:00 A.M. session at another studio. I arrived at destination #2 about 10 minutes early, so there was time for more coffee . . . and there is never enough coffee. The client arrived 20 minutes late and handed me his copy, surprising me with the announcement that he wanted a character voice (but had no idea what it should sound like and told me to come up with something appropriate). I recorded it and made my lunch appointment with a potential client in the nick of time. After lunch, I returned to my studio and checked e-mail for any work that had come in. There were scripts for three car dealers, two scripts for a retail store with another 'After-Christmas Sale' emergency, a concert spot and a request from a high school radio station for some free liners. Of course, they all wanted the audio delivered by the end of the day. In the home studio there are no producers and no clients, just me, so it's much faster work, and everything was recorded and delivered via Internet within four hours."

He continues, "At this point I thought I could relax, until the phone rang. My session from the morning had reworked the script and decided to do two radio ads and a television ad, but it had to be finished before morning. I doubled my fee, drove 30 miles, recorded the new scripts, and arrived back home around 10:30 P.M. I'm constantly scurrying, but I like coming through at the last second to make everything work out."

> **Voice acting has all of the benefits of regular acting work without the hassle of the makeup, costumes, and lighting.**

abounds. The professional voice actor will rely on an agent to take care of the all the legwork, such as marketing and arranging auditions. Voice artists don't have to ensure that their physical appearances mesh with the characters they are playing, and this relieves a lot of the pressure typically placed on performers. It's a rare occupation that stresses being heard and not seen, but there's still plenty of recognition to be found behind the scenes.

Prepare for Success

If you've followed the typical voice actor track of first breaking into radio as a production assistant, intern, or spokesperson for local businesses, you've gained the experience necessary to start marketing your voice. Voicing local radio commercials is the best way to get noticed by agencies looking for new talent. Even though it's possible to break into the field with no experience, most professional voice artists have a background in communications, and have completed internships at their college radio stations and are accustomed to being in front of a microphone. Some voice agents even recommend that actors who are starting out train in production skills (editing and learning the computer software used in sound studios) and then seek out employment in radio production to immerse themselves in voice spots.

Getting Your Foot in the Door

To really get your name out there, it's almost a necessity to create a demo tape to submit to agencies containing various reads: hyper voice, soothing voice, and maybe even an accent or two. There's minor progress to be made in terms of seeking out auditions and networking, but an agent is really the best "in" to getting jobs, and you'll be able to use those golden vocal chords for something less strenuous than beating down doors. Always adding to your demo, larger agencies have your name on file and know where to turn when looking for the perfect "mid-to-upper thirties, two-small-children-at-home, drinks-coffee-and-does-Pilates-every-Wednesday" voice to reach their target audience.

Biggest Challenges and Best Perks

The downside of being a voice artist is that everyone knows it's a pretty sweet gig, and almost everyone has a voice, so there's a plenty of competition in the market. Acting assignments are typically short—they range from one day to perhaps a few months—so actors frequently experience periods of unemployment between jobs. However, when the gigs do roll in . . . well, let's just say no one has ever complained about being paid to read out loud for a few hours. It's not exactly easy money, considering the number of hours of searching that a beginning vocal actor has to put in before they find their niche, but landing a commercial role or a studio contract can make this dream job become a reality.

WEDDING PLANNER

A (Relatively Typical) Day in the Life

This high-stress profession may seem more light-hearted and frou-frou than it is. Couples hire wedding planners to help out with both the big picture (the overall look and feel of the wedding) and the tiny details (how many people they can afford to invite, who will sit where, and what the place cards will look like). Some planners coordinate the reception while the couple attends to the ceremony. A consultant can log plenty of hours securing a locale, designing the décor scheme, tracking down invitations and favors, and negotiating the prices for these services. A consultant often makes appointments for the couple with caterers, bakeries, or photographers, and may pre-screen musicians or DJs. They might book limos, hire an officiate, coordinate a post-wedding brunch, and assist with honeymoon planning. Talk about details! Other couples might hire a consultant for the wedding day only. There, the planner simply works with vendors (ensuring the caterer is on track and that the photographer knows who is who), and does any damage control. If someone spills a glass of wine on the bride's dress, the consultant will know how to clean it. If the hair stylist doesn't show up, she knows how to do a decent French twist, or at least knows how to fake it.

A wedding planner's day is never the same. One day they are visiting hotel ballrooms, the next they are meeting prospective clients. Organization, flexibility, and creativity are hallmark traits. A flair for sales will help, too—as a planner needs to sell his/her services to potential clients, then use some smart negotiating with vendors to score the best deals on his/her client's behalf. Because a wedding consultant brings repeat business to vendors,

An Extreme Day in the Life

Wedding planner Carolyn Russom of I Do Desert Weddings.com says her job takes her well beyond the basics. She braces herself for extreme days on the job like this one: "With just two hours before the 5:00 P.M. ceremony on an April afternoon, the bride was getting ready and the groom was nervously pacing in the hallway. On my way to do some last-minute set ups, I noticed the cake had not arrived. It was only a few minutes late, so I wasn't too worried – yet. I went off to check on the florist and banquet staff. By 4:00 P.M., I peeked back in: Still no cake. I called the baker's cell phone but she didn't pick up. Guests would be arriving in a half hour. Before pursuing a back-up plan, I went to make sure the bride had everything she needed. My assistant had been with the couple and their families all afternoon, but the bride likes to be reassured that everything is going smoothly. It wasn't, but I sure didn't tell her that. The last thing I wanted to do is upset her an hour before her dream wedding. I called the baker again. Her van had broken down five miles from the wedding site, she couldn't get a tow, her cell phone was dying, and the cake was beginning to melt in the heat! I sent my assistant in my SUV to pick up the baker and the cake, while I stayed with the bride so she didn't suspect that something was wrong. When they all arrived 45 minutes later, the ceremony had already started. We brought the cake through a back door so the guests wouldn't notice and quickly set it up and decorated the table, finishing just 10 minutes before the reception. Later that night, the bride and groom commented on how beautiful everything was, especially the cake. Neither had any idea what had happened to get it there!"

> **This high-stress profession may seem more light-hearted and frou-frou than it is.**

he/she often receives discounts he/she can pass on to clients. Ideally, this trims wedding costs and saves the couple time and headaches.

Prepare for Success

A planner without a business background might consider earning an MBA, as organizational and financial skills are a must. Creativity is also essential; a planner who adds special touches and a signature style to each event will soon stand out from the competition. A website helps attract new business, as will a presence at bridal shows. More than anything, however, experience counts. The more weddings a planner has done, the more creative they will become. As a planner learns the art of negotiating, he/she can save clients more money. (And happy clients are the best word-of-mouth referrals.)

Getting Your Foot in the Door

Consultants often come to the field through other related jobs, such as catering, event planning, floral design, or public relations. Some with a business background choose this as a second career. Then there are those who start off by planning their own wedding, move on to those of close friends, and eventually print up business cards advertising their services. Strong planning, budgeting, and negotiating skills are more important than an eye for flowers. Competition is fierce and it takes years to build a reputation and important connections with suppliers. An apprenticeship (possibly unpaid) or internship under a successful planner would provide a coveted opportunity to break in and learn the ropes.

Biggest Challenges and Best Perks

Playing the role of mediator, negotiator, counselor, and financial planner takes a special kind of person—one with tact and grace. A finesse in handling the many personalities that just one wedding throws at a planner—especially the bridezillas and their moms—is essential. Marketing your services to couples is tough. Many would rather attempt to do it themselves than go to the expense of hiring a planner, so scoring a meeting and convincing them it's a wise investment can be difficult. Busy consultants work most weekends of the year. But the hugs and thank-you notes from couples after the wedding make it all worthwhile. Wedding planners feel honored to be a part of these seminal moments, and take pride in a job well done. Successful wedding planners may eventually book high-budget weddings, celebrity weddings, or destination weddings, in which travel costs are covered. Planning an affair on a tropical island or in the Tuscan countryside definitely has its perks.

Professional Profile
Avg. starting salary $27,680

Avg. salary after 5 years $33,200

Avg. salary 10-15 years $44,300

Jargon
B2B Bride-to-be

G2B Groom-to-be

Are you Interested In?
Weddings, catering

Related College Majors
Event planning, event management, logistics management, finance, sales

For More Information
Association of Bridal Consultants:
www.bridalassn.com

Coordinator's Corner:
www.coordinatorscorner.com

The Knot:
www.theknot.com

SCHMOOZING

AGENT (SPORTS, MODELS, ACTORS, WRITERS)

A (Relatively) Typical Day in the Life

If you've ever seen the movie *Young Guns*, then you probably remember the line: "I'll make ya famous." That line defines an agent's job in a nutshell. Agents represent athletes, writers, models, actors, producers, performers, and other would-be celebrities. When choosing clients, agents look for something new, different, and charismatic about a person's work. Agents spend their waking hours attempting to find work for each client, ideally more high-profile and lucrative work. Even after the client has been picked up by a movie studio, sports team, or publishing house, an agent's work is not done. Agents negotiate to get the best deals, hammering out all contractual points with their clients' best interests in mind. Agents make a standard 10 to 15 percent commission on each of their client's paychecks—when they're getting work. It can be a thrilling, but financially unpredictable, livelihood.

Most agents go to endless streams of meetings, and haggle, network, and keep tabs on who's who in the industry and what that means for their clients. When they're not busy scouting out opportunities for their clients, they are assuring them that their next big break is just around the bend. Agents encourage, strategize, entertain, and advise their clients as they would their friends, all while maintaining professional relationships. No matter what specialty agents have, they work hard to promote and market talent. An ability to function under pressure and compromise are essential.

While many agents are self-employed, most start out at the bottom, working their way up in talent agencies. Along the way they learn tenacity, communication skills, and the ability to sell ideas effectively. Even when their

An Extreme Day in the Life

Jessica Faust is cofounder of BookEnds, L.L.C., a New Jersey–based literary agency that represents diverse types of work. Her most extreme days are when she receives an offer from a publisher to buy one of the books she represents. "Everything else you had planned for that day is set aside and you need to be as accessible as possible, which means interrupted meetings and lunches if necessary," she says. When she was approached by romance author Christine Wells, who had just received an offer from a major publishing house, she jumped into action for two extreme days: "I actually had Christine's proposal under consideration for quite some time but hadn't had the chance to read it. Immediately upon receiving her e-mail, I dropped everything else and started reading the proposal. It was good, very good. So I asked her to e-mail the entire manuscript. It didn't take long for me to realize that not only was this a very well-written book, but . . . [also] by an author I'd love to represent. I offered representation and Christine accepted late on a Thursday afternoon. My job on Friday morning was to get her book in front of as many editors as possible. I spent the day calling and later e-mailing the manuscript to a number of editors, with the caveat that they would let me know Monday morning whether or not they were interested in making an offer. Come Monday afternoon, we had two offers and a number of editors who really loved her work. Monday was spent negotiating the contract to see which publishing house would give Christine the best deal. In the end, we made the decision to sell two of Christine's books to Berkley Publishing."

'I'll make ya famous.' That line defines an agent in a nutshell.

workdays are officially over, they must keep social, often attending cocktail parties where they schmooze with potential business partners. Agents are always busy working behind the scenes so their clients may bask in the limelight.

Prepare for Success

A college degree is preferred for entry-level positions at most agencies—though the major itself is less important. Marketing or communications backgrounds are good bets. English would work for a literary agent, or sports management for the aspiring sports agent. There's no stringent regimen to prep for this job other than a desire to work like a dog to be a great agent.

Getting Your Foot in the Door

An internship is a common first step, followed by moving slowly (possibly through mailroom and receptionist jobs) toward an assistant position. Count on long hours of administrative and gopher work while learning the business. An agent in training studies contracts, negotiations, the craft of client interaction, and ways to gain new clients. People skills, a thick skin, and a flair for the art of persuasion are signature agent traits, as is an uncanny ability to sniff out new talent. Agents, for all their hard-ball negotiating skills, also need to possess sensitivity. Fragile egos and hurt feelings will need their attention. Basic business skills and strong leadership qualities will help too.

Biggest Challenges and Best Perks

Much of the difficulty of being a successful agent is developing your own contacts, strategies, and techniques—as other agents will never share their own. Saying no to people is an undeniable part of being a top agent. With their reputation on the line for each person they take on, agents need to believe in new clients wholeheartedly. New agents tend to pursue new talent, looking for that gem in the rough that will bring in fame and fortune. Many agents become jaded by the lack of glamour, the snail's pace progress, and the menial responsibilities. If the long hours and low pay don't break you, the high demands, aggravation, and attitudes just might. However, an agent's job does have its moments. Parties, industry events, and general schmoozing are all part of the game. Meeting successful people often results in invitations to the places they go and the affairs they host. There's always the reward of seeing a client's career take off. The connections agents make in their careers come in handy if they ever decide to leave, which many do before long.

PROFESSIONAL PROFILE
Avg. salary: Varies

JARGON
Trades The daily and weekly periodicals of the industry
Rolling calls The rapid succession of calls assistants make on behalf of their bosses. Once the conversation begins, assistants hit the mute button take notes.

ARE YOU INTERESTED IN?
Sports, reading, fashion, acting

RELATED COLLEGE MAJORS
Marketing, communications

FOR MORE INFORMATION
Association of Talent Agents:
www.agentassociation.com
Association of Author Representatives:
www.aar-online.org

BAR/CLUB MANAGER

A (Relatively) Typical Day in the Life

Managing a bar or club is a high-profile job, but don't let anyone tell you that it's all fun and glamour. Daily responsibilities might include anything from lugging cases of beer up a flight of stairs to cleaning up spills and/or ejecting obnoxious patrons. In addition, the workday schedule is erratic, usually extending from late afternoon to late into the nights, with weekend shifts making up a regular part of the weekly work schedule. At the end of the night, bar and club managers are responsible for the profitability and smooth functioning of the venue. As a result, club managers have a significant degree of input on the persona and operation of the club and can impress their sensibility on the patrons' experiences, ensuring that everyone has a great time. However, their creative input must not be at the expense of sacrificing the attention to detail that the day-to-day aspects of the profession require.

Managers are responsible for assembling, managing, and paying staff, as well as opening and closing the club or restaurant. More senior managers might also be responsible for ordering supplies and managing inventory. In addition to these duties, managers have significant input into promotional efforts that make the public aware of the club or bar. Many managers are given complete latitude to determine and advertise events. Open mic nights, happy hours, and ladies' nights are examples of events that many club and bar managers find to be successful in attracting new patrons.

Bar or club managers must be comfortable with people: from the professionals with whom they work—accountants, wait staff, suppliers, and government regulators (including representatives from the liquor, fire, sanitation, and health departments)—to the patrons they entertain. They must also be comfortable claiming responsibility and enforcing authority as the primary liaison between the owners of the establishment and the

An Extreme Day in the Life

Jennifer Kay is part owner and manager of Down the Hatch, a popular pub located in the heart of New York City's Greenwich Village. A 12-year veteran of the business, Jennifer says she sort of fell into it: "I never thought this is what I would be doing. I was an English and psychology major in college, studied abroad, everything. I started working here part-time as a bartender, DJ, barmaid—I stuck around and eventually became a manager after seven years." Jennifer says a willingness to work your way up is the key to success in this profession. She says, "Like any job, you need to be willing to start from the bottom. Having bar experience is essential." Some of Jennifer's most extreme moments on the job have nothing to do with managing the bar at all: "One time we had a sewage line burst, flooding the basement where my office is. Water was slowly creeping toward my computer hard drive—I had to tie garbage bags around my shoes to wade through the muck—imagine the smell and the sight of it! It happened during a very busy time for the bar—at 6 P.M. on a Saturday during college football season. We had to close the bathroom but our customers took it in stride. They are very loyal." For Jennifer, being able to help people have a good time while doing "something different every day" makes the mucked-up days on the job completely worth it.

> **One of the most enjoyable aspects about being a club or bar manager is the creativity the profession entails.**

employees. The ability to work autonomously and think on your feet is essential for success in this profession.

PREPARE FOR SUCCESS

There is no specific educational requirement to become a bar or a club manager, but most managers have a high school education, and many of them have also completed college accounting, finance, or management coursework. Work experience is more important than educational requirements. Employers seek people who have experience managing others and keeping track of large budgets and inventories and who have demonstrated a strong sense of responsibility in past jobs. Financial analysis skills—basic cost benefit analysis, for example—are important for club and bar managers to propose interesting, yet fiscally sound marketing schemes. Managers must understand local regulations and accounting procedures to ensure the establishment functions legally and smoothly.

GETTING YOUR FOOT IN THE DOOR

The best time to break into the hospitality industry is in the summer, and especially in the months before the Christmas season. Most people network their way into staff positions at bars or clubs, working as bartenders, waiters, and bar backs. Aspiring managers usually work their way up from staff positions and learn the ropes by managing the establishment under strict supervision for two to three nights for no pay. There is usually a three-month probationary period when loose supervision and limited responsibilities are offered before full-scale management responsibilities are turned over.

BIGGEST CHALLENGES AND BEST PERKS

The long work hours can be a major downside to this profession. Since bar and club popularity levels are cyclical, when owners see any dip in profits the first person blamed is the manager. Only certain establishments offer any benefits whatsoever, and some managers complain that there is little challenge to the job once they have smoothed operations and reinvented locations. On the upside, one of the most enjoyable aspects about being a club or bar manager is the creativity the profession entails. Most managers work closely with owners on developing marketing strategies based around theme nights, entertainment, advertising, and special events. A great working atmosphere with opportunities for some fun social interactions with patrons is another major perk. Managers may eventually buy some sort of stake in the bar or club; this new role of ownership seems to provide the spark many need to keep the party going.

PROFESSIONAL PROFILE
Avg. starting salary: $20,500
Avg. salary after 5 years: $33,900
Avg. salary 10 to 15 years: $56,800

JARGON
Top shelf Behind the bar, this is where the premium quality liquor is kept on display until someone orders it

Bouncer The guy checking IDs in front of a bar or club and also there for security purposes

Cover The amount you have to pay to gain admission to a bar or club

ARE YOU INTERESTED IN?
Nightlife, entertainment

RELATED COLLEGE MAJORS
Hospitality, business management, marketing, advertising

FOR MORE INFORMATION
National Bar and Restaurant Association:
www.bar-restaurant.com/contact.html

Nightclub & Bar Magazine:
www.bar-restaurant.com/

BOOKING AGENT

A (Relatively) Typical Day in the Life

When you pay 15 bucks to see a musician or a band or a comedian take the stage, there's a good chance that a booking agent set up the event. Booking agents, sometimes called talent agents, serve as the complete behind-the-scenes representatives for performing artists of all kinds. In larger markets and when high-profile performers are involved, this can be a cutthroat industry that leaves agents both exhausted and exhilarated.

Before any actual booking ensues, however, booking agents must convince clients to take advantage of their services. This involves a little self-promotion. After all, when performers sign on with a booking agent, they agree to pay the agent a percentage of their earnings from every show the agent secures. So the performers must be absolutely convinced that the agent is going to make a 110 percent effort to find the best venues for the best prices on the best nights with the best tours. The performers, in other words, need to believe that booking agents are prepared to act as their tireless advocates.

Agents spend a large portion of their workday on the telephone, haggling with club managers, negotiating with concert hall managers, gathering details from music festival organizers, squaring contractual details with band managers, record label execs, and anyone else who might need to be involved. Because they're in charge of promoting the shows they line up, booking agents also get on the horn with newspapers, magazines, record stores, music websites, poster makers, and college kids who are willing to plaster a town with fliers for the price of two Big Macs and free tickets to the show.

Organization, clearly, is a critical skill in the booking agent game. As a booking agent, you'll want to be aware of as many clubs, concert halls, stadiums, festivals, college events committees, bands, and venue managers as you can. You'll also need to manage schedules. Book hotel rooms. Arrange meals. Yep, there's a lot to keep track of, but it's the fast pace and vast volume of work that keeps many agents at the top of their game.

Prepare for Success

Even if you work for a larger company, as an agent you are a business unto yourself. You need to seek out potential clients, hook them, book them, establish professional connections, manage budgets, handle promotions, arrange schedules, and oftentimes give artists creative advice on projects, image, and large-scale marketing decisions. In other words, a solid background in business goes a long way. A handful of higher-ed institutions even offer specific degrees in the business side of the performance industry. If your school doesn't offer something like this,

An Extreme Day in the Life

Eva Alexiou, owner and agent at Philadelphia's Fata Booking Agency, says that it's difficult to pinpoint any one extreme day because every day has its own bursts of intensity. "Everything we do is extreme here," she says of Fata, which has a client list of about 20 rock bands. "Everything from working with a promoter to negotiating the money you need, establishing the room's sound condition, dealing with a band's management to suit everyone's demands to keeping the band's morale high. Anytime you work with money and people, it's extreme."

try to land an internship with a booking agency or, at least, finagle your way into a spot on your college's events programming board. Real-world experience will give you a knowledge base that agencies and clients will expect you to have.

Getting Your Foot in the Door

Just when you think you've networked enough, network some more. The performance industry is always in flux, so it never hurts to make your presence known again and again. It goes without saying that if you booked a show that's happening 15 minutes from your apartment, it's good business to swing by. Let's not forget that there's always another great band or comedy act just waiting to be discovered. Keeping yourself in the mix can require a lot of evening and weekend work; after all, most concerts and performances don't take place during your typical nine to five day. For this reason, getting your foot in the door as a booking agent often means foregoing that coveted eight hours of sleep and sacrificing many a quiet night at home in front of the boob tube. For your time, however, you'll get to see a lot of great acts, hang out with a lot of fun people, and, most likely, get a lot of free drinks.

Biggest Challenges and Best Perks

Everybody has expectations—the performers, the club owners, the record labels, and you. As a booking agent, it's your job to try to bring all those expectations together peacefully and in a manner that best serves your clients' interests. Along the way, though, you might find that not all parties agree on the best way to move forward. Fata Booking's Eva Alexiou bluntly states, "If you have to deal with arguing and people having issues with their dealings, then obviously this makes you want to rip out your eyeballs." So, a level head and a long fuse can be tremendous weapons against those on-the-job frustrations.

Any frustrations are (usually) worth it when an event or tour is successful. If the band is happy, the venue management is happy, and all of those CDs and t-shirts and posters are flying off the vending shelves, then a booking agent gets to enjoy a rush of satisfaction. Other perks? This is not a monotonous job. One day you're negotiating a show at a club in Berlin and the next you're checking out bands at a festival in downtown Chicago. You also get free entry to a lot of shows and a ton of free CDs, too.

Professional Profile
Avg. salary: Usually commission based, 10 to 20 percent of total event earnings

Jargon
Soft-seater An upscale performing space with a guest capacity larger than a nightclub and smaller than an arena

Are you Interested In?
Music, media, entertainment

Related College Majors
Music management, business administration, marketing, communications

For More Information
Book Live Music:
www.booklivemusic.com

Music Biz Academy:
www.musicbizacademy.com

Entertainment Booking Agent:
www.executivevisions.com

BUYER

A (Relatively) Typical Day in the Life

Being a professional buyer is a glamorous, powerful job in many respects. However, the glitter and glitz should not cloud the hard work and keen intellect required to make it in this competitive field. Professional buyers examine goods and work within reasonable budgets to make competitive bids for products to resell. Don't underestimate the amount or the scale of necessary negotiations. People who are comfortable with negotiating are ideal for this profession. The decisions a buyer makes—color, size, quantity, and price—are some of the most important in determining whether a company makes a profit in a given year. The power to influence sales, beat competition, and earn high profits through their own actions gives many buyers satisfaction in a high-pressure position. It's the closest thing to gambling, including picking stocks. Buyers don't do much research—they have to go with their tastes and gut feelings. Buyers must have confidence in their choices, be able to assert their preferences, and defend their selections.

Buyers work long and sometimes unusual hours and travel to fashion shows, industry conferences, seminars, and trade shows. They investigate producers' lines and place orders, usually with a limited amount of discussion.

An Extreme Day in the Life

Valerie de Charette is an associate merchandiser for Macy's young men's urban wear line. She loves her job but warns that breaking into the industry isn't easy: "I always knew I wanted to do something in fashion. The way it usually works is that companies recruit students from fashion institutes. After I graduated from Harvard I started working as a buyer, then merchandiser manager for DrJays.com, an urban wear retail outlet. I was lucky—I snuck in through a backdoor." She says the most exciting moments on the job are seasonal: "The two biggest seasons for buys are the spring and fall. Twice a year the younger market goes to Vegas for the Magic Convention to showcase their spring and fall lines. Everyone is there. Jay-Z is walking around, there are booths for Ralph Lauren, Polo, Nautica. . . .You get to see tons of celebrities, and there are lots of great parties. Lil' Jon was standing behind me holding his cup trying to get into one of the parties. I saw Anna Nicole Smith dancing on a hotel balcony." According to Valerie, celeb sightings are par for the course in this profession: "There are always celebrities around. You'll run into Jay-Z or P-Diddy in the showrooms, or different sports celebrities endorsing a line. That's a cool perk—you get to meet people you think are exciting." In her current role, Valerie works as part of a steering committee/recommendations office for the Macy's buyers. "We go around the market and see if there's anything new and fabulous the buyers should buy. We can see how all [seven] regions of Macy's are doing so we can give advice to any and all regions based on what's working or not working in other regions, and we can direct the brands if we see there is something missing from the stores." Her advice for people who are trying to break into this profession is simple: "Try to do a training program at one of the big companies. Most of them are two years long, and you rotate through four different jobs in four different areas. What's cool is that you get to see how all sides of the business works. After you have training, you can get a job anywhere."

It's the closest thing to gambling, including picking stocks. Buyers don't do much research—they have to go with their tastes and gut feelings.

Professional buyers work with retail salespeople to get feedback on how choices they have made responded to the market. This back-and-forth dialogue is important to a buyer's understanding of any problems the sales force has moving the product. While buyers will sometimes come into conflict over purchases and sales, the profession is so grueling that many find themselves sympathetic to one another in spite of that conflict.

Prepare for Success

Almost any college major can prepare you to become a buyer; it depends on what you want to buy. A book buyer might have been an English major; someone who buys hospital supplies might have majored in biology. Any college major with a background in business or managerial skills will be prepared for the career. All employers require new employees to learn the specifics of their own businesses. Large companies usually have internal buyer training programs lasting from one to five years that expose new employees to all aspects of the business.

Getting Your Foot in the Door

Many trainees begin as salespeople and learn about inventory policy, stock maintenance, and shipment checking. Aspiring buyers receive extensive training on proprietary computer and inventory-tracking systems. The ability to plan ahead, predict consumer habits, and make difficult decisions distinguish those who emerge successfully from training programs. Buyers who continue in the profession find it helpful to achieve the professional designations recognized in each state, such as certified purchasing manager (CPM) and certified purchasing professional (CPP). To become an official purchasing agent for the government, applicants must pass a two- or three-part exam.

Biggest Challenges and Best Perks

Working as a buyer, regardless of the industry, is a high stress, high-octane position. Maintaining confidence and smooth negotiation skills can be daunting in the face of demanding clients and disgruntled customers. Markets often prove to be erratic and inconsistent, and it takes a resilient spirit to weather these concerns. Fortunately, those who do are able to embrace a career that promises much fun and excitement. Buyers may consider themselves arbiters of good taste with highly valued opinions. Frequent travel is another benefit and professionals find themselves rubbing elbows with high-powered clientele.

PROFESSIONAL PROFILE
Avg. starting salary: $31,100
Avg. salary after 5 years: $56,700
Avg. salary 10 to 15 years: $100,000

JARGON
Actuals A physical commodity that is bought or sold, such as corn, silver, or soybeans

Basic product An item that is consistently bought or sold and has few style changes made over the years

ARE YOU INTERESTED IN?
Fashion, retail, business

RELATED COLLEGE MAJORS
Fashion merchandising, merchandising and buying operations, marketing, business administration and management

FOR MORE INFORMATION
National Contract Management Association:
www.ncmahq.org

CAR SALESPERSON

A (Relatively) Typical Day in the Life

The global automotive industry is fiercely competitive and car salespeople labor at their dealerships' frontlines fighting consumer fear of being hoodwinked, bamboozled, swindled, and ripped-off. They offer a product that millions of consumers want to buy, but the stereotypes of slimy salespeople who take advantage of people can make it difficult for them to get the sale.

The best among them log long hours—50 to 60 hours per week, including many nights and weekends—researching car features, studying sales techniques, and working leads to provide impeccable customer service. They are always on the move, scouting prospective customers, staying in touch with past clients, and building relationships with referral sources. Ultimately, this is a people business. Introverts need not apply.

On a typical day, car salespeople check their calendars for appointments and prepare by gathering necessary documents or making sure the cars are washed and ready to go once the customer signs. They add new contacts to their client databases and make plans to reach out to prospects by phone, regular mail, or e-mail. Car salespeople frequently make dozens of calls daily to prospective customers who have made past purchases from them. As a salesperson you might hang out around the dealership's repair department and talk to people about the problems they are having with their current vehicles and what they want in their next car. Car salespeople do whatever they can to get customers behind the wheels of cars they are likely to buy. They take the car or paperwork to the customer's office

An Extreme Day in the Life

Ishmeal Kamara, a former car salesman in Columbus, Ohio, says that interest in cars and resilience are the keys to success in a field where "over-researched" customers, and those who believe every car salesperson stereotype can dampen the spirits of even the most well-intentioned salesperson. "They've read every consumer report, watched every *Car & Driver*, downloaded every piece of information on the car from the Internet, and are rude and nasty even before you say a word. The challenge is to overcome that person and serve the next person with a smile."

He says that professionals must go the extra mile for clients—literally. "On my wildest day, I got there and had to drive 50 miles to go to another dealership to get the exact car that the customer was looking for. I brought it back and they weren't completely sold on the vehicle. They changed their mind on what they wanted. I took them out in the car to go eat and paid for their lunch. We came back and I sold them on it, but they didn't bring any of the paperwork. I had to drive another 40 miles to their house to get the paperwork to prove income, homeownership, [and] car insurance. Then we came back and couldn't get them approved with their credit score. I had to ship all the paperwork overnight mail to the guy's mother in Florida so she could co-sign. It was a two-day car sale."

But that wasn't all. "In between the breaks, you are rescheduling appointments or giving them to another salesman hoping you can split the sale. During this six-hour period you're not eating, you're not drinking, and you are on the move. At that point, you can't do anything to mess up the sale because you have three managers breathing down your neck."

The only time salespeople want to be at their desks is when they're closing deals.

or pick them up and drive them to the dealership when necessary. The only time salespeople want to be at their desks is when they're closing deals.

Prepare for Success

College coursework in fields such as marketing, finance, sales, psychology, and public speaking is becoming more common. However, enthusiasm for cars and vast product knowledge are the best preparation for a prosperous career in car sales. The most successful people in the field love what they are selling and know the automobiles like the back of their hands. They also possess the communication skills to share that passion and information with customers. Their zeal becomes infectious.

Aspiring car salespeople can sharpen their product knowledge by reading industry publications such as *Car & Driver* and *Consumer Reports*. They can give you a better understanding of the vehicle and prepare you to respond to the concerns and questions of customers. Reading car manuals and taking the inventory out for a spin also boosts your knowledge and gives you nuggets of information to use when wooing customers.

There's also no substitute for working long hours in this relationship-driven business. Deepening your car IQ and reaching out to prospective customers is a full-time job and then some.

Getting Your Foot in the Door

Car sales positions aren't extremely difficult to come by because turnover in the field is high and you can get the job with just a high school education or equivalent. The application process typically includes several interviews with sales and human resources managers. You'll also need a valid driver's license, authorization to work in the United States, and be able to pass pre-employment background screenings, drug tests, and credit checks. Some dealerships require a personality profile evaluation as well. You can inquire directly with dealerships or scan postings on online job sites for opportunities.

Biggest Challenges and Best Perks

People pose the biggest challenge in this field where so much of your success hinges upon how well liked you are. Facing rejection after rejection can batter your self-esteem and your wallet if you are paid on commission in proportion to the dealership's profit on each sale. Even if you're making a comfortable amount by your own standards you may still fall short of the quotas your company expects. Plus, working nights and weekends can put strain on relationships.

On the flip side, if you excel in car sales you'll be compensated well with hefty commissions and all the trappings that come with a higher income. Car salespeople also appreciate the freedom they have to plan their own days when sales are going well.

PROFESSIONAL PROFILE
Avg. starting salary: $29,400
Avg. salary after 5 years: $43,600
Avg. salary 10 to 15 years: $70,250

JARGON
Demo A test drive

Green pea A new salesperson

Roach A customer with bad credit

ARE YOU INTERESTED IN?
Cars

RELATED COLLEGE MAJORS
Marketing, communications, business management

FOR MORE INFORMATION
American International Automotive Dealers Association:
www.aiada.org

National Automotive Dealers Association:
www.nada.org

CASINO HOST

A (Relatively) Typical Day in the Life

A casino is a business like any other, and like all successful businesses, a casino relies on the inflow of capital to stay afloat. Those "complimentary" shrimp cocktails don't pay for themselves—the money has to come from somewhere. It comes from the $20 you just dropped in ten minutes at the nickel slots, the $50 your buddy dropped in the blink of an eye at the craps table, and the $200 your other buddy who couldn't make the trip gave you to put on red 63 (or was it black 36?). While it's true that some people get lucky, make no mis-

take: The house always wins. If you stay long enough, you'll see this adage in action. So why is the gaming industry such a lucrative one? Simple: marketing. Lots of money is put into attracting tourists to the casino. And while advertising campaigns and entertainment features are great for getting customers into the hotel and bodies onto the casino floor, keeping them on the floor is the job of the casino's most effective secret weapon: the casino host.

A casino host's job is not unlike a host at a restaurant or a concierge at a hotel. In a nutshell, it's up to you to keep the players—especially the high rollers—happy, a tall order when you consider the fact that the house always takes in more money than it pays out. But it's a job that successful casino hosts do with impressive ease. Casinos, like a lot of companies, like to know who their best customers are, and do what they can to keep them. It's the job of the casino host to establish a rapport with the players. The host is the face of the casino, and just to ensure that the players keep rolling out the dough, the host has a coterie of comps (or freebies) to give away as incentives to keep playing.

An Extreme Day in the Life

Gregory J. Gorla is an administrative operator at the Wynn Las Vegas Race and Sports Book. He has been working at his current job since the property opened in April of 2005. He couldn't be happier about the direction his career has taken: "I used to work for Philadelphia Park Racetrack and when I was in college at Johns Hopkins I took an economic class about the city of Las Vegas—it was a lot of fun! We actually took a four-day field trip to Vegas. I always wanted to live out here so I left Philly Park and moved here. I got hooked up with my current boss through a mutual friend at Bally's/Paris for my first job. When I got hired at Wynn I left, and then months later my current boss left Bally's/Paris to work at Wynn too!"

Greg says his job is full of extreme moments: "For me, everything is pretty memorable because I work with sporting events. My most memorable moments are when certain teams cover a point spread that wins the company lots of money or when other teams cover a point spread that loses the company lots of money."

Whether they're winning or losing, there's never a dull moment in this profession. "The casino business is always going to be alive and well. No matter how badly things may be going in people's lives, they have that dream that if they hit it big at the casino everything will work out fine. People love to gamble!"

It's not always easy to make people happy in an industry that can take so much while giving so little back, but casino hosts do a pretty good job of it.

Prepare for Success

An interest in casinos or the gaming industry is surely one of the basic pre-qualifications of any aspiring casino host. Beyond that, there's no standard path that leads to a career as a casino host. It's a customer service job, but one that takes a special level of finesse. It's a job for which interacting with people is one of the main job descriptions. To perform this aspect of the job well, casino hosts should develop a knack for reading people, understanding and empathizing with them, and being an all-around likable person. There's no hard-and-fast rule about what kind of educational background is required of a casino host, but a background in business or management could be helpful.

Getting Your Foot in the Door

There's no lock on the gaming industry. There are age restrictions regarding who can and cannot be on the casino floor, but assuming you're old enough and without a criminal record, getting a job in a casino should be no more difficult than getting a job at a hotel or nice restaurant. There's a limited amount of real estate in the United States on which it's even possible to attain a gaming license. Towns with casinos are casino towns. Positions aren't falling off trees, but they're definitely out there. Once in the door, it's up to you to figure a way up the ladder.

Biggest Challenges and Best Perks

One of the toughest parts of the job of any casino host may surprise you: it's the comp, or rather, to whom to give the comp. There are all sorts of little complimentary amenities that any player can get, including free drinks and food for just being on the casino floor, but these are not really comps. A comp is typically something of a little more value; this can range from dinner at the hotel restaurant, to tickets to a fight or a show, to a free stay in a luxury suite. These freebies are not really free. Comps are directly proportional to the amount of money the casino host expects the player to wager on the floor. The casual player should never expect to be given a genuine comp under normal circumstances. Still, this raises the issue of whom and when to comp, and it can be a very difficult line to walk. It's the job of the host to walk that line. Along the way, they meet all sorts of fascinating people from all over the world. It's not always easy to make people happy in an industry that can take so much while giving so little back, but casino hosts do a pretty good job of it.

Professional Profile
Avg. starting salary: $35,000

Avg. salary after 5 years: $44,000

Avg. salary 10 to 15 years: $65,000

Jargon
Whale A rich gambler who will spend large amounts of money at a casino

Are you Interested In?
Gaming, business

Related College Majors
Hospitality, logistics management, public relations, business administration

For More Information
American Gaming Association: www.americangaming.org

CURATOR

A (Relatively) Typical Day in the Life

Curators collect, exhibit, interpret, maintain, and protect objects of historical and aesthetic importance primarily in museums, libraries, and private collections. Curators are responsible for the safety and proper presentation of the works. On a day-to-day basis curators create exhibitions, acquire works for the collection, meet with and educate trustees, label exhibits, accurately and carefully keep track of inventory, and oversee research on collection pieces to make certain the integrity of the piece is maintained (such as dating tests for fossils

or X-ray analysis of paintings to determine origin). These varied and wide-ranging duties require someone with a mind attuned to details. Another facet of a curator's job is educating the public about the objects and publicizing the exhibitions. Curators direct internal museum research on pieces and invite academics to join in the study. The literature you pick up at a museum or the audiotapes you listen to were written by and prepared by a curator. Grant writing is another area of responsibility for most curators, and all of them should have excellent written communication skills. In addition to classification and preservation skills, curators have to coordinate the tasks of a full, dedicated staff, which can be an unexpected side of the profession. People who are interested in becoming curators

An Extreme Day in the Life

Jacob McMurray is the senior curator at the Experience Music Project museum in Seattle. According to Jacob, "the two most important skills for a curator to have are the ability to become an expert in a subject quickly, and the ability to tell a story in visual terms. Exhibitions, in essence, are artfully crafted lies; the nature of an exhibition requires complex truths to be distilled down into a few simplified narrative threads." Jacob believes that the best curators are often the ones who simply fall into the profession. He says, "The traditional view of a curator is an individual with a lifelong passion or professional interest in a particular subject. I personally feel that this type of person is often the wrong type of person to be creating an exhibition. An expert in a particular subject is prone to focus on minutiae and not on general threads that will appeal to a wider audience. A generalist who is able to quickly learn the salient points in a topic, will naturally focus on narrative threads that are more accessible to a wider group of visitors, thus ensuring enjoyment by all." When it comes to unusual moments on the job, Jacob's got them in spades: "One of the strangest experiences that I've had as a curator occurred recently. The Comedy Central cable television channel was planning a roast of William Shatner, who played Captain James T. Kirk on *Star Trek*. One of the objects we have on display in the Science Fiction Museum and Hall of Fame is Captain Kirk's command chair prop from the series. In any case, Comedy Central found out that we had the chair on display in the museum and wanted to borrow it for their roast, so that William Shatner could sit on it during the filming of the show. As a general rule, such a use of an artifact would be frowned upon, but the collector proposed use of his artifact, so we went forward, under strict guidelines. I was able to fly down to see the filming of the roast, and I have to say that seeing William Shatner ride onto the soundstage on a white stallion, and then take his rightful seat in the command chair of the Starship Enterprise was quite surreal."

As new artifacts arrive at our institution, it's like Christmas every day. I can't imagine a more enjoyable job than being a curator.

should note that during lean-funding years, the position involves much more grant writing, publicity, and fund-raising than it does collection maintenance and acquisition. Extra time spent at social functions to raise money can be significant.

Prepare for Success

Few curators start college with the expectation of becoming curators. For many, the profession seems to appear out of thin air. Both graduate education and practical experience are required for people who wish to become curators. Aside from an extensive knowledge of history and art, it is useful to have a basic understanding of chemistry, restoration techniques, museum studies, and even public relations. Curators must also be skilled in aesthetic design, organizational behavior, business, and fund-raising. Many employers look favorably on foreign language skills as well. To become a collection manager or a curatorial assistant, a master's degree is required. To become a curator at a national museum, a PhD and five years of field experience are required.

Getting Your Foot in the Door

The market is competitive, and academic standards are very high for this profession. Many start out in curatorial assistant positions, as well as collection manager jobs (which are more task-oriented) to gain experience and begin making connections that will prove invaluable later in their careers. A significant number of people get jobs through the recommendations of their professors. Networking skills are crucial for this position. Nearly all curators find it helpful to engage in continuing education. Research and publication in academic journals are important for advancement in the field.

Biggest Challenges and Best Perks

In the early stages of the career, the hours are long; the pay is low, if any pay is forthcoming at all. Some curators find that they are unable to spend enough time with the art they love because of their obligations to do publicity, fund-raising, and grant writing. Curators who can manage a staff and the details of their job are, for the most part, successful in and excited by their choice of career. Jacob McMurray explains, "My favorite aspects of being a curator are that my job is always changing, I'm always learning new things, and, as new artifacts arrive at our institution, it's like Christmas every day. I can't imagine a more enjoyable job than being a curator."

PROFESSIONAL PROFILE
Avg. starting salary: $26,400
Avg. salary after 5 years: $35,270
Avg. salary 10 to 15 years: $66,050

JARGON
Deed of Gift A signed document transferring title of a piece without monetary consideration

Provenance The office of origin or original source of the materials in an archival collection

ARE YOU INTERESTED IN?
Museums, art, history

RELATED COLLEGE MAJORS
Art history, chemistry, public relations, business administration

FOR MORE INFORMATION
American Association of Museums:
www.aam-us.org

Independent Curators Incorporated:
www.ici-exhibitions.org

Smithsonian Institute:
www.si.edu

EVENT PROMOTER

A (Relatively) Typical Day in the Life

Promoters develop marketing strategies for events that range from rock concerts to international chess tournaments. They work with television, radio, special-events coordinators, ticket sellers, reviewers, bulk mailers, and local merchants to market a product. Few other professions place such a premium on creative thinking. Traditional advertising and marketing strategies can often prove too expensive for the standard entertainment event. Promoters work on a team in which people with different skills—artistic, financial, copywriting, and statistical—come together to produce a seamlessly integrated strategy for getting the word out about a product.

On a day-to-day basis, promoters research, model, and examine target demographics; conduct focus groups, do interviews, make phone contacts, travel, and pitch ideas. The ability to successfully pitch ideas is very important to anyone considering a future in this profession. In addition, promoters need listening and organizational skills, charm, and style. A great promoter will bend over backward for both the paying guests and the talent. Going the extra mile in hospitality for your act is a crucial part of keeping guests and talent coming back in the future.

Promoting is like gambling—a high-risk, high-return industry in which it is amazingly easy to lose your shirt because of one poor decision. In many cases, the difference between a financial bloodbath and a smash hit is solely the ability of the promoter, so the pressure is high and rapid career swings are not unusual. People bond while scrambling to find inexpensive media outlets, dashing to events that moments before were mere ideas, and running to coordinate all the details, but the relationship means nothing if the project is unsuccessful. A promoter cannot afford to be associated with a failed marketing strategy.

Two years is a significant period of time in the life of a promoter. By then, a number of projects have gone from idea to completion, a number of them have stalled or failed somewhere during the process, and some of them never developed into anything beyond a mere idea. Individuals who have worked at a variety of agencies either start

An Extreme Day in the Life

Charisse Nichols is the GenNext Director for CenterStage (Maryland's state theater in Baltimore). She's tasked with "creating an underground image" that will attract a hip and youthful audience to the theater's various productions. "What attracted me to the position is that I get paid to be a big thinker who creates projects that are out of the box." Since rising in the ranks from her days as a part-time box office clerk ten years ago, Charisse has had a number of hectic days trying to make something big out of very little. "Working for a nonprofit, everything is done on a shoestring budget, so many days you spend trying to find sponsors who will give either money or items to cut costs." Last year she was given two weeks and $2,000 to plan a "friend-raiser" that would draw 800 "young, hip, beautiful people" to CenterStage. "In one day, I had to get a donation from a wine sponsor of twenty cases of twelve bottles of wine, get a Balinese dance troupe from DC to perform for free, work with a graphic designer to come up with a design for the invitation and the web page announcement, meet with the marketing group to make sure all of our sponsors were happy with the promo copy, and put together items for 300 gift bags. This was just one day." Don't worry: She pulled it off.

The difference between a financial bloodbath and a smash hit is solely the ability of the promoter.

their own firms or consolidate their strength at the top of their current one. Client satisfaction is the telling point for whether the promoter, at this point, will continue to be successful or will decline. Some individuals who specialize in certain types of entertainment marketing—sports events, concerts, or movies—can fall victim to the cyclical nature of public opinion. Individuals who have ridden the elevator up during the boom period of one specialty area may find themselves in a helpless free-fall if that field flops.

Prepare for Success

No undergraduate degree is required to enter this occupation, and rightly so—no undergraduate degree would properly prepare you for it. Understanding demographics, business, and publicity is important, but the two most valuable traits are creativity and an ability to be in touch with your audience. It takes a particular type of person to become a promoter; confidence and flamboyance help immeasurably. A successful promoter has an unlimited imagination that outmatches the most limited budget.

Getting Your Foot in the Door

Every state has at least one large promoter and several smaller, specialized promoters with long records of success, so this field can be very difficult to break into. Most concert promoters start out in college, where they can establish contacts with talent buyers and bands who come to play at the school. Booking agents are the most important contacts for promoters. An act can always find another promoter, so establishing and maintaining solid relationships with talent and agents is of utmost importance.

Biggest Challenges and Best Perks

The profession is project-based, which can mean unpredictable hours and an unsteady workload. The helter-skelter mix of people working to produce an event can turn into a clash of egos, ideas, and concepts. You'll be put on the chopping block for your bad ideas, and the fall from grace can be swift and merciless. Many people who have endorsed failures or passed on enormously lucrative projects have quickly found themselves seeking work in other professions. The farther up the ladder in this industry one wants to go, the more cutthroat it gets. Many promoters, even the best, suffer burnout.

While the hours can be long and the future uncertain, the field can be financially rewarding for those few individuals who achieve star status. In addition, many promoters take advantage of their contacts to start their own businesses with as few as one or two steady clients.

PROFESSIONAL PROFILE
Avg. starting salary: $21,300
Avg. salary after 5 years: $32,600
Avg. salary 10 to 15 years: $51,700

JARGON
After party The party that follows the main entertainment event, usually by invite only and lasting late into the night
VIP Very important person and/or the sealed off section of a venue accessible only to very important people (i.e. celebrities, special guests, or the guy picking up the tab)

ARE YOU INTERESTED IN?
Music, media, entertainment

RELATED COLLEGE MAJORS
Advertising, marketing, business management

FOR MORE INFORMATION
Pollstar:
www.pollstar.com/
Selling Power Magazine:
www.sellingpower.com/homepage/index.asp
Winning Strategies:
www.winningstrategies.com/

GUIDANCE COUNSELOR

A (Relatively) Typical Day in the Life

Few careers are as potentially rewarding—or as frustrating—as that of a guidance counselor. They help guide and structure children's educational and vocational direction as they pass through a potentially unstable and confusing time in their lives. It can be frustrating because you will have limited power to make students follow your advice, and often you will face students who don't want to think about the future. Counselors try to understand what motivates their students' as well as their skills and desires. Many counselors become surrogate parents for their students. Individuals who aspire to enter the field should be aware that emotional as well as intellectual demands come with the territory.

As most guidance counselors spend more than a third of their time in consultations with students and parents, prospective counselors should be comfortable with teenagers and have excellent communication skills. Another 25 percent of a guidance counselor's day is spent administering and evaluating tests. Guidance counselors use the

An Extreme Day in the Life

Nicole Oringer has worked as an independent counselor for the last 13 years. "I started my career as a teacher, and while I loved teaching, I enjoyed my relationships so much with my students and their parents that I decided to become a guidance counselor. After receiving two master's degrees, I worked as a high school guidance counselor for five years, before opening up my own practice. High school guidance was a wonderful training ground for me, but I felt frustrated by the job's constraints. I had to spend many hours working on schedules and helping students in crisis, which was emotional. I found that the best part of the job was the college piece—it's usually quite positive because the outcome of this counseling is: You're going to college!" For Nicole, becoming an independent counselor was a way for her to focus on the aspect of working with students that she truly enjoyed. "Becoming an independent counselor was a great move—I spend my time doing what I love to do—working with students and their families and visiting colleges. My philosophy is that colleges admissions is a match to be made and not a prize to be won, so I really spend time talking to families about choices, and not just going to schools that they have heard of. The longer I do this, the more I use my counseling skills as it is necessary for me to function as a counselor to the student and his or her family, and as a matchmaker, intent on discovering the right choices for students, based on major, special talents, special needs, or personality." Overall, Nicole is very happy with her chosen career: "The best part of my job is hearing how happy my students are at their schools. It is a privilege and a risk to be intimately involved with these families at such a stressful and pivotal time in their lives. It is enormously satisfying to watch a student mature as he or she explores goals, academic passions, college choices, and extracurricular dreams; to listen to a parent who calls to say that their child is so happy, that the college fits like a glove; to hear the shrieks of joy coming through the telephone as a student relays the good news about a college acceptance."

The most important skill a potential guidance counselor can bring to this profession is the ability to relate to adolescents.

results to provide context for existing records of academic performance, teacher evaluations, and a better overall understanding of students' needs.

Some guidance counselors call the continuing education they receive from the students with whom they work the most interesting feature of the profession. People who don't love the profession usually leave quickly; guidance counselors have one of the highest initial attrition rates of any profession in this book—a staggering 60 percent within the first two years. Careers that require this degree of emotional commitment can be rough on those individuals who are not prepared to make one on a regular basis.

Prepare for Success

A bachelor's degree is required to become a high school guidance counselor, and some states require that the candidate have a master's degree as well. To work in public schools, guidance counselors also typically need to be licensed. Coursework should include social studies, psychology, and communications work, with an emphasis on public speaking. Courses dealing with education are important, too; many private schools require that guidance counselors teach courses in addition to performing their counseling duties. A background in statistics and mathematics is important for evaluating students' standardized tests. By far the most important skill a potential guidance counselor can bring to this profession is the ability to relate to adolescents. They need to be able to listen, be honest, and have both an open mind and a sense of humor.

Getting Your Foot in the Door

The early years are the most trying years for guidance counselors. The full emotional impact of helping guide teenagers through difficult personal decisions and life-changing options presents itself to the new hire. Individuals must learn to keep personal and professional decisions separate while maintaining warm relationships with students. This juggling act is difficult to manage, particularly in the first few years when older students are making critical decisions but have no reason to trust in your ability to help them.

Biggest Challenges and Best Perks

Many guidance counselors consider both the biggest challenges and the biggest perks to be one and the same: the students. Counselors work with adolescents who are typically in a state of flux and turmoil. Students are dealing with changes and major life decisions and though often in need of guidance, they are sometimes wary of heeding advice. Guidance counselors are their cheerleaders, support system, and at times the swift kick in the behind teenagers require. This results in a frustrating but ultimately extremely satisfying profession.

HOTEL MANAGER

A (Relatively) Typical Day in the Life

A hotel manager oversees all of the daily operations of a hotel, from staffing to coordinating fresh-cut flowers for the lobby. Many managers, over time, are given long-term responsibility for negotiating contracts with vendors, negotiating leases with on-site shops, and physically upgrading the hotels at which they work. Hotel managers usually relish the ability to put their own distinctive style on the hotel experience.

When things fall apart, though, no one is a hotel manager's friend. Hotel managers can feel great about their positions, create strong relationships with regular customers, and maintain an amicable working environment, but should the bottom line waver and financial woes occur, the first neck on the chopping block is the hotel manager's.

People in the hotel management profession often need to juggle the administrative, aesthetic, and financial decisions that constitute daily life on the job. A hotel manager's position as a liaison between the ownership and the staff can be difficult and isolating. However, people who can put up with the long hours, high degree of responsibility, and variety of tasks emerge with a solid degree of satisfaction and a desire to continue in the profession. Part of life as a hotel manager can be similar to life as a doctor, as managers can be called to duty at any time of the day or night. Hotel managers must handle any and all emergencies, and individuals who wish to remain in the profession must be quick-thinking and decisive.

An Extreme Day in the Life

Kevin S. Bousquet has been a hotel manager at the Interlaken Inn in Lakefield, Connecticut, for 23 years. Though there are some days that test his patience, he enjoys the people who pass through his doors. As good as he is at his job, however, there are some things that are beyond his control. He recalls, "About 10 years ago, we were looking at the weather report on a very busy evening; the forecast called for severe thunderstorms, and there was even a tornado watch. As luck would have it, I had a very elegant event planned to take place under our tent outside. I tried my best to convince the coordinator of the event to move the party inside. After several hours of deliberating, I finally agreed to continue with the original plan and service the party outside. Ten minutes before the party started, the sky opened up with the worst storm that I had ever seen. The winds were so strong that fully set tables were blown all over the backyard. After the storm, all of the guests and employees waded through 10-inch deep water gathering enough supplies so the function could still be carried out. That evening when the party was completed, and as the guests were leaving, they informed me it was the most fun they had ever had going to an event and would remember it forever. On 90 percent of the days, I love my profession. What I love most about my position is how I can impact a guest's experience—that is the most rewarding experience a hotel manager could have."

Prepare for Success

Hotel manager hopefuls typically go to hotel management school right at the start of their careers. Those who don't should garner as much practical hotel experience as possible. Each chain or specific hotel puts new employees through its own training programs, so people applying for jobs should learn all they can about the scope and functioning of the specific hotels where they wish to work.

Candidates should have a good organizational and financial background, excellent communication and interpersonal skills, and strong self-discipline. They should also be extremely detail-oriented; when running a hotel, there is no such thing as an unimportant detail. Good managers drive themselves to improve and upgrade the hotel at every available opportunity, so knowledge of the competition always comes in handy.

Getting Your Foot in the Door

Aspiring hotel managers used to begin at the reception desk, as part of the wait staff, or as members of the cleaning staff before being able to work their way up the ladder. Since hotels have become more commercial properties and the duties of hotel managers have expanded, this avenue of advancement has more or less closed. Nowadays, experience is gained and connections forged during the first two years, which constitute a type of apprenticeship in which theoretical coursework is fleshed out by practical experience. The path up the totem pole is pretty simple: The better you are at what you do, the more responsibilities you are given.

Biggest Challenges and Best Perks

The initial years of a hotel manager's apprenticeship can often be thankless ones. Little input is expected from the aspiring managers on issues of design, decor, or promotion. The hours are long, the sleep is little, and the pay is low; satisfaction levels, unsurprisingly, are below average. Satisfaction levels typically begin to leap as hotel managers jump from job to job. Getting positions with increasing responsibility means two- to three-year stints at different hotels, learning a variety of skills—staffing, negotiation skills, event planning—and then moving on. At this point, managers' input on larger issues begins to be taken seriously. By the time a hotel manager has racked up 10 or more years in the business, pay is extremely competitive, workload is efficient and responsive to management and client needs, and satisfaction levels are high. Although the early years can be racked with uncertainty and a lack of control, those who stay with the business can create their own home away from home.

LOBBYIST

A (Relatively) Typical Day in the Life

Whether lobbyists work for a large organization, a private individual, or the general public, their goals and strategies tend to be similar. First and foremost, lobbyists must be adept at the art of persuasion. They must figure out how to sway politicians to vote on legislation in a way that favors the interest they represent. This means tailoring appeals to specific individuals as well as to group voting blocs. Lobbyists also occasionally lobby one another. When opposing groups find a common area of interest and can present a united

front, they are extremely effective. Lobbying can be direct or indirect. Direct lobbying means actually meeting with members of Congress and their staffs, providing them with information pertinent to a bill being voted on. The lobbyist imparts his or her information with the help of graphs, charts, polls, and reports that he or she has hunted up or created. Needless to say, this is usually information that the politician may not otherwise have access to and casts the matter in a light favorable to the interest the lobbyist represents. Sometimes, lobbyists will even sit down and help a politician draft legislation that is advantageous for their interest.

Maintaining good relations with politicians who can be relied on to support the lobbyist's interest is key. While their employers cannot make large campaign donations, lobbyists can raise money from other sources for reelection campaigns and be affiliated with political action committees. The resulting core of relationships a lobbyist has with the decision-makers of this country is what makes a lobbyist worth hiring. To be successful, the lobbyist must be well-informed, persuasive, and self-confident. Indirect lobbying, sometimes referred to as grassroots organizing, is a bit less glamorous. Grassroots lobbyists enlist the help of the community to influence politicians by writing, calling, or demonstrating on an organization's behalf. This means long hours spent on the phone and writing let-

An Extreme Day in the Life

Mary Kinney is a Legislative Advocate with Platinum Advisors, LLC. "Starting at a very young age, I was always very interested in politics. Once I got to college I began taking all of the appropriate courses and then interned every summer in the State Capitol. Every school year I volunteered for my party doing voter registration. I spent a summer in DC as an intern with a pollster." Her dedication and experience paid off: "Lucky for me, a lobbying firm took a chance and hired me on a three-month probationary basis after college. I survived and was hired full-time and took on some pretty hefty clients in my first year." Mary's most extreme moments on the job are usually seasonal: "Lobbying is definitely a seasonal sport. From January through late August, most lobbyists are busy harassing legislators for a vote. There are committee hearings and floor votes (both the Assembly and Senate) and then you get to lobby the Governor! Our busiest time of the year is August. This is the last month to get a bill passed out of the Legislature and signed into law by the Governor. We call this month 'hell month' . . . it's a lot of last minute writing, negotiating, and hustling that requires late nights and early mornings. The fate of a bill can turn on a dime, often at the last hour of the last day of session. This requires a lot of last-minute negotiating of the language of certain bills or, 'gutting and amending' as we call it in the biz. It only lasts a month, but it seems like forever and when it's over, most lobbyists would agree, the five month 'recess' is much appreciated."

Lobbying is definitely a seasonal sport.

ters, trying to rouse the community to get involved. These lobbyists also report to politicians about the concerns and reactions they have gotten from community members. Grassroots lobbyists may also use media—writing articles for newspapers and magazines and appearing on talk shows—to generate interest in and awareness of their issues.

PREPARE FOR SUCCESS

A major in political science, journalism, law, communications, public relations, or economics should provide future lobbyists with a solid foundation. Working in a government or political office, especially as a congressional aide, takes you into the front lines, but it may also be useful to start out in a law or public relations firm. Lobbying is a profession brimming with people who have changed careers. Lobbyists are required to register with the state and federal governments.

GETTING YOUR FOOT IN THE DOOR

Many lobbyists also come from careers as legislators; former politicians often capitalize on their years of government service and their connections to old pals still in office. This is the "revolving door" that recent legislation has begun to regulate. Indeed, networking is the name of the game in lobbying, a profession in which people are hired as much for whom they know as for what they know. Someone who can schmooze at high levels will start his lobbying career from a high perch, while others face a long hard climb upward. Although there is no corporate hierarchy, this also means that there is no ceiling for individuals who do well.

BIGGEST CHALLENGES AND BEST PERKS

Lobbyists tend to work long hours; working between 40 and 80 hours per week is the norm. When a bill is up for vote, lobbyists will usually work through at least one night. Professional challenges are heightened in a tight economy where accountability is a must and choices on spending fall under the microscope. The least attractive part of being a lobbyist may be the less-than-spotless reputation of the profession. While many lobbyists are undoubtedly scrupulous, the staggering amounts some high-profile lobbyists can earn causes some degree of mistrust.

Job security for lobbyists grows proportionally with every year of experience. By networking in Washington, DC, lobbyists become increasingly valuable to their organization, leading to higher salaries and professional recognition. Lobbying cannot be legislated out of existence, as it is protected by the Constitution. Honest lobbyists work hard to promote causes they believe are important and worthwhile, and that can be its own reward.

PROFESSIONAL PROFILE
of people in profession: 106,000
Avg. hours per week: 55
Avg. starting salary: $21,400
Avg. salary after 5 years: $53,500
Avg. salary 10 to 15 years: $85,600

JARGON
Roll Call A formal "yea" or "nay" vote on a bill or amendment taken by each legislator during session

Watchdog group A part of government or an interest group whose job it is to review the actions of other parts of government or groups, and raise the alarm when something is amiss

ARE YOU INTERESTED IN?
Politics, activism

RELATED COLLEGE MAJORS
Political science, journalism, law, communications, public relations, economics

FOR MORE INFORMATION
American League of Lobbyists:
www.alldc.org
Greenpeace:
www.greenpeace.org
Women in Government Relations:
www.wgr.org

PUBLICIST

A (Relatively) Typical Day in the Life

A publicist gets press coverage for his or her client. Publicists are often the intermediaries between high-profile personalities and members of the media. They usually want their clients to receive positive acclaim, but many publicists surveyed noted the old adage that "the only bad publicity is no publicity." Politicians and captains of industry require a little more specific spin on their press—they want to be seen as forward-looking and confident—but other professions are less picky, as in the case of rock stars who reveal sordid details of their nightlife to cultivate rough images. Publicists also perform damage control and attempt to counteract any undesirable press coverage their clients receive. This position as "last line of defense" is what distinguishes the adequate publicist from the extraordinary one. Good publicists can transform scandal into opportunity and create valuable name recognition for their clients. Publicists don't work only for famous people. Sometimes they work for a little-known person or industry and generate press coverage. If a company desiring publicity is hampered by its esoteric nature or technical jargon, the publicist must translate its positions into easily understandable language.

A major part of the publicist's day is spent writing press releases and creating press packets, which have photos and information about the publicized person or company. Publicists spend a lot of time on the phone. They operate under hectic conditions and must adhere to strict deadlines that coincide with publicity events, such as the release of a movie or the publishing of a book. They have to ensure that they get the appropriate information to the media in time for the event for which they are generating publicity, such as a record release or automotive sale. They must always be available for comment (even when that comment is "no comment") and remain friendly with members of the media, juggling the demands of both their clients and the reporters on whom they depend. Most publicists are initially attracted to this field because of its perceived glamour. They soon find out that they have to roll up their sleeves and work hard; but at the end of the day, they do get to go to the hottest parties in town: the ones for their clients.

An Extreme Day in the Life

Joe Wiggins, vice president for urban publicity and video promotions at TVT Records, has been working in the field since 1998. As he can attest, the life of a publicist includes many hectic days. One particular experience that stands out took place on August 29, 2004, in Miami—the setting of the MTV Music Video Awards. "I had an artist named Pitbull, and he was performing on the pre-show," Wiggins says. "And then I had two other artists—Lil' Jon and the Ying Yang Twins—and they were performing for the main show. There was a lot of coordinating, and I had to handle it. The main thing was to make sure everybody was where they needed to be at the right time. And the show was live, so there was no room for error." Though there was plenty of running around, the performances went off without a hitch. "Yeah, I survived," he says. "But that was stressful."

PREPARE FOR SUCCESS

The most appropriate bachelor's degree for a publicist to hold is in communications, but employers also look favorably upon business degrees. In college, aspiring publicists should study public relations, public speaking, and writing. Depending on the publicist's desired area, other elective courses may include labor relations, economics, and politics. Candidates should also have some experience with copyediting. Pick up a copy of *PR Newswire* or *Public Relations Journal* to learn more about the field.

GETTING YOUR FOOT IN THE DOOR

Most publicists recommend that you intern at a firm before plunging into this job—a low-responsibility position lets you see the pace of the profession firsthand. Besides, it helps to make as many contacts as possible in this "it's-who-you-know" field. Some publicists have graduate degrees, although employers don't require you to have them. All publicists start at the same entry-level positions and work their way up. Experience is the key to obtaining a good job, especially in the entertainment industry, which is the hardest to break into. The music industry is most likely to acknowledge and reward fresh insight given by new employees.

BIGGEST CHALLENGES AND BEST PERKS

The biggest challenges of being a publicist are the long hours and low pay (at least initially). However, by the time seasoned publicists have made enough contacts and pitched enough good stories, they can relax a bit. Although they are still working long hours, they can begin to enjoy the glamour factor. Many publicists have a lot of influence over the media. Some of the best ones start their own firms or become entertainment television hosts on the small cable networks.

PROFESSIONAL PROFILE
Avg. starting salary: $29,400
Avg. salary after 5 years: $51,000
Avg. salary 10 to 15 years: $69,600

JARGON
Pitching the story Term used to describe the process of convincing a media organization to cover a particular news item

ARE YOU INTERESTED IN?
Media and entertainment

RELATED COLLEGE MAJORS
Communications, business, marketing, public relations and advertising

FOR MORE INFORMATION
National Council for Marketing and Public Relations:
www.ncmpr.org
Public Relations Society of America:
www.prsa.org

REAL ESTATE AGENT/BROKER

A (Relatively) Typical Day in the Life

Buying or selling a house or apartment is one of the biggest decisions of a person's life, and real estate agents and brokers help people navigate what can be a confusing process. Although both are often called real estate agents, agents and brokers perform different tasks. The broker has more administrative responsibilities. When people want to sell or rent property, they usually call a real estate agent. The beginning of an agent's career is spent on the phone as well as looking at and showing properties with the hopes of finding buyers and sellers. This is a difficult time for agents, as they have not yet established reputations. They rely on the name of their firms to attract clients. There is lots of variety in the daily routine, but these beginners must be prepared for long hours and no commissions as they learn the ropes. A large chunk their day may be spent on the phone obtaining listings for their agencies. Agents also arrange to advertise the properties they are showing and may visit all of the properties before showing them to clients. Agents need to know about everything from floor plans to heating systems to cesspools—they are matchmakers and must know both sides of the equation. It's also important for agents to be familiar with the neighborhoods in which they work so they can properly advise their clients about a property's fair market value. A good real estate agent is informed about things such as schools, tax rates, and public transportation systems and should be aware of going mortgage rates. A real estate agent must manage delicate price

An Extreme Day in the Life

Andre Kelly Sr. has been in the real estate business for more than 20 years. The diversity of the industry and the ability to make a lot of money are what attracted him initially. "There are so many areas you can concentrate in and make money: residential homes, cash flow investment properties, commercial property, foreclosure assistance, property management. All of these areas I've worked in at one time or another." Licensed as a real estate agent in Tennessee and Louisiana, Mr. Kelly says there are a lot of positives and negatives in this industry: "Buyers are liars. They lie about where they work, how much they get paid, and their credit history. Sellers are liars too. They lie about taxes, mortgages, and repairs in the home. As a real estate agent you are dealing with buyers and sellers, and you have to know how to do due diligence and check things out for yourself." It doesn't stop there. A real estate agent has to coordinate many elements to close a deal. "You have to have great negotiation skills. You'll be dealing with shrewd investors who only care about ROI and absentee owners who don't return your phone calls. Contractors are greedy vultures—if you don't know how to deal with them they will wring you dry. You have to deal with title companies and insurance companies; you'll help figure out zoning issues, set possession dates, and even help arrange the moving logistics. A good agent will work all this out. 'Hassle-free housing'—that's what a good agent provides." Despite these challenges, Mr. Kelly loves his job: "Real estate is the best vehicle for diversity, challenge, fun, risk, and profit, and it does good for the community both socially and economically. Every day I hand the keys over to a client I'm happy. Who can I help today? That's my vision."

'Hassle-free housing'—that's what a good agent provides.

negotiations when an interested buyer and seller hook up. An agent also coordinates the closing when a property is sold, which means the actual signing of papers and transfer of a property's title.

PREPARE FOR SUCCESS

The basic requirements for becoming a real estate agent are a high school diploma and communication skills. However, more and more people are entering the field with college degrees, and some colleges even offer courses in real estate. These may be helpful, as would other business courses, but most of the learning takes place after you've entered the field. In fact, many real estate agents come to the field from other careers because of the flexible hours or the potential for part-time work. However, before you can be considered a realtor, you must have a real estate license. Every state requires that brokers and agents undergo a series of examinations and accumulate some experience before granting them this license. Each state does have its own test; therefore, if you want to work in a different state, you need to pass the state-specific exam.

GETTING YOUR FOOT IN THE DOOR

Networking is a large part of the job—most real estate agents develop a group of attorneys, mortgage lenders, and contractors to whom they refer their clients. Membership in the National Association of Realtors facilitates networking, but membership is limited to licensed agents. Marketing savvy also helps, and aspiring real estate agents should be prepared to pay for their business cards, mailings, some open-house ads, glossy brochures, and even the snacks or rental furniture at the showings. Establishing a client base in the area market is key to any real estate agent's success.

BIGGEST CHALLENGES AND BEST PERKS

The nomadic trend in U.S. life and the ever-expanding population have prompted the real estate industry to grow at higher-than-average rates. The downside is that the market is always under the influence of economic fluctuations, and the biggest complaint realtors have is the resulting lack of stability in their incomes. Real estate agents cannot expect to earn steady paychecks, since their pay is based on commissions, which may vary greatly. On the upside, real estate agents enjoy flexible hours and the ability to earn significant commission on successful deals. Seasoned agents often advance to the highest levels of their firms, working with blue-chip properties with even better commission structures. Many successful agents eventually strike out independently and start their own firms.

PROFESSIONAL PROFILE
Avg. starting salary: $21,010

Avg. salary after 5 years: $52,860

Avg. salary 10 to 15 years: $84,000

JARGON
C-Suite The top executives in real estate companies who make all the important business and policy decisions

ARE YOU INTERESTED IN?
Housing, investment strategies, sales

RELATED COLLEGE MAJORS
Real estate, business administration, management, marketing

FOR MORE INFORMATION
Century 21:
www.century21.com

National Association of Real Estate Brokers Inc.:
www.nareb.com

National Association of Realtors:
www.realtor.com

RESTAURATEUR

A (RELATIVELY) TYPICAL DAY IN THE LIFE

Owning a restaurant is a demanding labor of love. Restaurateurs need to be leaders and jacks-of-all-trades whether they own a Dairy Queen at the side of a road or a five-star dining room. Expect long hours, as restaurateurs are often the ones who open up and lock up at night and deposit the day's take in the bank. A restaurateur arrives before the staff to look over the log book—a journal in which the managers jot down key activity from the day and night before. The book is one way for an owner to find out which items need to be ordered, any maintenance problems that need to be addressed, customer compliments and complaints, staff issues and scheduling conflicts, and ideas for improvements. Next stop is a daily review of the accounting records. If there's time before the doors open, a brief discussion with the managers and stock check might be on the agenda. Keep in mind that all this work takes place before the restaurant even opens for the day!

Once guests start arriving, restaurateurs get ready to schmooze with guests. They need to remember names and faces so they can make returning customers feel special. If regulars prefer a certain table or always order a post-dinner coffee, the restaurateur makes sure they get it. Simple gestures like these help hard-working restaurateurs build up repeat business. They act as hosts, chatting with guests and making sure they are enjoying their meal. Before they leave for the night, restaurateurs may help close out the registers and lock up. At larger, fancier restaurants, restaurateurs may scale back their daily involvement to meetings with key managers and surprise visits to ensure all is running smoothly. In cases such as these, they will lean on general managers and depend on them to run tight ships while the restaurateurs keep a keen eye on the books.

An Extreme Day in the Life

Steve Spinello got his start in the restaurant business in his mid-twenties and owned an Italian restaurant in Chicago for more than 20 years. While this career is known for long, extreme days, Steve says they became easier to handle as he gained more experience. One of his most memorable experiences happened less than a year into his career: "It was one of those nights when we ended up extremely short-staffed. My host called in sick before the dinner rush and the sous chef cut his hand when we started getting busy and left for the hospital. Not an hour later, one of the waiters heard his girlfriend had just walked out on him and he ran right out the back door! I had to fill in for everyone at once. I was back in the kitchen trying to help out. Then I would run out and seat people and try to get meals onto the right tables while they were still hot. I started thinking about back when I was a waiter and I dreamed of owning a restaurant so I could sit back and watch everyone working. Ha! That night I began to doubt if I should own a restaurant at all. I wanted to just walk out because I thought maybe I was in over my head. Somehow we made it through but it was one of the toughest nights I've ever worked." Steve's career choice was reaffirmed a couple days later, however. "I opened up the newspaper to see a great review of my place. The food critic had been in on that night and didn't mention a thing about the craziness. Only that the pastas were great and the service was welcoming."

Prepare for Success

A college degree in business, hospitality management, or the like will make a solid background for the aspiring restaurant owner. Strangely, few actually take this formal educational route, choosing instead to cut their teeth working various jobs within the industry. There's no substitute for hands-on experience. Even a formal education normally requires an in-house externship for graduation. Success in this business often stems from working under the best until you open your own. Be a great waiter, host, bartender, cook, and manager and you will likely make a great owner—especially if you take the time to learn the business aspects.

Getting Your Foot in the Door

Start small (normally in the front of the house as a waiter) and work your way up to a general manager. Practically an owner-in-training, general managers run the front of the house and act on the owner's behalf when he is away. You may need to restaurant hop to work your way up. Be ethical, punctual, a team player, and provide great customer service. Play the networking game and job offers will find you. If opening a new restaurant, the owner faces the monumental tasks of obtaining financing and choosing a wise location. Then he hires staff, establishes relationships with wholesalers, and oversees the restaurant's design, from decor to menu. Failure rates for new restaurants are high, and an owner must make sure his establishment keeps pace with the times and consistently operates at a high level.

Biggest Challenges and Best Perks

New restaurants are highly susceptible to failure, primarily due to poor cash flow management. Owners who make it may be stressed out and tired, working 80-hour weeks and making only enough money to stay afloat. They rarely take time off and work like mad to pay off their loans. Managing staff members can be tough. Restaurateurs live the business and often have little personal life outside of it.

On the other hand, running a successful restaurant means people in the community know you and you know them. You are able to provide guests with a great eating-out experience and host people in the special place you've created. Praise for your masterpiece is music to your ears.

Professional Profile
Avg. starting salary: Varies

Avg. salary after 5 years: Varies

Avg. salary 10 to 15 years: Varies

Jargon
Backer Someone who provides the restaurateur with the financing to open up a restaurant; also the first to see the profits

Are you Interested In?
Cooking, food

Related College Majors
Business management, hospitality management, operations management, culinary arts

For More Information
National Restaurant Association:
www.restaurant.org

Educational Foundation of the National l Restaurant Association:
www.edfound.org

RETAIL SALESPERSON

A (Relatively) Typical Day in the Life

Retail salespeople can do their jobs from behind a counter, over the phone, or even by visiting their clients personally, whether they're right down the hall or on the other side of the world. Most salespeople pitch their products dozens of times a day, five days a week. Whatever the product, they must convey confidence and goodwill, because making a sale requires a trusting consumer. People in sales must be ready to deal with rejection and with disgruntled customers. Since products and market conditions change constantly, salespeople must adapt if they want to survive. The tremendous rate of change in fields such as consumer electronics and, particularly, computers can be as overwhelming as it is exciting. In these complex and fluctuating economic times, both the local mom-and-pop shops and behemoth superstores have multitiered levels of staff to supervise their operations, and often the training and hiring is done from within. The salesperson on the floor of the ladies' lingerie department, for example, may very well be destined to move into commissioned sales, management, finance and auditing, operations, e-commerce and IT, merchandising, buying, or entrepreneurship.

Skilled salespeople know the products they are selling and understand their customers' needs. Salespeople often say they want to help people find what they need and bristle at accusations that they are selling just to make commissions. After all, salespeople are a necessary part of a dynamic capitalist economy. Moreover, many salespeople truly

An Extreme Day in the Life

Ann Palumbo has worked as a retail sales professional for the past 20 years. She cautions, "Retail is a very different animal than most people think. Some people think 'Oh, you work in Bloomingdales; it must be very glamorous.' In fact, working at a retail store entails a lot of pressure to meet your sales goals." Some days on the job are more hectic than others: "It can be very fast-paced and then there are times when it's boringly slow. There will be times when you're all standing around waiting for the next customer. You have to be able to work in both paces." For Anne, the best part of working in retail sales is the opportunity to connect with customers. "The best part for me is really building a rapport with a customer. They can get their stuff online but when they come into a store they want to be schmoozed and complimented; it fulfills a need for one-on-one attention. I sell hats and sometimes people are not sure about what they want so I'm there to support what they're looking for—is it the right color? Is it the right shape for their face? Customers are looking for guidance and a little bit of handholding. I have a customer who follows me from department to department. We'll keep track of events in each other's lives—that's an important thing for a lot of women. They're looking for a common thread. I think that's what's most rewarding about this career—that touch of humanity." However, Ann readily points out that this career is not for everyone: "Retail isn't for you if you're not competitive and you don't have a hard shell. You can't let little things get to you. You have to understand that you're not always going to meet the nicest person. You're dealing with people from the outside world. . . . There will be good days and bad days."

[Salespeople] are only as good as their previous month's sales figures.

enjoy the human interactions as much as the more palpable thrill of closing a sale. For some salespeople, the demands of travel detract from the time they can spend with their families; others enjoy the travel or find they can work from home. A good sales record leads to a better job with a better salary and, often, extra incentives such as higher commissions. Nevertheless, even the best salespeople often work constantly because they are only as good as their previous month's sales figures.

Prepare for Success

The sales profession demands experience over education. A specialized degree is not necessary to pursue a career in sales. An understanding of the product is important no matter what you sell, but the salesperson must learn to communicate well with clients, whether it's face-to-face, over the phone, or by letter or e-mail. Ambitious salespeople may study marketing and sales techniques at college or business school either before or during their sales careers. Most salespeople devote their sales-related reading to specialized journals dedicated to the professional salesperson or to the individual markets they serve. The amount of time salespeople devote to their jobs depends on what they sell and on their own personal needs.

Getting Your Foot in the Door

Getting into retail sales is easy, and the growth opportunities can be significant. The skills involved in sales transfer well to other careers. However, entry-level sales jobs may pay minimum wage, often without a commission. Practicality, persuasiveness, and tenacity are qualities esteemed in managers, and many salespeople use their job as a stepping-stone to consulting or management positions. In addition, some salespeople may be recruited into positions as manufacturer's field sales representatives for products they were formerly selling at the retail level. A change in product lines or entry into a new area can spell a need for rapid reeducation about the product and the best way to sell it.

Biggest Challenges and Best Perks

The grind of frequent rejection and the constant interaction with others can be tiring, but for some, the triumph of making a sale can be its own reward. The best salespeople develop personal strategies for being a convincing salesperson, no matter what it is they happen to be selling. Proven salespeople can negotiate higher commissions or more lucrative accounts. Seasoned professionals have settled into management positions and may be responsible for a sales force or important accounts. Veteran salespeople may be able to cut back on their hours while still bringing in significant business to the company. Others may be drawn to the travel and business opportunities of international sales.

Professional Profile
Avg. starting salary: $17,700
Avg. salary after 5 years: $23,504
Avg. salary 10 to 15 years: $35,300

Jargon
Footfall Consumer traffic into a store or area of a store

POS (point of sale) The physical location where a product is displayed

USP (unique selling proposition) The real thing that makes a product stand out, for example taste or packaging

Are you Interested In?
Sales, customer service

Related College Majors
Marketing, business management, communications

For More Information
Bloomingdale's:
www.bloomingdales.com

National Retail Federation:
www.nrf.com

TOUR GUIDE

A (Relatively) Typical Day in the Life

Tour guides are educators. Their number one obligation is to provide customers with compelling information in an engaging manner. To do this, tour guides must cultivate a deep knowledge of the topic at hand. They also need to be comfortable fielding a wide range of questions from public.

Location has a lot to do with the precise duties of a tour guide. After all, tour guides can be found everywhere from a historic home, to the Gettysburg National Military Park. Sometimes guides have to lead a tour of the same site eight times in one day; others, like a backwoods adventure through the Badlands, can last several days and bring about unique adventures each time. Depending on the site, guides can lead their tours by foot, bus, canoe, or anything else that effectively carries people across the areas being toured.

Tour guides do more than simply lead tours; they collaborate with colleagues to devise and implement educational programs and services. They may also design off-site presentations and events. In addition, tour guides are often involved in promoting tours, selling tickets, and other administrative chores associated with the educational programs offered at the facilities at which they work.

Ultimately, tour guides make use of three very important skills: an ability to obtain and retain a deep well of information, an ability to communicate effectively with others, and adaptability. This last skill is especially significant. After all, a guide never knows when a tough question or a know-it-all patron or an unexpected thunderstorm is going to change the dynamic of the tour. However, like an actor, the tour guide must keep command of the stage. The show must—and will—go on.

An Extreme Day in the Life

For more than three years, Alex Narvaez has been the lead educator at the Lower East Side Tenement Museum in New York City. His job includes leading tours, preparing educational programs, and giving off-site presentations for the museum (which promotes "tolerance and historical perspective through the presentation and interpretation of the variety of immigrant and migrant experiences on Manhattan's Lower East Side"). He tells us about one particularly memorable experience: "We visited the Department of Mountainview Correctional Facility in Amerdale, New Jersey, as a part of an off-site presentation. The presentation was intended to help teachers communicate to their students (most of whom were young, male first-time offenders) that history is important and people have a productive place in society and can contribute to history through their own lives. After our presentation, a teacher got up and said, 'A lot of these kids feel like the world owes them something, and that they are the only ones who have it tough. The folks you talked about [in this presentation] lived through horrible depressions and had next to nothing. We can tell these kids that life is tough and you survive and you have to seize the day, because no one is going to hand you a wonderful life. You have to do it yourself.' That was one of the most powerful moments I've experienced, especially since one of the inmates was right next to us as the teacher spoke."

Tour guides must cultivate a deep knowledge of the topic at hand.

Prepare for Success

Remember always that a tour guide is an educator; we simply cannot emphasize this enough. As far as education jobs go, a good tour-guide gig can be as competitive as any. After all, you're not the only one who wouldn't mind spending all day wandering around the Art Institute of Chicago or Seattle's Experience Music Project. So how do you land the job? Knowledge is power in this profession and a steady diet of history and culture courses will give you a solid foundation upon which to build. Don't rely solely on course work. Real-world experience—whether as an intern at a local historic site or as a tour guide for your college's admissions office—will allow you to grow more comfortable talking to the public, fielding questions, and adapting to the unexpected twists and turns that come with the job.

Getting Your Foot in the Door

Show up on the job prepared to be a jack-of-all-trades. This means not sighing when they say that you'll need to spend the morning photocopying promotional brochures or selling tickets. Many facilities that cater to tourists are understaffed and survive only because of the staff's teamwork mentality. Knowledge of technologies can go a long way; after all, the Internet continues to offer valuable avenues for education and marketing, and many organizations—particularly smaller ones—are behind the times. Don't forget that tourists speak many languages. If you have a working knowledge of Spanish or Chinese, for example, use it to make yourself a more marketable employee.

Biggest Challenges and Best Perks

Tour guides are not always the highest paid members of society, and, depending on the particulars of the job, they may have to log a lot of weekend hours in their early years. There's no predicting what sort of people are going to end up on a tour. One tour may be full of kind and attentive foreign tourists, and the next may include a pair of blowhards who offer contradictory or dismissive comments at every stop of the tour. Maybe it includes a couple of old ladies who insist on touching the paintings at a museum. Your job is to keep your cool and maintain order—at times, this can be a pain in the neck.

Most times you have the opportunity to talk about something in which you're very interested, and you have an attentive audience to boot. In this type of job, you're always meeting new people and hearing about their own stories. Because no group of tourists is ever the same, no tour is ever the same either—and this variety is something tour guides cherish. What could be better than that?

Professional Profile
Avg. salary: $50 to $150 per day

Jargon
Cultural tourism Travel for the purpose of learning about cultures
Educational programming Activities conducted in partnership with formal education institutions

Are you Interested In?
History, foreign cultures, travel

Related College Majors
History, area studies, hospitality and tourism

For More Information
World Federation of Tourist Guide Associations:
www.wftga.org

TRAVEL

DIPLOMAT/ATTACHÉ/FOREIGN SERVICE OFFICER OR SPECIALIST

A (RELATIVELY) TYPICAL DAY IN THE LIFE

The Foreign Service represents the United States around the world. Members interact with local governments as emissaries of the United States and staff United States embassies and consulates. The Foreign Service handles all problems of Americans abroad, including negotiating on behalf of United States companies who wish to do business abroad; providing information about the host country; and issuing replacements for lost documentation. Foreign consulates also issue visas to foreigners wishing to enter the United States. These tasks consume a minimum of 30 hours of the work week; since additional internal duties including writing reports and attending social functions can take up another 40 hours per week, people who are looking for a sinecure are ill-advised to enter the Foreign Service.

Diplomats are posted to positions abroad for terms of two, three, or four years with nine-month stateside stints every two to four years, but they can be recalled by the State Department at any time. Divided into two tracks of Foreign Service Specialist and Foreign Service Officer, applicants select a path best suited to their specialties. While Foreign Service specialists assume trade-specific posts, Foreign Service officers are generalists who select one of five career tracks—economic, public diplomacy, consular, management, and political—but may be called upon to serve on any track

An Extreme Day in the Life

Laura Kennedy is a career member of the Foreign Service with the rank of Minister-Counselor. She previously served as an Ambassador and Deputy Chief of Mission abroad and is currently serving as a member of the Board of Examiners of the Department of State. One of Laura's most extreme moments on the job happened right after September 11th: "I was sent as Ambassador to Turkmenistan, a country sharing a long border with Taliban-run Afghanistan and itself ruled by a dictator, Saparmurat Niyazov. Turkmenistan had earlier cooperated with the Taliban regime although it had never formally recognized that government. We were extremely anxious to enlist the Turkmen government in the effort to drive the Taliban from power, but we also knew that our serious differences over human rights issues constrained our ability to cooperate with this government. So we focused on Turkmenistan as a humanitarian relief corridor to Afghanistan and were able to keep alive valuable lifelines to this extremely isolated country with our educational exchange programs and our support to the beleaguered NGO community." Despite these successes, "A failed assassination attempt against Niyazov in 2002 made our relations more problematic. Although the U.S. government had absolutely nothing to do with the attack, President Niyazov was nevertheless suspicious. He had been furious that we had given a visa to an opponent of his regime, who was later arrested as the alleged ringleader of the failed coup. We demanded due process for those arrested and we used every means available to censure the violations of their human rights. We did manage to obtain the release of an American citizen who had been arrested in the aftermath of the failed plot. But most of those arrested were subjected to abuse and hideous show trials; to this day, they remain hidden in prison from the outside world." Laura's advice for students considering this career is simple: "Take advantage of all opportunities to meet diplomats and read about the work of the State Department. [And] work on your foreign languages."

Strong communication skills are absolutely essential for anyone thinking about entering the profession.

for the duration of their employment. Much of your working hours will be spent handling reports: assembling facts, writing, proofreading, and reading. Reading is fundamental and if your writing isn't up to snuff, you'll be selected out—fired, that is. Strong communication skills are absolutely essential.

Prepare for Success

To enter the Foreign Service, you must be an American citizen between the ages of 20 and 59. Although there is no educational requirement to become a Foreign Service officer, the vast majority of applicants hold a bachelor's degree or higher. Applicants must pass the competitive Foreign Service exam, offered once a year in most major urban centers and at consulates abroad. Individuals who pass take a secondary exam, which includes a day-long assessment: a physical, a rigorous background exam, and a final review of all the candidate's strengths and weaknesses. Candidates are expected to be familiar with another language, but fluency can be acquired after posting.

Getting Your Foot in the Door

Strong preparation for the Foreign Service exam is the best way to break into this profession. Individuals who pass all the tests are given a ranking and put on a list of eligible candidates for future postings. At most, a few hundred slots open up each year. Be aware that if no position opens up within 18 months, you will have to begin the process all over again. Most candidates do not receive officer status upon hire. Halfway through their probationary period, which lasts roughly four years, new diplomats are expected to have made significant headway in learning a foreign language. Each year, appointees receive ratings from their supervisors. Recommendation for promotion depends on the officer's perceived potential for greater responsibility along with the availability of positions at higher levels.

Biggest Challenges and Best Perks

Until 1924, the Foreign Service was staffed only by individuals in the upper class. The wages were so low that no one else could afford to take a position. While the Rogers Act in 1924 provided reasonable wages and democratized the process of entering the Foreign Service, new specialists can expect to work long hours for a wage that turns out to be pretty low if calculated hourly. Despite these issues, more than half of Foreign Service officers pursue lifetime careers in the Foreign Service. They enjoy the responsibility that comes with the position: The ability to look at a host country from the inside, write a considered opinion of the state of that country, and have it seriously regarded by officials making decisions about international relations.

Professional Profile
Avg. starting salary: $39,691*
Avg. salary after 5 years: $45,000
Avg. salary 10 to 15 years: $89,000

*Current starting salaries for Foreign Service officers range from $39,691–$54,794, depending on education and experience. Further details can be found by visiting: http://www.careers.state.gov/officer/benefits/index.html#salary

Jargon
Danger pay Special compensation a diplomat receives for working in areas where violence, political or otherwise, is prevalent

Are you Interested In?
Foreign policy, diplomacy, travel, international relations

Related College Majors
English, foreign language, government, geography, international history, economics

For More Information:
U.S. Department of State:
www.state.gov/employment

United Nations Headquarters:
www.un.org

Foreign Policy Association:
www.fpa.org

ESL INSTRUCTOR

A (Relatively) Typical Day in the Life

Anyone who enjoys learning different languages, traveling overseas to immerse themselves in different cultures, and meeting new people has probably considered teaching English as a Second Language. Increasingly, teaching ESL has become a valid career choice in its own right, rather than something to do while figuring things out. As a result, aspiring ESL teachers face stiffer competition for the best jobs (better pay, more desirable locale). You'll need to bring your A-game to the job boards.

Teaching ESL is a specialty within the much larger realm of teaching English to non-native speakers. Those who teach English as a Second Language do so to students who are learning it in a primarily English-speaking environment or in a country where English is one of several main languages. ESL is also taught in the United States—mostly at community colleges but also at private universities; be sure to check course catalogs.

In this profession—which attracts many recent college graduates—wages are (ideally) enough on which to live, but not enough on which to live it up. Some countries—Taiwan, Japan, and especially Korea—pay better than others. Jobs are also available in other areas of Southeast Asia, in addition to Eastern Europe and the Middle East. With their standard 15- to 30-hour workweek, teachers have time for exploration and travel but not the cash to do so luxuriously. Few return to the States with a fat savings account, but they do have memories, a new appreciation for another people and culture, and even a decent amount of job offers in case they ever decided to return.

You should spend the days before applying to and leaving the country to take an ESL position by researching as much as you can. Knowing as much as possible about the area in which you'll be teaching is critical. In addition to checking safety conditions, you should try to acquire information on the history and daily life of the region so your transition goes that much smoother. Once you're there, teaching will consume your time. When you're not in the classroom, you will be working on lesson plans, grading homework, attending staff meetings, and working to

An Extreme Day in the Life

When he was a senior in college, Jay Mok served as ESL instructor in South Korea as a part of a community service program at Harvard University. Though he went on to pursue a career in business, he is grateful for the life-changing experience. He says, "My first day as an ESL instructor was the most exciting. It was my first time teaching ESL without knowledge of my student's native language, my first time instructing adults, and my first time teaching such a large number of students. Due to the loose structure of the program, I also had quite a bit of freedom regarding how to teach the classroom. But methodology was the last thing on my mind on that first day. I was nervous and had butterflies in my stomach as I introduced myself and asked my students to do the same. While scrambling to prepare the first lesson, I remembered the teaching style of one my favorite chemistry teachers. As I followed my notes, I emulated my old teacher and engaged the class. Soon I felt the butterflies vanish and the attention of 20 adults focus on my words and the chalkboard. Three hours later, as my new students thanked me on their way out of the classroom, I felt quite a bit of satisfaction [from] the small difference I was starting to make."

ESL teachers face stiffer competition for the best jobs (better pay, more desirable locale). You'll need to bring your A-game to the job boards.

adapt to a new life on foreign soil. English language fluency is naturally essential to success, as is flexibility, confidence, and passion for learning about a new culture. It's also highly recommended that you do your best to learn the language of the country in which you will teach. It will help you not only in day-to-day situations, but also help you gain a greater understanding of your students.

Prepare for Success

It is no longer possible to secure a job as an ESL instructor by merely being a native English speaker and having a bachelor's degree. Most entry-level jobs now require an ESL teaching certificate in addition to a college degree. The certificate can be acquired in a three- to six-week course and allows you to teach in private schools such as Berlitz, Kaplan, and International House. It also helps determine if you're cut out for the job. Knowing a second language will also help boost your resume.

Getting Your Foot in the Door

Meeting (and impressing) people in the ESL world is the gateway to new opportunities. Arrive for your ESL position armed with an open mind, knowledge of the country, and a supply of teaching materials, which could be tough to buy outside of the United States. Those who dig the ESL experience might consider earning a teaching diploma, which is offered in Britain and recognized throughout Europe and Asia. The intensive course ranges from three months to one year and is required for many higher-level (the director of a school, for instance) and better paying positions. Those who want to teach at the university level will need a master's degree.

Biggest Challenges and Best Perks

Dealing with culture shock and homesickness are some of the biggest challenges of this profession. Even those who love their host countries may start to feel differently six months later and begin to miss the comforts of home. Coming back to the United States can be shocking as well. Teachers miss their students and friends abroad and find people at home cannot relate to their experiences. On the upside, becoming an ESL teacher takes travel to another level. You'll be totally immersed in a country and many find it exhilarating to make the transition from outsider to insider. Americans in foreign countries stand out, sometimes (and hopefully) earning them a certain level of popularity. Moreover, teaching is a skill you can take anywhere with you, and patience is a great quality to nurture.

Professional Profile
Avg. starting salary: Up to $1,500 per week (U.S. dollars)

Varies from country to country

Jargon
PPP Stands for presentation, practice, and production; an approach to grammar lessons based on the idea of presenting small items of language to students, providing them with the opportunity to practice it in controlled ways, and finally integrating it with other known language to communicate (production)

Are you Interested In?
Travel, foreign languages

Related College Majors
Foreign language studies, education

For More Information
ESL Magazine:
www.eslmag.com/modules.php?name=RssFeed

ESL Employment:
www.eslemployment.com/dcforum/DCForumID12/153.html#

American TESOL Institute:
www.americantesol.com/

MISSIONARY

A (RELATIVELY) TYPICAL DAY IN THE LIFE

The primary job of a missionary is to "spread the word," so to speak—to introduce as many people as possible to the religion of the mission and to offer those people ample opportunity for conversion. This involves lots knocking on doors, shaking hands, handing out religious tracts and sacred texts, holding meetings, and venturing into unfamiliar areas. These unfamiliar areas are not necessarily in foreign countries. It's true that missionaries often have the opportunity to work abroad, but you're just as likely to find a missionary traveling around rural areas of the United States, tending to organizational duties in a big-city office building, or even proselytizing over the Internet. In fact, missionaries often split their time between actual "missions" and taking care of the administrative duties that allow those missions to occur.

In many cases, your religion will determine what kind of missionary work is available, if any at all. Faiths such as Christianity and Mormonism have especially organized and powerful missionary movements that span the globe, penetrating even the remotest regions of the earth. Other religions engage in little or no missionary work. Judaism, for instance, is explicitly uninterested in recruiting converts, though it does sponsor outreach efforts to reconnect with ethnic Jews who've drifted from the religious practice of Judaism.

While converting nonbelievers is the main goal of a missionary, social work is often involved as well. This is particularly true for missionaries who are placed in Third World countries. They may bring medicines to the ill, offer English language classes, and help community members erect churches, schools, infirmaries, and homes. Missionaries can visit a community for just a week or two, or they may sign on for extended stays of months or years. They can also travel alone or in teams, depending on the funds available and the structure of the sponsoring organizations.

An Extreme Day in the Life

Whether done as a career or undertaken as a temporary volunteer endeavor, missionary work involves days that can be long and unpredictable. Bryan Swiss spent two years as a volunteer Mormon missionary in Russia during the mid 1990s. While there, he and a partner missionary were sent to the city of Podolsk to spend a week assessing the likelihood of starting a Mormon church there. He explains, "We went exploring to the far south[ern] border of the city. As we were about to head back, we saw a lone man exiting a parking structure. We decided to introduce ourselves and share our message. The man told us he was interested in knowing who we were and what we did, and listened intently to our brief explanation. Imagine our surprise when at the end of the conversation, the man announced to us that he was in fact the mayor of the city, and promptly produced his business card! He was impressed with our earnestness, and felt that our organization would be a positive addition to the city. He instructed us to call his secretary and schedule an appointment with him the following week. After that, we met frequently with the mayor and other city government officials to lay the foundation for establishing a church group in their city. Given the political climate in Russia at the time, this was quite a feat. If anyone had told me in high school that by age 20 I would be wearing a suit and conducting negotiations with high-ranking Russian officials, I don't think I would have believed them!"

Missionaries are able to invest themselves in work that **carries great personal conviction.**

Prepare for Success

Strong faith is the most important prerequisite to becoming a missionary. This is exactly what a mission organization or church is going to need to see before they send you off into the world to represent them. Therefore, get your hands on the holy book of choice and start studying. Volunteer work—whether helping out with clerical duties at a mission's headquarters or distributing tracts in your neighborhood—is a great way to get your feet wet in the field. If going abroad is your goal and you know where you'd like to go, spend time learning about the culture—its people, history, politics, and beliefs—because doing so allows you to show your dedication and prove you are knowledgeable when you make your case for the position.

Getting Your Foot in the Door

Expanding your knowledge of a specific country or region can lend you the expertise needed to land repeated assignments to your location of choice. It goes without saying, therefore, that proficiency in a foreign language or two can be a tremendous help. Meeting and associating with other missionaries may open up additional opportunities. Most important, you must be able to demonstrate your ability to establish a good rapport with people, including people from radically different backgrounds from your own who may be less than sympathetic to the ideas you're sharing with them. For this reason, the best missionaries are those who can think quickly on their feet and are capable of withstanding occasional bouts of social discomfort.

Biggest Challenges and Best Perks

When you do missionary work, you wear your beliefs on your sleeve—and you often encounter people who are dismissive of these beliefs. Rejection is part of a missionary's daily life, and it's not always easy to swallow. It can also be difficult being away from your family, friends, and culture for long stretches of time, particularly if you're working alone. The hours are typically long and vacations can be hard to come by.

But there are certainly perks. "Knowing that one's labors have improved and enriched the lives of others brings the missionary deep satisfaction," says Bryan Swiss. "Missionaries develop a strong sense of purpose and self-esteem, and find opportunities to make decisions about who they are, what they want from life, as well as how they will conduct their personal lives." In other words, missionaries are able to invest themselves in work that carries great personal conviction. They're often able to do this while living in interesting locations, working with intriguing people, and learning about new cultures.

MOTIVATIONAL SPEAKER

A (Relatively) Typical Day in the Life

Motivational speakers believe that they can change lives by uttering the right words. They aim to move crowds with entrancing stories and advice. They inspire people to live their dreams, get in shape, become financially secure, and have some fun. They come from all walks of life but share an ability to win applause and dollars with their presentations. They are their message.

Many motivational speakers are solo-preneurs, which means that they are responsible for crafting and delivering compelling speeches along with booking engagements, coordinating travel, and invoicing clients. They must balance the delivery of inspirational messages with the nuts and bolts of small business operations. In the beginning, much of their days are filled with hustling to get the next gig.

They also spend significant amounts of time getting better at their craft. They earn credentials, join trade organizations, find mentors, watch tapes of leading speakers, and practice speeches in front of the mirror. Many also package their expertise in books, CDs, videos, and other products to earn additional income.

They also must stay motivated themselves. There are days when they aren't feeling so peppy, but they must still step out in front of audiences and deliver a motivational tale. Sometimes they have to fake it and convey a vibrant spirit that they don't feel. In other instances, they have to psych themselves up with their own encouraging speeches. Ultimately, motivational speaking is performance, and the show must go on.

An Extreme Day in the Life

Mark Adams was a college basketball coach for 17 years and sales professional and trainer for 6 years before he became a full-time motivational speaker. Now he uses his own experiences in sports and business to connect with diverse audiences at client companies, including Wendy's International, Goodwill Industries, and U.S. Bank. "I love what I do so much and the rush is so overwhelming. It's like coaching. There's nothing like winning a college basketball game. When you walk off the floor, there is an adrenaline rush. I missed coaching. I missed that adrenaline rush. When I speak and get a standing ovation that's like walking off that court with a championship in sight."

Coaching prepared Mark well for motivational speaking by putting him in front of audiences of boosters, alumni, and media representatives on a daily basis. He started out by speaking free as a means to market his program, but now he gets paid to give dozens of speeches a year to business audiences who appreciate his straight-shooting advice. "Most days I work very hard. I pride myself on preparation. I spend time e-mailing and telephoning different members of the organization who are going to be in the audience. I ask pointed questions about their personal and professional challenges. I use their quotes to frame my presentation and gear it toward their issues. Most speakers come in with a canned presentation. I come in with a customized message. If I have a competitive advantage, that's it. I interview 5 people per event for 40 or 50 presentations a year."

He advises aspiring motivational speakers to "constantly challenge yourself to remember where you failed and where you were successful." It's the school of hard knocks that builds credibility with audiences, not untested philosophies, he explains.

It's the school of hard knocks that builds credibility with audiences, not untested philosophies.

Prepare for Success

You don't need any particular educational background to become a phenomenal motivational speaker. In fact, some popular speakers have only graduated from high school. Deep life experience, including a few notable failures, losses, and difficulties, can go a long way toward endearing you to audiences. In this arena, people aren't impressed by theories. They want to hear about how you fell, but then got up, and how they can too. Experience isn't everything. You also need to present your life in a compelling fashion, and that takes practice. Aspiring motivational speakers should get in front of any audience they can. Volunteer to speak in front of community organizations so you can practice different presentation styles, incorporating humor into your speeches, and get comfortable speaking in front of audiences. Organizations such as Toastmasters International give members weekly speaking opportunities and provide manuals and other resources to help them improve presentation skills.

Getting Your Foot in the Door

You'll have to create your own opportunities in this competitive field by offering your services free to community organizations or hosting your own seminars. These early unpaid opportunities will give you experience, testimonials, videos, and other promotional aids that will allow you to secure paid speaking engagements in due time. You can't be shy about letting people know you are available. Tell your friends and family. Contact speakers' bureaus, nonprofit organizations, and businesses that could benefit from your expertise. Promote yourself with websites, brochures, and other marketing materials. A well-placed business card can help your cause.

Biggest Challenges and Best Perks

Motivational speakers work long hours. Audiences can be skeptical and resistant to their messages and vocal about their displeasure. Speaking engagements can be few and far between. When things are good, the breakneck pace of presentations can wear speakers down. They sometimes have to travel extraordinary distances between engagements and can't always afford top-notch accommodations.

Still, many of them love the flexibility of being their own boss and working day in and day out to improve the lives of people who are struggling personally and professionally. The whole aim of the job is to encourage, inspire, instruct, and motivate audiences. Motivational speakers enjoy the opportunity to travel extensively and meet fascinating people at each stop along the way. No two days are alike and they never know with what new challenges audiences will present them. Plus, there are financial rewards. Some speakers earn thousands of dollars per gig once they are well established.

Professional Profile
Avg. salary: $1,500 per lecture (national-level speakers)

Jargon
Canned For speakers, a standard speech or presentation

Flop sweat Fear of performing

Gross fee The total fee charged for a booking, including agents' fees

Are you Interested In?
Motivating, life coaching, public speaking

Related College Majors
Communications, psychology, organizational behavior

For More Information
International Speakers Bureau:
www.isbspeakers.com

Professional Speakers Association:
www.professionalspeakers.org

Toastmaster's International:
www.toastmasters.org

NEWS CORRESPONDENT

A (Relatively) Typical Day in the Life

News correspondents, coveted positions of print and broadcast journalism, are reserved for top-notch, experienced reporters who generally live and work (at least temporarily) wherever the news is happening—across the country and around the world.

News correspondents gather, organize, investigate, and report on news stories in real time from wherever they are stationed. Usually assigned to a post in a large U.S. or foreign city, they are caught up in the action of the current events they have been sent to cover—from the heat of war to signs of peace negotiations, from elections and natural disasters to business scandals, and even from the inauguration of a new pope to a royal wedding. If they are working for large organizations, then reporting is their main concern, either via videotaped or live transmissions of stories for broadcast, or reporting in the field and racing back to a satellite office to file it (i.e., get it back to their home newsroom) for print. Correspondents who work for small organizations may be a one-person newsroom, charged with editing film and tracking down news in nearby locales or, in print journalism, taking photographs, writing headlines, and suggesting layouts to accompany their stories. Technology has changed correspondents' lives, making it much easier for them to keep in touch and exchange information with their colleagues back in the United States.

The ideal correspondent is one tough cookie: persistent, probing, poised, and resourceful. They need to be in good physical condition and of sound mind. Broadcast correspondents must be camera-ready rain or shine, day or night—often with little time to prepare. They must look and sound refreshed and calm, even in the face of world tragedies and disasters. Pressing deadlines and the pressure to get bigger and better stories make the work of a news correspondent stressful and hectic. Long, irregular hours are a given, and correspondents lead lives that revolve around their careers. Assignments can be dangerous, and other people on the scene (onlookers, police, other media) may impede on their tasks.

An Extreme Day in the Life

Atika Shubert is a CNN news correspondent currently based in Tokyo. She began her career in 1997 as a freelance newspaper journalist in Indonesia, before joining CNN as a field producer, and later becoming a television correspondent. Extreme days have been many, but one of her first assignments, covering public protests in Indonesia sticks out because of the incredible violence. "Every day, tens of thousands of people gathered on the streets, demanding a change in government. Violent confrontation was inevitable. . . . It was the first time I heard gunfire, the first time I smelled tear gas, the first time I saw a baton being used to beat someone down. It was chaos. And it was terrifying. My colleague pulled me aside and gave some advice: 'First, stay alive. Then, tell the story.' We ended the day in front of the morgue. By this time, I was having second thoughts about my chosen profession. He stopped abruptly. 'Don't go in if you don't want to,' he said, opening the thick steel door and stepping inside. I stared after him for a few seconds. 'I thought you weren't coming in,' he said. I told him, 'I just wanted to know what's behind the door.' That's how I knew I was in the right job."

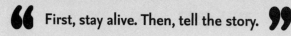
First, stay alive. Then, tell the story.

Prepare for Success

Get on track early with a bachelor's degree in journalism (broadcast or print) or mass communications. Some employers also look for majors in English, history, political science, economics, or international business. They demand practical, hands-on experience from school newspapers or broadcasting stations. Related summer jobs and internships are becoming the norm; do as many as you can. A job or internship with a well-known name in the business will build credibility, contacts, and experience. Most correspondents start out as general assignment reporters or copyeditors at small publications or broadcast stations. Large publications and stations prefer to hire reporters who have several years of experience.

Getting Your Foot in the Door

Bring word processing skills, computer graphics know-how, and desktop publishing skills to your first job. Continue to hone your research skills, analytical thinking skills, and your knowledge of politics, government, and current affairs. Most correspondents have worked their way up from newsroom reporter or TV news anchor positions through hard work, dedication, and powerful reporting skills. Others find advancement opportunities by moving to larger newspapers or stations. Proficiency in another language (or two) can boost your qualifications, as can a master's degree in journalism.

Biggest Challenges and Best Perks

Whether it's a forest fire or gunfire, news correspondents have to be ready to hop on a plane at a moment's notice. Their unpredictable, and sometimes life-threatening, life on the go is filled with an endless stream of unfamiliar people and places. You may not know where you're going, what you'll find there, what kind of news will transpire, or when you're coming back—this can take a toll on personal relationships. Feeling like you're constantly surrounded by disaster, trauma, and death can also be challenging.

That said, most correspondents live for unpredictable moments, and if asked they'd tell you that waiting for news to happen or showing up late to the scene is what is most frustrating. To thrive in this profession you have to truly love it and most do. Travel attracts many folks to this profession, as does the constant excitement and unpredictability. Correspondents are the first on the scene and get an up-close, insider's view of events that most people only see on television. With this comes a sense of pride and importance and, in rare cases, journalistic fame and fortune.

Professional Profile
Avg. salary: $31,320

Jargon
File The process of sending a report back from a location

Slug A key word that sums up the news story

Are you Interested In?
Current affairs, politics, travel, writing

Related College Majors
Journalism, communications, English

For More Information
National Association of Broadcasters:
www.nab.org

Radio/Television News Directors Association:
www.rtnda.org

Society of Professional Journalists:
www.spj.org

PILOT

A (Relatively) Typical Day in the Life

The job of an airplane pilot carries considerable prestige, responsibility, and risk. Airline pilots often find themselves in different time zones, climates, and cultures on an everyday basis. Pilots literally have the lives of their passengers in their hands. The physical and mental demands are rigorous. The ability to remain calm under pressure is crucial, as is perfect vision, hearing, and hand-eye coordination. Before every flight a pilot must check and file flight plans, ensure that there is enough fuel, secure the approval of the air traffic control personnel of the Federal Aviation Administration (FAA), and check weather and flight conditions. The airline pilot, or captain, is assisted by a crew consisting of a copilot or a flight engineer, and an appropriate number of flight attendants for the size of the aircraft. Another important "member" of the crew is the automatic pilot, an electronic device that is programmed to fly the plane. Even when the automatic pilot is on, it is the pilot's responsibility to remain alert to problems that may affect the flight. During the flight, the pilot maintains radio contact with ground control stations to report on altitude, speed, weather conditions, and a host of flight details.

With minimal retraining, the airline pilot can make the transition to other areas of aviation. Helicopter pilots work with television networks and radio stations to deliver traffic and accident reports. They also work for air taxi

An Extreme Day in the Life

Brannon Boone got his first pilot's license at age 17. After graduating from Louisiana Tech in 2001, he was hired as a pilot for Great Lakes Airlines and was promoted to captain in 2005. "My most memorable experience on the job would be the day I started IOE (Initial Operating Experience) for my first airline job as a first officer (copilot). IOE is the first time you get to 'fly the line' or carry passengers after weeks of grueling hours in a classroom and simulator. I was extremely excited. My first flight was a short hop from Cheyenne, Wyoming to Denver International Airport. I arrived at the airport early that morning, and did my job of preflighting the aircraft as well as receiving all the weather information and flight plan for the captain. Once we had the aircraft prepared for flight, we began accepting the passengers. As soon as the people were boarded, I just jumped right up in my seat and was ready to go! My captain turned to me and asked, 'Are you going to secure the door and give your passenger speech?' Considering that this 19-seat turboprop did not require a flight attendant, I had no idea I would also have to assume that role. I was so nervous as I stumbled through the speech that I once again forgot to close the main cabin door! At this point all the passengers looked really nervous and were completely silent. I told them not to worry—it's my first day, hoping to add some humor to the situation. I don't think they thought it was very funny. It was an exciting and [a] very memorable day that I will never forget." Brannon's advice for aspiring pilots is simple: "Go after your dream! Although the airline industry has had some rough days lately, there is promise of plenty of future hiring. There are also many other opportunities in aviation. Do your homework and select the path that is best for you, and I promise you will have numerous rewarding experiences."

Pilots literally have the lives of their passengers in their hands.

services, sightseeing operations, mail delivery, and rescue services. Agricultural pilots are involved in farm maintenance techniques such as crop dusting, fertilization, and insect and weed control. Pilot instructors teach company airline pilots regulations and procedures. Chief pilots supervise the training of new pilots and handle other administrative work; test pilots test new planes; and executive pilots work for large corporations that own or lease planes for company use.

PREPARE FOR SUCCESS

At least four years of college are preferred for individuals seeking entry to this profession. FAA-certified military and civilian flying schools provide adequate practical and classroom training, and some colleges and universities offer degree credit for pilot training. Applicants for the commercial airplane pilot's license must have 250 hours of flying time and successfully complete rigorous testing, including a physical examination, a written test given by the FAA, and a practical test. Before receiving an FAA license, pilots must be rated according to the kind of plane they can fly—single-engine, multiengine, or seaplane—and for the type—Boeing 707 or 747. Airline pilots must also have an airline transport pilot's license, for which a minimum of 1,500 hours of flight time, including night flying and instrument time, are required. Most airline pilots start out as flight instructors and move to "feeder" airlines before becoming major airline pilots. Many airline pilots begin their careers with military aviation training.

GETTING YOUR FOOT IN THE DOOR

In the long run, seniority counts in this profession, so young pilots are advised to buckle their seat belts, enjoy the ride, and keep racking up those hours. Prospective pilots must work long and hard at accumulating required flying time. They must be focused and determined to complete the various stages of what is a rigorous routine to an ultimately satisfying career. When applying to the airlines for pilot positions, apply to as many as possible. This will give you a chance to work on interview skills and learn more about the industry. Pilot recommendations are another good way to get noticed. If you know a pilot at an airline in which you are interested see if they will write a letter of recommendation for you.

BIGGEST CHALLENGES AND BEST PERKS

The biggest challenge of this profession is the training and time investment it takes to break in—once in, pilots tend to be very satisfied with their jobs and remain in them until forced to retire. The main professional concern of new pilots is amassing flying hours, including pilot-in-command, night flying, and instrument time, to make it to the next position. Such professional visibility and prestige comes with significantly more responsibility and a better pay scale.

RELIEF WORKER

A (Relatively) Typical Day in the Life

Reaching out to others across the globe in the wake of a natural disaster does not make for a traditional career path. Relief workers don't act alone, however. Most are employees of or volunteers at large organizations with global networks in place that kick into high gear whenever disaster strikes. These organizations gather and distribute food, water, clothing, supplies, and other necessities, along with the work crews needed to help survivors pull through the crisis and get back to living a life closer to normal.

As you can imagine, it's not an easy task. Relief workers bring experience and knowledge to areas that need them most, along with their supplies. They have a keen sense of when to lead and when to follow instructions and an ability to adapt to intensely challenging situations. Integrity, accountability, an adventurous spirit, and a readiness to live in poor conditions to provide a basic level of health, safety, and comfort to others is crucial.

Workers' jobs vary based on the location and their expertise. Jobs range from administering medical aid, providing emotional support, and caring for children, to on-site administration, needs assessment, and coordination with local authorities and other nongovernmental organizations (NGOs). Once basic needs have been met, relief workers sometimes stay on to tackle family reunification, long-term self-sufficiency, sustainability, disaster prevention and preparedness, and community rehabilitation. Each NGO operates under its own set of principles. Many rely on donations to continue their work.

An Extreme Day in the Life

After the Indian Ocean tsunami of December 2004, relief worker Andrea Woodhouse worked in Aceh, Indonesia, as an advisor and aide to the cabinet minister who coordinated the international emergency response. "It's hard to describe how devastated Aceh was: 168,000 people died; 500,000 people lost their homes; roads and bridges were destroyed; entire villages were wiped out. Many Acehnese people had lost their entire families. We lived and worked out of the governor's mansion, which was turned into the headquarters of the relief effort. I slept on the floor and bathed with dirty water that we had to disinfect daily. Our days began at 5:00 or 6:00 A.M. and went until 1:00 or 2:00 A.M. The minister led government departments racing against the clock to feed, clothe, and give shelter to tsunami survivors and coordinate with the military, United Nations, and the hundreds of relief organizations that flooded into town, all while dealing with journalists, press conferences, and delegations from donor countries. By far the most extreme part about Aceh, though, was seeing the strength and resilience of ordinary people. One evening, I was talking with Ben, an Acehnese man who worked as a guard and housecleaner. We had become friends, but he spoke little about his tsunami experience. That evening he got out his wallet and showed me a photo of his wife and his three children, all of whom died in the tsunami. He said, 'For a month afterward, I couldn't eat. I prayed all the time. But we have to accept what has happened and go on.' I learned a lot from people like Ben, and walked away from Aceh feeling humbled at how much human beings can overcome."

Relief workers often live under the same or similar conditions as those they are helping.

Prepare for Success

A desire to help and a willingness to give up a comfortable life at home would seem like all it would take to become a relief worker. That's the greatest misconception about this field. Since aid agencies work on a global scale, some have international workforces in which hopefuls compete for jobs against people from across the globe. Many employers insist on previous experience, but you can't get experience without a job, right? This dilemma is especially common in relief work. Count on starting from the very bottom as an intern or a volunteer. Programs such as the Peace Corps provide a nice starting point with good training, language classes, and a strong support system. Specialized skills and a college degree in areas like anthropology, agriculture, nutrition, political science, epidemiology, international law, human rights, social work, or the sciences are a good foundation.

Getting Your Foot in the Door

It's important to network and build contacts for this career. Get your name out there by going to conferences and forums, meeting as many higher-ups as you can, and building a good track record by working in meaningful jobs in international cross-cultural relief work. Get someone you know to give you a glowing reference. Learn as many new languages as you can and look for ways to take on more responsibility. If there is an organization, a locale, or a type of relief work you favor, start building a resume that is representative of it. Some relief workers get experience at home (a nurse, for example) and highlight that experience when looking for aid jobs. Engineers, agronomists, environmentalists, logisticians, linguists, and medical professionals are valued for their highly technical knowledge, as are IT specialists. There are places for writers and researchers too, in putting together grant proposals and reports. Not everyone can be out in the field.

Biggest Challenges and Best Perks

Relief workers often live under the same or similar conditions as those they are helping. Your health can easily be compromised when living in devastated areas. Beyond the physical discomfort, many relief workers live with the frustration that they aren't doing enough and question their impact on the big picture. Knowing that they can return to a safe, comfortable life back at home makes many feel guilty. In addition, family and friends may not understand their work or why they do it.

Relief work can be incredibly rewarding on a personal level. Some say they've "lived more life" abroad in six months than they have at home. You'll probably run through the entire range of human emotions on a daily basis. As an aid worker, your perspective and values will change. You will affect people's lives for the better and have the chance to witness the amazing perseverance of those faced with tragedy.

SHIP ENGINEER

A (Relatively) Typical Day in the Life

Ship engineers are responsible for holding vessels together at sea. They keep a close watch over engines, pumps, generators, boilers and ventilation, heating, cooling, and electrical systems below deck. Being conscientious and self-motivated helps in this field because you will not have constant prodding from a superior to get the job done. Frequently, you will stand watch alone and must be confident in your ability to monitor ship systems, changing weather conditions, and other dynamics that affect the safety of crew and passengers.

This is an ideal job for mechanically oriented people who are fascinated by the design, function, repair, and maintenance of machines and tools. You'll monitor various gauges and dials to control ship systems. You also determine what types of maintenance should take place and do it. When things go wrong, you'll get to the root of the operating error, determine a course of action and fix the problem yourself or supervise other repair people. Beyond technical skill, you'll need strong written and oral communication skills to aid coordinated action among groups of people.

You'll spend extended periods of time out at sea and some damp and cold conditions are to be expected. However, many of the discomforts of merchant mariner life have been alleviated in newer ships that have sophisticated controls over air-conditioning, heat, and soundproofing. Plus, amenities such as e-mail and more comfortable sleeping quarters make the time away from home more bearable.

An Extreme Day in the Life

Hugh Curran began his seafaring career at the ripe old age of 15 when he made a summer voyage to the Caribbean as the engine boy on a ship. Now in his sixties, Hugh has vivid memories of life at sea, particularly the time he spent as chief engineer of a large container ship that departed from New York and sailed east around the world in 88 days with stops in Rotterdam, Saudi Arabia, Singapore, Hong Kong, and other locales. He's also witnessed the dramatic ways technology has transformed the profession since the days when ships were so long they had to use big box girders to limit the longitudinal stresses. Today, one large container ship with a 19-member crew does the work that it took 15 ships with 55-member crews to do back in the day, he says. However, the tremendous crew reduction means that there are fewer people working to address problems when they arise. "Difficulty occurs when the ships maneuver in close port areas or restricted channels. Most ships require two senior engineers to be in the machinery room at all times during these maneuverings because sometimes things happen that you don't want to happen—difficulties with machinery that controls the main engine from the bridge. Things like that are always stressful. The big thing that everybody dreads is fire at sea in these massive ships with minimal crews. A fire has to be contained and localized very quickly because once it gets out of hand there aren't enough people to fight it. You need to be sure that areas vulnerable to fire are well maintained. Even worse than that would be a fire in very heavy inclement weather, which can lead to a loss of control and cause problems with the steering."

You're in charge of your day with very few people to watch over you.

Prepare for Success

Ship engineering positions are regulated by the U.S. Coast Guard, which is part of the U.S. Department of Homeland Security, so aspiring engineers must obtain an engineering officers license. Graduating from the U.S. Merchant Marine Academy or one of six state maritime academies is a great first step toward the license. Getting into the academies is competitive so students should take the most rigorous courses available in high school and do well in them so they stand out in the applicant pool. If you decide later in life to enter this field, you can also obtain an engineering license without graduating from a maritime academy by gaining five to eight years of ship experience and meeting other regulatory requirements. Frankly, it is very difficult to pass the written test without formal preparation. Additionally, a physical examination, drug screening, and National Driver Register Check are required for licensure.

Getting Your Foot in the Door

Earning an engineering license does not guarantee you a job in this selective field, but the time you spend in a maritime academy or working aboard a ship will bring you in contact with people who can alert you to new job opportunities and recommend you for positions. Like any other job, you should make every effort to meet people who currently or previously worked in the area in which you are interested. Present yourself professionally and ask them for tips on getting a foot in the door. The maritime academies also offer helpful job placement support.

Biggest Challenges and Best Perks

Working with machinery on moving vessels exposes ship engineers to cuts, blows, exhaust fumes, abrasions, and other work-related injuries. Ship engineers have fallen from ladders in the engine room, been struck by unsecured heavy objects, been burned by hot pipes, and been poisoned by fuel vapors. They can also experience anxiety related to being confined aboard a ship for extended periods of time and the rigid discipline and routine of ship life. Plus, their absences from home can create tension in personal relationships.

For the right person, this can be a very fulfilling lifestyle. Many thrive on the autonomy of ship engineering. You're in charge of your day with very few people to watch over you. You'll also get to see the world and experience camaraderie on the ship. The job pays well, offers ample vacation time, and has a fair degree of predictability, which lowers job-related stress.

Professional Profile
Avg. salary: $57,290

Jargon
Coasters Shallow-hulled ships used for trade between locations on the same island or continent

Freighter Any sort of ship that carries goods and materials from one port to another

Tanker A vehicle carrying large amounts of liquid fuel

Are you Interested In?
Ships, sailing, travel, machinery, tools

Related College Majors
Naval architecture and marine engineering, mechanical engineering, civil engineering, electrical engineering

For More Information
International Ship Electrical and Engineering Service Association:
www.isesassociation.com/

U.S. Navy:
www.navy.com

U.S. Coast Guard:
www.uscg.mil/uscg.shtm

SOMMELIER

A (Relatively) Typical Day in the Life

When customers in an upscale restaurant want to order a bottle of wine with dinner, they may feel overwhelmed or unfamiliar with the selections offered on the wine list. When this is the case, they may ask the sommelier for advice. Sommelier is the French term for cellar master or wine steward. Sommeliers are individuals with a love of wine and are eager to share some of their knowledge with customers. They can describe the regions, grapes, vineyards, and vintages of an assortment of wines. The best sommeliers talk to, not at, their customers and enjoy when customers tell them about a bottle they have recently tasted. Sommeliers either help to create the wine list or compile it on their own; they also recommend wines that suit customers' tastes and price ranges. Even individuals who are knowledgeable about wine may benefit from a sommelier's advice; after all, many sommeliers travel yearly to different regions to choose wines for their restaurants, and they have tasted all the items on the wine list, and know which wines go best with which entrees.

Many patrons are easily intimidated by wines and do not understand the terminology used to describe them. The sommelier must be ready to coax from them a description of their preferences and be understanding of their budgetary limits. When they select a wine, sommeliers bring it to the table with the appropriate glasses and pour it for the customer to taste. Sommeliers should encourage patrons to smell the wine first and should describe its

An Extreme Day in the Life

Wining during dining is only one of the responsibilities of a sommelier, and it's far more likely that customers are going to provide more daily excitement than the bottles themselves. Former sommelier Christopher Miller, now a wine education consultant, remembers some of his more colorful nights on the job: "During the 'big spending' days of the late 1990s, I was a sommelier at the 21 Club in Manhattan. I had many memorable experiences during my tenure there, including high-fives from Matt Dillon for choosing such a fine wine for him, or being told by Jon Bon Jovi that, of course, I'm an excellent sommelier: 'Look the size of your nose!' (I never was a fan of his music)."

He continues, "My favorite story was when I got 'trapped' pouring wine at a party that included Bill Cosby and Allan King. As I poured Mr. Cosby's table, he jumped up and began a speech that was basically a comedy routine; I had to freeze and blend into the scenery. Mr. Cosby continued along for a bit, and was finally interrupted by Allan King. During Mr. King's dialogue, Cosby stole his lunch and played other adolescent tricks on him; very fine entertainment. Being a sommelier has allowed me to enjoy world-class and rare wines while observing such memorable moments, including being stopped by the Israeli Secret Service for pulling a knife as I walked into the dining room to open and pour the prime minister's wine. The Secret Service discovered that the knife was attached to a corkscrew and allowed me to continue doing my job. The job isn't conducive to family life, but it is a great adventure and the only way to taste some of the greatest wines of the world without being a 'trust-fund' kid. And yes, I served wine to them too!"

Sommeliers must bring the wine to life for patrons before it even touches their palates.

components. In a sense, sommeliers must bring the wine to life for patrons before it even touches their palates.

PREPARE FOR SUCCESS

While no formal training is required to become a sommelier, professionals in the field utilize a host of skills. A good sense of taste and smell, as well as a detailed memory, complement the business, management, and communication skills required of a good sommelier. A sommelier must also know the finer points of wine service (which include proper table etiquette, decanting, and glassware positioning) and the proper protocol for serving brandies, liqueurs, and cigars. Many aspiring sommeliers gain this knowledge as servers or bartenders at fine restaurants. In these positions, they typically read books about wine and attend tastings in their free time until they feel confident enough to cover for the restaurant's sommelier one or two nights a week. Most sommeliers begin by working under another sommelier's guidance; apprenticeship under a master is the best way to learn about the wines worth stocking. Individuals who seek more formal training attend sommelier education programs, generally offered at colleges and culinary schools in metropolitan areas.

GETTING YOUR FOOT IN THE DOOR

It doesn't matter how individuals learn the ropes; certification by The Court of Master Sommeliers—the only internationally recognized organization for certifying restaurant wine professionals—helps immensely when you are looking for a job. They offer annual wine education programs and testing in the United States. Individuals who are knowledgeable about wine may consider hosting tasting dinners or teaching wine-tasting classes to build their repertoire of different wines, and those who are more experienced may write about their experiences for industry publications, such as *Food & Wine* magazine, to gain notoriety.

BIGGEST CHALLENGES AND BEST PERKS

A sommelier's life is pretty blessed; extensive and frequent travel is part of a sommelier's career, and not many people complain about a long day tasting fine wines. People enter this profession because they have a "taste" for it, and nearly all beginners report great satisfaction with their career choice. This is not to say that the job is easy; the task of creating the wine list for a restaurant requires diligence and creativity and entails finding the best suppliers of the choice inexpensive wines and the higher-priced vintages. Many years of experience are needed for a sommelier to earn the necessary reputation to advance in the field, and the education can predictably be quite pricey. It's nice work if you can get it, but it's not to be undertaken lightly.

PROFESSIONAL PROFILE
Avg. starting salary: $29,900
Avg. salary after 5 years: $33,900
Avg. salary 10 to 15 years: $34,500

JARGON
Crush The time of year when the grapes are picked and processed

Fat Refers to a wine of higher than average alcohol content

ARE YOU INTERESTED IN?
Wine, travel, cooking

RELATED COLLEGE MAJORS
Hospitality and tourism, business management, culinary arts

FOR MORE INFORMATION
The Court of Master Sommeliers:
www.mastersommeliers.org

Food & Wine **magazine:**
www.foodandwine.com

Sommelier Society of America:
www.sommeliersocietyofamerica.org

SPORTS REFEREE

A (Relatively) Typical Day in the Life

From the little league to the pros, referees may be the most loathed figures in sports. Players and coaches aren't shy about showing their displeasure with bad calls, and fans have been known to spew choice words across the field or court to get referees' attention. However, game after game, week after week, refs trudge across the country to officiate games. They see themselves as upholding the integrity of the game, and they may be on to something. They are the ones who enforce the rules, blow their whistles for fouls, and throw yellow flags for violations. Without their moderation, games could quickly get out of hand, especially with competitors fiercely vying to win.

Officials must stay on their toes, make snap decisions, resolve conflicts, and objectively call the game, which is, of course, much easier said than done. Many college- and professional-level referees worked their way up from high school officiating positions. Some even began as volunteer refs for youth recreational leagues and moved up over time. Along the way they learned to control the chaos of sporting events, urge good sportsmanship, and keep the booing from getting them down.

The confidence to work in sometimes hostile conditions comes from careful preparation, a solid grasp of the rules, and a reverence for the game. Great refs spend hours studying the game. They meet with other officials to discuss rules, fundamentals, and philosophies. They attend training sessions and watch game tapes to evaluate their officiating and prepare for upcoming contests.

An Extreme Day in the Life

A college basketball referee who asked to remain anonymous enjoys playing an integral role in the sport he loves. He says the profession allows you to meet great people and forge unbelievable friendships. Plus, you're really well taken care of from the moment you arrive at the game in everything from security to administration. "A lot of us have played the game and I just like being a part of the atmosphere. The game can't go on without us. All of our preparation and study of film comes into play. Our veteran guys have developed a rapport with coaches and know how to manage the game. We watch a lot of tape and break down film. Regardless of where you're officiating, the key is seeing plays, managing games, controlling the benches, and being approachable by the coaches. We can't be argumentative with coaches. We all know that the coaches aren't going to agree with everything you call. You have a rapport and listen. You cannot be influenced by what the coach says, [or] whether the people are going to boo you. You have to make sure your integrity is intact and you can't show any favoritism for one team or another."

He says the greatest difficulties in this job take place off the court. "The biggest challenge is getting from one location to the next with all of the things going on with the airlines. Some places you can drive to, but usually you have to fly. If you're working two to three games per week you have to make sure you get proper rest from game to game. If you miss a flight, that's when the pressure comes in of trying to figure out a secondary plan."

The profession allows you to meet great people and forge unbelievable friendships.

Prepare for Success

Aspiring officials must be students of the game and commit significant time and energy to learning the sport's intricacies. Websites, reference books, and game tapes can help would-be referees sharpen their rules knowledge and learn more about what it takes to succeed in the field. Training clinics, association meetings, and networking with other referees can also boost the likelihood of success.

Beyond the mechanics of the game, officials need to be physically fit to keep up with the players in sports such as basketball, baseball, soccer, and football where a lot of ground is covered. Then there's the expressive side of the business. Referees also have to remain cool in very stressful, emotionally charged settings—coaches poking their fingers in refs' faces, fans hollering "baaaad caaall," and worse.

Getting Your Foot in the Door

Contrary to popular belief, refs don't just show up in stripes with a whistle hanging around their necks. In many cases, they've survived competitive auditions at referee camps that coincide with sports camps. They pay a fee of anywhere from $25 to $500 plus travel and lodging expenses to officiate games at the camps where they are evaluated by veteran officials. The evaluators carefully assess the aspiring officials' hand signals, physical fitness, knowledge of the rules, and composure. Officials also must take written examinations before stepping onto the floor.

Biggest Challenges and Best Perks

The hectic pace and logistical challenges of working multiple games per week can be taxing. Rowdy fans and disgruntled players and coaches are another source of job stress. No one cheers for the officials and great calls are often greeted with silence. On the upside, refereeing sports can be very lucrative. Some college officials earn $2,000 per game before taxes and expenses. Professional refs can earn much more depending on the sport. However, most referees say they are in the field for the love of the game. Many are former athletes who sought a way to stay close to the sport. The view of a sport's contest doesn't get much better than the referee's. The friendships that referees make and the networking they do over the course of the season is another perk.

PROFESSIONAL PROFILE
Avg. salary: $40,000

Compensation varies widely by sport and level with some youth games paying less than $10 a pop and some college games paying $2,000 for two hours of work.

JARGON
Line drive In baseball, a hit that is level

Steal the round In boxing, a flurry of activity at the end of a round to make up for a lackluster previous round

Trifecta In basketball, a three-point basket

ARE YOU INTERESTED IN?
Sports

RELATED COLLEGE MAJORS
Sports management, physical education

FOR MORE INFORMATION
National Association of Sports Officials:
www.naso.org

National Intramural-Recreational Sports Association:
www.nirsa.org

Referee, The Magazine for Sports Officials:
www.referee.com

SPORTS WRITER

A (Relatively) Typical Day in the Life

Games, meets, and matches aren't all hot dogs and foul balls for sports writers. Although most athletic events take place in the afternoons or evenings, there's a lot of prep work involved before the clock starts. After deciding what event to cover in person, you'll have to travel to the location. That can mean heading to the local high school to cover Friday night football or halfway across the world to cover the Olympics. After flashing your press pass, you'll get the kind of access to the game and players that make most fans green-eyed. Pre-game prep can include anything from locker room interviews, to catching the mood of the players before they hit the field, to coordinating with your photographer to snag a prime location for the best action shots, to reviewing team and player stats that could be pertinent to your write-up. Once the buzzer sounds, you have to be all eyes and ears to catch the play-by-play—and if you're lucky, a colorful interaction between coach and referee or a tense moment between players.

Post-game, it's crunch time. Deadlines loom, and in addition to preparing the article on the event you just covered in person, most likely you're responsible for write-ups on stats and games you weren't able to attend. You will have to set foot in the office to file your story and to follow up on scores that are not yet available. This might include calling coaches to get the scoop on how their team ended the day, or following up with colleagues to get their coverage. After submitting your information to the editors, it's time to wait for them to review and get back to you with any questions, suggestions, or corrections they have. Nights can be long and there's no heading home until your article has been approved and submitted to layout.

An Extreme Day in the Life

Jen Gaynor spent eight years covering high school and college sports for the *Times of Trenton* in New Jersey and Dorf Feature Services. "I started writing my senior year of high school. By the fall of my freshman year in college, I was writing up to four stories a week." A lot more goes into preparing these articles than meeting word counts and deadlines—including a lot of mileage. "I've seen about 90 percent of New Jersey from the driver's side of my car." Jen didn't immediately jump into the position. It took "just [more than] a year to get into sports; four months later, I wrote my first story: a feature on a track-and-field official at the Atlanta Olympics." Although every day on the job proved valuable, the lessons that really stand out to Jen were more intangible. "You will learn a great deal just by listening. Don't ever take criticism about your work to heart." One day in particular proved to Jen how all the hard work and effort could pay off. "I am a huge soccer fan and I followed the U.S. Women's National Soccer Team while I was in high school and college. The team was playing in Hershey in the summer of 1999 and I badly wanted to cover it." She not only covered the game, but also reached an important milestone in her career. "When I had first started at the paper as a high-schooler, I went to a U.S. game and a reporter I really looked up to was covering it. Years later, I felt like I had come full circle and had finally come into my own." Is it worth the pressure and late nights writing and revising? Jen says the reward was "in the form of thank-yous from parents and players."

The clock can be a sports writer's biggest enemy—it's not uncommon for the deadline to be 11:00 P.M. and the game to end at 10:30 P.M.

Prepare for Success

Generally all publications require undergraduate degrees in journalism, although it is possible to get in on experience alone. In addition to studying print media, it helps to actually put your skills to work on the school newspaper or complete a summer internship while still in school. Although a degree gives you the basics, most of the skills needed to go really far in this career are gained on the job, so even a part-time position will get you the experience you need when you're just starting out. Obviously, it's necessary to have more than a passing interest in sports—you must have a vast amount of knowledge about player stats, rules and regulations, and history. A background in creative writing can be extremely helpful, since sports writers are famously colorful with their words and need to be able to make the reader visualize each play.

Getting Your Foot in the Door

It helps to start local and work your way up. Summer internships or entry-level positions with your hometown newspaper build up your resume and introduce you to people who can open doors for you down the road. Most local publications are eager to find someone to cover the Friday night high school football game. These positions are generally in high demand, and acceptance relies heavily on your portfolio, so the more bylines you have the better. Look for websites that accept original contributions from freelancers so you can get some work under your belt.

Biggest Challenges and Best Perks

It can be very difficult to get your foot in the door to become a sports writer. It can take years of part-time or freelance work before you snag a full-time exclusive position. Even if you are only working locally, there is a lot of travel involved. Once you move up the ladder, you might end up with the same schedule as a professional athlete—a different city every couple of days. Don't expect many perks such as free tickets and autographed gear—journalistic ethics are strongly enforced in this field. The clock can be a sports writer's biggest enemy—it's not uncommon for the deadline to be 11:00 P.M. and the game to end at 10:30 P.M.

Professional Profile
Avg. entry level salary: $29,051

Avg. salary after 5 years: $34,602

Avg. salary 10 to 15 years: $47,043

Jargon
Caroms Rebounds

Curtain raiser A story written about an event before the event occurs

Dinger Home run

Are you Interested In?
Creative writing, sports

Related College Majors
Journalism, communications, English

For More Information
American Press Institute:
www.americanpressinstitute.org

ESPN:
www.espn.com

Society of Professional Journalists:
www.spj.org

TALENT SCOUT

A (Relatively) Typical Day in the Life

You don't need to be able to carry a tune or strut down a runway to recognize talent when you see it. Some people never would have made it into the public eye if a scout hadn't spotted them. Depending on what form of talent you're looking for (models, actors, musicians), you have to spend a lot of time in the same places they do—clubs and bars, community theaters, open mic nights, and so on. Of course, some people don't even know they're destined for fame and fortune until a scout approaches them. Charlize Theron was discovered by a scout after arguing with a teller in Los Angeles. Aside from roaming hotspots searching for the next big thing, scouts also spend time arranging screen tests or auditions for their clients, contacting agents to let them know of new talent, and maintaining files on all clients detailing their individual abilities/attributes and any past experience. Most scouts work for production companies or record labels and spend a lot of time meeting with creative directors and executives to find out exactly what look or sound they want to develop. There's no room for waking up on the wrong side of the bed in this industry—you have to be on from the moment you start your day. Depending on the scope and nature of the search, your day could stretch well into the night as you wait for that local band to finally take the stage or fly across the country to catch a stand-up routine. Sometimes, scouts make the talent come to them by staging open calls. There's no shortage of people waiting to be discovered, so the scout's job is never done.

An Extreme Day in the Life

Duane Gazi is the director of scouting and development at Trump Model Management and has been in the model scouting business for 16 years. He's never had any doubts about his calling: "When I was 11 I told my mother I wanted to work at Ford Models. It became my sole determination to make it happen." Breaking into the industry wasn't easy. "I would call the agencies and pretend I was casting a show and they would send me the girls' model books. This is how I memorized all of the models' names." For Duane, "it only took one person" to believe in him and "give [him] a chance." After that, everything was a whirlwind. He says one of the most exciting aspects of the job is the opportunity travel to around the world. "I've been to 24 countries in Europe and Asia, 16 cities in Canada, every state in the U.S. except Alaska and Hawaii, and several countries in South America. Work-wise, Moscow is very productive. The girls there are all tall, gorgeous, and thin." When it comes to just kicking back and relaxing, Holland is the place to be. "It's the one place where you immediately feel welcome. There's a very progressive, liberal vibe." Besides being an international jet-setter, a talent scout comes into contact with some pretty amazing people. "I've met a lot of people I admire and I'm able to meet them in normal circumstances. I met Madonna face to face and talked to Meryl Streep. This is one of the best perks of the job." For Duane, the best advice he can offer an aspiring scout is: "Know what you want to do and why you want to do it. You can bluff your way in, but this business is about substance, and you need to know what you're talking about. [Above all] trust your instinct. If you wait too long, someone else will have already said yes."

There's no room for waking up on the wrong side of the bed in this industry—you have to be on from the moment you start your day.

Prepare for Success

There's no specific degree out there that teaches you how to spot talent, but it doesn't hurt to have some business acumen under your belt to help you navigate the world of contracts and commissions. Majors such as business studies or marketing can prove helpful. Skills in negotiation and schmoozing are key. Most scouts learn their trade on the job and start out as assistants or mail clerks, so any summer job or internship you can get at an agency will help you get the grunt work out of the way early. Renew your subscriptions to all the entertainment and gossip rags and remember to pay your cable bill—to find what's up and coming you have to know what's on its way out. Since you're going to have to work your way up from assistant or junior scout, it's best to have good typing, filing, and phone skills that make you stand out above the rest.

Getting Your Foot in the Door

It's difficult to get into the business without knowing someone—even if it's just the janitor who can slip your resume under an agent's door. As with most jobs in the entertainment industry, it's all about networking. You generally need the recommendation of someone in the know, so anyone who knows anyone associated with the agency you're trying to break into should become your new best friend. Don't be reluctant to start at the bottom. If you're lucky enough to skip the stereotypical mailroom initiation, you're still going to be low on the totem pole. Check with temp agencies that specialize in staffing companies in the industry and make an excellent impression on anyone who bothers to make eye contact with you.

Biggest Challenges and Best Perks

This is no nine to five job. In fact, depending on how far up the ladder you go, it might be best to keep a change of clothes handy for nights spent on your office couch. Even if you do manage to leave the office, or even take a day off, don't count on ever being off the job. Your clients have the same drive you do and won't take getting your voice mail very lightly. On the contrary, the ultimate reward is seeing your discovery win an Academy Award, even if they forget to mention you in their acceptance speeches. There's no room for waking up on the wrong side of the bed in this industry—you have to be on from the moment you start your day.

Professional Profile
Avg. salary: $45,000

Varies depending on commission structure

Jargon
Comp card An 8 by 10 photo sheet containing images of talent in various poses. These are used to obtain modeling, television, and acting gigs.

Are you Interested In?
Fashion, entertainment, music

Related College Majors
Marketing, public relations, business management

For More Information
Association of Talent Agents:
www.agentassociation.com

Casting America:
www.casting-america.com

Talent Managers Association, Inc:
www.talentmanagers.org

TRANSLATOR/INTERPRETER

A (Relatively) Typical Day in the Life

Translators take a document written in one language and write it in another language; they work on legal documents, business-related documents, journalistic work, or literary texts and are usually paid by the word. Interpreters do the same thing except they listen and translate messages as others speak them; they are normally paid either by the hour or receive salaries as full-time staff in settings such as the United Nations, international businesses, or perhaps within the legal system as court interpreters. Translating and interpreting require extreme professionalism, dedication, knowledge, and attention to detail. Interpreters must be flexible, as they may be called to work at any hour of the day or night, and they must be willing to withstand the significant pressure of attending diplomatic or business meetings. Translators, however, usually have time to refer to dictionaries and other reference tools and to polish the final product. In recent years, stricter deadlines have made translating a high-pressure job. A variety of working environments exists for translators and interpreters; many of them find work in academic fields, either studying or interpreting foreign texts. Although literary translation has the most room for creative expression, literary translators must be just as careful as technical translators.

Prepare for Success

A broad general education and professional background may be extremely useful; it's always best when translators and interpreters possess as much knowledge in as many areas as possible. Technical translators must naturally possess excellent technical writing skills, but special certification is not required. Federal court translators

An Extreme Day in the Life

Translating is a profession that brings new challenges and exposes people to diverse environments on a daily basis. The professional with whom we spoke has practiced both domestically and abroad, putting her linguistic skills to the test, often in tense situations. She says, "Once I interpreted a conference between the principal and a mother whose family had just moved to the United States. She was very frustrated because the school wanted her to place her daughter at a more age-appropriate level so that she could catch up and learn English, while the mother said that she had already taken the equivalent of this grade in her home country. The student was two grades ahead of other students her age and the school felt that it would be a disservice to her if she remained in the present grade because she was not doing well. The conference was stressful because both parties were frustrated and the mother was emotional, but in the end the mother agreed to think it over." The stress and excitement that this career often generates is not limited to parent-teacher conferences. "The most extreme moment was probably being an interpreter when my friends and I went to a caracol, or a center of government for the Zapatistas in Chiapas, Mexico. First, I had to convince the guard at the gate why he should let us in and then we sat at the junta (or head of government) in order to get a pass to walk around the area and then we talked with a junta leader for two hours while he told us the history of the Zapatista movement." Intense.

This is a position for individuals who have a love for language.

must be completely fluent, even in the slang of their second language, and must pass the federal certification examination if they work in Haitian Creole, Navajo, or Spanish. Potential translators must not overlook the importance of cultural studies, as it is invaluable to understanding the nuances of any work that needs translating. Therefore, courses in history, anthropology, and politics are as necessary as courses in grammar and conversation. Time spent studying abroad while in college is also an essential part of an applicant's resume.

GETTING YOUR FOOT IN THE DOOR

The process of becoming a translator for the United Nations or other government agency is very structured and predictable. Individuals seeking the greatest opportunities for employment should be fluent in English and in three of the official languages of the United Nations: French, Spanish, Arabic, Russian, or Chinese. There are numerous job opportunities for individuals who are fluent in other languages. Applicants may have a language degree, preferably a bachelor's or master's degree, but an academic degree does not make translators or interpreters. Applicants need to live abroad so they can immerse themselves in the language and need specialized training. Employers prefer candidates who have exceptional fluency in at least two foreign languages. Before interviewing for a position, candidates are normally required to undergo a series of tests to ensure language proficiency. The interview culminates in an inquiry into the applicant's knowledge of the applicable region's culture and background. Computer skills, including familiarity with computer-assisted translation (CAT) software, are essential for translators.

BIGGEST CHALLENGES AND BEST PERKS

Although the future of translation shows immense growth, the field has become extremely volatile. Pressure from foreign translators and interpreters and the general economic downturn have made translation a somewhat uncertain career. Interpreters in courts especially are suffering from statewide budgetary restrictions that have pulled funding for their services. However, translators who weather the storm can look forward to higher salaries and satisfaction. This is a position for individuals who have a love for language. Continual recognition and perpetual advancement are not likely to occur in this field. Interpreters deciding to remain in the field do so because of liberal benefits, increasing flexibility, and security. For some translators, such as individuals who are employed by the United Nations, there is a slow but positive advancement in salary, benefits, and title—a system that rewards continued employment.

PROFESSIONAL PROFILE
Avg. starting salary: $32,600
Avg. salary after 5 years: $41,600
Avg. salary 10 to 15 years: $64,234

JARGON
Relay Means indirect interpretation; rather than translate directly from the source language to the target language, an interpreter may work from a colleague's translation

Pivot In relay interpreting the pivot interpreter is the interpreter who works directly from the source language and whose translation will serve as the basis for other interpreters who work in other languages

ARE YOU INTERESTED IN?
Foreign languages, travel, grammar

RELATED COLLEGE MAJORS
Foreign languages, area studies, romance languages and literatures, linguistics

FOR MORE INFORMATION
U.S. Department of State:
www.state.gov/employment

American Translators Association:
www.atanet.org

National Association of Judiciary Interpreters and Translators:
www.najit.org

TRAVEL WRITER

A (Relatively) Typical Day in the Life

Do you like the idea of traveling to exotic locations, exploring new cultures, wearing out your sneakers as only a hard-core tourist can, and then writing about all of it? If so, it's possible that you're cut out to be a travel writer. This is a profession made specifically for someone with a sharp pencil, an adventurous spirit, and a willingness to do a whole lot of work for—at times—not too much dough.

Travel writers come in all shapes and sizes, covering territories both near and far, specializing in topics as diverse as wine and government, and bringing in earnings that range from mere vittles to a respectable salary to—for the lucky few—a very generous contract with lots of royalties. Some travel writers work for newspapers, others for guidebooks, and still others freelance, which means there's no telling what sort of publications they'll be writing for (a guidebook one month and a travel agency website the next). Then, of course, there's Paul Theroux, Bill Bryson, and Jamaica Kincaid—the literary luminaries of the genre. Whatever the venue, this is a brand of writing that requires very keen eyes and ears for understanding the intricacies of culture. Travel writers are adept at picking up on local details—a unique aspect of the local patois, a distinctive herb in the meals, an unusual alliance of religion and economy, and so on.

Because there's no telling what experiences are going to turn up the kind of details for which you're looking, travel writers need to be prepared for long days of exploring, researching, and simply getting from place to place. Other skills needed include the ability to interact with people, conduct interviews, live on the cheap, read a map, and keep a cool head in uncomfortable situations. Strong knowledge of a foreign language is a big plus as well. Don't forget the value of specialization. The industry veteran we interviewed says, "[Travel writers] must know about what they write, be it history, a regional destination, cruises, cuisine, wine and spirits, adventure travel, motorcycling, or

An Extreme Day in the Life

Tom Griffith, known to his readers as T. D. Griffith, is a seasoned travel writer who has authored articles for dozens of magazines and newspapers, as well as guidebooks for industry heavyweights such as Fodor's. Though he specializes in the Dakotas, Montana, and Wyoming, his work has taken him all over the United States and to 40 countries worldwide. During his travels he has "had experiences and met people that still have [him] shaking [his] head." There was the time he went "barreling through waves on a catamaran off the coast of Barbados." Then "walking five miles down the valley below Lauterbrunnen, Switzerland, where more than 70 waterfalls cascade from the glaciers above." Oh, and then "riding every roller-coaster in Las Vegas in one afternoon, including all 4 rides atop the Stratosphere in 45 minutes." Let's not forget "[riding a] helicopter up Mount Haleakala in Maui and descending into the crater of the largest dormant volcano in the world. Then riding Harleys on the Road to Hana with 617 curves, spectacular cliffs, and 54 one-lane bridges." It's not all adventure, though. He also mentions that a looming deadline can lead to an extreme day or two. "Omnipresent deadlines are a fact of life in this world," he says.

This is a profession made specifically for someone with a sharp pencil and an adventurous spirit.

several dozen other niches—all of which have publications devoted to them today."

Prepare for Success

Practice makes perfect—or at least professional. Writers of any genre figure this out early on and enroll in as many writing-intensive courses as their schedules can handle. English, journalism, history, political science, and foreign language courses can help a travel writer build the right skills.

If you want to know what great travel writing looks like, you should pick up a copy of *The Best American Travel Writing*. Grab a few travel guides while you're at it. If in a perfect world you'd be exploring and writing about the remote villages of Guatemala, then pick up the Fodor's guide to Central America and see how other writers have managed to do just that. Don't be shy about giving it a shot yourself. Write for your school newspaper, local rags, websites, and blogs—take advantage of any opportunity to build your portfolio.

Getting Your Foot in the Door

Young travel writers should spend time cultivating relationships with publishers and editors. Even if there's nothing available when you first query an editor, a good first impression can lead to an assignment a few months down the road—or at least a friendly referral to another editor. Get in touch with other writers, too. Like you, they have their ear to the ground and may know of a gig that's perfect for you. There are a variety of regional and national professional associations out there that might be worth joining too. These associations can help you build your network and expand your opportunities.

Biggest Challenges and Best Perks

You don't have to dig too hard to find stories about the tribulations and, sometimes, outright dangers endured by writers traveling in remote corners of the earth. Then there's the meager pay earned by many of the young writers who produce those handy guidebooks that tourists love. There are language barriers, countries with limited or no cell phone service, and the loneliness of extended solo travel. For this reason, travel writers must, by design, have thick skins and an itch for adventure.

You also have plenty of perks coming your way—especially if you land an assignment in a location you've been dying to visit. Each day will offer you the chance to see new things, talk to new people, and dig a little deeper into another culture. In other words, you'll get paid to see the world and write about it.

PROFESSIONAL PROFILE
Avg. salary: Varies

JARGON

Kill fee The amount of money publications pay to writers when articles they were assigned to write are canceled

Litotes The use of understatement for the purpose of emphasis

ARE YOU INTERESTED IN?
Writing, travel

RELATED COLLEGE MAJORS
English, journalism, history

FOR MORE INFORMATION
Literary Traveler:
www.literarytraveler.com
Society of American Travel Writers:
www.satw.org
Travelwriters.com:
http://main.travelwriters.com

ROLL UP YOUR SLEEVES

ACTIVIST COORDINATOR

A (Relatively) Typical Day In the Life

"Some look at things as they are and ask why? I dream of things as they never were and ask why not?" The words of the British playwright George Bernard Shaw strike at the heart of the basic motivation behind activism. No one ever became an activist with dreams of maintaining the status quo. That's what politicians are for. The role of the activist is to organize, assemble, gain influence, and eventually persuade those in power to alter the state in which we live. It's a tall order, but one that is within the grasp of those willing to make the sacrifices necessary to have their voices heard. The first steps—organization and assembly—fall at the feet of the activist coordinator.

The first thing you should do is dispel any notion you may have that activist/volunteer work is glamorous. As a coordinator, you are responsible for doing the grunt work associated with keeping the organization, well, organized. The type of work that you'll be doing will differ based on the nature and size of the organization. Larger non-profits will employ a number of volunteers (or paid employees) whose job it will be to help you with your daily tasks. If you're lucky enough to have a couple of these workers on hand, you're going to get a little help with the most menial of your tasks: licking and stamping the envelopes, folding flyers, doing the e-mail campaigns, and cold-calling donors. If yours is a more grassroots outfit, all of this work, and whatever other planning may be required for upcoming events, demonstrations, and fund-raisers are likely to fall squarely on your shoulders, and you're likely to be paid less, not more, for your trouble.

An Extreme Day in the Life

Kymberly Perfetto is a volunteer coordinator for TIME'S UP!, a New York City–based nonprofit devoted to using "educational outreach and direct action to promote a more sustainable, less toxic city." Kym describes TIME'S UP! as "a very grassroots organization. The organization works more as a collective so it's really up to the group to have initiative to get things done." One of their more high-profile projects involves helping to organize New York City's version of a truly global phenomenon: Critical Mass. An event that began in San Francisco, Critical Mass is a large-scale demonstration in which hundreds—sometimes thousands—of cyclists come together for a ride through city streets. It is at once a protest in favor of bicyclists' equal rights on city streets, and against the car-induced air and noise pollution with which all New Yorkers are familiar. While Critical Mass is by far the most visible of the events Kym helps to organize, she recalls an event of slightly smaller, but no less meaningful proportions that occurred following the death of a 14-year-old boy: "He was struck and killed by an SUV in Far Rockaway. TIMES UP! organized a memorial ride for him, and put up a 'ghost bike' at the place where he was killed. Upon arriving in Far Rockaway, his family was shocked and excited to learn that 100 or so cyclists they had never met had ridden all the way out there for their son's memorial. His mother cooked up all this food for everyone and we all had a picnic on the beach. It was a truly amazing event."

A small group of thoughtful people could change the world. Indeed, it's the only thing that ever has.

Prepare for Success

Before setting a goal to make the world a better place, you have to first understand what needs fixing. At the risk of stating the obvious, it would help if you had an interest in and an understanding of current events. Regardless of the scale of your ambitions, your first concern should be local, starting with you. Educating yourself is priority number one. While it's not absolutely necessary for you to go after a degree, don't be surprised if your liberal arts education (with a concentration in your field of interest) proves to be an undeniable asset in finding a paid position inside your nonprofit of choice. After all, these organizations don't have money to burn, and if they have to give it away in the form of salary, they're more likely to give it to somebody they feel has a strong understanding of the cause they're trying to further.

Getting Your Foot in the Door

Oftentimes, you'll find that the door is not open, but rather entirely off its hinges. Nonprofits—especially those that are either charitable in nature or devoted to a specific cause—are almost always looking for volunteers to lick envelopes or pass out flyers. Their only criteria will likely be that you have a genuine interest in their cause and a willingness to give up your time and put up with the most monotonous and menial tasks in the name of furthering that cause. Oh, and you'll be doing this for little or no money (at least at first). Simply call up the agency you're interested in and let them know you're available. Chances are you'll get your first assignment before you even hang up the phone.

Biggest Challenges and Best Perks

Do you know what the problem with altruism is? Don't say the money. (You're right; there isn't a whole lot of money to be spread around, but that's something you have to expect and accept long before you decide to make this your life.) The real problem with altruism is that the politics of change are far slower than you'll want them to be. The rewards—while many—are not always apparent and they're never immediate. This can be especially tough if you, like many, became an activist out of pure idealism. Nothing can damage idealism like the realities of slow progression, and few things are more damning to a cause than a bunch of disillusioned idealists. However, as Margaret Mead reminds us, one should never doubt the possibility that "a small group of thoughtful people could change the world. Indeed, it's the only thing that ever has."

Professional Profile
Avg. salary: Mostly volunteer

Jargon
Cycles of protest Denotes the patterns of rising and falling action experienced by individual movements as well as the tendency of movements to generate other movements

Movement cultures The shared values and behaviors by which a social movement differentiates itself

Organizing vs. mobilizing Mobilizing refers to the process by which leaders can get large numbers of people to join a movement; organizing refers to a process in which people come to deeply understand a movement's goals and empower themselves to continued action on behalf of those goals

Are you Interested In?
Current affairs, politics, travel, writing

Related College Majors
Political science, history, communications, English, economics, area studies, environmental science

For More Information
Activist News:
www.topix.net

Idealist.org:
www.idealist.org

The Intellectual Activist:
www.intellectualactivist.com

AU PAIR/NANNY

A (Relatively) Typical Day In the Life

If you love children and don't mind things getting a little messy sometimes, this is the job for you. Au pairs (or nannies) are professional child care providers who help busy parents (often those who work full-time) take care of their kids. This might include dropping them off at school, shuttling them to various appointments, doing the family's grocery shopping, and more. Au pairs go just about everywhere with the children for whom they care, so the job requires a lot of energy, creativity, and patience. In addition, sometimes the job involves household duties, so it's important that you be willing to be hands-on at all times.

"Live-out" nannies usually need to wake up very early to travel to their clients' homes and take over child care while parents prepare for work. Some au pairs (especially those who have been hired from abroad) live with the families for whom they work, particularly when children are very young or just when it's the most convenient arrangement. Nannies see the parents off, make sure they have their instructions and information for the day, prepare breakfast for the kids, and get the kids ready for the day ahead. Nannies usually go to the park, library, or museum, or to playdates that are set up in advance for the child. They make sure to head back home to ensure children eat their lunch, and they might do some light cleanup, read children stories, or have them take naps. If applicable, nannies pick up children after school and accompany them to any after-school activities or appointments. Depending on the situation or arrangement, nannies might also prepare dinner for the children or for the whole family, make sure the children do their homework, and get the children ready for bed. During vacations, some nannies even travel with the families for whom they work.

An Extreme Day in the Life

Katherine Long worked as a nanny for a family in Maine the summer after she graduated from college. "To get started, I looked into a couple of different organizations. Anyone who is getting an au pair is pretty wealthy, so most of these agencies cater to high-end clientele. I ended up with a local family I used to babysit for in high school. The children I was in charge of were 4, 7, and 12 years old." Although she was not a live-in nanny, Katherine says the responsibilities of the job required her to be available and alert at all times: "I went to Nantucket with the family on their vacation. Nantucket sounds ideal but when you're in charge of three kids, you're there for work." Katherine's favorite aspect of the job was the kids themselves: "Being a nanny is just a great opportunity to hang out with kids and do all the fun stuff they do—swimming, biking, riding, tennis." Her advice for people considering this profession is to be selective about the clients for whom they will work. "The reason I went with a local family is that you need to know if the family is going to be a good fit for you—never go into this job blindly. It's definitely different from a desk job. It has its ups and downs, and there are moments when you're running around after three kids trying to make sure they don't kill one another that the idea of a desk job seems kind of nice."

Prepare for Success

A college degree is not required to become an au pair or nanny, but many clients will want you to help their children learn a second language or correct homework, so be sure to highlight you language skills, travel experience, and good grades on your resume. If you are looking for work as an au pair in another country, it would be helpful to familiarize yourself with the language of your destination country. In addition, references are always necessary, so look for individuals in your life who would be able to speak knowledgeably and highly of your experience and character. Knowledge of first aid is important, since you may be the only person with a child during an emergency. Caring for children can require a lot of patience and energy, so it's important to plan any of your after-work activities around an even, set schedule that leaves time for rest and a good night's sleep.

Getting Your Foot in the Door

Many people become au pairs for the experience of living abroad and taking in another culture. The best way to get a job in another country is through an agency or someone you already know, to ensure safe working conditions and to minimize the risk of a bad work arrangement. Agencies such as the International Au Pair Association can provide information about qualifications, appropriate training, and advice on finding a job. Know what your requirements are before you start looking, on issues such as housework, cooking, how many (and what age group) children you feel comfortable caring for at once, and whether you'll be live-in or live-out. The registration, screening, interview, and sometimes training process can take some time, so start your research as early as possible.

Biggest Challenges and Best Perks

The constantly busy and changing schedule that caring for a child entails may be one of the biggest challenges as well as one of the best perks. If you love working with children, this job allows you to do that all day, but keeping up with the children can be a challenge itself! Hours can be long, and maintaining a patient and kind demeanor can be difficult when you or the child is cranky. Many au pairs find themselves having less authority than the parent when it comes to decisions and discipline, although they often spend more time with the child than the parent does. On the contrary, there can be a lot of flexibility in this profession, and some nannies work out arrangements that free up their time for other interests such as classes, auditions, or travel.

Professional Profile
Avg. live-in salary: $532 per week

Avg. live-out salary: $590 per week

Varies greatly depending on locale and breadth of established responsibilities.

Jargon
Play date A scheduled time period in which parents arrange for children to play together for a few hours

Are you Interested In?
Babysitting, child care

Related College Majors
Child care and support services management, child development, early childhood education

For More Information
International Au Pair Association: www.iapa.org

Au Pair in America: www.aupairinamerica.com

International Nanny Association: www.nanny.org

AUTO MECHANIC/CAR DETAILER

A (Relatively) Typical Day In the Life

If you have a car, chances are that sooner or later your engine's going to overheat. That means (assuming he or she has a good track record) an auto mechanic's job is never done. It's a dirty job that can carry a negative reputation—did my car really need a new starter when I just brought it in for an oil change? Having a garage full of cars means being able to diagnose the mysterious thumps, clangs, and shakes symptomatic of a car when it's "sick." Being able to locate the problem quickly and accurately can mean the difference between repeat customers or an empty shop. After talking to the owner about the problem, electronic diagnostic equipment can be hooked up to the car to detect some problems, but most often experienced mechanics can sniff out problems on their own. If computers are used in the diagnosis, the results are compared with acceptable standards to see if they deviate. After finding the problem, it's time for repair—or, if the part in question is worn or damaged beyond saving, it's time to replace. Although most mechanics encourage regular tune-ups and maintenance, most of their clients wait until their cars' problems have hit critical points. For routine inspections, mechanics test certain systems and try to find problems before they cause breakdowns. Repair shops are a power tool addict's heaven—hoists, pneumatic wrenches, welding equipment share space with the everyman's toolbox, screwdrivers, pliers, and wrenches. Larger shops have technicians that specialize in one automotive system—electrical, fuel systems, or refrigeration. Occasional cuts and burns are common as so much of the work is hands-on. There is some paperwork involved in the job as well. State inspection records must be maintained, insurance forms completed and submitted, and books kept up-to-date.

An Extreme Day in the Life

Mechanics have been compared with physicians, with one small exception—doctors are always working on the same model. Although he received top-notch training, mechanic Mike Daley says "the greatest challenge is keeping up with new technology." Mike got his start as an apprentice after taking training classes, then worked his way up. It wasn't what he always wanted to do. "I was good at it, so I chose it," he says when asked how he ended up under the hood. His first job was as a "grease man," doing nothing but oil changes day in and day out. It took five years of entry-level work to reach the position he is in now. To stand out from other prospective hires, Mike recommends "electrical classes, vocational school, and technical school" but also warns that at least at his shop, there are "many more mechanics applying than we have positions for." After admitting that "the money is good and the benefits are great," Mike also confesses that he has arthritis "from using [his] hands so much." He advises that people considering the field make sure they understand that "this line of work takes a toll on your body." The bigger the test, the greater the reward at the end of the day. "The most significant project I have done is working on a huge piece of construction equipment. It was a DC-10, a huge bulldozer . . . over 20 feet high." The task? Rebuilding it "from the engine to the transmission." Moving from taking apart junked cars as an apprentice to working on a bulldozer so large that "[his] car could fit in the bucket" was proof that his skill level had advanced along with his title.

Being able to locate the problem quickly and accurately can mean the difference between repeat customers or an empty shop.

Prepare for Success

Automotive training schools provide training in the technology increasingly pervading this profession. They combine classroom instruction with hands-on practice and generally last from six months to one year. Some automobile manufacturers also offer two-year degree programs, with the in-class curriculum supplemented by "labs" in a dealer's service department. While many mechanics choose to take this route, equally common are those who learn all they know by assisting experienced mechanics and tinkering in their own garage. It's not really a field you can break into without already having a fairly extensive knowledge of what goes on under the hood. Most shops require their mechanics to be certified, which requires 1,000 hours clocked working on cars and passing a written exam. Internships emptying oil pans are easy to secure for students working toward their certification.

Getting Your Foot in the Door

Aspiring mechanics who become part of a training program can rely on the assistance of their instructors to find internships, but even self-taught mechanics should seek entry-level positions, paid or unpaid, to get their foot in the door. It doesn't hurt to have a few "clients" to vouch for you, neighbors that you rescued on the highway or friends who have a penchant for running over nails on the interstate. For those looking for careers that don't tie them to a shop—a pit crew mechanic, for example—it takes years of clocking hours to become the absolute best in your specialty before you can move up to the races.

Biggest Challenges and Best Perks

A mechanic is everyone's best friend. You can not only make sure your own wheels last as long as possible, but also become very popular with your neighbors. It's a dirty job with its share of hazards, but mechanics take every precaution to ensure their own and their coworkers' safety. Mechanics generally pull in a good salary for all their labor. Most people who enter the field can expect long-term careers. A repeat customer is the biggest compliment a mechanic can receive. The real challenge is keeping up with the ever changing technology the automotive manufacturers develop in each new model, from hybrids to on-board navigational systems.

PROFESSIONAL PROFILE
Avg. starting salary: $13,940

Avg. salary after 5 years: $22,830

Avg. salary 10 to 15 years: $32,450

JARGON
Drive train All the moving components of the car as a unit, including the engine, clutch, transmission, driveshaft, differential, axles, and wheels.

ARE YOU INTERESTED IN?
Automotive history, design, mechanics, power tools

RELATED COLLEGE MAJORS
Automotive training, automotive engineering

FOR MORE INFORMATION
American Automobile Manufacturers Association:
www.aama.com

Automotive Service Association, Inc:
www.asahop.org

BREWMASTER

A (Relatively) Typical Day In the Life

Brewmasters are the people behind the beer that flows from barroom taps worldwide. Yes, this means that they'll most likely do an on-the-job beer tasting once or twice a day to make sure taste, aroma, color, and clarity are consistent from batch to batch. Sobriety is a virtue in this profession, so don't expect to find brewmasters chugging their product all day long. Brewmasters are responsible for choosing raw materials, coming up with new recipes, and overseeing all aspects of the brewing process to make sure the beer that's being produced is up to snuff. In many cases, this means that a brewmaster will manage a team of brewers and assistants—some of whom may hope to fill the position of brewmaster one day.

In this field, size really does matter—at least in terms of how a brewmaster's day is filled. At larger breweries, the duties described above—tasting, experimenting, and overseeing a staff and basic production—may be more than enough to keep the brewmaster occupied all day long. At smaller breweries, however, where the workload is a little lighter, brewmasters may get involved in packaging, marketing, touring, adding malt to the grinders, moving boxes and barrels, and even working a few shifts as bartenders.

If a restaurant is attached to the brewery, brewmasters may also get together with the restaurant manager to select menu items that'll go best with the beers being produced. After all, brewmasters—like winemakers, chefs, and other culinary artists—are always thinking about taste. For this reason, the two most important traits in a successful brewmaster will be a discerning palette and a healthy nose.

Prepare for Success

Nothing's going to teach you how to make good beer like trying to make good beer. This means buying a book that teaches you the ins and outs of ingredients such as barley, wheat, hops, yeast, and so on, and picking up a home

An Extreme Day in the Life

Alan Pugsley, brewmaster for Maine's Shipyard and Sea Dog breweries, does much more than just brew beers. He also sets up brewing systems all over the world. On one job, he and his colleagues had just a few weeks to get the brewery up and the beer flowing. "Everything was going along just fine and a brewing date was set. But then we met a hitch." The refrigerating equipment was delayed. This meant that boiled wort—an ingredient used in brewing—might not be cooled to the temperature necessary for yeast to be added and fermentation to occur. "We brewed anyway," he says. But they didn't manage to cool the wort enough. "This is where we started to rack our brains. I had seen these 'ice block' stores down the street where huge blocks of ice were sold. The fermenting vessels were open top so if we were able to suspend these ice blocks indirectly in the wort somehow we could cool it down further. So we bought some very large rolls of food grade polythene, purchased many 50-pound blocks of ice, wrapped them in the polythene, sanitized the bags and suspended them in the fermentation vessel to try to cool down the wort so we could pitch the yeast and start fermentation, all of this while doing everything in a very sanitary manner in an open room at about 80 degrees!" It worked. "Innovation is a brewer's necessity at times!"

Innovation is a brewer's necessity at times!

brewing kit and giving it a shot. Kits range from rudimentary to elaborate, so select one that matches both your wallet and skill level. You'll want to develop keen senses of taste and smell—not only to judge the beer, but also to assess the individual ingredients that you're putting into the mix. This is what an employer will be looking for when you hit the job market. At large breweries, an employer may also look approvingly on brewers with specific educational training, like a PhD in brewing biochemistry. (Yes, a handful of universities worldwide really do offer this degree.) Brewers and brewmasters can also increase their marketability by acquiring certification and training through organizations like the Master Brewers Association of America.

Getting Your Foot in the Door

In this industry, experience is key; you have to put in your time if you want to climb the ladder. Most brewmasters start out as apprentices, assistants, or brewers. Through hard work and networking at all the beer fests your schedule can fit, you'll put yourself in a position to rise in the ranks or snag a coveted brewmaster position. Some of the hard work we're talking about involves rigorous experimentation—after all, if you manage to come up with an award-winning beer, your future in the field suddenly looks much brighter.

Biggest Challenges and Best Perks

Let's face it—there are only so many breweries in the world, and each one (unless it's huge) probably has only one brewmaster. What this adds up to is a competitive market. Those who rise to the top must have a combination of enterprise and patience. Enterprise is important because you need to make your beer better and more distinctive so that you are more likely to earn the sort of loyal following that guarantees job stability. You need massive amounts of patience because to make those delicious beers, you'll have to carefully test plenty of combinations, sort through ingredients that are nearly (but not quite) identical, and figure out what small detail is off when the beer has an unintended color, taste, or smell.

The payoff is that you get the satisfaction of knowing that you've created a beer that you and your clientele find very satisfying. Day in and day out, you work to maintain the quality of a product that, in many rights, is yours. While there can be some monotony to the job, there's also a lot of creativity. Brewmasters often use their imaginative palates to perfect recipes for the flagship and the seasonal ales that many breweries feature. Yes, brewmasters very often get to sip on beer morning and night—sip being the operative word.

Professional Profile
Avg. starting salary: $30,000
Avg. salary 10 to 15 years: $60,000

Jargon
Sakéry A brewery that makes sake
Sakémaster A sakéry's equivalent of a brewmaster

Are you Interested In?
Beer, food, chemistry

Related College Majors
Biochemistry of brewing, agricultural and biological engineering, food science, culinary arts

For More Information
Brewer's Association:
www.beertown.org
The Brewmaster's Castle:
www.brewmasterscastle.com
Institute and Guild of Brewing:
www.igb.org.uk/title.asp

CHEF

A (Relatively) Typical Day In the Life

Chefs have earned a celebrity status that penetrates the banquettes of the world's finest restaurants to rural backyard barbecues everywhere. Although the glitz and glamour enjoyed by recognizable faces may overshadow the thankless toil many career kitchen-dwellers experience, people who become chefs tend to have very high levels of satisfaction with their professions. Although it's grueling work, would not dream of doing anything else. Long hours, painstaking attention to detail, and constant proximity to food are the keystones of this job. The profession rewards the talented and the daring people who can see opportunity and grab it.

A supportive camaraderie exists within the community of chefs, especially in urban centers. Most start out knowing absolutely nothing and apprentice under experienced chefs who teach them how to run a kitchen. Chefs work long and unusual hours; this makes it difficult for them to socialize outside of working hours. The result is limited opportunity to meet others, particularly if they live in areas where there are only a few chefs.

The daily life of a chef's career in the first few years is devoted to education. Few chefs survive cooking school and many don't anticipate the physical demands of the profession: lifting heavy pots, being on your feet for eight hours, stirring vats of sauces, and rolling pounds of dough. Many chefs specialize in a certain type of cuisine. It is difficult for new chefs to have their skills recognized without first establishing a history of success in a variety of workplaces. Chefs who leave the profession do so with heavy hearts; they genuinely enjoy the companionship of fellow chefs, the creativity involved in working with food, and the aesthetic beauty and gustatory delights of the profession. They sometimes leave because of the lack of opportunity, the daily pressures (which can be considerable), and the low wages for those who do not advance immediately to positions of authority.

An Extreme Day in the Life

According to the professional with whom we spoke, "extreme" is a word that is often synonymous with the life of a chef. An unyielding pace and constant strive for perfection coupled with the heat creates an intense, feverish work environment. The line cook said, "Life in a restaurant, and more specifically [the] kitchen, can be completely unpredictable. Kitchens move quickly and as it's an accident-prone environment, it can be rather dangerous. During my tenure it wasn't unusual to see bad burns, with fellow chefs dropping pots of boiling liquids on themselves or worse, [on] their peers. Of course, I suppose this shouldn't be too surprising after working a 10-hour shift on a packed Saturday night. Conditions can be trying as you'll find yourself wearing long-sleeved jackets and such attire on very hot summer nights. I quickly developed an affinity for improvisation, which came in handy on nights when the oven broke or the fish was questionable. Despite all the pressures (and the odd safety concern) the extreme days did make my career choice worthwhile. Often I'd reflect at the end of a horribly busy, incredibly unsmooth night of service and realize that we had achieved real unity in the kitchen. And of course, kitchen chaos definitely leads to some good stories and bragging rights about survival to other chefs."

A supportive camaraderie exists within the community of chefs.

PREPARE FOR SUCCESS

While the profession used to offer a direct progression for people who were new to the field—they would begin as preparation chefs, move on to assistant chefs, then get a chance at running their own kitchens—it is becoming more difficult to become a head chef unless you demonstrate exceptional talent, have amazing creativity, and can secure financing. There are more than 550 cooking schools in the country, and employers are beginning to impose higher academic standards on their prospective employees. Some employers are even turning to organizations such as the American Culinary Federation, which has certified a mere 70 of these 550 schools, for recommendations. Most training programs are practical; cooking, preparation, working as part of a team, instrument maintenance, and personal hygiene (yes, that is a course) are taught as part of basic cooking principles. Programs last up to four years. Specialization is important in this industry for people who are looking to work at swankier restaurants.

GETTING YOUR FOOT IN THE DOOR

Many chefs start out as cooks, assistant chefs, preparatory chefs, and unpaid interns, sacrificing long hours for low wages to gain the practical experience necessary in a number of fields before they can assume positions of responsibility in a professional kitchen. Some people start these positions while finishing up their second, third, or fourth year at a culinary academy. Successful chefs are able to listen carefully, work hard, and take advantage of opportunities to demonstrate their skills to advance in the profession.

BIGGEST CHALLENGES AND BEST PERKS

The physical demands of cooking are both strenuous and daunting. Chefs are on their feet while slaving over hot stoves for hours on end. Additionally, the kitchen moves at a fast, frenetic pace and the pressure to serve sumptuous food in a timely manner remains constant. Of course, dull moments are rare, and many thrive on the adrenaline rush that results. Furthermore, chefs often have lower food bills, as many restaurants offer their chefs complimentary "family" meals. There is always the pleasure of having served satisfied customers a memorable meal.

PROFESSIONAL PROFILE
Avg. starting salary: $25,636
Avg. salary after 5 years: $34,918
Avg. salary 10 to 15 years: $41,600

JARGON
Expeditor People in this key role are the link between the customers and both the wait staff and the line chefs; they ensure that food reaches diners in a timely fashion

Garde-manger The chef in charge of cold foods, including salads and dressings, buffet items, and cold hors d'oeuvres

ARE YOU INTERESTED IN?
Cooking

RELATED COLLEGE MAJORS
Culinary arts, bakery science, food science

FOR MORE INFORMATION
American Culinary Federation:
www.acfchefs.org

National Restaurant Association Educational Foundation:
www.nraef.org

National Restaurant Association:
www.restaurant.org

FLORIST

A (Relatively) Typical Day In the Life

Roses are red, violets are blue—if that's the extent of your knowledge of nature's greenery, a job in the floral industry may not be for you. However, if you know the difference between a petal and a pistil, if you have an eye for arrangement, and if you don't sneeze at the mere mention of magnolias, then this industry wants you. The role of the florist is to create a more pleasant, beautiful place to live. Think about it. Almost every special occasion provides an excuse to fill the room with flowers; these include births, weddings, anniversaries, graduations, holidays, bon voyages, and more. Parade floats, pageant winners, and Derby horses are draped in flowers. Flowers can also brighten sad times and help a person cope with an illness or loss. A florist has the opportunity to bring a lot of pleasure to the world.

Most florists own their own shops or work in the floral departments of grocery stores. Florists don't just arrange flowers. Presentation is only half of a florist's job. That said, to cultivate a regular client base, florists must be able to arrange skillfully and beautifully dried, artificial, and live flowers into bouquets or arrangements that suit the tastes and needs of their clients and occasions. They also have to know how to grow, cut, and clean a flower. Florists in smaller operations may also need to grow or purchase flowers, do the bookkeeping for the shop, and make deliveries. Being a florist is not always a bed of roses, though. The week of Valentine's Day is probably the most stressful time in the life of a florist (and potentially the most profitable). It's like the post office during Christmas.

An Extreme Day in the Life

Surprisingly, the work of a florist doesn't always come up roses. Kathleen Benken works at the floral business started by her husband's family in 1939 and describes her typical day. She says, "I walked in at 7:30 A.M. to six orders [that] have printed overnight. One employee has called in sick and the wholesale houses call to say that some of the wedding products, ordered weeks ago, did not make the flight from Miami and may or may not be in later that week. No one told us we were out of leather leaf, a staple in the floral industry. The compressor in the front cooler froze up, freezing the arrangements on the left side. There are 26 orders that need to be done by 11:30 A.M. in order to make the pool delivery. A driver comes in and sheepishly says he dropped one of the arrangements for the funeral starting at 10:00 A.M., and can I hurry up and fix it? The credit card number for a final wedding payment has been declined and the phone to the bride has been disconnected. The greenhouse informs me they have no ficus trees available for the wedding rental tomorrow. The only remaining help I have is an employee whose kids keep calling to say they are beating each other up. She is now in tears. I burn my hand on the glue pan trying to set up a few extra funeral baskets. My lunch order is delivered late and is all wrong and cold. We get through the orders by 3:00 A.M., I take care of the bride, the flowers, the credit card, the broken arrangement, call the sick employee, redo the frozen flowers, call the wholesale house to say thanks for getting the flowers here today after all, and the greenhouse finds the ficus trees. It's a challenge sometimes, but there are few things that come close to the joy that flowers bring."

It's a challenge sometimes, but there are few things that come close to the joy that flowers bring.

Large weddings (the month of June, in particular) can also be a stressful time for some florists.

Prepare for Success

Some community colleges offer classes in floral design, but if you really want to be a florist, you need the heart and hands-on experience. The American Institute of Floral Designers offers aspiring florists the chance to be accredited in floral design. Prospective members must send in pictures of their arrangements and then do a live showing in front of AIFD judges. The AIFD also offers grants for student research in the area of floral design. AIFD accreditation gives you a higher standing in the world of floriculture.

Getting Your Foot in the Door

Most florists start off as apprentices in flower shops. After years of learning the trade, some move on to open their own shops. With the right resources, almost anyone can open a store, but it's your ability and reputation that will keep the store open. Affiliating with a company or website such as FTD can help you connect your business with other florists, and drive traffic to your store, and word-of-mouth marketing definitely comes in handy around those floral crunch times (i.e., weddings, proms, and Valentine's Day).

Biggest Challenges and Best Perks

The first few years of a floral arranger's career are filled with learning which flowers go with which other flowers and assorted greenery. Beginning florists might find themselves in a few not-so-glamorous positions, ranging from work as floral delivery people to selling roses on the side of the road. It's only when an amateur florist has put in the proper time and training that they're rewarded with the sunnier side of life among the flowers. Established florists may try to expand their businesses by adding stores, or arranging the flowers of large-scale, high-profile weddings, parties, and other special occasions. Florists don't rake in the cash as a rule. Most are in the business because they love their work. They love flowers and plants, and they love knowing that they've added a little color to someone's life.

Professional Profile
Avg. starting salary: $13,440
Avg. salary after 5 years: $19,480
Avg. salary 10 to 15 years: $23,560

Jargon
Red & white combined Within the trade there is a standard of what each flower or flower colors represents, in this case, unity

Are you Interested In?
Gardening, nature

Related College Majors
Floral design, floriculture, horticulture

For More Information
The Society of American Florists:
www.safnow.org
American Institute of Floral Designers:
www.aifd.org
FTD:
www.FTD.com

FUNERAL DIRECTOR

A (Relatively) Typical Day In the Life

There's no standard day in the life of a funeral director. At any given hour or on any given day, a call can come in saying that someone has died and the body needs to be retrieved. Retrieval is just the beginning. What follows is multiday process that demands careful work and long hours—turning your attention to both the dead and the living.

Those scenes you see in movies of funeral directors (or morticians or undertakers, as they're also called) standing over a corpse in the middle of the night, preparing to embalm it—actually happens. Funeral directors are in charge of embalming, refiguring, dressing, and putting makeup on bodies. Preparing the body, however, counts for just a fraction of the responsibilities on a funeral director's docket. A funeral director must sit down with family members of the deceased—people who are often grieving, shocked, or distraught—to help them make appropriate, prudent decisions in a swift and an organized manner. These decisions include deciding where and when the services should occur, what they should entail, whether cremation is desired, and whether pallbearers are needed. The funeral director also takes care of getting an obituary in the paper, making arrangements with the cemetery, reserving a hearse, and decorating the venues that will host the memorial service, burial, scattering, and/or wake.

A funeral director is also an expert when it comes to bureaucratic chores such as obtaining a death certificate, notifying the Social Security Administration, or securing the paperwork needed to take a body over state lines. Let's not forget that at the end of the day, running a funeral home is a business, and that means that a funeral director also needs to think about billing, paying the necessary taxes, and launching an occasional marketing campaign.

No doubt, the life of funeral director can be a hectic one. Ask anyone in the profession and you'll hear the same thing: All the work is worth it when you know you've been able to help a family come to terms with a loved one's death and get on with life.

An Extreme Day in the Life

Dorrence Benta, who has been a licensed funeral director for 27 years, works for New York City's family-owned and operated Benta's Funeral Home, Inc. She says that every day is an extreme day in her profession. "A day in the life of a funeral director is largely unpredictable. On a daily basis a funeral director can find him or herself conducting and supervising funerals, engaging in funeral conferences to arrange funerals, contacting hospitals, nursing homes or medical examiners, transporting remains, embalming, securing properly completed death certificates from physicians, filing documents with proper authorities, arranging travel for decedents, and many other responsibilities." Other responsibilities? Sure. Securing finances, dealing with insurance companies, educating clients on legal matters such as Social Security death benefits, working with casket providers and florists, and gathering information for the program. "Multiply the above activities times (on average) three to four families per day," she says. "By the day's end you slide into bed without fear of insomnia. But then, guess what? Funeral directors are subject to receive calls in the middle of the night to respond to a need for services."

If you have a weak stomach or get easily spooked, this **might not be the profession for you.**

Prepare for Success

If you want to be a funeral director, you're going to need some specific training, most likely a four-year degree in mortuary science. (Some schools offer focused two-year programs as well.) This is a field of study that covers anatomy, embalming, psychology, business, and more. Don't rely solely on college courses to get you ready for your career. If possible, try to land a summer position with a funeral home, even if it's just helping out with the phones. You not only get some insider's knowledge of how things work, but also establish relationships with professionals in the field. Don't underestimate the importance of networking. Many funeral homes are small, family-run businesses; becoming "one of the family," so to speak, could well be your way to break into the profession. All funeral directors have to take an exam to become licensed by the state in which they intend to practice.

Getting Your Foot in the Door

Even with a degree in mortuary science, there's a good chance that you'll need to spend a few years as an apprentice before you get to don the title of funeral director. Take advantage of your apprenticeship period to watch how an experienced director relates with mourning clients; learn about various religious, spiritual, and cultural customs of which your clients will expect you to have knowledge; get a respectable haircut and pick up some new professional clothes; and work your butt off to impress your employers, so they'll want to keep you on the staff after the apprenticeship ends.

Biggest Challenges and Best Perks

If you have a weak stomach or get easily spooked, this might not be the profession for you. After all, preparing a body for presentation includes draining all of its blood, replacing the blood with embalming fluid, washing the body thoroughly, applying cosmetics, perhaps repairing disfigurements—in other words, spending a lot of time with a corpse. Other challenges come simply from managing the checklist of tasks that must be accomplished before, during, and immediately after a funeral. Because death is unpredictable, you may need to be on call 24/7, working nights and weekends when needed.

Without question, this is hard work. But it's never monotonous. Each family has its own concerns, each obituary its own details, and each body its own requirements. In fact, each day will demand a unique combination of creativity, sympathy, and science. In other words, funeral directors have the opportunity to use their varied skills to provide families with a memorable occasion to say good-bye to their loved ones. This, funeral directors will tell you, makes it all worthwhile.

Professional Profile
Avg. salary: $45,960

Jargon
Restorative arts A hot topic in undertaking, this refers to the ability to rebuild or repair remains during the embalming process

Are you Interested In?
Anatomy

Related College Majors
Mortuary science

For More Information
National Funeral Director's Association:
www.nfda.org

American Board of Funeral Service Education:
www.abfse.org

HAIRSTYLIST

A (Relatively) Typical Day In the Life

To be a professional hairstylist, you have to be able to invest yourself in making other people look pretty darn good. Many hairstylists work in salons, side by side with other stylists, as well as manicurists, pedicurists, waxers, shampooers, cosmetologists, aromatherapists, or even massage therapists. In most salons, stylists are expected to be up on the latest styles and the newest techniques. Not all stylists work in salons, though. Some work in the entertainment industry, preparing actors, actresses, and models for the roles they'll play onstage, on-screen, on camera, or on the runway; in this scenario, stylists often need to have knowledge about the latest and the oldest and most unique hairstyles around.

Whatever venue they work in, hairstylists can expect to cut, color, trim, tint, shave, shampoo, and otherwise style hair. They also advise clients in the ways of personal hair care. This requires a thorough knowledge of the products that line the shelves. (Hairstylists also do their part to promote the products that line the shelves.) Most stylists know a thing or two about wigs and hair extensions, as well—the shapes, styles, fits, and fibers that are available.

Styling hair, as does all salon work, requires a firm foundation in people skills. After all, if a client comes in for shampooing and coloring and a complete style makeover, the two of you might spend hours chatting away. The more questions you ask, the better you'll be able to make suggestions. Your ability to connect with your customers will ultimately determine whether or not those customers decide to return to your chair.

It's worth noting that within the "personal appearance" industry—an umbrella that covers hairstylists—nearly 50 percent of the workers are self-employed, according to the Bureau of Labor Statistics. If you think you might want to be among this 50 percent, use your early years in the field (those years when you're working for someone else) to soak up as much information as possible about how all aspects of the business are run, from advertising to product purchasing to keeping the books. Then, when you decide to strike out on your own, you'll be ready.

An Extreme Day in the Life

Stephen Adams describes himself as a "salon owner/creative director/stylist/platform artist." Headquartered in Minneapolis/St. Paul, he owns Moxie Hair Salon and Art Gallery, a business dedicated to the creative mind, to great haircuts, and the ongoing education of the stylists who work there. He also travels "all over the country and sometimes out of the country" to work as a platform artist, which means "coloring, cutting, and styling hair on beautiful models." This is one of his favorite aspects of the profession. He says, "The evening fashion shows are crazy and wild with so many models and teams of hair and makeup people scrambling around trying to get everything done in time, for the show must go on. I love doing show work because it is where I get to be very creative and make the hair into art. By building new styles with wefts of hair and extensions of color, the model will be transformed into someone else before your very eyes."

There's no denying that hairstyling can be an art form. "

PREPARE FOR SUCCESS

All states require some sort of certification—most likely, graduation from a state-recognized beauty school. Stylists also need to pass a state licensing exam, which often includes written and practical components. One you pass the tests and have the necessary qualifications in hand, you'll be ready to start earning money for your skills. If you're looking to break your way into high-end hairstyling, you might consider matriculating to an apprenticeship that allows you to work under a notable professional in the field. Though this will make you low man (or woman) on the totem pole for a year or two, it'll also help you build a strong professional network and give you a close-up view of how the big dogs do it—two invaluable gifts. Even if your aspirations aren't pulling you toward some fancy metropolitan salon, be prepared to tackle easy tasks at first and slowly work your way up.

GETTING YOUR FOOT IN THE DOOR

Increasingly, hairstylists find themselves working in salons that do more than simply cut and style hair. Beauty salons now offer manicures and pedicures and waxing; day spas and health resort facilities can provide everything from therapeutic massage to yoga to holistic health advising. As the realm in which hairstylists work expands, so do the opportunities to increase your marketability. Many vocational schools offer the kind of training and certification in specific areas such as aromatherapy that could give you an edge when it comes to scoring a pay raise, promotion, or position at the salon next door.

BIGGEST CHALLENGES AND BEST PERKS

Watch someone who's really good at styling hair, and there's no denying that hairstyling can be an art form. This is part of what makes the profession so compelling. It's also one of the profession's great traps. Hairstylists must remember that they are there to satisfy the customer, not—alas—themselves. To be perfectly honest, even if they do exactly what the customer asks for, there's a chance that the customer won't be satisfied. So, picky, prickly, pugnacious customers will, on occasion, require great feats of patience on your part. For every complainer, you're going to have 10 customers who absolutely rave about how you've styled their hair. Helping customers feel better about their appearance is one of great boons of this gig. If you're a people person who just happens to be wiz with the scissors, then this is a profession that's specially made for you.

Hairstylists often work long hours, including evenings and weekends. If you prefer to work a set schedule, this might not suit your lifestyle. However, if you can handle some Saturdays in the salon, a career in hairstyling gives you a great opportunity to pick up 40 hours a week without conforming to the nine to five mold.

INVENTOR

A (Relatively) Typical Day In the Life

Inventors are some of the icons of American history; the image of Alexander Graham Bell inventing the telephone in a relatively primitive lab is firmly imprinted on our national consciousness. Inventors industriously work to create new products for the American public. Today, however, with the rising costs of engineering and development, most invention occurs in corporate labs and research and development departments. Still, 20 percent of U.S. patents are issued each year to private inventors. A skilled inventor can still transform good ideas into significant sums of money.

Whether working in a lab or from home, an inventor's daily responsibilities can be summed up in one word: invention. There are great rewards in designing a product that is better than any that have come before it. But developing a useful product is only the first step in the process. The inventor must also be able to negotiate a favorable licensing contract with an established manufacturer, or else have the wherewithal to become an entrepreneur and go into the business of manufacturing his or her ideas. Designs that are developed must avoid infringing on existing patents, and investors must protect themselves from others who would copy their existing design. Knowing the fields or backgrounds of inventions makes inventors' lives much easier when they both develop new products and assess the value of inventions they are developing. Many inventors continue to work as research scientists and engineers while they develop their ideas, and these are the fields that most return to if they are unable to make it as inventors. Many return to inventing over and over again, accumulating successes and failures over the years. The

An Extreme Day in the Life

In an interview with *Smithsonian* magazine, Amy Smith, who holds a master's degree in mechanical engineering and teaches at MIT, talks about her work to help solve everyday problems for families living in the developing world. Currently, she is working in Haiti to help figure out how to convert post-processed sugar cane fibers into a fossil fuel source.

"Well, it's not very romantic, but I think our charcoal project is going to have a huge impact, because it allows you to have a clean-burning fuel without cutting down trees. We're planning large-scale dissemination in Haiti. There's no glitz factor to it, but it's probably going to make a huge amount of difference."

Smith, a 2004 MacArthur Fellowship recipient, also runs MIT's IDEAS Competition, in which student engineers design projects to make life easier in the developing world.

"Obviously, access to safe drinking water is a huge problem, and lack of access to opportunities, and general poverty. But if you get people safe drinking water, and then they still have no way to earn any money to feed their families, you still have a problem. And if you give them better methods of agricultural processing or ways to create clean energy, but there's still drinking water that makes them sick, you still have a problem. There are too many interrelated issues, so solving one problem won't completely change the lives of millions."

Source: http://www.smithsonianmagazine.com/issues/2006/september/qanda_smith.php?page=1

The first idea an inventor develops is often not the best one, but the experience gained with each try can be invaluable to later efforts.

first idea an inventor develops is often not the best one, but the experience gained with each try can be invaluable to later efforts. Two-thirds of all inventors never see any profits from their creations. Still, a good idea can be worth pursuing, and a very lucky few will reap the rewards of owning and operating a business that allows them to make a living on their creations.

Prepare for Success

In addition to being creative, successful inventors must also be effective businesspeople. With rare exceptions, a background in science or engineering is a must. Many private inventors spend years working as designers for private corporations before they develop the ideas that let them set out on their own. Experience in product design and development is crucial, as is knowledge of the new product's potential market. Years working in industry or in academic research are the best methods to acquire the skills of a successful inventor.

Getting Your Foot in the Door

The key to being a successful inventor is establishing manufacturing and distribution relationships. This makes it much easier to generate profits from additional inventions, and it allows the professional to spend more time focusing on inventing and less on pounding the streets looking for business contacts. Some inventors solicit the help of a marketing agent to establish those relationships; however, their fees can be exorbitant, ranging from 20–50 percent of the licensing sale. At the very least, aspiring inventors should participate in inventor trade shows, which is a perfect forum for testing your ideas out on the public and meeting the right people who can help you take your idea from concept to creation.

Biggest Challenges and Best Perks

As a full-time career, inventing provides an uncertain living for all but the most talented. Developing new products is time-consuming and often expensive, and income doesn't start to flow until a marketable prototype is ready. On the other hand, a successful inventor's operation probably resembles a small business. While very few inventors make it to this point, those who do reap the rewards of owning and operating a business that allows them to make a living on their creations.

PROFESSIONAL PROFILE
Avg. salary after 5 years: Varies
Avg. salary 10 to 15 years: Varies

JARGON

Patent The exclusive right to manufacture, use, or sell an invention for a certain number of years.

Sit on your invention When a company purchase a license to manufacture an invention, but never takes it to market.

ARE YOU INTERESTED IN?
"Tinkering," puzzles, trivia

RELATED COLLEGE MAJORS
Science, engineering, mathematics

FOR MORE INFORMATION
United States Patent and Trademark Office:
www.uspto.gov

American Society of Inventors:
www.americaninventor.org

Yankee Invention Exposition:
www.yankeeinventionexpo.org

MAKEUP ARTIST

A (Relatively) Typical Day In the Life

If you've ever taken a bad picture and been annoyed, imagine how someone in the public eye feels when their bad photos are viewed world-wide! This is one of the reasons makeup artists are invaluable to their clients: They style the most visible part of the body. A steady hand and warm disposition are crucial in this profession in order to make the client feel comfortable. Strong time-management skills are also key: If you miss an appointment, you could lose business.

A makeup artist's "typical day" varies widely. If the client is making a TV or studio appearance, then you are likely to report to the same place a few times a day to prep him or her for the show. If you work independently on the sets of movies, commercials, and music video shoots, you may spend the whole day—with lots of down time—on set retouching and adjusting your work. Your day could also be spent at a client's house doing makeup for one for a big event, or for twelve for a wedding party. On a slow day, you might clean your materials, attend a trade show, call around for more business, take a class on a new product or technique, or just shop for new materials. The life of a makeup artist isn't just mascara and lipstick, however: Some makeup artists are called upon to "age" characters in movies with plot timelines that span many years, create fake bruises and wounds for violent or accident scenes, and turn humans into aliens for sci-fi films. Whatever the project, the end result is always the same: a reinvented face ready for its close-up.

Prepare for Success

Many makeup artists have a degree or certification in cosmetology, which gives you a strong foundation (no pun intended!) in application, products, ingredients, and techniques, and gives your client or employer confidence that you are a trained professional. Certification is not absolutely necessary, however, as some makeup artists just discover they have skill in the field and start working without any prior coursework. Many beauty institutes promise job-placement assistance, so be sure to ask about that before you enroll anywhere. If you need some work to pad

---

An Extreme Day in the Life

In an interview with Gurl.com, makeup artist Vanessa Mojica talks about some of her favorite and least favorite aspects of the job:

"Meeting a lot of fabulous people is probably the most interesting and best part of my job! I have made some great friends working at Fredflare.com, as well as other jobs I have done on location. It is always great to meet other creative people and be able to come together and make something amazing." On the other hand, "trying to convince people they want the wrong look for themselves is very difficult. I try to make all my clients happy but at the same time, I have to select a style that will fit their face and features. I haven't run into anything that rough, but with this job you have to be up for anything. You have to expect crazy and fun things to happen."

Source: http://www.gurl.com/showoff/spotlight/qa/0,,693924,00.html

Seeing a client beam after you've worked your makeup magic may be one of the most rewarding perks of this profession.

your resume, consider working for free at a few events, such as a friend's wedding. This will give you some concrete references and photos, which are a great way to attract new clients.

Getting Your Foot in the Door

A good way to get your foot in the door is to assist a more established artist, or work as an entry-level employee for a salon or makeup company directly. Working on your own can give you the freedom to pick and choose assignments and clients, but you need a strong initial client base— or an alternate source of income while you start out. These junior positions are usually not well paid, but will help you gain experience and contacts. Solo makeup artists have to drum up their own business, so putting the word out among your friends, acquaintances, and family is a good idea. Make sure that you understand what your clients want and give yourself enough time for each assignment—doing a great job is the best advertisement. Also, keep your own appearance up: Since you are selling the illusion of beauty or cosmetic enhancement, your clients will appreciate that you look the part.

Biggest Challenges and Best Perks

Life as a makeup artist is not without its challenges. Days can be grueling and long, and tempers can run high. Makeup artists occasionally have to deal with clients' unrealistic visions of themselves and how they should look post-makeup. It's a challenge to dispel these ideas kindly yet firmly and bring the client around to realizing what is actually possible. On the upside, seeing a client beam after you've worked your makeup magic may be one of the most rewarding perks of this profession. Working on lavish film sets or TV shows with car services and fancy dinners can also be a great perk. makeup artists often travel with a client/employer, so location can be a perk as well. The life of a makeup artist involves a lot of variety—in tools and materials, in industry, and in assignments—and for many artists, this is the main perk.

Professional Profile
Avg. starting salary (retail setting):
$12–20/hr

Avg. starting salary (photo shoot):
$25–65/hr

Avg. starting salary (entertainment production): $50–$200/hr

Jargon
Corrective makeup Makeup application technique resulting in the minimized appearance of blemishes

Are you Interested In?
Beauty, art

Related College Majors
Cosmetology

For More Information
The Makeup Artist Network:
www.makeupartistnetwork.com

National Association of Screen Makeup Artists and Hairdressers:
www.nasmah.org

Makeup Artist Magazine:
www.makeupmag.com

MASSAGE THERAPIST

A (Relatively) Typical Day in the Life

A massage therapist is not a career for the shy (you'll need to tell complete strangers to take their clothes off and get under a sheet), the restless (complete concentration at all times is a must), or anyone with hang-ups about making skin-to-skin contact with people off the street who might call to schedule an appointment. Fortunately, most people who believe in the healing power of the human touch come to this field with an open mind, ready hands, and a desire to help others. A massage therapist is charged with reducing stress, relieving muscle aches and pains, and lulling clients into a state of blissful relaxation—all with the right moves of the hands and fingers.

In training, a massage therapist learns not only techniques for kneading and working different muscles groups, and how to perform different types of massage—from the long, sweeping strokes of Swedish massage to the gnarly work of kneading several muscle layers in deep tissue massage—but also skills that ensure professionalism. Adjusting massage techniques based on client feedback, focusing on requested muscle areas, and paying attention to the client's specific needs are things that come with time, practice, and dedication. Hospitals, chiropractors' offices, medical clinics, spas, resorts, salons, health clubs, offices, conventions, professional sports facilities, and private homes (in the case of out-call therapists) are just some places where massage therapists report to work, bringing their signature calm demeanor.

Prepare for Success

Friends and family will line up out the door to volunteer as guinea pigs for massage practice, so it's easy to find willing subjects for the aspiring therapist to use as skills-building clients. Learning different types of massage—hot stone, sports massage, prenatal, chair massage—or types of related treatments—Reiki, reflexology, facials—adds versatility to a massage therapist's portfolio and increases demand. Choosing a school is an important first step. Take the time to find a school that shares your philosophies and will help you develop an area of specialization that interests you. A school with a strong track record of job placement upon graduation will serve you well. Note that each state and/or city or town has different requirements for massage therapists; schools should ensure each student understands and fulfills local requirements.

An Extreme Day in the Life

The first months, or even years, in this field can be a big adjustment. Your most extreme days may happen in the midst of gaining experience and getting into your massage-giving groove. Jenessa Pascoe is in her first year as a massage therapist in San Francisco, having recently earned a certification from massage school and a license from the state. She balances her out-call massage business with her continuing education, as well as part-time jobs at a spa and a chiropractor's office. "Clients like out-call massage because they don't have to deal with traveling to and from a spa or being in an unfamiliar environment. It's a novelty and a luxury that fits into our culture where food and other items are delivered to our doors. . . . I always ask if they have an iPod hookup so I can bring the music I have on mine and use it at their house."

> **A massage therapist is not a career for the shy, the restless, or anyone with hang-ups about making skin-to-skin contact with people off the street.**

Getting Your Foot in the Door

Building a client base by providing out-call massage services in clients' homes is a good way to get started. When it's time to interview at a spa, gym, or health center, it's smart to mention that your clients will come with you. Private practice requires owning a portable massage table and other supplies, but your mobile business can build quickly through word-of-mouth referrals and smartly placed advertisements. Always carry a stack of business cards and don't be shy about passing them out. Self-promotion is an important quality of a massage therapist who is working to build steady clients.

Biggest Challenges and Best Perks

Massage is physically demanding and those who practice must be in good shape. Masseurs must be ready for any personality or body type to walk into the treatment room. Having a thick skin will come in handy as clients can be critical if the massage isn't exactly the way they want it to be. Those running a private practice have additional challenges of bookkeeping, traveling for work, building a loyal client base, and knowing how to pre-screen clients to avoid awkward or even dangerous situations.

A soothing environment—candles, aromatherapy, and peaceful mood music in many cases—beats a hectic workplace of ringing phones and clacking computer keys any day. A client who has just received a massage looks transformed after an hour on the table, and a good massage therapist finds that to be a big reward of the profession. If you work in a spa, you may receive discounts on services, and you'll always know who to call if you need a healing massage of your own.

PROFESSIONAL PROFILE
Avg. salary: $50,093

Varies considerably based on number of customers, amount of tips, and whether services can be privately contracted. Spa owners can earn considerably more.

JARGON
Breema performed on the floor while the recipient is fully clothed. It consists of rhythmical and gentle leans and stretches that lead to deep relaxation, increased vitality, and stimulation of the self-healing processes of the body

Trigger point therapy applies pressure to cause instant muscle relaxation

ARE YOU INTERESTED IN?
Holistic medicine, health, meditation

RELATED COLLEGE MAJORS
Massage therapy

FOR MORE INFORMATION
Massage Network:
http://massagenetwork.com

Massage Today:
www.massagetoday.com

Massage Therapy 101:
www.massagetherapy101.com

PEST CONTROL TECHNICIAN

A (Relatively) Typical Day In the Life

Pest control technicians spend their days out in the field facing off against the creepy crawlies that turn most people's stomachs. Roaches, rats, and termites are just a few of the pests they seek to contain daily. Warmer climates offer up the most diverse range of creatures that pose serious risks to human health and safety. However, pest control professionals nationwide are devising more effective ways of eliminating the threat with tactics from pesticides and traps to physical barriers and sanitation upgrades. The trend is moving toward the integration of several pest-fighting measures to keep rodents and insects at a distance.

As a pest control technician, your job would be to find, identify, repel, control, and in some cases destroy vermin. You'd have to call on your understanding of their biology and customs to determine the most effective course of action. Your arsenal could include potent restricted-use pesticides that are regulated by the U.S. Environmental Protection Agency (EPA), mechanical traps that stop pests in their tracks and microchip-implanted baiting stations. You may also need to collect and dispose of dead pests.

This physically demanding job will have you reaching, bending, kneeling, and crawling during indoor and outdoor inspections and treatments. Often you'll be wearing heavy gear including respirators, gloves, and goggles to protect yourself from toxic pest control chemicals and the critters themselves. You can expect a 40-hour week of fighting infestations and traveling to client sites. Rats and roaches don't limit their forays into homes and businesses to regular hours so some technicians work nights and weekends.

An Extreme Day in the Life

Scott Leeman, a pest control technician in St. Louis, Missouri, spends his workdays hunting down pesky insects and rodents, but always keeps people foremost in his mind. "We're using a product that is strong enough to kill so people are concerned with safety. There's a very simple rule to live by and that is the label on the product you're using is the law. It is very specific and our company is also very involved in how to safely apply treatments and take care of things. It's not only selling a product, it's explaining a product to make sure the customer is comfortable with what's happening."

What's comfortable for the client isn't always comfortable for the technician, and pest control workers frequently go out on a limb to meet customer's needs. Scott has faced off against wasps, squirrels, and birds at death-defying heights. "The tough part is climbing way up on a ladder and doing the job so that we don't get hurt and so the customer is satisfied. For instance, a customer had yellow jackets coming in and out of the chimney and the source of the problem was a 40-foot-high nest. Also, birds, squirrels, and raccoons get in from the attic. You don't want to get in a position where you have a chance of hurting yourself."

Sometimes mysterious pest problems closer to earth are just as unsettling. "The other difficult kind of job is when there's an odor and you're trying to find it. You want to do a through inspection without harming the home. That's the hardest one—when you can smell the odor, but just can't find its source."

> You'll see some nasty things in this profession—the pests themselves and some of the gruesome damage they've done.

Prepare for Success

About 40 percent of pest control technicians have attended college, but high school graduation or equivalent is usually enough qualification for the field. Aspiring pet control technicians should brush up on their basic math and chemistry skills, which you'll need to mix up pesticide cocktails to fight the vermin of the day. You'll also need strong communication skills to win the confidence of distressed clients who want pests out of their homes and workplaces as fast as possible with as little disruption to their daily routines as possible. You'll need to explain your strategy and the associated costs in a clear and compelling fashion. Physical fitness and good health is also critical in this field as technicians often have to work in extreme temperatures and bad weather. A strong stomach also helps. You'll see some nasty things in this profession—the pests themselves and some of the gruesome damage they've done.

Getting Your Foot in the Door

Turnover among pest control workers is high, which bodes well for people seeking employment in the field. The industry is desperate for people and a quick search on Internet job sites such as Monster.com will yield hundreds of postings from employers seeking pest control technicians. Your local newspaper's job classified section is another great way to hunt for opportunities. Finally, aspiring job hunters should check with the pest control associations in their region for leads.

Biggest Challenges and Best Perks

Pest control technicians work in some of the most unpleasant conditions around. They're chasing down mice in hot attics and inspecting cold, dingy crawl spaces. Their job is to seek out the disease-carrying pests that everyone else avoids. Many of the tools of their trade are toxic and must be handled with care. Plus, they pay isn't spectacular although it tops minimum wage fast-food jobs.

There's also a great deal of independence in this field. You are out and about for the vast majority of the day, devising pest control strategies. You're working with your hands and aren't stuck in an office contending with paperwork and petty politics. Plus, there is the emotional payoff of knowing you've helped make a home safer for a family by eliminating the rodents and insects that plagued it.

Professional Profile
Avg. salary: $10–16 per hour

Jargon
Certified applicator A person qualified to use restricted-use pesticides

LD50 The chemical dose calculated to be lethal to 50 percent of the organisms in a specific test situation

Target The site or pest receiving the control measure

Are you Interested In?
Insects, sanitation, public health and safety

Related College Majors
Entomology, chemistry, math

For More Information
National Pest Management Association:
www.pestworld.org

PestWeb:
www.pestweb.com

U.S. Environmental Protection Agency:
www.epa.gov

RESTORATION EXPERT

A (Relatively) Typical Day In the Life

Imagine that after cleaning out their attic, John and Jane Smith were thrilled to discover an original Winslow Homer painting hidden behind a wall of junk. Their excitement quickly waned, though, because the painting was so worn—a tear across the top half, rampant discoloration, a cockled canvas—that it wasn't even worth hanging on the wall.

This is the sort of scenario for which a restoration expert lives. A restoration expert's job is to make a work of art or document look as it did when it was brand new. They are problem solvers who combine artistic appreciation, scientific acuity, and surgical precision to tackle the task at hand. There's no telling what exactly that task will be. The craft of restoration can be applied to paintings, paper documents, photographs, frames, and 3-D art. The problems can include acid damage, adhesive residue, color and pigmentation deterioration, stains, tears, holes, flaking, folding, cockling, water damage, fire damage, smoke damage, insect damage, and any number of defects caused by neglect. Determining how exactly to fix the problem—or problems, as is often the case—requires a thorough understanding of the chemical composition of the original materials used in the work, as well as the makeup of the solvents, cleaners, and fibers you intend to apply.

This is a profession for the meticulous. While each day will likely bring unique challenges, these challenges will be handled in a slow, careful fashion. After all, that canvas you're working on might be worth 20 grand. Though a lot of restoration work occurs in the quiet solitude of a lab, restorers also have the opportunity to work with clients and consultants from major museums, galleries, and private collections. Restoration experts play a vital role in the world of art—past and present.

Prepare for Success

Most restoration facilities are filled with people who hold fine arts or art history degrees. Therefore, step one is to get yourself an education that schools you in the materials, practices, philosophy, and history of art. This is important because restoration experts take great pride in returning a work of art to its original state—and the more you know about historical periods and methods (not to mention specific artists themselves) the better you'll be able to identify what the work's original state was. After college, many restorers land apprenticeships at facilities where a seasoned pro (or two) is at the helms. You can consider this phase two of your restoration training. Outside of

An Extreme Day in the Life

The Madisonian Gallery's Edward Fritzi is not only a longtime restoration expert, but also a court certified art expert witness and a fine art appraiser. For him, every piece of art he restores brings its own challenge and excitement. He says, "The adventure and thrill of discovery in locating, evaluating, and restoring fine art is typically found in the details of the weave of a canvas, the press of the paper, the confidence of a brushstroke, the design of a monogram, the extent of prior restoration, or the degree of freedom in the design. These elements and more are critical in determining the authenticity and value of a fine work of art and carefully restoring the work, be it for preserving a long lost treasure, insurance, estate valuation, or a charitable donation to a museum."

Restoration experts do for a piece of art what physicians do for the human body.

formal education and apprenticeships, spend your Saturdays walking through museums and galleries and talking to the people who work there. Using your spare time wisely can help you bulk up your knowledge base as well as establish some relationships that can lead to a larger client list in the future.

Getting Your Foot in the Door

Let potential clients know you're serious about your work by becoming a member of professional organizations such as the American Institute for Conservation of Historic and Artistic Works (AIC). If you strike out on your own, presentation is critical. That means creating public relations materials, business cards, and a website that lets the public know you can be trusted with their masterpieces. Don't expect that all your business will be local. Catch the art world's eye and you—like many of the most revered professionals in the field—may be receiving calls from archivists, dealers, and collectors coast to coast. Continuing to develop your skills with various techniques, materials, and mediums will only increase your marketability.

Biggest Challenges and Best Perks

For decades there's been talk of restoring Leonardo da Vinci's Mona Lisa. Why the itch to restore it? Over the course of centuries, restoration experts have applied protective substances like resin and varnish to the surface of the painting; these substances, like a thick layer of tartar on your teeth, have caused the painting to yellow and discolor over time. So far, the Louvre doesn't want anyone to touch it. Even if the Louvre did give the nod, it's likely that very few restoration facilities would be willing to take on the project because there's no telling which restoration techniques would work best on a 500-year-old work of art. Who wants to be known as the person who destroyed one of the world's most cherished paintings?

True, most restoration experts don't get to work on a Leonardo da Vinci, but they do work on significant documents, maps, and pieces of art, which can also be stressful. Each motion must be well-planned, delicate, and precise. On the flipside, restoration experts do for a piece of art what physicians do for the human body. That is, they have the ability to examine, diagnose, and remedy its problems, essentially, breathing new life into the piece. Because each work of art is unique, each work day is unique as well. There's no telling what combination of solvents, science lessons, and historical tidbits will come into play. All your efforts will add up to a finished product—that fully restored Winslow Homer, let's say. Knowing that you're responsible for a fully restored Winslow Homer—well, that's quite a perk.

Professional Profile
Avg. salary: $37,320

Jargon
Accretions An accumulation of foreign matter on the surface of the artwork that affects the artist's design

Foxing Reddish-brown stains caused by metal particles in the paper

Inherent vice Deterioration of an object as a result of its original construction

Are you Interested In?
Museums, art, history

Related College Majors
Fine arts, art history, chemistry

For More Information
American Institute for Conservation of Historic and Artistic Works:
http://aic.stanford.edu/

Association of Restorers:
www.assoc-restorers.com

The Fine Arts Conservancy:
www.art-conservation.org

SEAMSTRESS/TAILOR

A (Relatively) Typical Day In the Life

Tailors and seamstresses do more than just sew; they help their clients look and feel great. From custom tailoring to dress and suit making, the focus is on getting the clothing to fit the way the client intended. This takes a sharp eye for detail and the tenacity to be painstaking about quality. A typical day could involve opening your shop for business and reviewing garments that will be picked up that day and confirming your orders/client fittings for the day over e-mail or by phone. The next step might be a visit to the garment district for fabric, a sewing machine part, or some trimmings. Then back to the shop to meet with clients picking up altered clothing or fitting a made-to-order garment. Some professionals travel with artists or entertainers for special events, so a trip to a hotel to do last minute alterations on a wedding gown or performance outfit could be the last stop in your day.

Prepare for Success

A college degree isn't absolutely necessary to become a successful tailor or seamstress, but taking a degree or courses in dressmaking, drawing, and design can save you a lot of time spent figuring out technique and how to translate your ideas onto cloth. Young graduates with promise are often scooped up by the big name fashion houses to design and sew for them, which a great way to get experience in the field. Many successful tailors and seamstresses get their starts apprenticing or interning for a designer, so do some research to figure out what area interests you so you can get internships that best suit you.

An Extreme Day in the Life

"Be as pretty as you can be, but know as much as you know." This philosophy pretty much sums up the business savvy of B. J. Hunnicutt, retired owner of a tailoring shop in Salisbury, North Carolina. Ms. Hunnicutt first heard this phrase when she was a student studying dressmaking at a local college, and it has been the mantra underlying her career as a professional seamstress for the past 50 years. "I got started with sewing when I was 13 as a student in one of the local 4-H clubs. The first piece I made was a bra. There was no cup and it was flat as an egg! From there I started sewing on the pedal machine and began trying to make dresses for my sister." At college, Ms. Hunnicutt studied dressmaking, home décor, and upholstery. Some of her most extreme moments on the job have also been the most recent, occurring as the result of changes in the tailoring and dressmaking profession. She explains, "Today's fabric lines don't match when you hook it on the loom and you can't cut the cloth properly. All the cloth-making factories around here are closed now and most of that business has been outsourced to other countries. So quality fabric is more expensive and harder to get. I finally closed the shop because of fabric issues." However, for those willing to tackle these difficulties, the profession can be quite gratifying. "Explore all avenues before you venture in and develop expertise in more than one area. Ask yourself: 'What age and category am I going to cater to?' Figure out where you are going to get your machinery and fabrics and try to develop relationships with companies in your area. You have to have a passion for what you're doing. Keep abreast of new trends and be willing to diversify."

You'll have to strike a delicate balance between the fantasy that clothing can be, and the reality that the professional eye sees.

Getting Your Foot in the Door

The best way to get started in the profession is to intern or assist a designer or another seamstress/tailor. If you succeed in this role, you can either become employed with a company or build up the contacts and know-how to start your own business. Staying open to changes in the industry is also important. Take workshops or classes periodically to keep up with new equipment, fabrics, and techniques.

Biggest Challenges and Best Perks

The biggest challenge of this profession may be staying on schedule without sacrificing quality: You can expect to put in some long nights juggling several deadlines back to back. Another challenge involves being the voice of reason in your business dealings: perhaps a favorite pair of trousers can't be altered to a client's size, or the dress design they've ordered doesn't suit the fabrics they've selected. You'll have to strike a delicate balance between the fantasy that clothing can be, and the reality that the professional eye sees. Clothing can be a touchy subject in any circle.

The thrill of seeing a dress or suit that you made from zipper to hem may be one of the biggest perks of this profession. The job involves very close attention to detail and a constant awareness of your clients' wishes and budgets. Seeing your efforts come together in a finished product provides a huge sense of accomplishment. The variety of assignments and sometimes settings is another perk; you get to interact with new people and possibly travel to interesting locations on a regular basis.

Professional Profile
Avg. salary: $25,392

Varies based on skills and experience, also on whether or not you're working as an independent contractor

Jargon
Baste To hold pieces of fabric together temporarily with long loose stitches

Braid A decorative trim

Are you Interested In?
Sewing, fashion, sketching

Related College Majors
Apparel design, fiber textiles, weaving arts, fashion design

For More Information
The Home Sewing Association:
www.sewing.org

Professional Association of Custom Clothiers:
www.paccprofessionals.org

SPORTS THERAPIST

A (Relatively) Typical Day In the Life

Many people enter the field of physical therapy with dreams of zigzagging across the country on team jets and becoming the trusted confidants of celebrity athletes. However, most physical therapists—even those who specialize in sports-related injuries—have a less glamorous life and treat injuries with ice packs, electrical stimulations, and ultrasounds. The field's lasting allure comes from the challenge of rehabilitating patients whose lives have been damaged by injury and pain. On a typical day, a sports therapist might meet some patients for the first time and work on evaluating their conditions. In other cases, the patients are there for treatment, and sports therapists spend time doing anything from neuromuscular re-education to flexibility exercises to core stabilization. Common sports-related injuries include damaged rotator cuffs, torn knee ligaments, herniated disks, lumbar strain, and ankle sprains.

You'll also need to stay on top of technological advances in the field because innovative treatment techniques are developed all the time. Even NASA-developed rocket technology has been adapted to treat spinal cord and traumatic brain injuries. Old-school techniques such as performing a passive range of motion by slowly moving a hip, knee, or ankle joint around are still in effect, though.

This hands-on field may be called physical therapy, but practitioners say psychology plays a major role as well because an array of emotions—fear, anger, pity, and more—are experienced by patients. Some patients' whole identities are tied up in their athleticism, and they have a hard time coping when an injury keeps them on the sidelines. Often the physical therapist ends up supporting people in the emotional part of the recovery as well.

An Extreme Day in the Life

John Alexander, who practices at a physical therapy and sports rehabilitation center in South Carolina, says the field is mentally and physically challenging. "The most extreme day would be having more patients than time to treat them. You end up spending a very small amount of time with a lot of different patients, and you may or may not feel like you've done anything but time management. Sometimes if you have a lot of patients who need a lot of joint mobilization or soft tissue mobilizations, those can get very tiring to your hands and wrist. As a therapist you have to be aware of your own body mechanics so that you are performing treatment and mechanics carefully so that you don't put yourself in a position where you can be injured. Low back strain can occur from being in an awkward position. Transfers are another big one. If your patient is large and you're kind of small you're almost helping them pick themselves up especially if they are at a low functioning level. Mostly, it's more mentally challenging especially when you're trying to figure out why a person is experiencing the symptoms they are experiencing. Another challenge would be patient relations. A lot of time the patients don't want to be there because they've heard horror stories about physical therapy. We get called physical terrorists or they say 'I'm going to pain and torture today,' instead of PT. You have to be a good motivator. Sometimes I even feel we should go back and get a degree in psychology because you spend a lot of time one-on-one with a person. They really open up to us and let out frustrations, sadness, joys, and the whole spectrum of what they're feeling."

The physical therapist ends up supporting people in the emotional part of the recovery as well.

Prepare for Success

Before you decide to enter physical therapy school, shadow some therapists in different settings such as sports clinics, hospitals, or home health. You'll get to see the range of opportunities available within the field and see if it's something you want to pursue further. Oftentimes, people discover that the field is quite different from what they imagine. You must earn a bachelor's degree before applying to a physical therapy school. You can major in anything as an undergraduate as long as you take all of the prerequisites for a graduate physical therapy program. Schools have different entrance requirements and curriculums so you need to research your options to find the best fit and submit a strong application. Graduate physical therapy programs are offered at the master's and doctoral levels so you could earn master's of science in rehabilitation or a doctor of physical therapy degree.

Getting Your Foot in the Door

As a part of your physical therapy coursework, you'll spend several weeks working through rotations in a hospital and other therapy settings. Take advantage of this opportunity to meet working therapists who can become part of your network and offer valuable job-hunting leads and advice. Some students even win job offers as a result of their work. Also, attend career fairs where you can gain even more exposure to potential employers. The American Physical Therapy Association's website offers resources for prospective physical therapists, including details on its National Student Conclave, a career development event.

Biggest Challenges and Best Perks

Physical injuries can be devastating for athletes whose success in sports is an integral part of their identities. The therapists guiding them through the recovery process can become the target of great hostility even though they're working to improve the athlete's mobility or help them recover from a surgery. The physical demands of the job are significant as well and the therapists may need some therapy themselves after straining their backs and hurting their wrists treating patients.

Many physical therapists say the rewards far outweigh the challenges. The heartfelt thanks they receive from patients make all of the headaches and hassles worth it. The feeling you get when discharging someone who has successfully completed therapy and can do more than when they came in is unmatched, especially when the patient previously suffered chronic pain.

Professional Profile
Avg. starting salary: $48,480
Avg. salary after 5 years: $57,330
Avg. salary 10 to 15 years: $70,050

Jargon
Contusion Crushing of tissue
Reconstruction Rebuilding of a body part or joint
Strain Disruption of muscle fibers

Are you Interested In?
Sports, medicine

Related College Majors
Physical therapy, nutrition, human growth and development, psychology

For More Information
American Physical Therapy Association:
www.apta.org
National Academy of Sports Medicine:
www.nasm.org
National Rehabilitation Association:
www.nationalrehab.org

PERSONAL TRAINER/FITNESS INSTRUCTOR

A (Relatively) Typical Day In the Life

Personal trainers generally work one-on-one with clients to develop fitness regiments that match their goals. Trainers must keep their clients motivated, focused, and challenged, teaching them how to workout safely through proper use of equipment and techniques, and helping them set new goals when benchmarks are reached. Some or all of these happen during each training session. While some clients meet with their trainers several times a week, others meet only occasionally when they feel like they need a morale boost and a fitness analysis. Many trainers are also are able to suggest nutrition guidelines to clients who are focused on weight loss. The best personal trainers are equipped with in-depth knowledge of health, fitness, weight loss, and nutrition.

Fitness instructors teach group or private classes in gyms, fitness centers, health clubs, spas, or studios. With the wide assortment of classes that most gyms offer, an instructor can teach anything from traditional aerobics, to kickboxing, African dance, Pilates, spinning (high-speed stationary biking), capoeira, and even hip-hop.

A trainer's typical day consists of meeting with clients, making appointments, finding new clients, preparing for class, teaching classes, and working out. They may work with their gyms to develop new classes or may work for several gyms teaching variations of the same class. Both trainers and instructors also attend staff meetings. The work schedule in this kind of career is built around fitness classes or appointments. You may have two days off in the middle of the week but work weekends. Or you may work six or seven days a week, but less then eight hours each day.

A good trainer or instructor will have tons of energy and will be able to communicate and make a connection with a variety of different people. Additionally, they need to have a solid understanding of the human body—its muscle groups, respiratory functions, how it burns calories, how it exerts itself and then recuperates, and how it responds to cardiovascular conditioning and strength training. Trainers and instructors need to stay on top of the health and safety issues involved in what they do, in addition to learning new skills to ensure they will be able to offer clients whatever is new and hot on the gym circuit.

An Extreme Day in the Life

Andy Petranek has been a personal trainer and fitness instructor for 15 years and is the owner of the private training gym Petranek Fitness in Santa Monica, California. He specializes in teaching an athletic conditioning class called Crossfit. Petranek says he has an extreme day once or twice a week. He says, "[I am] at work by 5:30 a.m. I teach two classes back to back, one at 6:00 A.M. and one at 7:00 A.M. After that, I'll have as many as 15 clients on a really heavy day. Then, I'll teach one more class from 6:30 to 7:30 P.M. Somewhere in the day, I usually do my own workout." The toughest part is when a client gets frustrated in a class because they are unable to do something and storms out. "My job as a coach is to constantly put things in front of you that you can't do," Petranek says. "Hopefully they come back and reconfront that." Petranek says "[My] best days are when people get something they have been struggling with. Or they have a personal breakthrough in their performance. That's what makes me light up."

Trainers and instructors find it thrilling to see a transformation in their clients, both physically and mentally.

PREPARE FOR SUCCESS

Most personal trainer jobs require national certification, which can be obtained after completing a program through various organizations. The certificate is usually good for two years and can be renewed by attending continuing education classes. Some receive initial training from a career college or fitness institute, though a bachelor's degree is preferred. Popular majors for this field are exercise science, physical education, exercise physiology, sports medicine, biomechanics, or kinesiology. Additional knowledge of first aid, CPR, and nutrition makes for a top candidate.

GETTING YOUR FOOT IN THE DOOR

If you belong to a gym or fitness center, that's a good place to start. Talk to the manager about what he or she looks for in a new hire. Visit other fitness centers and ask about their preferences in a top candidate as well. You may start out teaching one class, or even assisting a teacher, or with a few friends as your first personal training clients. Many personal trainers open their own fitness centers or studios.

BIGGEST CHALLENGES AND BEST PERKS

Though most trainers and fitness instructors are energized by their profession and all its physical requirements, sore muscles and exhaustion can catch up with you. You may have a day with classes back to back and little time to eat, rest, shower, or get outside for a breath of fresh air. Clients who are in a bad mood, make excuses, or don't want to be there can put a crushing weight on your day. Clients who skip appointments are frustrating for wasting your time. For those who wish to do this full-time, it's hard to get enough work, and even if you do, the pay tends to plateau early.

You'll certainly look great and be in shape as long as you're in this career. Trainers and instructors find it thrilling to see a transformation in their clients, both physically and mentally as they reach their fitness goals. You'll meet many different people, always have a place to work out, and be around coworkers who are as fanatical about staying fit as you are. If you work at a posh gym, you may receive discounts on fitness gear or spa services.

PROFESSIONAL PROFILE
Avg. starting salary: $28,000
Avg. salary after 5 years: $36,000
Avg. salary 10 to 15 years: $50,000

JARGON
Back cycling Cutting back on the number of sets, repetitions, or amount of weight used during an exercise session

Circuit training Going quickly from one exercise apparatus to another to keep the heart rate up

Freestyle training Training all body parts in one workout

ARE YOU INTERESTED IN?
Health, fitness, nutrition, exercise

RELATED COLLEGE MAJORS
Exercise science, physical education, sports medicine, kinesiology

FOR MORE INFORMATION
National Athletic Trainers' Association:
www.nata.org

National Exercise Trainers Association:
www.ndeita.com

WIG MAKER

A (Relatively) Typical Day In the Life

Life can get downright hairy for a wig maker with six new heads to cover and a panicked Broadway star who fell asleep after the show with gum in her mouth. It can take anywhere from 15 hours to 2 weeks of patience (not to mention some very nimble fingers) to make one wig. The tools range from the exotic—hair from the tails of specially bred Chinese horses—to more commonplace items like needles and curling irons. Technique hasn't changed much from the days of colonial wig makers, and most people in the trade today have had their skills passed down from generation to generation. The hair is either synthetic, from horses, or donated by people. The most lucrative markets that a wig maker can get into are theater, film, or opera. Simple scene changes can require wigs—there's hardly enough time to create the perfect updo in the 30 seconds allotted for costume changes. With each custom order, a long process begins. Measurements must be taken from the eventual wearer to create a model head. After the head has been cast, it's covered with nylon netting and the knotting begins—hair is knotted to the netting in groups of four to five hairs at a time. An experienced wig maker can pull off about 30 of these knots a minute. After their creations are complete, wig makers who work for the theater can expect to attend technical run-throughs, which can take up to 12 hours, to watch their work in action and make sure things are exactly as the director intended. Wondering whether blondes, brunettes, or redheads have more fun? Your local wig maker can help you answer this age-old question once and for all, though it'll cost you—because of the tedious work involved, handmade custom wigs can set you back up to $2,000 each.

An Extreme Day in the Life

Growing up, Ryan Fischer was more likely to have his head stuck between the pages of a science book than under any wig he had been fashioning. Wig making wasn't his lifelong dream by any stretch of the imagination. He went to school to become a scientist, and somewhere along the line he found himself drawn to the theater. Twenty-one years later, he still remembers his first wig-making job like it was yesterday. "I had to build a custom wig for the lead soprano [in an opera]. It took me twice as long to do as [it] should have but I wanted it to be perfect. I delivered it on time and was commended for my attention to detail. It is to this day still one of my proudest jobs and one of my prettiest wigs." Since the early days, Ryan has worked on countless projects for countless heads, but it's difficult for him to pin down a single moment that outshines the rest. "I have a picture of my first wig, and there are award-winning shows from *Cats* to *Munchkin-land*, and I remember sitting down with people who have said, 'We're not going to pull this off; we don't have the budget.'" Later, he remembers those same people calling him a miracle worker. He remembers the ovations—the standing ovations—and the struggles he had to overcome to make it all possible. While these were all significant moments, Ryan finds the greatest feeling of pride in the present: "I'm still here, I'm doing it, I'm still following that dream and still making it a reality. And like so many shows, I have no budget, but I'm somehow making the whole thing look so good, so polished, so dazzling."

As a freelance artist, your next job depends on the success of the one you just finished.

Prepare for Success

An MFA in costume and makeup or theater arts will get you entry-level experience with wig making and design. The theater industry is one in which mentors are priceless, especially in a field as exclusive as wig making. Although classes in costuming and makeup offer introductory sections on the art, the only way to hone your skills is to spend day after day with an experienced craftsperson. Most wig makers also get certification in cosmetology. Knitting, sewing, or rug making are good ways to practice the skills necessary to create a top-notch wig, as the stitching involved is very similar to those used in these familiar hobbies. In addition to hair, wig makers can be responsible for creating fur or whiskers, so it helps to have a good base of reference to draw upon when asked to create the more unusual pieces.

Getting Your Foot in the Door

As with many fields in the performing arts, most positions are earned by starting at the bottom. If you want to be even eligible for an internship or assistant position, you have to have some kind of experience, usually gained from working behind the scenes on college plays or community theater. Though the competition may be small in numbers, there are only so many successful wig makers that have the skills necessary to train a novice. You're going to have to be aggressive in your attempts to get your foot in the door and set your sights on gaining an apprenticeship with one of these luminaries of the business.

Biggest Challenges and Best Perks

It can be a little unnerving to realize that thousands of people are going to see your work, but there's no better motivation to make sure not a single strand is out of place. As a freelance artist, your next job depends on the success of the one you just finished. Being successful in a narrow field (there are only three or four wig makers that supply all of Broadway) is a tribute to the perseverance and training it takes to make a living in this profession. There's interaction with people who share your creative interests—actors, directors, costumer designers—and perks like free access to shows, keeping your own hours, and seeing your name in the list of credits.

Professional Profile
Avg. salary: Varies depending on the type of wig, length of hair, and type of cap used to knot the hair. Custom-made wigs usually start at $300 to $400 each.

Jargon
Full-hand ventilation Labor-intensive wig-making process in which hair is hand tied to cap. It takes as many as 50 to 60 hours and uses as many as 4,000 hairs

Are you Interested In?
Theater, sewing, knitting, beauty, fashion

Related College Majors
Fine arts, theater, costume and makeup, cosmetology

For More Information
Hair Stylist Resource Center:
www.hair-news.com

International Academy:
www.iahd.net

Professional Beauty Association:
www.probeauty.org

THE GREAT OUTDOORS

ANIMAL CONTROL OFFICER

A (Relatively) Typical Day in the Life

"If it walks, crawls, swims, or flies we cross paths sooner or later," says animal control veteran Michael Melchionne. That's right, we're not just talking about picking up a stray poodle or helping a tabby cat find his way out of a tree. We're talking about spiders, snakes, snakehead fish, bats, deer, wolves—you name it. In fact, just look at the info offered to prospective animal control officers in Michigan and you'll find documents such as the "Ferret Health Advisory Sheet," "Salmonella in Reptiles," and the "Proper Disposal of Animal Carcasses Brochure." Basically, an animal control officer is the person called in whenever some creature, dead or alive, ends up where it shouldn't be or poses a danger to humans.

This is a job that mixes slow days with absolutely hectic ones. In a single morning, you may be called to get a bat out of a downtown delicatessen, fetch a rattlesnake from a backyard, and pick up a dog that's running scared at the edge of the interstate. The next morning, however, you may be sitting around headquarters, fielding phone calls and catching up on your municipal law reading. Municipal law? That's right. Today's animal control officer is not the dogcatcher of old, but rather an animal expert working in the fields of public service and law enforcement. For instance, animal control officers increasingly devote their time to animal cruelty complaints. The broad reach of the profession means that, on any given day, an officer could be in touch with the police department, the town clerk, the health department, and any number of other public offices.

Even if you're an animal lover, you'll need to be a people person to make it in the animal control arena. The distraught owners of a lost cat, the angry neighbors of a dog abuser, the frustrated paramedics who can't get into the house of a sick person because the pit bulls are in a frenzy (uh, see below) are among the small fraction of people an animal control officer must calm and assure. Of course, you'll also need to know your animals—what sorts of tranquilizers, traps, and treats will work best in any number of situations. As you can probably tell, there's no predicting what a day in animal control will bring—and that's exactly why animal control officers love it.

An Extreme Day in the Life

"Every time the phone rings it could be the beginning of the biggest call of your life," says Michael Melchionne, the chief animal cruelty investigator for Stafford Township in New Jersey. A 32-year veteran of animal control, he's had his fair share of adrenaline-pumping experiences. "I got called to a first aid call one time. People couldn't get into the house because of two pit bulls. The firemen had the hook and ladder set up on the second floor because they couldn't get access. I got up on the hook and ladder. The fireman, who was a friend of mine, pushed me through the window over a hot radiator; I hit the floor, and there were two pit bulls there. I started giving them direct commands while fending them off with a rabies control pole. They retreated into a back bedroom. Turns out there were three people overdosing inside. All three people were saved and the dogs were contained."

If it walks, crawls, swims, or flies we cross paths sooner or later.

PREPARE FOR SUCCESS

There's no doubt that a degree in zoology or veterinary medicine—or any animal-related science, for that matter—gives you an edge in this field but it is not a prerequisite. In fact, the best way to prepare for an animal control career (and, in many states, the required way) is to serve a sort of apprenticeship. Basically, this means spending time riding along with animal control officers, volunteering in humane societies, observing veterinarians, and sitting down with law officials to get a handle on the nuts and bolts of local ordinances and policies. It's also worth noting that a clean rap sheet is required; after all, you're joining the ranks of law enforcement. Most employers also ask you to take an extensive physical exam. So you better start eating those carrots and doing those push-ups.

GETTING YOUR FOOT IN THE DOOR

You fare better when you know more. This means that all the work you did familiarizing yourself with the laws regulating the sale of small turtles and the use of rats in research facilities and the burden of responsibility in a dog-bite situation will facilitate quick and effective decision making—particularly when you're in a high-stress situation. This also keeps you from overstepping the boundaries of the law. State and national organizations offer certification and specialized training courses—credentials that can only help when the boss is looking for someone to promote.

BIGGEST CHALLENGES AND BEST PERKS

Climbing through a second-story window while two snarling pit bulls snap at your hands and face is the sort of challenge that comes with the territory for an animal control officer. Danger aside, this job can also involve plenty of sadness. Just ask any of the many animal control volunteers who ventured to New Orleans after Hurricane Katrina: Dead and injured pets were everywhere. But it's not all somber. Animal control officers are often involved with helping animals find their way back home, saving animals from unpleasant circumstances, and transporting wild animals to more suitable environments. As a matter of fact, it's not uncommon for an animal control officer to be treated like a hero. Needless to say, you'll rarely be chained to a desk.

PROFESSIONAL PROFILE
Avg. salary: $39,000 to $51,000, annually

Salaries vary according to geographical regions and budgets. There is potential for job advancement and higher earnings in supervisory positions as chief investigators, shelter managers, or executive directors.

JARGON
At large Off the owner's premises

ARE YOU INTERESTED IN?
Animals, law enforcement, public service

RELATED COLLEGE MAJORS
Zoology, veterinary medicine

FOR MORE INFORMATION
National Animal Control Association:
www.nacanet.org/

State Animal Control Associations:
www.animalsheltering.org

The Humane Society:
www.hsus.org/

ANIMAL TRAINER

A (Relatively) Typical Day in the Life

You may remember seeing a commercial for trash bags in which an elephant triumphantly raises a heavy bag of trash to demonstrate the bag's amazing strength and flexibility. Someone had to train that elephant, since trash bags are not common in the wild grasslands of Africa. Professional animal trainers are the patient and devoted individuals responsible for every turn, trick, or stunt an animal actor performs.

Animal trainers care for their assigned animals and get them ready for roles in movies, commercials, or television shows, as well as live shows at amusement parks, Sea World, Las Vegas, and educational shows for children. Trainers are also employed in zoos, wildlife preserves, education centers, and rescue facilities. Some canine trainers work with dogs used for detective work or prepare them to work with disabled individuals. They also help pet owners properly train their dogs, cats, or other furry friends.

Because alligators, bears, and cocker spaniels don't speak English, trainers need to learn and practice modes of communication that animals understand. They need to be able to command respect from the animal while maintaining respect for the animal. Conveying what they want an animal to do and getting them to do it the same way every time can take Jedi-like mastery. A strong commitment to animals is essential for people in this profession. Good public speaking skills, showmanship, animal knowledge, the ability to improvise, and deep focus are also important. Theatrical backgrounds come in handy for trainers who are part of a show. Others are strictly behind-the-scenes players and are more like off-camera coaches who walk their animal through each scene. Some people are attracted to animal jobs as a way to avoid working with people. Be warned: Many animal jobs involve contact with the public. Even jobs in Hollywood require cooperation with directors, producers, and other actors.

Trainers need to be in good health and physically fit. Knowledge comes from observing and participating hands-on in the actual handling, training, care, and maintenance of animals. The compassionate care of real animals, exotic or domestic, is part of this career path. Some trainers work with the same animals for years—even decades—so long-term dedication comes with the territory. Be prepared to go where the jobs are because there aren't many.

An Extreme Day in the Life

Dawn Prentiss, CPDT, runs her own dog training business called Semper Fido in Brooklyn, New York. As a pet dog trainer, there are days she doesn't officially work teaching classes or consulting with clients because she deals with the day-to-day task of running a business. Saturdays and Sundays, however, tend to be her most extreme days, starting at 6:00 a.m. and ending (if she's lucky) by 6:00 or 7:00 P.M. Those days she gives private, group, and pet owner lessons almost constantly. One of her biggest hurdles of the day is the three-hour puppy obedience, adolescent obedience, and agility class. She says, "Managing a class with six dogs of different sizes and temperaments can be quite the challenge. Managing the dog owners who often don't listen is an even bigger challenge!"

A job as an animal trainer could easily vie for a spot in the top 10 list of most exciting jobs of all time.

PREPARE FOR SUCCESS

Most colleges don't offer animal training programs, but a bachelor's degree is becoming a more common prerequisite for jobs, especially those in animal management. Consider a degree in zoology, animal psychology, biological sciences, or veterinary studies. Many private companies also operate animal training schools open to people 18 years and older with strong backgrounds in the sciences, math, and English. Training schools cost thousands of dollars and cannot guarantee job placement, but participants come away having learned from pros through observation and hands-on experience. You'll need to balance a love for and dedication to the animals with the drive to work your way up in the field.

GETTING YOUR FOOT IN THE DOOR

If you have a job in mind, contact people working in your area (local zoos, Humane Society, veterinary clinic, and animal rehabilitation centers) about requirements for a position. It may be a good place to volunteer. Although volunteering often involves little direct contact with animals—you'll be cleaning, answering phones, filing papers, and running errands—it will demonstrate a serious commitment to future employers. Internships and apprenticeships are even better, though these are not handed out casually. With some experience, you may find an opening as an assistant.

BIGGEST CHALLENGES AND BEST PERKS

Professional animal training comes with a mystique that can propel those in the field to a superhero-like status. Even superheroes must contend with the job's darker side. Feeding dinner to big cats isn't as simple as opening a bag of cat chow. Be prepared to euthanize rats, rabbits, pigeons, and other small critters for your feline friends' meals. Trainers often spend considerable parts of their days cleaning up excrement, and to top it off, the pay is low. People who are new to the field may receive hourly wages instead of annual salaries. Life as a trainer carries a real risk of injury or death. Trainers also have to deal with the illness or death of the animals they train. The job can be emotional, stressful, and life-threateningly dangerous. On the flip side, a job as an animal trainer could easily vie for a spot in the top 10 list of most exciting jobs of all time. To spend your workday one-on-one with Bengal tigers, African lions, spotted leopards, grizzly bears, monkeys, camels, kangaroos, eagles, dolphins, elephants, or family pets is not only thrilling, but also an honor. It is a field many find desirable, but it takes a special person to stick with it for the long haul. Those who do stick with it would never dream of giving it up.

PROFESSIONAL PROFILE
Avg. starting salary: $15,000
Avg. salary after 5 years: $23,000
Avg. salary 10 to 15 years: $45,000

JARGON
Service Dogs Trained to pick up objects, open and close doors, and operate light switches; some service dogs even pull individuals in wheelchairs

RELATED COLLEGE MAJORS
Animal management, animal psychology, zoology, veterinary studies

FOR MORE INFORMATION
Association of Pet Dog Trainers:
www.apdt.com/

Exotic Animal Training School:
www.animalschool.net/

The Humane Society:
www.hsus.org/

COACH

A (Relatively) Typical Day in the Life

Coaches fill many roles for their players, whether they are high school teachers who coach football after class or former world-class players who began coaching after they retired. Despite the defeats, disappointments, and countless sleepless nights, there's nothing they'd rather be doing.

Coaches teach skills, proper form, techniques, and fundamentals of the game and train their athletes to perform at their best in the heat of competition. They scout and recruit players and push those players to their limits through fitness exercises and mental exercises. Coaches who manage teams also get athletes to work together and find winning team chemistry.

Coaches spend their time planning programs, watching videos, reviewing notes of previous games (or rival teams' games), managing practice sessions, running drills, and coaching games and calling plays. Boosting morale by giving pep talks, post-game talks, and celebrating victories come with the territory.

Coaching requires immense commitment to the game and to each individual player. The best coaches are also good teachers, leaders, and communicators. Their teams hold a deep respect, even reverence, for the guidance that coaches give, even when they disagree with it. While some coaches are known for their outrageous tempers, the good ones hold sportsmanship in high regard (and may be punished for their outbursts if they don't).

The specific sport and the age level of the players have a substantial impact on coaching styles and techniques. Coaching individual sports differs somewhat from coaching team sports. Many coaches stay sharp by attending conferences and conventions to meet other professionals and learn new methods of training, injury prevention, and player motivation. Coaches are often away from home for long stretches of time and need to develop routines that revolve around practice, games, and strategy sessions.

Prepare for Success

Playing a sport, and playing it well, is the most common precursor to coaching. After a successful playing streak on some level, many coaches begin their careers as assistant coaches, eventually moving on to head coach

An Extreme Day in the Life

Alex Altman took a leave of absence without pay from his job in commercial real estate to coach the boy's tennis team at Trevor Day High School in New York City. He had coached the year before but flew back across the country to coach one more season with the players, who went on to earn back-to-back New York independent school league titles. Altman's interaction with one particular blocked player encompassed the coaching experience for him: He helped the player transition from someone unable to deal with the intense pressure from team members, family, and friends and who lost matches because of that pressure, to a team player who was able to move past his block, remember how much he enjoyed the game, and feel accomplished by competing and actually winning. Altman's real reward was when "[the player] found his confidence and discovered he had it within himself to win. When it came time for the trophy ceremony at the end of the year, I could see how happy he was. And having a little part in that was my biggest thrill as a coach."

Coaching requires immense commitment to the game and **to each individual player.**

positions. Having worked for a youth league or summer camp as a coach fattens a resume too. Public school positions as head coaches and sports instructors usually call for a college degree in a major like exercise and sports science, physiology, kinesiology, nutrition and fitness, physical education, and sports medicine. Private schools may be more lenient if the applicant has good participant experience, passion, and superb knowledge of the game. First aid training is also a good idea. Expect stiff competition for entry-level positions.

Getting Your Foot in the Door

Becoming a coach at the professional level is an extremely lofty goal, especially for someone who has not played as a professional athlete. After an 18-year career as a Major League baseball player and a player in the National League, Joe Torre retired to manage the Mets before eventually serving as manager for the Yankees. That's the kind of experience we're talking about. Coaches on any level need to build strong track records and reputations as great leaders, coaches, and role models so they can move up the ranks. During the season, they need to design and perfect strategies to garner consistently dazzling results. They need to network like mad to develop relationships that may catapult them to higher positions. Specializing in one area of coaching, maintaining a winning record, recruiting high-profile athletes, and not being afraid to toot their own horns are essential for coaches who have set their sights on the big leagues.

Biggest Challenges and Best Perks

The anguish coaches feel about losing is small compared with witnessing a player's disappointment in him or herself, watching a selfish player alienate the team, or having a player suffer a major injury. Coaches need to decipher which athletes will respond to which type of coaching to perform their best. The wrong technique applied to the wrong type of player can be disastrous. Coaches' salaries lean toward the low side; long, grueling hours, emotional burnout, and little opportunity for growth are the norm. However, being able to help players achieve their best is worth all the blood, sweat, and tears. Coaches may just be one of the most admired and influential people in their players' lives, especially if those players are children. It can be extremely gratifying to run into a former player years later, and hear the telltale "Hey, Coach!" followed by the player's gratitude for making such a difference in his or her life. Off-season downtime is another bonus, and winning a few championships never hurts either.

Professional Profile
Avg. starting salary: $17,890
Avg. salary after 5 years: $27,880
Avg. salary 10 to 15 years: $42,250

Jargon
Playbook A collection of plays to be used by a team during a particular game

Are you Interested In?
Sports

Related College Majors
Sports science, physiology, kinesiology, physical education, sports medicine

For More Information
National High School Athletic Coaches Association:
www.hscoaches.org
United States Olympic Committee:
www.usoc.org

FARMER

A (Relatively) Typical Day in the Life

Few other occupations provide the variety of physical work, productivity, and intangible rewards associated with farming. Part of the high return rate of family members to the profession of farming can be attributed to an emotional attachment to the lifestyle; people who choose it often wouldn't opt to do anything else. Most farms employ fewer than 30 workers, and a sense of family pervades many of these communities. Farmers tend to specialize in one or a limited number of crops. The producer chooses his crop based on the climate, land, market, and history of growing in the region. Each crop utilizes different types of equipment, and each piece of equipment requires different maintenance and personnel decisions. Farmers make difficult decisions about how to allocate resources and deal with unanticipated problems, such as insect infestation, drought, and fire. Over the course of any year, regular equipment and land maintenance requirements must be made. Self-motivation is a must because those farmers who don't take advantage of downtime to take care of long-term projects can find themselves relying on unreliable machinery or storage facilities. Farmers also arrange for the storage, transportation, purchase, and sale of produced items and negotiate and coordinate all agreements relating to them.

Prepare for Success

For some people, owning or running a farm is a childhood dream, fostered in their high school Future Farmers of America organization or their neighborhood 4-H youth educational programs. For many, farming is the family business. Operating larger, less-centralized farms, however, requires more study. It is recommended (and

An Extreme Day in the Life

Though farming can be an onerous profession, the job definitely provides its share of unpredictable moments. Farmer Shanti Nagel says, "One morning I was woken up before sunrise with cries that the cows were gone! We all hauled out of bed, pulled on all the clothes we could find and made our way to the cow barn. The search began, looking down to see where the hoof prints led. We followed them to the back of the barn where a board had been forced loose. We kept following the trail of prints, manure, and warm cattle scent out through the back of the farm and down the highway. Their trail crossed over the highway into the local golf course! The cow hoofs had done a terrible number on the baby green grass, tearing a 10-foot path. Still we saw no cows. The path was easy to follow with all the destroyed grass. We jogged the entire golf course length and at the far end of it, perhaps over a mile in, we finally caught sight of the herd. They had discovered that they very much enjoyed the new, well-tended golf course grass. I guess it beats their supply of winter straw back in the barn." After finally locating the missing cows, the process of getting them back to the barn was another saga. "One person in the front called out to them and the rest of us flanked them from behind. With sticks waving in the air we kept them moving at a good pace, running to catch the few that tried to make a break for it. Crossing back over the highway with 30 cows was an exciting moment. Stopping traffic, moving them from behind, and making sure we didn't lose any was teamwork at its best. After hours of this we finally got them all safely back into the barn. We fixed the loose board and still it wasn't even time for breakfast!"

[Farmers have] an emotional attachment to the lifestyle; people who choose it often wouldn't opt to do anything else. "

sometimes required) that people who want to run their own farms attend a two- or four-year agricultural college located in the state in which they want to work. All states have land-grant colleges with agricultural programs whose course catalogs include dairy science, farm economics, horticulture, crop science, and animal science.

GETTING YOUR FOOT IN THE DOOR

The beginning farmer is responsible for crop tilling, fertilizing, composting, and harvesting. Many take classes at local agricultural colleges or rural community colleges with agricultural programs or courses sponsored by large farming concerns, to gain increased responsibility on the job. Some farmers choose to gain certification as an Accredited Farm Manager (AFM) through the American Society of Farm Managers and Rural Appraisers, although these certifications are more encouraged than required. Work is rigorous and challenging and requires a variety of managerial, scientific, and practical skills.

BIGGEST CHALLENGES AND BEST PERKS

Even with modern advances in farming technology, the work can be grueling and may require critical decision-making skills and many long, thankless hours. Long-term planning of crop yields and profits is extremely difficult, as production and income are determined by a combination of weather, disease, price fluctuation, and domestic and foreign subsidy, and tariff policy. Farmers have a higher-than-average level of daily anxiety; the physical hazard is the worst—farming ranks among the most dangerous professions.

Most farmers enjoy what they do and certainly enjoy what they produce. Farmers who have taken the requisite courses, shown ability in managing other workers, and demonstrated ambition and energy will often purchase their own land, using their successful experience as an asset to secure financing. Individuals who have found areas of specialization—such as harvesting, storage management, or soil analysis—continue their education through conferences and conventions and see commensurate increases in pay.

PROFESSIONAL PROFILE
Avg. starting salary: $12,296
Avg. salary 5 years: $30,157
Avg. salary 10 to 15 years: $42,100

JARGON
Reaper Plough that is pushed to cut grain

Cultivator Device that mixes up soil and weeds mechanically

Thresher Device that separates seeds and chaff

ARE YOU INTERESTED IN?
Agriculture, horticulture

RELATED COLLEGE MAJORS
Agricultural business and management, agricultural mechanization, agricultural technology management, agriculture, agronomy and crop science, feed science, grain science, livestock management, soil science

FOR MORE INFORMATION
American Society of Farm Managers and Rural Appraisers:
www.asfmra.org

American Dairy Science Association:
www.adsa.org

American Farm Bureau:
www.fb.com

FISHERMAN

A (Relatively) Typical Day in the Life

The world of commercial fishing bears no resemblance to the leisure fishing depicted in beer commercials, where guys lounge around on docks waiting for something to bite. The hours are longer, the physical demands greater, and the stakes much higher.

On a typical day, your boat might drag a heavy frame with a dredge or mesh bag attached across the seafloor to catch scallops, clams, oysters, and other shellfish. Wire or wood cage-like traps can also be used to catch bottom dwellers such as lobsters, crabs, and shrimp. If you're a hook-and-line fisherman, you might use a rod, fishing line, and hooks with lures or bait attached. Then you might help sort fish species on the deck, pack fish in ice, or cut a shellfish's meat out of the shell. You might also dress fish, which is slicing them open, bleeding them out, cutting out the entrails, and washing them.

The days are long. Day boat fishermen may go into the ocean at 8:00 A.M., stay there for 18 to 20 hours, sleep for a few hours, and get up to do it all over again. It's not unusual to work 20 consecutive days before getting a day off. Trip boat fishermen may be offshore for 2 to 14 days, working virtually around the clock. Owners hire crews for a full season or for another contracted period of time; you are expected to stand and move heavy objects for the duration of your shift. All crew members are expected to pull their weight, abide by safety rules, and stay positive despite weather and other adverse conditions. Plus, you won't have much privacy. Crews eat, sleep, and work in very close proximity. Toilets, when available, are often partially exposed. Some vessels do have private showers and toilets.

An Extreme Day in the Life

Tom Rudolph has spent many intense days on the water as a crew member of fishing boats in New England and now serves as the research director of the Cape Cod Commercial Hook Fishermen's Association. He's learned the ins and outs of one of the most physically demanding jobs around. "I've heard many captains express frustration with a new crew member who doesn't get that fishing is more than a job. It's a lifestyle choice. Captains are extremely hard working, very skilled, and very individualistic. They make hay while the sun shines. When the fishing is good, they will deprive themselves of everything from sleep to time with family, and that's basically the way it has to be. You catch up on your rest and take care of personal business when it's windy or when the fishing dries up. If you want to be successful, you can't walk away from good fishing."

Tom says that many people are attracted to the extremely hard physical labor of commercial fishing and the challenge of working on a moving platform. "Fishing isn't regulated in the way that many fields are. There's no one saying you get a break every eight hours. Sometimes you can't even really find a few minutes to take a drink of water, especially when you're new to the business and you're not very fast. Then you have to push it that much harder and you don't get the work done fast enough to give yourself a break. Fishing is all about efficiency and you don't learn the shortcuts until you've been at it for a while. An experienced fisherman only has to move something once whereas an inexperienced person will move it three times. Working on boats is not for everybody."

Fishing is more than a job. It's a lifestyle choice.

Prepare for Success

For every story of commercial fishing success, there are several more tales ending in poverty, injury, and even death. Just to get started crew members may need to spend up to $500 on special apparel like all-weather gear, rubber boots, gloves, wrist covers, and sleeping bags to help you get the job done more comfortably. You'll also need to do some investigation to find out which captains pay well, treat their crews with respect, and are attentive to safety measures. Ask about the boat's safety procedures and equipment because many fishermen have died of treatable injuries because their boats weren't properly equipped and the injury occurred far away from hospitals. Get a signed contract or work agreement that clearly outlines your job responsibilities and compensation before accepting a position. Crews generally are paid a daily rate or earn a percentage of the boat's catch.

Getting Your Foot in the Door

Every fishery is different, but knowing someone within the organization who can give you a recommendation is always a big help. Some aspiring fishermen have gotten gigs by going down to the docks day after day and making their faces known to the crews and captains. They got their first cracks, did well, and were hired again. Some fisheries have a more rigid process akin to apprenticeships. Many of the United State's healthiest fisheries are in Alaska and people step up to boat jobs after proving themselves onshore in fish processing plants.

Biggest Challenges and Best Perks

Fishermen say they love the opportunity to work with their hands and spend time on the ocean. The money's not bad either. Crew members typically earn between $30,000 and $60,000 annually. Owner-operator captains frequently rake in between $100,000 and $200,000 per year. Both have the satisfaction of knowing that they earned every penny while testing their mettle against nature.

Commercial fishing is also extremely dangerous. The Bureau of Labor Statistics' annual census of workplace fatalities reported that 48 fishermen died on the job in 2005 and that the profession's fatality rate was 30 times higher than the rate of the average worker. Economic pressures and fatigue often worsen safety conditions. Owner-operators who are anxious about their abilities to catch enough fish to cover equipment, crew wages, and bills may take greater risks.

Professional Profile

CREW MEMBER
Avg. salary: $30,000 to $60,000, commensurate with experience

OWNER-OPERATOR CAPTAINS
Avg. salary: $100,000 to $200,000, depending on the size of the operation

Jargon
Long lining In commercial fishing, an extremely long line has hundreds or even thousands of baited hooks

Trawling Method of fishing that involves actively pulling a fishing net through the water along the sea bottom behind one or more boats

Are you Interested In?
Fishing, sailing

Related College Majors
Aquaculture, aquatic biology, marine biology, marine science

For More Information
National Fisherman:
www.nationalfisherman.com

The Fisherman's News:
www.fishermensnews.com

Maritime Fisherman's Union:
www.mfu-upm.com

FORESTER

A (Relatively) Typical Day in the Life

If you have visions of foresters strolling through the woods, talking to animals, and hugging trees, you've got another thing coming. This profession is engaged in the more arduous pursuit of manipulating natural processes to create favorable conditions for making consumer products. In other instances, they're sending dying trees to the chopping block and spraying insecticide on healthy ones to stave off impending attack by bark-burrowing beetles. There are industrial foresters, wood procurement foresters, extension foresters, research foresters, and consulting foresters. They're all charged with different tasks related to the management of the roughly 747 million acres of U.S. forestland.

On a typical day, a consulting forester might advise several private landowners on questions about timberland and wildlife. He might go on a timber cruise and take a systematic inventory of the timber by species and product type, estimating volume and grade of timber to arrive at a monetary value. A consulting forester could also write up a risk analysis plan that describes timberland dangers such as hurricanes, fires, and insects and propose measures to reduce the hazards. You also might find yourself counting stumps as a part of an investigation of a timber trespass situation or conducting an estate appraisal to uncover the tax implications of a client's death.

An industrial forester might meet with several logging contractors in a day and discuss what's happening at the sites, make sure the right tree is cut into the right kind of product, and check that certain species are being sorted and piled for particular mills. They may also ensure that best practices are followed to preserve the soil and water conditions. Later in

An Extreme Day in the Life

Eddie Drayton has held field, management, and consulting positions in the forestry business for nearly 40 years. He's in partial retirement now but is still drawn to the natural magnificence of the outdoors. "One of the more pleasing aspects of the job is just walking in a beautiful stand of trees—the majesty of the trees, serenity of the surroundings, listening to the wood peckers, turkeys, coyotes, and hawks. Or rounding a curve in a road and seeing a beautiful doe deer with a couple of fawns or a majestic buck with a big rack of antlers or a flock of turkeys feeding in a patch of grass."

But on other occasions the danger of this profession stands out in Eddie's mind. "Some of the scarier aspects are almost stepping on a cane brake rattle snake. Almost equally as bad is stirring up a yellow jacket nest and getting stung several times. Occasionally as I am waiting in a real wet marshy area, I hear an alligator make a sound then pop up out of the water. There is some danger working in these areas, but not as much as people would think. Animals, especially snakes, don't want to bother or be bothered. They're not just waiting to strike and put their poisonous venom in you."

Supervising logging operation is another trying aspect of the job. "In a 39-year career, I have experienced three people who were killed in logging operations. The most dangerous part is having a limb fall out of a tree. A jagged limb falling 50 or 60 feet can be like a missile. One of the jobs of the forester is to make sure the logging operation is operating safely—checking for safety equipment and following safety procedures. That is the most tragic part of working in forestry—seeing someone killed or maimed in a logging operation."

A major job benefit is the satisfaction of knowing that your work is environmentally sound.

the day he might switch gears and go on a reconnaissance mission of the company's land looking for insect damage, beaver damage, wind damage, or disease.

PREPARE FOR SUCCESS

Foresters must obtain a four-year degree from an accredited forestry school where they learn about plant physiology, tree species, forest economics, market forces, agronomy, and biology. Mathematics is another key part of forestry education because the profession requires use of complex formulas to measure volumes of trees in the woods. Even judging wood quality requires a combination of physiology, entomology, and mathematics skills. Additionally, foresters need engineering skills to build roads and bridges and understand boundary line surveys. Experienced foresters say English skills also are valuable because you need to communicate your findings clearly to colleagues and clients. However, there's no replacement for real-life experience when you're forced to improvise and respond in real time to environmental challenges. Practical experience through internships or summer jobs can really set aspiring foresters apart from the pack.

GETTING YOUR FOOT IN THE DOOR

The Society of American Foresters is a spectacular resource for would-be foresters. The 100-year-old organization's online career center includes internship and job listings. What's more, the site features a job seeker tool kit that includes cover letter, resume, interviewing, salary negotiation, and company research advice. Student members of the organization can join work groups on topics that include fire management, wilderness management, and soil conservation so they can learn more about the field. Aspiring foresters also should check campus career fairs for companies and government agencies that might employ foresters.

BIGGEST CHALLENGES AND BEST PERKS

Foresters spend most of their workday outdoors, which many describe as a challenge and a perk. Sometimes they have to walk long distances through densely wooded areas and contend with insects, animals, heat, humidity, bad weather and other potential hazards. However, foresters speak of the joy that comes from seeing life grow and being out in the forest with the wildlife.

A major job benefit is the satisfaction of knowing that your work is environmentally sound. New trees are planted even as forests are thinned to produce consumer products. You're helping to boost the economy and quality of life through the production of boxes, toilet paper, newsprint, and more. At the same time, the forests you tend are pumping out oxygen, recycling water, consuming carbon dioxide, and providing wildlife habitats.

PROFESSIONAL PROFILE
Avg. salary: $56,146

JARGON
Controlled burn A fire set by foresters to stimulate certain areas of a forest and jump-start the growth of certain trees, such as sequoias, that need fire to break down the seed coat

ARE YOU INTERESTED IN?
Nature, trees and wildlife conservation

RELATED COLLEGE MAJORS
Forestry, plant physiology, agronomy, biology, environmental science

FOR MORE INFORMATION
The Society of American Foresters:
www.safnet.org

Global Association of Online Foresters:
www.foresters.org

HORSEBACK RIDING INSTRUCTOR

A (Relatively) Typical Day in the Life

When you hear the words "horse," "stable," and "mud," do you immediately start thinking about your future in the professional world? If so, then the diagnosis is official: You're suffering from Gotta-Be-a-Horseback-Riding-Instructor syndrome (also known as Equinitis). You need to contact the owner of a private stable, the operator of a summer camp, the manager of an equestrian school, or the chair of a university's equine studies department as soon as possible.

The duties of a horseback riding instructor can include developing and implementing training programs, offering on-site demonstrations, preparing safety programs, cleaning stables, tending to the horses, and, of course, conducting practice sessions for everyone from the novice to the experienced rider. Quite often, instructors work for recreational facilities, offering brief lessons to customers before leading them on hour-long—or sometimes day-long—treks through the forest or countryside. However, there are many types of work in this field. For instance, some instructors serve as trainers for professional or competitive riders, helping these riders advance their technique, adjust after physical rehabilitation, or prepare for the challenges of a specific event. Other instructors place the bulk of their focus on training the horses.

If you're considering a career in horseback riding instruction, you're probably already aware of the fact that it is not always a glamorous job. Sure, leading a group of four freshly trained riders along a creek bed on a breezy, late-summer day sounds sweet, but your days will also be spent cleaning up after horses and slogging through mud. Your chores might also have you working indoors or (more likely) outdoors, rain or shine, early in the morning or well into the evening, and very often on weekends. However all the rough conditions are worth it because you get to care for horses, ride horses, and teach others to ride as well.

Prepare for Success

In this line of work, there's simply no substitute for hands-on experience—and lots of it. This means spending time at stables, in saddles, and anywhere else that you're likely to get exposure to horses. If you can, pick up

An Extreme Day in the Life

Kim Kennedy, a 30-year industry veteran, is owner, trainer, and instructor at central Illinois's Topline Farm. She says, "Each year in early winter I body clip all of my horses. This is a tedious job. One year, when I had about 15 horses to clip, I found myself getting more creative with each horse, so that instead of clipping their entire body down to the same length, I sheared patterns into their coats. I had a very nice black horse named Rockford and when it came time to clip him I did so in a striped zebra pattern. The contrast was obvious and I thought it cute—until, at the last minute, the horse that I was planning to take and ride in a clinic with one of our Olympic riders became lame and Rockford was the logical replacement. I was so afraid of his freakish appearance—as I now saw it—and wasn't prepared for everyone to have a good sense of humor and find him darling. In the end, though, I was spared the embarrassment. I actually became popular."

Let's be honest—this job can have its grimy moments.

seasonal work at summer camps or parks that offer horseback riding adventures. Even if you spend the bulk of your time with a bucket (instead of the reins) in hand, you'll be building your pool of experience. Some schools offer equestrian clubs (or even an equine studies major); if your school happens to be one of them, signing up is a no-brainer. If not, check around the campus and local community for extracurricular or volunteer opportunities that'll help you build the skills you hope, one day, to use to pay the bills. Many instructors are willing to host apprentices—all you have to do is ask.

Getting Your Foot in the Door

To increase the chances of vocational mobility, instructors can earn certification from professional organizations such as the American Riding Instructor Certification Program (ARICP) offered by the American Riding Instructors Association. The ARICP includes written and oral exams and, for upper-level qualifications, submission of a video that demonstrates your abilities. Moreover, through the ARICP, an instructor can become certified in 14 specialty areas, such as dressage, side-saddle, and reining. To broaden your marketability, diversify the range of riding styles you're able to teach. Therefore, if trail riding is your forte, devote some time to bulking up your knowledge of show and competition riding. At the professional level, this is an increasingly competitive industry. The more you can do, the better you'll fare.

Biggest Challenges and Best Perks

Biggest challenge? Convincing yourself that this really is your dream job on those chilly, rainy, early mornings when you're working hard in the stables. Let's be honest—this job can have its grimy moments. If you don't like mud under your fingernails, then you won't like working as a horseback riding instructor. If you don't like self-motivation, you'll have trouble too. To make a career of it, many instructors are self-employed, which requires building and replenishing client lists, promoting the business, and keeping up with advancements in the field. It's a lot of work. But the payoff is huge: You get to live a life devoted to horses and to teaching others an appreciation of horses. If you're a person with a special connection with animals—with horses in particular—there's most likely no better way for you to make a living.

PROFESSIONAL PROFILE
Avg. salary: $20 to $250 an hour, depending on the services offered

JARGON
Hot A horse that becomes overly excited

Transition The act of changing from one pace to another.

ARE YOU INTERESTED IN?
Horses

RELATED COLLEGE MAJORS
Equine studies, zoology

FOR MORE INFORMATION
American Riding Instructors Association:
www.equisearch.com

Horse Illustrated:
www.horseillustrated.com

LANDSCAPE ARCHITECT

A (Relatively) Typical Day in the Life

If you are thinking about becoming a landscape architect, you should have an appreciation for nature, a creative flair, and a passion for working with your hands. You should also have strong writing and researching skills and an affinity for engineering and environmental sciences. All of these skills will be useful for mastering the art and science of the analysis, planning, design, management, preservation, and rehabilitation of land. Landscape architects apply their skills to site planning, garden design, environmental restoration, town and urban planning, park and recreation planning, regional planning, and even historic preservation.

The growing popularity of this profession is understandable. Where else could consecutive job assignments find you planning a site for corporate office buildings, managing a large wilderness area, and creating public parks that won't interfere with the natural environment? A landscape architect must work with all the other professionals involved in a project—architects, engineers, and construction contractors, for example—to make sure their design concepts will work with the actual construction. Surveys of the land at the site itself must often be made, taking into consideration complex factors such as drainage, slope of the land, and even how sunlight falls on the site. Once this is done, landscape architects spend the remainder of the project in the office, preparing presentations for clients that include cost estimates, sketches, and models. After a project is approved, landscape architects prepare even more detailed working drawings and outline explicitly the methods of construction and lists of construction materials. Some landscape architects even supervise the installation of their designs, although this is often left to a developer or separate contractor.

An Extreme Day in the Life

For Mary Palmer Dargan, life as a landscape architect frequently unfurls at a frenetic, bustling pace. CFO of a successful firm, Mary is involved in numerous projects that require her to shuttle back and forth between client sites. While her days might be packed, they are never monotonous. When we spoke with her, she was recovering from a particularly hectic workday that involved a 14.5-hour photo shoot for *Southern Accents* magazine. The day began with a consultation between the customers, the builder, and Mary. She says, "I visited the property, which was a prime site near two golf courses. We had a great jam session with little sketches of how to park the cars. The wife and husband were initially not on the same page but eventually worked things out. I then showed them some photos of step ramps and pretty steps of stone. We then agreed to draw up plans and import color photos to create a contractor packet." She then had to speed off to Balsam Mountain Preserve to solve the quandary of where to stockpile a large amount of soil from footings. By the time she was able to return to her office, her in-box had been deluged with 125 e-mails. Her schedule is unrelenting. She adds, "Tomorrow I'm meeting at the site of the future Cashiers Park with Commissioner Burrell and Commissioner-elect Mark Jones. I was volunteered to coordinate the park. We are in a hanging valley with a rising water table and want to solve the problem now before people's septic tanks start to rise out of the ground."

Job opportunities will be best for landscape architects who develop strong technical and computer skills.

Prepare for Success

It is a long road to becoming a licensed and professional landscape architect. Entrance into the profession requires a bachelor's or master's degree in landscape architecture, training, licensure (in all but five states), and specialized skills. During and after school, prospective landscape architects serve as interns to professionals in the field for a period of at least two years. Finally, they will have to pass the LARE (Landscape Architect Registration Examination) to obtain their licenses to practice landscape architecture as certified professionals. However, if they choose to take jobs with the government, the process can be somewhat shorter; the federal government doesn't require its landscape architects to be licensed.

Getting Your Foot in the Door

An ever-growing number of landscape architects are using computer-aided design (CAD) systems to assist them with presentations. Proficiency with this technology is becoming a requirement in the field. Larger-scale projects are often planned using geographic information systems technologies and computer-mapping systems. The use of computer-assisted design in the profession will continue to increase and job opportunities will be best for landscape architects who develop strong technical and computer skills. Knowledge of environmental issues, codes, and regulations will also give landscape architects an edge in the marketplace. Continued and growing concern for the environment should increase the demand for landscape architects, as the need to design environmentally sound development projects becomes even more pressing.

Biggest Challenges and Best Perks

The biggest challenge of becoming a landscape architect is the amount of time it takes to actually start practicing. The bachelor's degree in landscape architecture takes between four and five years to complete; a master's can take two to three years. This is followed by years spent interning under the guidance of a licensed landscape architect and studying for the licensing exams. Landscape architects who have lasted this long without switching career tracks should be enjoying the privileges of their experience. It is not unlikely to be an associate at a firm, and the more ambitious individuals may possibly have achieved the title of partner. Whether associate or partner, they are seeing an income that is at the top range of the profession. Landscape architects with 10 years under their belts and a talent for small business management often open their own firms.

PARK RANGER

A (Relatively) Typical Day in the Life

If you love the beauty of misty mornings outlined by hazy sunshine and the smell of dew and new beginnings, then a park ranger's life might be ideal for you. With more than 76 million acres of national parks in its care, the United States National Park Service and the park rangers it employs educate and ensure the safety of the millions of visitors who hike, climb, ski, boat, fish, and explore these natural resources.

The primary responsibility of the park ranger is ensuring safety. Rangers must strictly enforce outdoor safety codes and ensure the compliance of campers, hikers, and picnickers. Seemingly small details such as accurately completing registration forms at park offices become crucial links should a search-and-rescue mission become necessary. Park rangers are trained in first aid and rescue operations and are alert at all times to changing weather conditions, the progress and safe return of hiking or climbing groups, the condition of trails, the movement of wildlife, wind gusts, and forest fires. Besides the daily activities of communicating with visitors, answering questions, providing guided tours, rescuing park users who might have strayed too far, enforcing laws, and directing traffic, park rangers are often called upon to be conservationists, ecologists, environmentalists, and even botanists. Park rangers protect park's natural resources from vandals who destroy park property. Should a forest fire start, rangers may also assume the roles of firefighters.

Park rangers are empowered to arrest and forcibly evict those individuals who violate park laws. If you shrink from confrontation and lack the confidence and authority of a strong leader, then you may want to consider a different profession. Park rangers must be flexible enough to wear many hats in the execution of their duties. Strong people skills, the ability to work under pressure, in groups or alone, sometimes for extraordinarily long hours, and the patience of Job are the hallmarks of a fine park ranger.

An Extreme Day in the Life

In an August 2005 interview on Grist.org—a website for environmental news and commentary—Jordan Fisher Smith weighs in on his experiences working as a park ranger at American River Park, located in California's Auburn State Recreation area:

"I didn't know how close I would be to getting myself killed! When I got to this place, it looked so forlorn and hopeless. After I'd driven around for a week with the rangers, I wanted to leave so fast that I planned to transfer as soon as my year was up. Instead, I stayed for the rest of the time I was a ranger. The experience put to the test everything I believed as a ranger, and as time went on and I kept staying, I think I came to understand that if I couldn't love this place, what good was it to love a place that was supposedly perfect? This was the place that put my whole land ethic to the test, my whole idea of being a ranger. It was like working with the homeless or drug addicts or trying to rehabilitate juvenile offenders, or working with the aged. If you are caring for someone in a hospice situation, what is that about? It is an act of faith to invest yourself in something that does not promise to give you rewards. That was the great learning for me, and in fact it has given me rewards. My whole life is about this place."

Source: http://www.grist.org/advice/books/2005/03/23/dalton-noir/

Park rangers are empowered to arrest and forcibly evict those individuals who violate park laws.

PREPARE FOR SUCCESS

A college degree and/or the right combination of education and experience in park recreation and management will possibly get you into this profession. Job openings are few, and competition is fierce, so college credits in forestry, geology, botany, conservation, wildlife management, and other relevant subjects will go a long way in preparing you for a career that offers a multitude of possibilities. In lieu of a college education, competitive candidates may alternatively have at least three years of experience in parks and conservation and demonstrate an overall understanding of park work. A working knowledge of law enforcement, management, and communication skills also enhances one's prospects. Higher-level management positions may require graduate degrees.

GETTING YOUR FOOT IN THE DOOR

Part-time or seasonal work at national or state parks is an important stepping-stone to an entry-level park ranger position. Seasonal workers perform jobs such as manning information desks, trash collection, fire services, trail maintenance, law enforcement, and other unskilled tasks that are the core of the park ranger's life. Perform these well and you may make it into an entry-level position in the big league. A vast majority of high-level park rangers start out as entry-level drones. Thus the trail to promotion and high executive office starts with successful and thorough completion of every step. A keen grasp of the overall mechanics of the business can make you a sharper, more competent administrator. Promotions occur largely from within the ranks; salary is commensurate with responsibility. But a virtual lack of new job openings coupled with state and federal budget cuts mean that job seekers will have to look for work outside of the federally funded National Park Service, in other federal land and resource management agencies, as well as in state and local agencies.

BIGGEST CHALLENGES AND BEST PERKS

Ironically, one of the biggest challenges park rangers face is the actual task of finding a job. This not an industry prone to growth spurts and competition for coveted positions remains fierce. Those who do obtain employment may find the job isolating at times and will surely find themselves working in perilous conditions at some point. However, it is not surprising that job satisfaction is fairly high. After all, rangers do get to spend their time in some of the most beautiful settings the country has to offer. Furthermore, rangers have the added advantage of experiencing an amalgam of careers, from botanist and conservationist to tour guide and law enforcement. Perhaps best of all, they act as gate keepers to our natural treasures, helping visitors enjoy and gain respect for the outdoors.

PROFESSIONAL PROFILE
Avg. starting salary: $29,715

Avg. salary after 5 years: $36,330

Avg. salary 10 to 15 years: $56,890

JARGON
Wilderness First Aid (WFA) First aid plus some nursing, so as to be able to care for grave wounds or animal bites

ARE YOU INTERESTED IN?
Ecology, botany, nature, tourism

RELATED COLLEGE MAJORS
Geology, natural resources conservation, wildlife management, biology

FOR MORE INFORMATION
National Association of State Park Directors:
www.naspd.org

The Park Law Enforcement Association:
www.parkranger.com

SKI/SNOWBOARD INSTRUCTOR

A (Relatively) Typical Day in the Life

People who opt for a career in ski/snowboard instruction tend to be people who want to spend as much time as possible skiing and/or snowboarding; the instruction part is simply what gives them the location, freedom, and free lift passes to make that happen. Before skiers or snowboarders can even think about becoming instructors, they need to devote many hours over the period of many years to honing their skills in the snow. This is why most instructors will tell you that they've had skis strapped to their feet their entire lives.

Some instructors specialize in skiing while others go for snowboarding. You have cross-country skiing, downhill skiing, slalom skiing, slope snowboarding, and freestyle snowboarding, among other styles. Your customers may range from young snowboarders to old skiers and from beginners just learning to make turns to experts looking to perfect their technique. Some ski/snowboard instructors only train aspiring ski/snowboard instructors.

Instructing other people in the art of skiing and snowboarding requires more than just skill; you also need to know how to teach. This means that you have to get back to the basics. Next time you're on the slopes, imagine how you'd explain the fundamental movements required to make short turns. Do you have the patience to work with that kid who, for the thirteenth straight time, has fallen on his butt about four feet into a run on a gentle slope? Your days will be spent working with people who are dishing out a lot of money for your attention. You'll need to know your gear and equipment too, as your recommendations will be in high demand. People skills are critical.

As you might expect, ski and snowboard instruction is often seasonal work—unless, that is, you make it to the big time, and a company is willing to cart you back and forth between places like Colorado and New Zealand so you can catch each season. In some cases, instructors find off-season work in a resort or restaurant affiliated with the mountain where they give lessons. In other cases, they find alternative gigs in town or go elsewhere to take up seasonal work in some other field. For this reason, there can be a certain degree of instability associated with the life of an instructor. During those six months every year when they're practically living on the slopes, however, instructors are pretty stoked.

An Extreme Day in the Life

Dean Hunter, a New Zealand native, is cofounder of the Rookie Academy, which offers instructors-to-be top-notch "courses that ensure a complete range of technical and teaching skills." Working at the academy's twin headquarters in Wanaka, New Zealand, and Keystone, Colorado, he's experienced extreme conditions on some of the world's most revered mountains. Here's what he has to say about surviving an avalanche: "When an avalanche goes above you, the sound of it freezes you. Eerie, man—crack, vaump. Everything goes like quicksand and you try to make it to a safe point if you're lucky. If not, it swallows you up. It's just a blur. Life slows down. You try to get rid of your gear and swim to stay on top. Then it stops. All goes quiet. You are totally disoriented. If you're lucky, you have been pushed to the top and something is sticking out. Or you're buried and trying not to panic—trying to control your breathing, so you can live longer. Time goes so, so slow. Waiting. Waiting to be rescued from your snow coffin!"

During those six months every year when they're practically living on the slopes, instructors are pretty stoked.

PREPARE FOR SUCCESS

Good news: The best way to prepare for a career in ski or snowboard instruction is to spend every spare minute skiing or snowboarding. Bad news: You either need to find a second job quick or get down on your knees and beg your parents for a season pass to the nearest slope because these are not cheap extracurricular activities. If you haven't already, seek out a listing of student organizations at your college or community programs in your area; you might find discounted opportunities (and easy transportation) that will allow you to get in some good hours on the slopes.

GETTING YOUR FOOT IN THE DOOR

Many U.S. ski schools require their instructors to become certified by one of two professional organizations: the Professional Ski Instructors Association (PSIA) or the American Association of Snowboard Instructors (AASI). Both of these organizations certify training in safety, equipment, and snow sport pedagogy. To earn certification, be prepared to complete clinics and take a written exam. You also can't be certified until you've landed a job as an instructor. You begin with level-one certification and over the course of the years you work up to level three. Some schools for instructors allow you to pick up international certifications. This, of course, might open doors for foreign adventures in the future. Be aware, though, that membership in these organizations will require paying annual dues.

BIGGEST CHALLENGES AND BEST PERKS

In your early days as an instructor, you may need to be willing to crash in a two-bedroom cabin with twelve other people, drink watered-down beer, eat rice and beans for dinner, and find something else to do with yourself during the off-season. This might not be so bad when you're young and spry, but as you get older you may pine for something a little more fixed, or at least a little more private.

It's not unheard of to make a decent living off of ski instructing, though. New schools continue to pop up worldwide, which means that with the right certifications, pros could be busy for much of the year. Of course, this translates into a ton of skiing or snowboarding, which is exactly why instructors get into this business in the first place. By far, the biggest perk is waking up to fresh snow and knowing that, whether for pay or play, you'll be spending all day on the slopes.

VETERINARIAN

A (Relatively) Typical Day in the Life

Veterinarians provide medical services for animals. They also give advice to pet owners about the care and breeding of their pets. What many people don't consider is that veterinarians also protect humans from diseases that animals carry. Most veterinarians treat sick pets and provide routine checkups and shots for pets in private offices. Veterinarians must be tuned in to an animal's discomfort. They must be able to calm and reassure frightened animals. Since animals cannot communicate their symptoms, veterinarians must depend on their own and the owners' observations to make their diagnoses. Vets in private practice have to handle the business end of the practice, including scheduling appointments, sending specimens to labs, and taking payments from pet owners. Some veterinarians work with large animals, such as cattle, racehorses, or zoo animals. These doctors often spend a substantial amount of time on the road commuting to ranches and farms. They also work outdoors in all types of weather conditions. More frequently, however, they work in laboratory conditions very much like those of any hospital. Some vets work in the food industry, for the government, or both. They inspect meatpacking plants and check the livestock for disease. Occasionally, they perform autopsies on dead animals to determine what caused their death and how to prevent the problem from spreading to or afflicting other animals. Some vets research what diseases animals are susceptible to, and others explore what medicines can treat them.

An Extreme Day in the Life

Behind the scenes at a veterinarian's office, the animals sometimes run the show. "I remember when a local breeder started bringing all her dogs in to the practice," said Dr. Faye Smith, a small-town vet for more than 20 years. "Problem is, she bred mastiffs, giant 150-pound dogs, and we'd have 3 or 4 of them in the back at a time." One dog in particular, Napoleon, spent so much time in the office that he learned how to open the kennel doors. "The first time I walked back there and was greeted by this monster of a dog roaming the boarding area, I thought I was never going to be able to get him back where he belonged." Luckily, Napoleon was a gentle giant and happily settled back down. When an animal is in pain, however, even the mildest personalities can become extremely dangerous. "We were getting ready to lock the doors when an emergency case came in—a little Jack Russell that had been hit by a car," Dr. Smith remembers. "He was in shock and in pain, and we had to give him the thickest towel we had to bite down on or he would have ripped us to shreds." Later, after X-rays and some time to recover, the dog was "as sweet as ever." It's a rewarding profession, and the bond between pet and owner is so strong that people will go to great lengths to keep their animals healthy. "We've had diabetic animals getting insulin shots daily, just like one of us; owners [who] pay high prices for high-end organic vegan food; and people [who] come in asking for the latest high-tech robot mouse toy to keep their cat occupied while they're at work."

Veterinarians also protect humans from diseases that animals carry.

Prepare for Success

Veterinarians must have a doctor of veterinary medicine degree and be licensed by the state. It takes six to eight years to complete a DVM. During the first two years of the program, candidates complete general science studies at the college level. Most aspiring vets complete a four-year degree in biological or physiological science. A minor in business is useful for vets who plan to go into private practice. During their senior year of college, aspiring vets apply to four-year veterinary programs. Vet schools require a GPA of 3.0 or higher and high scores on the Veterinary Aptitude Test, GRE, or MCAT. Most of the 27 veterinarian schools in the United States are state funded, so applicants stand the best chance of being admitted to the school in their home state. Competition for a spot in a vet school is intense, and only half of those who apply are admitted.

Getting Your Foot in the Door

In the veterinary program, students acquire practical experience by working in clinics and assisting in surgeries. During the last two years of school, students do clinical rounds and go on to complete a three-year residency. Only then are they eligible to sit for the licensing exam. About 85 percent of those who take the exam pass it at some point. Some veterinarians who pass the licensing exam continue their studies in a specialized area. Technology for the care and treatment of livestock is creating more opportunities for vets. The demand for other vet specialists, like ophthalmologists, exists primarily in urban areas. Although many vets decide to specialize in something right away, others in the profession recommend that you get your feet wet first before choosing a specialty. Most veterinarians prefer working in urban locations. The field for farm animal vets, as a result, is relatively open.

Biggest Challenges and Best Perks

The biggest challenges facing veterinarians today is change. Changing animal health and welfare requirements are placing new demands on the veterinary profession. In addition, veterinarians—whose rapport with animals might be assumed—sometimes have trouble managing the expectations of their patients' owners. Despite the difficulties, veterinary medicine is a career in which most people remain until they retire. Few vets leave the field entirely. Being able to successfully diagnose animals' problems and care for them, not to mention earn the gratitude of the animals' owners, is one of the biggest perks of this profession. Occasionally, experienced vets take on assistants or begin teaching aspiring vets. Many vets find this to be the most rewarding time in their careers.

Professional Profile
Avg. starting salary: $46,339
Avg. salary after 5 years: $63,090
Avg. salary 10 to 15 years: $85,770

Jargon
Fading puppy syndrome When an apparently normal puppy gradually weakens and dies within a week or two of birth, generally due to infectious causes

Are you Interested In?
Animals, medicine

Related College Majors
Pre-veterinary medicine, biological sciences, physiological sciences, business

For More Information
American Veterinary Medical Association:
www.avma.org

Association of American Veterinary Medical Colleges:
www.aavmc.org

World Veterinary Association:
www.worldvet.org

LIVING ON THE EDGE

ADVENTURE GUIDE

A (Relatively Typical) Day in the Life

Adventure guides—whether they are trekking across the Himalayas in Nepal, caving through the underground world of Carlsbad Caverns in New Mexico, or leading a group of sea kayakers along the rocky coast of Maine—are all familiar with these five words: "You have the best job!" And most would agree—despite the nontraditional lifestyle they are obligated to lead.

Being outside and in an exotic locale is what draws many adventure guides to this career. The thrill of packing a bag and heading off to a tropical rainforest, jungle, forest, canyon, or desert is anything but predictable. Not all adventure guides work in the rugged outdoors, however. Bicycle tours through the city streets of Europe, jaunts through Napa Valley's wine country, island hopping on a yacht in Greece, or food-focused excursions through Spain are all offered by adventure guides of another sort.

While some positions call for a 9:00 A.M.–5:00 P.M. schedule (a guide who leads inner-city children on day hikes, for example), most guides adopt a schedule dictated by their employer's trips. If trips are 30 days long, employees are away from home for 30 days at a stretch, plus a day on each end for prepping and unloading. When they return, they may have a week or two off to unpack, revive, and get ready for their next adventure. Many jobs are seasonal—a guide might work as a rafting guide or a rock climbing leader in the summer, then as a snowboard instructor or dog-mushing guide in winter. Some guides live in two places, depending on the time of year. An experienced guide may eventually be able to pack up his or her skills and take them along to find a new job whenever the feeling strikes—or to open a guide business of their own. The more skills and variety of trips he or she has completed, the better.

Leadership is at the core of an adventure guide's job description. Part teacher, motivator, navigator, and first-aid caregiver, guides need to make split-second decisions based on the best interest of the group they are leading. Being a good role model, the ability to build morale and set an example through teamwork, diplomacy, and the ability to resolve conflicts quickly and fairly are also essential equalities. Risk-takers are attracted to this field. Spontaneity, courage, athleticism, and an innate sense of curiosity and wonder are common qualities of successful guides.

An Extreme Day in the Life

Rebecca Rusch is a professional Red Bull athlete who competes in endurance sports including long-distance mountain biking and trekking. When she took her first jobs as a climbing, whitewater, and backpacking guide, she was surprised at how expensive it was to earn the certifications her employers required. Though, "It was a big initial investment," she says. "It was totally worth it [because] I figured I was out there doing these activities and first aid and CPR were good things to know…you want to know that the other guides you're with are trained too, just in case something happens." Rebecca says those are the most extreme days. "I've had friends who are guides who have had to facilitate rescues out of the mountains. That would have been my worst nightmare—when you actually have to use that training when you're tired, scared, and in the middle of nowhere. Those are worst case scenarios, and fortunately they don't happen very often."

> Waking up on top of a peak and making a cup of coffee over an open fire while watching the sun rise over the pines isn't a bad way to start the work day.

Prepare for Success

Guides come to the field in both roundabout and straightforward ways. It never hurts to take outdoor education classes through companies like Outward Bound and National Outdoor Leadership School (NOLS). A college degree in outdoor recreation, outdoor/environmental education, or environmental science will round out a resume full of adventures. A variety of experience—by air, land, and sea—in as many locales as possible will make a guide more marketable. A love for working with people, foreign language proficiency, experience with children or the disabled, and search and rescue training can give guides an added edge.

Getting Your Foot in the Door

Drawn to this career by memories of family canoe trips or weekends in the mountains, many guides get their first "on-the-job" experience as kids. Teens (18-year-olds) with related experience can work summers as rafting guides, camp leaders, or wildlife educators. (Additional job openings are available to those 21 or older.) Many guide jobs offer on-the-job training for those who are hired, but certification may be required as it pertains to the position (life guarding for example). Schools that specialize in training adventure guides can use their connections and relationships to place graduates in entry-level jobs. A history of participation, education, and a willingness to go where the jobs are will be your, um, guide.

Biggest Challenges

Trip leaders and adventure guides are always the ones in charge, so even with co-guides or a leadership team, each guide is ultimately responsible for their group's health and safety—not to mention their enjoyment and their ability to come away having learned something about themselves. An ability to make informed decisions on the spot, manage emergencies in a calm and swift manner, and be a respected leader to all kinds of personality types is essential. While on a trip, guides are on call 24/7 and will find that privacy is a rare luxury. Being away from home and living out of a backpack can get old and pay is rarely above modest to average proportions. On the other hand, what many people consider a high-octane vacation is a guide's day-to-day job. Guides relish the variety and excitement inherent in their work. Waking up on top of a peak and making a cup of coffee over an open fire while watching the sun rise over the pines isn't a bad way to start the work day, and s'mores and ghost stories after a day in the woods isn't a bad way to end it.

Professional Profile
Avg. salary: $15,000-$30,000 per year (plus tips)

Jargon
PUDs (Pointless Ups and Downs) Refers to hiking trails which seem to be built up and down mountains for no other purpose than to make the trail harder

Stealth Camping Camping in a spot which is against the law or breaks the rules for the location

Are you Interested In?
Nature, travel, white water rafting, camping, hiking

Related College Majors
Tourism, environmental science, zoology, botany, geology

For More Information
Adventure Biz Success:
www.adventurebizsuccess.com

Back Door Jobs:
www.backdoorjobs.com

Adventure Divas:
www.adventuredivas.com

ARMED FORCES ENLISTEE/OFFICER

A (Relatively) Typical Day in the Life

You won't run into a wall of frustrating job searches if you're looking to join the U.S. Armed Forces: The Army, Navy, Air Force, Marines, and Coast Guard have 1.4 million active duty enlistees at any given time, and they are always looking for a few good men and women. Once you turn 17 years old, you can apply like the many millions who have done so before you.

When you join, you'll have to decide which branch of service suits you best since each branch has its own jobs, specialties, and overarching duties. Contact the recruiters, check out the promotional videos and marketing materials, and ask questions. Shop around for the best deal on college tuition assistance, enlistment bonus, and so on. To apply, you have to take a test, get a physical, find out where you will be stationed for basic training, and be sworn in. You'll eventually select a job (called a Military Occupational Specialty, or MOS), and, after completing basic training, start Advanced Individual Training (AIT). This is the specific training that applies to your MOS. You'll eventually be stationed somewhere (you may indicate a preference, but there are no guarantees) and dive into your military career. Whichever branch speaks to you, remember that the president is your boss. So don't screw up!

The life of an officer is slightly different from the life of an average enlistee; with a college degree and Reserve Officers' Training Corp (ROTC) experience under their belts, officers are eligible for Officer Candidate School (OCS), which paves the way for spots that are higher up on the command ladder, along with commensurate increases in pay and responsibilities. Those who enroll in the officer track at a military academy have their characters tested by intense military training, physical fitness training, military classes, as well as rigorous college curricula. Officers can be stationed in any of the 65 international army military bases, on a ship anywhere in the world, or at home in the states. They might work closely with members of the espionage community, civilian engineers, doctors, or politicians, as well as fellow officers and the enlistees under their command.

Prepare for Success

The armed forces love to promote from within. Enlistees who show promise and have paid their dues through time and effort should see their pay, authority, and responsibility increase with their rank. To become an officer, you

An Extreme Day in the Life

An E-5 in the Coast Guard based in Portsmouth, Virginia, is quick to point out that the Coast Guard is a great career for extreme days—at both ends of the spectrum. You'll have dull days full of routine tasks, maintenance, and drills that you've done hundreds of times. You'll also have once-in-a-lifetime extreme days that only someone in the military can expect to encounter and which are often the real draw to a military career. "I have to say, the day we stopped $110 million in cocaine from coming into the United States was one of the best. We were working in conjunction with the [Drug Enforcement Administration], U.S. Navy, and British Navy, but locating and seizing the contraband was still a daylong challenge. . . . I wish I could say it was all us, but we were all working together on the same mission to get it done. It was really cool."

This is one field where you will get to see the fruits of your labor.

can go through ROTC or Officer Candidate School, or you can graduate from one of the U.S. military academies.

As an officer, the world of the military's high ranks is your oyster. After four years on the job, officers are almost guaranteed a move up to first lieutenant or higher. Stellar personal conduct and professionalism have led commissioned officers to take the roles of generals, congresspeople, and senators after retirement from active duty.

Getting Your Foot in the Door

Before signing that enlistment contract, you need to be comfortable with the standard eight-year commitment that normally calls for two to six years spent on active duty and the remaining time spent in the Reserves. It's a give-and-take situation. Your selected military branch provides you with the agreed-upon job, rank, pay, cash bonuses for enlistment in certain occupations, medical and other benefits, occupational training, and continuing education. In exchange, you offer your service for the specified period of time.

Biggest Challenges and Best Perks

New soldiers should be ready to bear long months away from home at a stretch and also be willing to put their lives on the line to protect the country in the line of duty. (This alone requires more soul-searching than most entry-level jobs.) An ability to take direction without question and criticism without argument, honor authority in all its forms, conform as duty requires, and do a heck of a lot of calisthenics are also invaluable traits for people who want to join the military. By joining one of the military branches, you might get to see the world; assignments will take you to several destinations and you'll meet more people than you've met in your entire life. Your service will earn you money for college, along with knowledge, experience, confidence, and self-discipline. This is one field where you will get to see the fruits of your labor. Your newfound training and skills will apply to many civilian-related jobs from electronic/mechanical maintenance, engineering, and construction, to health care, communications, transportation, and media and public relations. Employers in the business world look positively on military backgrounds. It shows commitment, respect for authority, patriotism, a varied skill set, solid ethics, and an ability to function in both leadership and subordinate roles. You can also move up the ranks and create a long and rewarding career for yourself in the armed forces. For those who have what it takes, they need only look for open doors to find many before them.

PROFESSIONAL PROFILE

ENLISTEE
Avg. starting salary: $15,000
Avg. salary after 5 years: $24,000
Avg. salary 10 to 15 years: $40,000

OFFICER
Avg. starting salary: $28,000
Avg. salary after 5 years: $45,000
Avg. salary 10 to 15 years: $60,000

JARGON
Military Occupational Specialty (MOS) Job in which you choose to work while enlisted in the military

Advanced Individual Training Specialized training for one's MOS

OCS (Officer Candidate School) Upon completion, you are eligible for positions that are higher up on the chain of command, along with commensurate increases in pay and responsibilities

ARE YOU INTERESTED IN?
Soldiering, military history, defense

RELATED COLLEGE MAJORS
Air force ROTC, Army ROTC, Marine Corps ROTC, Navy ROTC, military science, engineering

FOR MORE INFORMATION
National Association for Uniformed Services:
www.naus.org

Veterans of Foreign Wars:
www.vfw.org

BORDER PATROL AGENT

A (Relatively) Typical Day in the Life

Following the attacks on the World Trade Center and the Pentagon in 2001, Congress approved a plan to consolidate a number of federal law enforcement and institutional bureaucracies into a newly formed U.S. Department of Homeland Security. Among the law enforcement branches of the DOH is the U.S. Border Patrol. It is the daunting—and often-times thankless—task of the border patrol to guard and protect the lengthy boundary between the United States and its neighbors to the north and south: Canada and Mexico.

Depending on which border you're stationed, and the frequency and manner of attempts to cross the bor-der, the typical day for a U.S. Border Patrol Agent varies. While the U.S./Canadian border is enormous, the rela-tively strong economy of Canada makes illegal crossings from the north far less common than those from the south where the less strong economies of Mexico and Central America provoke millions of migrants to risk crossing the considerably shorter, but far more hazardous, desert boundary between the United States and Mexico. Drug and contraband smugglers regularly attempt crossings from both the northern and southern bor-ders as well. It is the job of the border patrol to halt all illegal attempts to enter into the United States. They accomplish this, sometimes at great risk to themselves, through a variety of methods: Agents monitor major road crossings between the United States and neighboring countries; cars are stopped and checked (either randomly or on the agents' suspicion) for anything or anyone that should not be crossing into the country; and as the name suggests, a major part of the daily routine of the border patrol is to patrol the borders (by air, sea, and land) seek-ing out, detaining, and, when necessary, offering medical assistance to those attempting the long and treacherous crossing.

An Extreme Day in the Life

Michael Boyea has worked as a border patrol agent in Nogales, Arizona for eight years where he is current-ly a supervisor. "Border patrol is one of the most exciting jobs in federal law enforcement. There is a lot of dan-ger involved, but it is also very rewarding. It can also be very thankless." According to Boyea, "We're not always looked upon in a positive light by the public and people don't have a clear picture of what we're actually doing. They think we're just stopping poor, harmless people but in reality, agents encounter many criminals and felons on a regular basis. We get assaulted....There have been many instances where agents have received serious bod-ily injury and vehicles have also taken a lot of damage." While the job involves a distinct danger element, it's not adventurous all the time. Boyea explains, "Like many law enforcement jobs, there are times of boredom and times of pure adrenaline." Within the agency, "Special units allow agents to patrol on mountain bikes, four-wheelers, horses, and motorbikes. Other special units like SRT (Special Response Team) and BORTAC (Border Patrol's Tactical Unit) provide agents with lots of upward mobility." Boyea cautions aspiring agents to consider their options and level of commitment carefully before applying: "One of the job requirements for new agents is that you have to start out working in one of the four Southwest border states and...acquire a working knowl-edge of Spanish."

It is the daunting—and oftentimes thankless—task of the Border Patrol to guard and protect the United States' borders.

PREPARE FOR SUCCESS

There are very specific regulations and criteria for becoming a U.S. Border Patrol Aent. For starters, you have to be a U.S. citizen; be younger than 37 when you apply for appointment; have a valid driver's license; and pass a three-part examination that will test, among other things, your proficiency in Spanish. Additionally, a bachelor's degree in criminal justice, or relevant work experience in law enforcement, the military, or some other field that proves an ability to work through stress and adversity are required of any would-be agent. Beyond that, a sense of duty, patriotism, and a desire to serve your country—in a position that may at times make you unpopular to some of the same people you're assigned to protect—are all par for the course.

GETTING YOUR FOOT IN THE DOOR

If you meet the various requirements of age, background, language proficiency, and attitude, you're probably going to find that it's not all that difficult to get an appointment to the U.S. Border Patrol. This is not to say that standards are low. They're not. What's true, though, is that the current political environment, with its greater focus on protecting the United States' domestic homeland from all forms of encroachment and assault, has caused members of both political parties to call for stronger border security which means a patrol of expanding numbers.

BIGGEST CHALLENGES AND BEST PERKS

The boundary between the United States and Canada runs the length of over 5,000 miles of land and water. To the south, there's a boundary 1,951 miles long that stretches across regions which range from cities to desolate badlands. The border patrol is responsible for patrolling every inch of those boundary lines—a clear impossibility. When you add the dangerous, often unpopular nature of the work, it becomes readily apparent that it takes a special kind of person to become a U.S. Border Patrol Agent. However, if you have a sense of duty that leads you to sign up and defend our borders, the greatest reward lies in the satisfaction that comes with performing that duty. Not to mention the fact that you get to work outside riding ATV's through the desert. Pretty cool, eh?

PROFESSIONAL PROFILE
Avg. starting salary: $30,000+

Avg. salary after 5 years: $40,000+

Avg. salary 10 to 15 years: $50,000+

JARGON

Collar The process of arresting someone; it can also refer to an arrest itself

Tonk Term used by U.S. immigration officials to describe an illegal immigrant of any country

ARE YOU INTERESTED IN?
Law enforcement, military

RELATED COLLEGE MAJORS
Criminal justice

FOR MORE INFORMATION
U.S. Customs and Border Protection:
www.cbp.gov

United States Federal Government Jobs:
www.usajobs.opm.gov

Friends of the Border Patrol:
www.friendsoftheborderpatrol.com

CLOSE PROTECTION OFFICER (BODYGUARD)

A (RELATIVELY) TYPICAL DAY IN THE LIFE

A political convention, a rock concert, a quiet house by the lake: these are just a few situations in which bodyguards, also known as close protection officers, may find themselves working. Bodyguards accompany celebrities, politicians, millionaires, and public figures anywhere they go, and often face long hours and strange situations in the process. This career requires nerves of steel and quick instincts; while you could spend two weeks uneventfully shadowing your client, you are always expected to be keenly alert and able to act on little or no notice in order to ensure your client's safety.

A typical day could start out before sunrise or at midnight (depending on the event or shift you're working) with a trip to the gym where you might complete a long run to build endurance, or just a workout at home. If you work in a group, you might then report to your group and check the itinerary for the day or relieve another bodyguard who has spent the last several hours on duty. Then you're on the job, keeping close to your client at all times, holding hysterical fans or curious people at bay, monitoring all exits and arrivals at all times, and screening anyone who approaches. On a typical day, you will drive or accompany your client to meetings, family activities, and large social events without incident and often sit or stand for long hours watching their day unfold. But this job isn't

An Extreme Day in the Life

Bob Duggan is the founder and president of Executive Security International (ESI), Training Academy for Executive Protection, Special Operations and Protective Intelligence, located in Aspen, Colorado. In an interview conducted by *Combat Handguns,* Mr. Duggan explains how he came up with the idea for the training academy: "ESI evolved out of the Aspen Academy of Martial Arts, which I and several other martial artists founded in 1973." While working in Aspen, Duggan was often called to work for people who felt in need of personal protection. As the demand for his services grew, so did the realization that martial arts training was not enough to ensure complete physical protection to his clients. He explains that clients often "go out and find a martial artist, or a police officer, or a body-builder, because that's their image of what a body guard is—someone tough who stands in 'harm's way.' But catching bullets or punches is not really doing protection. . . . I didn't have sufficient training or background for what this profession required, and so I began to think about what it would take to build a training academy that covered the entire spectrum of protection work."

The list of common attributes of Duggan's most successful students is hefty: "Tenacity, perseverance, attention to detail. Extraordinarily sharp observation skills. Determined enough that this is something that they will do. That they'll put aside any diversion in order to get through it." He goes on to explain, "This is not an easy business to break into. It's just very hard. The ones who do make it share the same qualities . . . they are tenacious, persistent, [and] they are prepared to work their way through the various loops in the system in order to build a reputation, . . . a resume, and a clientele that will sustain them. Our graduates tell us that their training is indispensable in achieving those goals."

Source: http://www.esi-lifeforce.com/InterviewCH.html

just about waiting around and watching; you need to be in top physical and mental condition so you can be ready to protect when the time comes.

Prepare for Success

You don't necessarily need to go to school to be a bodyguard, but many agencies and private clients will require some sort of accreditation or training when you apply for a job, so it's in your best interests to secure the necessary certifications. If you've already worked for the police, the military, or a government agency, you may just need some training to fill in the gaps in your experience. There are bodyguard training centers that provide training in the many different areas that employers look for. Be sure to do your research before you sign up. Some required training may include close protection, anti-terrorism, first aid, sniping and special weapons, weapons disarming, unarmed combat, counter surveillance, explosives/chemical detection, risk assessment, and crowd screening.

Getting Your Foot in the Door

Aspiring bodyguards should visit websites like secretservice.gov, where the United States Secret Service lists job opportunities, requirements, and upcoming job fairs in cities across the country. Attend one of these fairs for a chance to speak to an actual agent/bodyguard and get an insider's view of the job. The Secret Service has age restrictions for applying, requires either a bachelor's degree or three years of service in the criminal investigative or law enforcement fields, and two 11-week training programs before hiring. There are also extensive medical exams and background clearance requirements, so keep these in mind as you prepare to apply for a job.

Biggest Challenges and Best Perks

The biggest challenge of this profession is the ability to put your life on the line in order to ensure another person's safety. This takes a level of bravery and commitment that few people have. Bodyguards must be alert at all times and pay constant attention to detail, even when everything appears to be safe. The hours can be extremely long (16-hour days are not uncommon) and may require you to work nights and weekends. Technology changes every day, so ongoing training in new weapons, forms of security, and technology is often necessary.

On the upside, you'll never be bored in this profession. Bodyguards are employed to cover a large range of functions, events, and situations, so the job is different every day. In addition, bodyguards go everywhere with their clients so extensive travel—sometimes for long periods of time—is another great perk.

PROFESSIONAL PROFILE
Avg. starting salary: $33,688

Avg. salary after 5 years: $56,148

Avg. salary after 10 to 15 years: $93,580-$187,160

Varies considerably depending on employer, location, and level of risk. Bodyguards employed by commercial companies are often paid a negotiated daily rate.

JARGON
Minder Someone who protects financial assets instead of a physical person

Principal The person being protected

Tactical Driving A school of driving that entails either avoiding attackers or disabling an attacking vehicle to allow for an easier escape

ARE YOU INTERESTED IN?
Firearms, law enforcement, martial arts, aggressive driving

RELATED COLLEGE MAJORS
Logistics management, criminology

FOR MORE INFORMATION:
Advanced Driving and Security: www.1adsi.com

The International Bodyguard Association: www.ibabodyguards.com

United States Secret Service: www.secretservice.gov

CIA AGENT

A (Relatively) Typical Day in the Life

The closest thing to being a spy, aside from playing one on television or in the movies, is landing a position with the Central Intelligence Agency (CIA). Be ready to jump through endless hoops to be counted among the chosen few in this profession. The CIA provides national security intelligence to senior U.S. policymakers. They collect information, analyze and evaluate it, and pull it together into written reports and oral briefings that they dish to top government officials. It's important enough work that the agency's director is appointed by the president.

There are several categories within the CIA in which you might find work. Many CIA employees have your standard desk jobs. If you're looking for more James Bond–style thrills, you should aim for a position in the National Clandestine Service arm. As sexy as this may sound, Hollywood-style undercover spy missions are far less common than, say, days when you strike up a chat with someone who may have a valuable tidbit of information. Much agents' time revolves around detecting surveillance to see if anyone is tracking their moves as they go about their work. It's not easy to gather information while looking over your shoulder to make sure no one is following you. You'll be driving along and taking notes, but it shouldn't look as if you are. You'll be walking a rigid, predetermined course on busy streets, but you need to look as if you're window shopping. You may leave a clue somewhere, but no one should be able to pick up on it.

To get into this type of work, you've got to be a model citizen who is passionate about international affairs. A good agent will live and breathe the CIA and will stand behind its mission through thick and thin. This CIA clandestine service job description from Federaljobs.net helps paint a picture:

"For the extraordinary individual who wants more than a job, this is a way of life that will challenge the deepest resources of your intelligence, self-reliance, and responsibility. It demands an adventurous spirit . . . a forceful

An Extreme Day in the Life

Lindsay Moran went to work as an undercover CIA case officer after graduating from Harvard and returning from Bulgaria on a Fulbright scholarship. Her book *Blowing My Cover: My Life as a CIA Spy* was released in 2004. In it, she talks about her brief but extreme career, full of days not unlike the one she described for us: "Probably my most harrowing experience as a CIA officer posted overseas in ethnic tension-torn Macedonia, occurred on what—to any outside observer—would have appeared like a relaxing bike ride on a breezy, blue day. In fact, I was en route, via my clunky old bicycle, to service a 'signal site,' a location where a CIA officer leaves a message—typically a chalk mark—for one of her recruited agents to spot and decipher. Once I'd finished making a charcoal slash across the base of a water fountain, my 'signal' to my agent, I was cruising downhill at a rather fast clip. As I rounded a turn, three camouflage-clad, heavily armed soldiers, who looked very much like the guerilla insurgents then wreaking havoc throughout the land, leapt into the brush at the side of the road. I could hear them readying their automatic weapons. My heart froze. Luckily, I spoke the Macedonian well enough to yell into the bushes, and convince them that they shouldn't shoot me. Later, I struck up a conversation with the trio, and even began targeting one of them as a potential foreign agent. In the mind of every CIA officer: He who doesn't destroy us might as well work for us!"

In the mind of every CIA officer: He who doesn't destroy us might as well work for us!

personality . . . superior intellectual ability, toughness of mind, and the highest degree of integrity. You will need to deal with fast-moving, ambiguous, and unstructured situations that will test your resourcefulness to the utmost."

Prepare for Success

Moran's book is just one of a handful written by former agents. They may be the closest thing to a behind-the-scenes look. Gather more info on the CIA's own website with suggested reading, job testimonials, agency requirements, some words about the culture, and a CIA personality quiz. That's where you'll also find very specific instructions for preparing a resume and applying for a job. You'll need a college degree for the most interesting jobs; consider a major in international relations/business, area studies, economics, math, or any of the sciences. Higher positions (overseas officers, intelligence analysts, etc.) require graduate degrees. Fluency in a language—particularly a Central Eurasian, Middle Eastern, or East Asian language—may increase your chances of getting hired.

Getting Your Foot in the Door

In the CIA's own words, in addition to the application, "applicants must undergo a thorough background investigation examining their life history, character, trustworthiness, reliability and soundness of judgment. . . . The agency uses the polygraph to check the veracity of this information." There is also a thorough medical exam that checks for both mental and physical fitness. U.S. citizenship is required. The interview process can be grueling but less so than the intensive, butt-kicking training for new recruits. Even before you graduate from college, you can pursue paid work opportunities with the CIA. These include highly competitive internships, scholarships, and co-ops, as well as graduate studies programs.

Biggest Challenges and Best Perks

Getting a job with the CIA is one tough nut to crack. You should be a law-abiding citizen with a record as clean as an angel's. Consider a backup plan as they report receiving more than 3,000 resumes a month. The lengthy application process can span two months to more than a year. Once in, undercover agents find that being cut off from friends and family and unable to tell them what they really do for a living can be a major downer. Isolation, loneliness, stress, and danger will challenge the best of them. On the upside, the CIA pays a competitive salary and offers a hearty benefits package. New appointees may have their moving expenses covered and may eventually get to travel the world. It is an honor to be offered a job with the agency, which is augmented by pride in serving your country and making it a safer place to live.

CRISIS NEGOTIATOR

A (Relatively) Typical Day in the Life

You're familiar with the scene: A man stands on the ledge of a 30-story building, a crowd gathers below, and police and rescue workers struggle to maintain crowd control while scrambling to inflate a giant air mattress in the event that the would-be jumper takes the plunge. Suddenly, there are two people on the ledge: the would-be jumper and someone new—the crisis negotiator. The crisis negotiator startles the would-be jumper, but the negotiator is smooth. The negotiator calms the would-be jumper by keeping him involved in a short conversation, if only for a few more minutes, before convincing him to step off the ledge to safety. Voila. Crisis averted.

It's rarely that simple.

In fact, one of the most high-pressure, challenging jobs in all of law enforcement is that of the crisis negotiator. It's a tough job, one for which there's no such thing as a typical day. If you're on a crisis negotiating team, you've been called in specifically because the situation has become too volatile for regular law enforcement to handle without risking harm to everyone involved. When such a situation does arise, it's the crisis negotiator's job to read the situation, understand the psychology behind it, and try to find a peaceful solution that avoids violence or loss of life. Negotiations last as long as the negotiator feels relatively in control of the situation. A single event may take only a few minutes; then again, it may take several days or more. Negotiators are not always successful, but more than the

An Extreme Day in the Life

In the mid-seventies, Jim Huegerich was a grad student in education who saw the opportunity to work on a crisis unit as "an excellent opportunity to learn how a community worked to support families and children." He says, "I agreed to do the job for two years." Thirty-two years later, he's the director of Crisis and Human Services for the Chapel Hill Police Department. "Most of the work we do is not in the field of formal hostage or barricaded subject negotiations. However, much of our work entails some manner of dispute or conflict resolution." It's stressful work. He adds, "The situations you respond to are unstable, intense, and frequently out of control." However, Jim and his team have a basic "commitment to the principle of the right of all people to have access to mental health services when facing a crisis, regardless of the ability to pay. This involves a belief in the benefit of crisis work, respect for the incredible surviving human spirit, and recognition of the benefit of working as a team." As fulfilling as the job can be, it can also be incredibly taxing. Jim Huegerich has a litany of horror stories any one of which could leave a person scarred. "There was the day that a mentally ill law student carrying 900 rounds of ammunition and a semiautomatic, high-powered rifle shot and killed two people and forever changed the lives of a whole community. There was the fraternity fire where an extended community grieved the deaths of five students while the rest of the community observed Mother's Day and UNC Graduation. There was the six-hour negotiation with the former state trooper who had a history of killing two people, and was on this occasion armed with several weapons and took his partner hostage; when the dust settled and things were defused, he leaned toward me and whispered the promise to kill me, the negotiator."

Crisis negotiators go into every situation with the understanding that someone's life is probably on the line.

quarter of a century since their methods were first implemented, they have played a vital role in saving the lives of countless law enforcement officers, hostages, suicidal subjects, and even criminals.

Prepare for Success

While there's not a standard path that leads one to the role of crisis negotiator, if you're interested in becoming one, you should be prepared to get a lot of training in a variety of psychological and strategic fields. While you're in college, try to concentrate on psychology, social work, and/or criminology if possible. In fact, don't stop at a bachelor's degree; for the intensity of this work, you really should consider a master's degree. While in school, seek out internships in psychiatric institutions. Volunteer to work with agencies who serve victims of crimes. This is a people-oriented job. The more early experience you can get interacting with people struggling with mental and emotional problems, the more prepared you're going to be when you're on the job.

Getting Your Foot in the Door

There are crisis negotiating teams on staff at the FBI and at some of the larger, well funded branches of local law enforcement, so, as in any field, it would make sense for you to first find out where the negotiators work. Getting your foot in the door at some of these organizations may not be as difficult as you might think. As is often the case in civil service, becoming a crisis negotiator primarily has to do with departmental need, an applicant's specific qualifications, and whether those qualifications meet the requirements set forth by the department.

Biggest Challenges and Best Perks

Law enforcement is a fundamentally dangerous line of work. Police officers go about their day with the understanding that what begins as the most mundane scenario can quickly turn violent or even deadly. Crisis negotiators don't even have the luxury of the occasional mundane scenario; they go into every situation with the understanding that someone's life is probably on the line, and even the most talented of negotiators is not able to succeed in talking everyone down. Regardless of how well-trained a negotiator may be, there will be unsuccessful missions and people will die. It's not an easy fact of the job to accept, but it's a fact nonetheless. However, there are few greater feelings of accomplishment than when you are successful and you and your team are able to defuse a situation that seemed destined to end in chaos and bloodshed.

PROFESSIONAL PROFILE
Avg. salary: $54,000 to $65,000 plus bonus incentives.

Tactical law enforcement job salaries depend on education and experience.

JARGON
Throw phone When there is no telephone accessible to the criminal subject, the SWAT team often delivers a telephone linked to the hostage site phone system.

ARE YOU INTERESTED IN?
Law enforcement, psychology of human behavior, mental health

RELATED COLLEGE MAJORS
Psychology, criminal psychology, social work, criminology

FOR MORE INFORMATION
New England Crisis Negotiators Association:
www.necna.com

Crisis Negotiation Associates:
www.crisisnegotiation.com

CUSTOMS AGENT

A (Relatively) Typical Day in the Life

Money laundering, child pornography, and gun smuggling are just a few of the crimes customs agents routinely investigate. Anything that crosses U.S. borders is subject to inspection by these criminal investigators, and they log long hours mining information from informants, probing evidence, and keeping tabs on suspected criminals. Enforcing more than 400 customs laws for dozens of government agencies requires a strong personality. In fact, you might need to be downright gutsy to do this job because even a routine day includes a mix of activities most people would find taxing.

A hypothetical but typical day begins with you strapping on your gun, badge, and credentials—necessities in this line of work. At the office, you may write up some reports for court or your agency and attend to other administrative aspects of the job. On the field, you investigate cases by talking to informants and industry experts or conducting surveillance on some unsavory character. You may also spend time in meetings briefing a prosecutor on the details of a case or planning the next step in an investigation with colleagues. You could be part of an intergovernmental task force on terrorism, counterfeiting operations, or even Super Bowl security. Don't think this job is just about mastery of modern detection methods, criminal codes, or interview techniques. You also need to be physically

An Extreme Day in the Life

Zachary Mann has been a customs agent for 19 years and fondly recalls the Blue Thunder lore that helped lure him into the business. Blue Thunder referred to the speedboats customs agents used back in the day when they were responsible for patrolling U.S. waterways and bringing down drug runners and other seafaring criminals. "I was interested in driving one of the boats and ended up being the captain of a blue thunder patrol boat," he says.

Beyond the thrill of high-speed boat chases and the adrenaline rush of drug busts, Zachary appreciates the opportunities he's had to indulge his curiosity and chart his own course. "You have a lot of say in how you investigate your case and you're going to be working with people who have more years of experience than you and others who are right out of school. As the lead investigator, you can decide how best to investigate and draw on the experience of your team. I think it's unique that you can pretty much decide what you're going to do. Of course, you have to show up, earn your pay, accept supervision, and do your job."

Zachary also says that the uncertainty of each day contributes to the job's allure. "You know what people say about law enforcement jobs: 95 percent is boredom and 5 percent is sheer excitement. One day I was sitting in my office when an agent from Tampa called and said he needed some assistance. He believed that some cocaine smugglers were in a particular hotel. We talked to the hotel management and confirmed the room and began surveillance. We even knocked on the door and spoke to the men. They invited us in, but we didn't have enough to arrest them. The next morning we got additional information, followed them around, and conducted a consensual search. We found tools of the trade and arrested three individuals."

fit and know how to shoot straight. Part of your day may be spent working out or unloading bullets in targets at the shooting range.

Prepare for Success

While a college degree isn't required to be a special agent, it certainly helps because of the complexity of the job and the fact that much of the applicant pool is college-educated. Any major will do—you never know when some highbrow art will be smuggled across the border suddenly making those art history courses you took in college relevant. Customs agents come from a variety of fields, including engineering, business, and the arts. Establishing good eating and exercise habits can also help equip you for success since applicants must pass a medical examination before being hired. Once on the job, everyday duties often require grueling physical exertion such as running, use of firearms, and exposure to severe weather. U.S. citizenship is another requirement.

Getting Your Foot in the Door

Would-be special agents should practice their investigation skills by grilling federal government recruiters at career fairs about job requirements and the application process. The federal government's official job site, Usajobs.gov, is another valuable tool for aspiring customs agents. Searching by series and entering "GS-1811" will pull up a range of criminal investigator/special agent jobs, including those within the U.S. Customs and Border Protection Agency. You can create an online resume and apply for jobs via the website, but don't expect to get hired right away. The process can take between 9 and 18 months. It's not all bureaucracy, though; exhaustive background checks are definitely in order for men and women who are signing on to protect our borders.

Biggest Challenges and Best Perks

Variety may be one of the biggest perks of this job. On any given day customs agents can wind up in Black Hawk helicopters, in high-speed patrol boats, or in the bowels of cargo ships loaded with illegal drugs. Location is also another perk, with 311 official ports of entry, including New York, Miami, and Los Angeles, and attaché agencies abroad in hot spots such as South Africa, Beijing, and London.

The biggest challenges, of course, are cracking the cases you've been assigned and staying mentally and physically sharp. You may work 12- to 14-hour days, constantly juggling a range of distinct investigative work: fact-finding missions, undercover and surveillance work, interviews, analysis, and reporting. Meanwhile, criminal ruses are becoming more and more sophisticated so agents have the added difficulty of learning new and better investigative techniques to catch them.

Professional Profile
Avg. starting salary: $42,000 to $53,000

Avg. salary after 5 years: $65,000 to $80,000

Avg. salary 10 to 15 years: $90,000 to $112,000

Jargon
Collar The process of arresting someone. It can also refer to an arrest itself.

Are you Interested In?
Law enforcement

Related College Majors
Criminal justice, criminal psychology, accounting

For More Information
United States Federal Government Jobs:
www.usajobs.opm.gov/

National Association of Investigative Specialists:
www.pimall.com/nais

DEMOLITION EXPERT

A (Relatively Typical) Day in the Life

If you enter the field of demolition work, you better be prepared to knock things down. Demolition crews raze structures ranging from small houses to enormous oil refineries—and a demolition expert is responsible for making sure this all goes off without a hitch. This means that you'll need to study the structure that's about to be demolished. What's it made of? In what direction do you want it to fall? What's the best equipment to use for the job? After all, you'll have everything from the wrecking ball to sticks of dynamite at your disposal. In essence, a demoli-

tion expert is an expert in the realm of physics, constantly assessing the physical composition of materials, the strength of materials, and the likely outcome when force from one thing (say, a 2,500-pound cast iron wrecking ball) comes crashing into another (say, a four-story apartment building with a brick exterior) at a certain speed from a particular direction.

Demolition experts are also successful salvagers. They keep their eyes peeled for wood, metal, and other materials that can be gathered and sold to scrap yards. As accomplished demolition expert Ron Dokell says, "demolition people" may have been "the world's first recyclers."

It's not likely that you'll be able to call yourself a "demolition expert" right off the bat. This is something to aspire to. Early in a career, demolition-experts-to-be work in the field, getting hands-on experience with the procedures and equipment central to demolition work. They may continue on this path or they may become estimators, foremen, superintendents, or project managers. A select few even become officers in the company. Whatever direction you take your career, you'll need to gain years of experience before you can officially don the "expert" badge.

Prepare for Success

"There are no books," says demolition extraordinaire Ron Dokell. "You learn this by going out there and gaining on-the-job experience." So if a career in demolition is your goal, you should find a summer job that'll let you get your hands dirty in the day-to-day work of demolition or some related field, like construction or restoration. (The National Demolition Association can be a good place to start your search.) While no book is going to turn you

An Extreme Day in the Life

Ron Dokell has quite a résumé. He's been in the demolition industry for fifty years. He's currently the president of the Houston-based Demolition Consultants. He's the previous president of the esteemed Olshan Demolition Company. For more than 35 years, he's specialized in demolishing "complex industrial structures," such as chemical plants, uranium mills, and oil production facilities. But the job that sticks out most in his mind did not involve a mammoth factory, but rather a legendary Las Vegas landmark. "Probably the most exciting thing we ever did was demolish the Dunes hotel," he says. This took place in October 1993 and involved a lot of high-powered explosives. Sure, explosives can be exciting, but what made this job particularly memorable? Well, the nearby Treasure Island hotel and casino, which was owned by the same company as the Dunes, was just opening its doors. In front of it, the Treasure Island had a full-sized pirate ship, which trained its cannons on the Dunes. As Dokell detonated a series of explosions, the cannons fired, making it seem as if they were responsible for the fall of the Dunes Hotel.

With each new building, you'll find a unique set of challenges.

into an expert, it doesn't hurt to put on your study cap and devote some hours to physics, chemistry, and mathematics—all disciplines that you'll need to have a handle on if you want to rise high in the field. If you do ascend into a managerial role, you'll have to be an ace at business, too. Demolition contracts are earned through competitive bidding, so your mind will never be far from the budget. And finally, try to meet as many people in the field as you're able. This is a growing industry, but in many areas of the country, the demolition business is very family oriented, and can be tough to crack into. So the more people you develop a rapport with, the more likely you are to land a position.

Students can join the National Demolition Association—found on the web at DemolitionAssociation.com—for just twenty bucks a year. This gives you an inside look at the people and jobs that comprise the field. It also gives you a subscription to a Demolition magazine, "the voice of the demolition industry."

GETTING YOUR FOOT IN THE DOOR

There's no better way to get your foot in the door of the demolition industry than by demonstrating a meticulous work ethic. The details matter here, so make sure you know the regulations, techniques, and precise expectations that the higher-ups have of you. And for the sake of yourself and all of your colleagues, ensure that you have a strong handle on the safety regulations that apply to the work you're doing. If you want to move up the ladder in this field, your coworkers need to trust the decisions you make—whether you make those decisions in an executive office or behind the bucket of a front loader. A good way to stay in the know about advancements in the industry is to attend the National Demolition Association convention, held each year.

BIGGEST CHALLENGES AND BEST PERKS

Wherever you can find powerful explosives, heavy equipment, flying debris, and collapsing structures, you'll also find plenty of opportunity for grave personal injury. This is why employers will value your attention to detail. So, when you're on the job, you need to remain focused at all times. A lapse in focus can put your future, your coworkers' futures, and the project's future in jeopardy. If you like this sort of detail-oriented work, though, you'll find great satisfaction in working with a crew of colleagues to tackle very large projects. And with each new building, you'll find a unique set of challenges. This keeps the days fresh. As Ron Dokell says, "The jobs aren't all the same, because buildings don't replicate themselves much."

PROFESSIONAL PROFILE
Avg. starting salary $28,000

(Please note that salary varies greatly depending on whether you pursue operative, estimator, or executive positions)

JARGON
Implosion The use of explosives on a building to cause it to fall inside the space of its own footprint

Nitroglycerin A colorless, poisonous, oily, explosive liquid, used in the manufacture of explosives, specifically dynamite

ARE YOU INTERESTED IN?
Explosives, physics, architecture, construction

RELATED COLLEGE MAJORS
Physics, engineering mechanics, engineering physics, mechanical engineering

FOR MORE INFORMATION
National Demolition Association:
www.demolitionassociation.com

Demolition Magazine:
www.demolitionmagazine.com

FBI AGENT

A (Relatively) Typical Day in the Life

The events of September 11, 2001 may have shifted the Federal Bureau of Investigation's priorities from traditional crime fighting to terrorism prevention, but its motto, "fidelity, bravery and integrity," still holds. Today, the FBI's more than 12,000 special agents are doing more counterterrorism and counterintelligence work than ever before. But combating the garden-variety violent crime and corporate fraud cases that have made headlines for years still ranks high among their typical duties. As an agent, your job is to enforce criminal laws and protect the nation from a range of foreign and domestic security threats.

Agents spend much of their time outside of the office meeting with sources and local law enforcement and conducting investigations for about half of the day. Agents working the white-collar or computer-intrusion beats may spend less time away from their desks. While out and about, you might investigate a corporate bribery artist who gives illegal "commissions" to foreign state-owned telecom carriers. You could serve a warrant to an unsuspecting hacker who has illegally accessed contact information, Social Security numbers, and other confidential information. You might also track down clues on a notorious killer and organized crime leader who has broken out of jail and evaded the police.

The rest of your 10-hour day is likely spent in the office at meetings or filling strenuous bureau requirements for documentation. The paperwork load is heavy and meticulous because the evidence you find needs to hold up in court. It also needs to be clear enough for someone else to pick up the investigation where you left off, in the event of your transfer or retirement.

An Extreme Day in the Life

Thomas O'Neill, chief division counsel for the FBI's Columbia Division, says there isn't a day when he doesn't wake up looking forward to his job. On normal days, the former attorney enjoys conducting surveillance, making arrests, and executing warrants in his regular territory. Then there are the days his team is flown off to other parts of the country to provide backup on high profile cases and events. In 1996, Thomas's team was dispatched across the country to help in an FBI effort to get 21 renegades who rejected the U.S. government to leave their compound in the hills of a 960-acre wheat farm and sheep ranch. The Freemen standoff in Montana was one of the longest federal sieges in modern U.S. history. "It was a big standoff in Jordan, Montana, that required around-the-clock surveillance. We spent two weeks there. You had to transport your whole team across the country. We manned a guard post waiting for some of the people to leave the compound. Since it was a high profile case at the time, you got to see daily clips on the world and local news. It was interesting to know that you played a role in that. It ultimately resolved with them giving up and coming out." Thomas was also one of hundreds of law enforcement agents dispatched to protect 11,000 athletes from 197 countries at the 1996 Summer Olympics. "As part of the SWAT team, we were in the yachting venue in Savanna, Georgia. To play a role in that event was incredible. The bombing occurred in the Olympic venue in Atlanta, but it ratcheted up everyone's attention level."

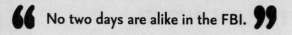
" No two days are alike in the FBI. "

Prepare for Success

The FBI's work in fields such as art theft, violent gangs, terrorism, espionage, cyber crime, white-collar crime, and more demands a workforce of multitalented agents who represent a variety of backgrounds. You must have a four-year degree to be a special agent, and the agency recruits people with expertise in accounting, computer science, engineering, intelligence experience, law enforcement, military, and the physical sciences. The FBI also looks for candidates who have foreign language skills, particularly in Chinese, Farsi, and Arabic. You'll also need to get in shape for this field. During the application process, everything from your 300-meter sprint time to the number of push-ups you can do will be tested. One thing you don't need to do to prepare for your application is learn to handle a gun. You'll learn this skill in training.

Getting Your Foot in the Door

The FBI's job site is the first stop for aspiring special agents. It includes career profiles, online job applications, internship opportunities, and recruiting event details. The website even includes a list of things that disqualify you from job consideration, including felony convictions, illegal drug use, and default on a U.S. government–issued student loan. Applications are processed through the field office closest to the applicant's residence, school, or workplace and all testing takes place in that field office. The online application is just the first of many steps in a hiring process that can take up to a year to complete.

Biggest Challenges and Best Perks

In the post-9/11 era, the FBI has shifted its emphasis from traditional criminal investigations to more counterterrorism and counterintelligence work. The stakes are high—your job is to prevent the next domestic terrorism act or foil espionage attempts. You have to do it without breaking the law and documenting every step you take to support prosecution in court. Talk about a challenge.

On the other hand, you have the satisfaction of doing something that matters: taking criminals off the street, preventing a crime from occurring, and protecting the innocent. You'll be at the forefront of investigative cases that make major news headlines and preoccupy the nation. You'll get to work closely with other critical agencies such as the CIA and NSA. No two days are alike in the FBI. Your wits are tested by bank robbers, kidnappers, terrorists, fugitives, and spies.

Professional Profile
Avg. salary: $48,890
Avg. salary after 5 years: $76,560
Avg. salary 10 to 15 years: $106,430

Jargon
EC (electronic communication)
A memo sent by an FBI agent

Are you Interested In?
Law enforcement, national security

Related College Majors
Accounting, computer science, engineering, physical sciences

For More Information
Federal Bureau of Investigation:
www.fbijobs.gov

FBI Agents Association: www.fbiaa.org

FBI National Academy Associates:
www.fbinaa.org

FIREFIGHTER

A (Relatively Typical) Day in the Life

A firefighter's job is one of society's noblest. S/he is charged with protecting people, their property, and their goods from destruction or damage due to fire. Firefighters must be able to perform strenuous physical tasks, such as carrying unconscious people down flights of stairs, directing the flow of a hose that carries 2,000 gallons of water per minute, or breaking down doors locked from the inside. The profession is very dangerous—more than one in four firefighters have to take time off for work-related injuries, ranging from slipped disks to disfiguring burns—and requires a strong sense of commitment to public service. Firehouses are manned around the clock. Firefighters must be able to deal with brief bursts of intense activity, then long periods of crushing boredom. The ability to go from scorching backdrafts to computer solitaire is an aspect of firefighting that is often glossed over in newspaper articles and movies. The hours are long for firefighters on duty; some have 24 hours on, then 48 or 72 hours off, and most city departments require firefighters to work an average of 48 to 56 hours per week.

Above all, firefighters must remember that their actions don't just affect themselves, but their colleagues' as well. More than most professions, each day is dependent not only on a firefighter's ability to handle themselves and their responsibilities, but to act as part of a team. This reliance on one another encourages close camaraderie among members of any firehouse, who share the unique professional bond of having been through dozens of life-threatening experiences together. The largest fire departments have many battalions and divisions, with lieutenants, captains, battalion chiefs, division chiefs, fire marshals, and investigators.

An Extreme Day in the Life

As you might expect, life as a fireman involves a tad more excitement that staring at a spreadsheet all day. Joseph Alaimo, a firefighter with Engine Co. 13 in Columbia, South Carolina, recalls a rough dawn: "Back when I was just a probationary fireman, a call came in at 4:00 A.M. for a house fire—there was heavy smoke and flames blasting out of every window on the first floor. As we tried to push our way through the front door, flames shot out from all sides. When it finally gave way, I fell onto what I thought was a lump of clothes, but was really a human body staring at me, obviously dead. I was getting burned from all sides as I watched this man burning in front of me. I had to keep moving, as we had reports of children trapped on the second floor. As we moved down the hallway, I imagined this is what hell looks like. I fought the flames, but it seemed... like a garden hose against a volcano. I started to have trouble seeing and realized the glass on my air mask was actually fragmenting because it was so hot. I looked at the wall and it was on fire, but thanks to my coat, it didn't burn through to my skin. I thought this was it, I couldn't go back at this point and I couldn't go on, and I started to pray to God. I got down and held the hose line over my head and let the jet stream of water blast straight up over me. I was toasted but alive, and had to get out of the house. I had so much smoke and steam coming off me that people thought I was on fire, but I did my job, and the fire went out. A life was lost at this job, but it was an experience that I think will keep me alive to save the next person from the fate of fire. It's truly the best job in the world."

It's hard to find a firefighter not intensely proud of what they do.

PREPARE FOR SUCCESS

To become a firefighter, you need to be between 18 and 31 years of age; you need a high school diploma; you must have corrected 20/20 vision; and you must pass the firefighters' examination, offered annually by local governments throughout the country. While many colleges offer courses in fire science, these classes are usually taken by firefighting professionals after they've been in the field for a while. At the beginning of their careers, firefighters are put through a rigorous three- to sixteen-week training program to learn firefighting techniques. Attrition rate is highest in these initial years—almost 25 percent choose to turn back. Many departments now require an Emergency Medical Technician (EMT) certificate as a condition of employment. Firefighters can become members of the firefighters' union and the International Association of Firefighters.

GETTING YOUR FOOT IN THE DOOR

The successful firefighter is an approachable communicator with the ability to take decisive action under trying circumstances. They make sure they are educated about technological or technique-oriented changes in firefighting through seminars, conferences, and conventions. Applicants who earn high scores on the written portion of the test and demonstrate physical dexterity, strength, and mental alertness should be able to find employment. The number of firefighters hired each year corresponds proportionally to population increases, so an awareness of shifting demographics can help the aspiring firefighter find a job in a promising location.

BIGGEST CHALLENGES AND BEST PERKS

The downside, of course, is the risk. But the danger is hardly a surprise to those going into firefighting, and is often a point of pride; it's hard to find a firefighter not intensely proud of what they do. In fact, one of the biggest satisfactions in fighting fires is just that—firefighters love their job. Once you make it past training, it's a very straightforward career progression until retirement—there's not much of a "corporate ladder" to climb. Although rookies are generally stuck with the late-night "graveyard" shifts, which may inhibit personal life at the beginning of their careers, ten-year veterans have more control over their hours and receive higher pay for basically doing the same job, and retirement is usually available at half-pay at age 50 for 20-year veterans.

FUGITIVE RECOVERY AGENT (BOUNTY HUNTER)

A (Relatively) Typical Day in the Life

For many of us, the term "bounty hunter" conjures up images of Boba Fett, the anti-hero of the *Star Wars* movies, making sure he got his bounty, Han Solo frozen in carbonite before shipping him off to Jabba the Hut. Of course, bounty hunters exist in this galaxy—and in this time.

Hired by bail bondsmen to track down criminal defendants who have missed a court date, bounty hunters, or fugitive recovery agents (the preferred term of those working in the field), spend much of their time pretty far away from the cubicle. In fact, if anybody's chained to the desk in this office, you can be sure that it's probably not the fugitive recovery agent. Technically, they're not civil servants, sanctioned members of law enforcement, or even necessarily licensed—but they're certainly not vigilantes. Nor are they glorified mercenaries, as their job name may imply. They do get paid for their services but they work within the law, often with cooperation from the local authorities who understand that fugitive recovery agents bring with them skills not necessarily taught at the police academy.

When a fugitive skips bail, the bail bondsman will call the fugitive recovery agent, who will then begin an investigation into where the assailant might have gone. This investigation may lead into some seedy areas of society. Wherever the trail leads, the bounty hunter's job is to find the fugitive, present them with the relevant paperwork (specific to the state) that identifies them as a fugitive, apprehend them, and return them to the bail bondsman who will typically pay the bounty of 10–20 percent (depending on the job) of the fugitive's total bail.

An Extreme Day in the Life

In an August 2004 interview conducted by CNN.com, Duane "Dog" Chapman talks about what it takes to be successful in the world of fugitive recovery, and how common misconceptions about his work abound: "Well, you got to, number one, want to do something right for America. Number two, you probably want to, you know, be good guy versus bad guy. And you got to have a lot of faith and a lot of patience."

When asked how he would respond to people concerned about vigilantism and whether or not his work interferes with normal law enforcement, Duane had this to say: "You know, after Andrew Luster [the Max Factor heir and convicted rapist Chapman tracked down] and not getting paid, a couple of people said, 'oh, he's nothing but a vigilante'. . .And so we said, you know what, let us show you what a vigilante really does, and let us show you the difference between a bounty hunter and [a] vigilante. So we've done that with these [new reality TV] shows. And I think that that word 'vigilante' will be completely taken out of our definition very soon."

Source: http://www.cnn.com/2004/SHOWBIZ/TV/08/26/bounty.hunter/

Fugitive recovery is dangerous work. While many subjects give in without a struggle, a bounty hunter can never take this for granted.

PREPARE FOR SUCCESS

You can't learn how to become a bounty hunter at your local college, but you can prepare in other ways. The best bounty hunters are going to be pretty good investigators. Assailants are not always going to be holed up at their grandmother's house, and since your primary occupation is based on the assumption that you can locate and apprehend fugitives, it would help if you had some skills in basic detective work. Additionally, knowledge of the streets, and the ability to establish rapport with all types of people from all walks of life could prove to be especially helpful. Not all states have a licensing system and not all bounty hunters who practice in those states carry licenses. But for the purposes of this profile, we'll only speak about those legitimately practicing the occupation. While it's not required, many fugitive recovery agents gain some of their skills from previous stints as members of law enforcement or as private detectives.

GETTING YOUR FOOT IN THE DOOR

The first thing you'll absolutely have to know is that different states have different laws. There are several states for which being a bounty hunter has either been outlawed or made irrelevant by the banning of the commercial bond system (without bail bondsmen, there is no bounty). Some states require that bounty hunters work with only one bondsman, essentially eliminating the freelance market. Other states require that all bounty hunters be licensed or at least go through specific training. Without a keen understanding of the bond system and other laws of your state, you may find that you're trying to get your foot in a door that doesn't even exist.

BIGGEST CHALLENGES AND BEST PERKS

We're all familiar with the lingo. Any news report regarding a fugitive on the lam always ends with the same cautionary message: The suspect should be considered armed and dangerous. Fugitive recovery is dangerous work. While many subjects give in without a struggle, a bounty hunter can never take this for granted; like a traffic cop, one has to approach every suspect with the utmost caution. Let it never be said, though, that this is boring work. It can be incredibly rewarding, although not necessarily financially lucrative. While some agents make a good living, many others end up working second jobs because they simply cannot support themselves through fugitive recovery alone.

PROFESSIONAL PROFILE

Avg. salary: Varies depending on volume and location. Generally, 10–50 percent of the bail bond contract but agents may charge up to an additional 20 percent if the fugitive recovery effort requires extensive travel.

JARGON

Bounty Hunter Also known as fugitive recovery agents and bail enforcement agents

Extradition The surrender by one state to another of an individual accused or convicted of an offense outside its own territory

FOR MORE INFORMATION

Bailbond.com:
www.bailbond.com

Fugitive Recovery Network:
www.fugitiverecovery.com

Bail Enforcement Education and Training:
www.bondforfeitures.com

LAW ENFORCEMENT OFFICER

A (Relatively Typical) Day in the Life

Sheriffs, state troopers, bailiffs, detectives, and cops on the beat are all part of the local law enforcement community—they are the men and women who bravely patrol the streets to protect lives and property while keeping the city safe and secure. What can be a demanding, stressful, and dangerous job, can also be quiet, monotonous, even boring. No matter the pace, police officers need to be prepared for any situation.

While sheriffs and state troopers are out cruising along stretches of major highways, the uniformed police officer is patrolling a specific area, responding to calls as they come in. When a crime occurs, detectives hit the scene and the sleuthing begins. Their investigations range from routine questioning to DNA analysis. On any given day, they might fill the role of a social worker, a psychologist, peace officer, and soldier. They are the first line of defense between criminals and their victims—a job that can be very stressful.

On a day to day basis, however, police work is mostly a series of routine checks that includes patrols, investigations, and paperwork. Even officers who work in America's biggest and most violent cities rarely draw their guns, much less fire them. Officers write and file dozens of reports and endure long, uneventful hours walking a beat or riding around in the patrol car. Still, local law officials must be prepared to handle any number of situations, from testifying in court to investigating violent crimes. As police officers work their way up through the ranks, their duties become more specialized. Seasoned officers serve as examples for the rookies on the force, providing critical on-the-job training and mentorship. Once an officer makes it to captain, he or she is eligible for consideration to become an inspector, police chief, or commissioner. Taken as a whole, it's a job most find to be worthwhile and fulfilling.

An Extreme Day in the Life

In a career that spanned more than 29 years in the line of duty, Danny Contreras worked his way up from patrolman to captain on a police force in Toledo, Ohio. During that time, he was cut with a knife, shot at, suffered broken bones, and cracked ribs. He rescued a man from being kidnapped, walked into a hostage situation, and nearly shot a man who was reaching under a mattress for what turned out to be a wad of bills. "I could go on and on," he says when asked about extreme days in the field. "But they're not all so bad. There are the good ones, too. I remember one time the guy in front of our patrol car was speeding, so we pulled him over. I had a partner with me that day, though we often worked alone. I went up to the car to ask him what he was doing speeding like that and he says, 'My wife's having a baby!' I said, 'Well, you're going to kill her before you get to the hospital driving like that.' So we put her in the back of our car and told the man we would meet him there. My partner drove and I got in back with the lady, who was really close to having the baby at this point. Afterwards, I had scars on my arm where she grabbed me and held on during that ride. We called the hospital to let them know we were coming so they were waiting for us when we got there. I think they delivered that baby while they were wheeling her in, it was that close of a call."

Law officials must be prepared to handle any number of situations, from testifying in court to investigating violent crimes.

Prepare for Success

If you want to be on the force, you need to be in good physical shape, with plenty of strength and adequate vision. After graduating from high school, you may want to think about getting a college degree in police science or criminal justice. Though it isn't required, it may give you an edge over other candidates. (Most forces require new members to be 20 or 21, so you'll have some time after high school before you can apply, anyway.) Police departments are also looking for shining examples of character; some will even ask candidates to undergo a psychological evaluation.

Getting Your Foot in the Door

As part of the application process, you'll need to pass a written exam, fitness test, drug test, background check, and in-person interview to be considered. Once you jump through these hoops, you'll need to go through training. This might mean a police academy, an apprenticeship, or some other training program. There, you'll learn the ins and outs of the various aspects of police work, including investigative procedures, self-defense, and the law, while fulfilling more minor duties such as directing traffic. Promotions require more education: A two-year associates degree to advance to sergeant, 96 credits towards a bachelor's degree to be considered for a lieutenant position, and a bachelor's degree to make captain.

Biggest Challenges and Best Perks

In addition to being thrust into dangerous, life-threatening situations, the stress of police work has been known to trigger depression, heart attacks, even suicide. In this field, it's easy to make the work your life and vice versa, so it's important to take your mind off the madness with outside past-times. Law enforcement officers need to stay physically fit—a challenge when you're glued to the front seat of a patrol car for hours on end, but necessary for days you need to jump a fence, scale a wall, and run two miles in a hot pursuit.

Police officers are pillars of the community; they find it personally fulfilling to keep the community safe and let justice prevail. Most officers get to know many people around town, and many businesses owners are happy to befriend them. Upon retirement, police officers receive a handsome pension (usually at half pay), which frees them up to pursue a second career or enjoy a modest retirement.

Professional Profile

OFFICER
Avg. starting salary $32,300
Avg. salary after 5 years $42,270
Avg. salary 10 to 15 years $53,500

DETECTIVE
Avg. starting salary $21,980
Avg. salary after 5 years $29,300
Avg. salary 10 to 15 years $41,710

Jargon
Taser A less-than-lethal-weapon in which two small electrodes are launched out of the weapon by a gas cartridge, giving them a range beyond point-blank and incapacitating the subject

Are you Interested In?
Law enforcement, public service

Related College Majors
Police science, criminal justice, criminology

For More Information
World Association of Detectives:
www.WAD.net

American Federation of Police:
www.APHF.org

Fraternal Order of Police:
www.GrandLodgeAFAP.org

LIFEGUARD

A (Relatively) Typical Day in the Life

If you love the beach, are in excellent shape, and want to save lives, a career as a lifeguard may be the job for you. Lifeguards work on the premises of pools, lakes, rivers, and beaches; they save swimmers who get in trouble and curtail risky water activities. Some lifeguards are also responsible for the general upkeep of the areas they supervise. This is a highly active job that requires constant surveillance and alertness, not to mention lots of physical activity.

A typical day begins with arriving to work at or before opening hours and setting up for your shift. This involves making sure you have your equipment, such as binoculars and a first aid kit in your tower, and checking the weather conditions for the day so you can be aware of any advisories. If you are responsible for tidying beach chairs or umbrellas, you might spend some time cleaning or organizing these. Once you're up in the tower or in your elevated chair, you are responsible for every person in your area. Therefore, you will spend a good part of your day watching them carefully; you need to keep an eye out for swimmers who go out too far, people who are affected by heat exhaustion, and anyone who is engaging in prohibited activities (prohibited activities include drinking from glass bottles, leaving children unattended, using drugs, public indecency, and swimming out too far in the water). If you see something dangerous from your tower, you either run out yourself or alert a lifeguard who is closer to the threat. Then you clean up your tower, pack it up, and try to get a good night's sleep so you can be rested enough to make the early shift again the next day. A typical day might also end with a vigorous workout to keep you in the top physical condition that the job requires.

An Extreme Day in the Life

Emma Heeschen has been a lifeguard for years in different capacities: at a YMCA center pool, a beach area at a local lake, a children's summer camp, and her high school pool. She stresses that while many people think being a lifeguard gives people an excuse to spend time at the beach for a living, she's experienced firsthand that lifeguards are "the first line of defense." While many days were disaster-free, filled up with swimming lessons and waterfront activities classes, Emma remembers the day she had her first save. "At the lake beach where I lifeguarded, I often had to watch my best friend's younger sister, who was not only a poor swimmer, but also had a rare disease that put her at a high risk for anaphylactic shock if she suffered any injuries, even the normal ones most kids have in the course of play. On one afternoon at the beach, she was pushed into the deep end and hit herself as she fell in—it was clear that she wasn't able to swim to the top or to shore." Emma swam out to rescue her. Fortunately, the grateful young girl was fine and did not require any medical help. Emma says, "The experience was an eye-opener, really bringing home the fact that the first real test of your strength, training, and preparation comes when you suddenly have to save a life."

Being paid to work in the sun is one of the biggest perks of this job.

Prepare for Success

Many positions do not require a college degree but do have very strict age and fitness requirements. A lifeguard must usually be at least 17 (private pools and beaches may have different rules), be certified in CPR, and trained in other lifesaving procedures. All of the positions have strenuous qualification exams, so it's important to exercise and perfect your swimming in both distance and speed. The job may require you to tow in the water people who are larger than you for considerable distances, so be sure to do strength and endurance training as well. In some areas of the country, lifeguards must be a part of the local fire department or law enforcement agency or be emergency medical technicians, so you may consider gaining experience in law enforcement, qualifying for fire department training, or training to be an EMT before you enter the field. Since a lifeguard must be alert and ready to jump into action at all times, you can further prepare yourself by organizing your activities around a set schedule that leaves time for rest and a good night's sleep.

Getting Your Foot in the Door

Many lifeguards try out for the position several times so they can pass the swimming, training, and written exams, so don't be discouraged if you don't qualify on your first application. Take a course in emergency medical services, work on your swimming and general fitness, and try again. Some people work seasonally as lifeguards while working the rest of the year in teaching and consulting positions; this is an option as well if you don't want to work in a physically strenuous job year-round. Visit the websites for your local beaches, rivers, lakes, or parks department to find out which agencies in your area hire lifeguards. If it's the local law enforcement or fire department, read up on their qualification requirements and be sure you meet them.

Biggest Challenges and Best Perks

The biggest challenge of this job is the stress involved with keeping track of your patrol area consistently throughout the day. The job demands a high level of physical fitness, and it can be difficult to maintain a lifestyle that keeps your body in shape. However, if you're an outdoors person or beach lover, being paid to work in the sun is one of the biggest perks of this job. The job requires constant alertness and action and no two days are the same. Many take advantage of seasonal lifeguarding opportunities to pursue other interests during their time off.

Professional Profile

Avg. salary: $16 to $20 per hour (seasonal)

Avg. salary: up to $27 per hour (full-time)

Jargon

Breaker zone The zone within which waves approaching the coastline commence breaking

Rip currents Different from an undertow, this is a powerful, channeled current of water flowing away from shore

Are you Interested In?

Swimming, law enforcement, public service

Related College Majors

Recreation management, public health

For More Information

American Red Cross Lifeguarding: www.redcross.org/services/hss/aquatics/lifegard.html

United States Lifesaving Association: www.usla.org

PARAMEDIC

A (RELATIVELY) TYPICAL DAY IN THE LIFE

Paramedics and EMTs are often the first medical people at the scene of an accident or a sudden illness; they give immediate care to heart attack victims, car crash victims, gunshot victims, and poison victims. They even assist in childbirth. The sick or injured are then transported to health care facilities in specially equipped emergency vehicles. When they arrive at medical centers, paramedics transfer their patients to nursing personnel and report their observations and treatment procedures to the attending physicians.

The guidelines or procedures that EMTs follow are directly related to their levels of training. The EMT-paramedic is at the upper rung of a three-level hierarchy. Paramedics administer sophisticated pre-hospital care. They are trained in the use of complex medical equipment, such as EKGs, and are capable of administering drugs both orally and intravenously. EMT-intermediates have more advanced training than EMT-basics, who bandage wounds, stabilize blood pressure, assist heart attack victims, and treat accident victims for shock. All three levels of EMTs can be talked through care procedures in the event that they are confronted with a difficult or complicated situation;

An Extreme Day in the Life

According to Jordan Coates, "an extraordinary day on the job would be one with zero calls. Zero calls mean zero sick and hurt people." Unfortunately for Jordan, six years working EMS has taught him all too well that "those days don't happen." Jordan began volunteering with emergency services when he was still in his mid-teens. "When I was 16, an elderly man at my church passed out and when the ambulance pulled up, a younger guy hopped out with the rest of the crew. He was a friend of my younger sister, and I later told him how interesting it was that he was working EMS and he invited me to volunteer as an 'explorer,' or uncertified member. A few weeks later I got on an ambulance for the first time and since then, I can honestly say that there's no other job that I would rather be doing." Once he had completed a 200-hour course load, Jordan became a certified emergency medical technician (EMT), which meant he could provide basic life support: airway control, CPR, defibrillation, hemorrhage control, oxygen administration, splinting, and the administration of a few basic drugs. In January of 2007, he became a fully trained paramedic. During the six years he's spent working in EMS, he's learned to expect the unexpected. "Shifts are so completely unpredictable in number and nature of calls that it's impossible to accurately predict what's in store for any given day. I had a day that started off with a DOA (dead on arrival), which includes telling the family that their loved one has died and taking the body to the morgue. That day also had a car accident that required us to land five helicopters in two separate fields around the scene to airlift five very hurt patients." As the intensity of the day dissipates, "it's hard not to think about the families of the dead or dying patients that you've treated earlier in the day. But every patient deserves compassion, and you have to put the bad calls in the back of your mind, trying not to think about them until you're not on duty. After getting off shift, you deal with the emotions of the day."

[Paramedics] have to be ready to hustle on a moment's notice, as someone's life may be on the line.

therefore, EMTs maintain radio contact with dispatchers and keep those dispatchers aware of the situation. Should the need arise, senior medical personnel (physicians) will then take charge.

An EMT's work can be richly rewarding, such as when a child is born safe and sound despite difficulties, or terribly sad, such as when a patient dies even after they administered proper care. Conditions are tremendously stressful, the hours are long and irregular, and salaries are low. Paramedics must be physically and emotionally strong enough to do back-breaking and sometimes dangerous work; they also have to be ready to hustle on a moment's notice, as someone's life may be on the line. Paramedics never know what conditions they might meet on any given day, so emotional stability is at a premium.

Prepare for Success

Training to become an EMT is offered by police, fire, and health departments, and also in some hospitals. Many colleges and universities offer non-degree courses and programs. Basic training to become a first-level EMT requires 100 to 120 hours of classroom sessions, plus 10 hours of internship in a hospital emergency room and 20 to 50 hours on field rescue or ambulance companies. An additional 35 to 55 hours of instruction are required in patient assessment, intravenous fluids, antishock garments, and esophageal airways for intermediate training. Paramedics usually undergo between 750 and 2,000 hours of training.

Getting Your Foot in the Door

As is often the case, the real training comes with experience. Although registration is not generally required, it does enhance the possibility of advancement and employment opportunities. Certified EMTs must renew their registration every two years. This requires remaining active in the field and meeting a continuing education requirement. Paramedics who want to advance to operations manager, administrative officer, or executive director of emergency services must leave fieldwork.

Biggest Challenges and Best Perks

The life of a paramedic is one of high stakes and high anxiety. They are constantly placed in tense, highly emotional situations where every second can be critical. Physical and mental exhaustion are par for the course as are gruesome encounters. Despite the stress and unpredictable conditions, it is a vital profession and at its very center is concern for the human condition. Paramedics are caregivers, agents of calm, and at their best, life-savers. Nothing could be more satisfying.

Professional Profile
Avg. starting salary: $19,040
Avg. salary after 5 years: $24,030
Avg. salary 10 to 15 years: $31,600

Jargon
Rapid Sequence Induction (RSI) A process that allows an EMT to intubate conscious patients by sedating them so they don't instinctively resist.

Cardiopulmonary resuscitation (CPR) Emergency first aid for an unconscious person whose breathing and pulse cannot be detected

Are you Interested In?
Medicine, health, public service

Related College Majors
Biology, nursing, public health, pharmacology, epidemiology, medical technology

For More Information
National Association of Emergency Medical Technicians:
www.naemt.org

National Registry of Emergency Medical Technicians:
www.nremt.org

PRIVATE INVESTIGATOR

A (Relatively) Typical Day in the Life

Whether residing at 221 Baker Street in nineteenth-century London or walking the dark streets of Sam Spade's San Francisco, the private investigator is one of the most popular prototypes in all of modern fiction and cinema. Revered for their unmatched intellect, their willingness to take chances, and their capacity to get to the heart of a crime, it's no wonder that real-life private detectives find it difficult to live up to their romanticized counterparts. Who wouldn't?

While the common perception of the private eye is that of a lone wolf and renegade patiently waiting for the next client to darken their doorway, only about 25 percent of all the people working in the field do so as independent contractors. Today, the majority of all private investigators are permanent employees who work on behalf of organizations and corporations with the regular need, and the means to pay, for an in-house investigative department. They may work in cooperation with criminal defense attorneys trying to prepare adequate defenses for their clients, at the behest of large corporations looking to prevent embezzlement within the rank and file, for insurance companies protecting themselves against fraudulent claims, or as financial investigators creating individual profiles of would-be investors for employers. Of course, there are still plenty of freelance private detectives out there offering all sorts of services to private citizens who come to them with problems for which they cannot, or choose not

An Extreme Day in the Life

Richard "Bo" Dietl spent the first 16 years of his adult life as a highly decorated member of the New York City Police Department. As a homicide detective, he worked on some of the city's most high profile cases, making more than 1,500 arrests. When Bo retired from the force in 1985, he became the founder and CEO of Beau Dietl & Associates, a private investigation firm that provides a variety of security services to clients large and small. Already well-known for the duties he performed as a civil servant, it wasn't long before Bo's public persona began to take on national proportions. Featured in an article penned by the screenwriter for *Goodfellas* in *New York* magazine, Beau Dietl & Associates was catapulted onto the national stage. The young company was being called upon to improve the security standards of some of the country's largest corporations, and its outspoken CEO was fielding regular requests to appear on various media programs. As a private investigator, Mr. Dietl soon found that the attention he was receiving was a double-edged sword. While his regular appearances on popular programs such as WFAN's Imus in the Morning have given Bo an outlet to speak directly to some of the nation's most powerful politicians and businesspeople, he says there's always the danger that "you become too high profile, and some of the more conservative companies begin to look on you as too flashy, or over the top." Dietl insists his main responsibility is to his clients, and while he rarely holds his tongue on other subjects, he exercises complete discretion when it comes to the job. "I don't want people to think if they hire me the next thing they're going to see is their case on TV." This mentality, along with his personal connection to New York City, has enabled Dietl to continue to work as a public personality in a typically private business.

Private investigators have a knack for surveillance and observing the most minute details of a given situation.

to, get help from local authorities.

Prepare for Success

There's really no formal training to become a private investigator, although most states require some type of licensure. It should come as no surprise that many of people who work as private investigators are former law enforcement employees, have been in the military, or have worked for the federal government. It's also common for private detectives to have college degrees. This is by no means a requirement, though. Generally, there are a number of traits private eyes have in common: They have a knack for surveillance and observing the most minute details of a given situation; an ability to interact with people and interview and interrogate them without appearing abrasive; and a willingness to do a lot of legwork. With the amount of paperwork that this job can entail, it would be helpful if you weren't afraid of occasionally hunkering down at a desk to get the job done.

Getting Your Foot in the Door

There are as many ways to get started as a private detective as there are fields worth investigating. A lot of times, private investigation comes to you, not the other way around. You have a career in a field, end up working alongside an investigator, find you have a knack for the job, and bingo: Your foot is in the door before you even knew it was there. If you want to take a more direct path, your best shot is to pursue a position with a private investigating agency. Whether you fall into this profession or pursue it actively, working alongside other PIs will help you learn the ins and outs of the business.

Biggest Challenges and Best Perks

Any job that involves criminal or unsavory elements can be dangerous work, and being a PI is no different. While at times the work may feel impersonal, it's important to remember that you're usually going to be investigating a person; whether the cause is frivolous or genuine, people don't like it when anyone, especially a stranger, is checking up on them. While people love to read stories and watch movies involving private detectives, you'll find that many people don't like them so much in real life. It's not always easy to be unpopular—add the element of danger, and there are any number of occupational hazards that may occur. That said, if you're the right kind of person, it's far from boring work. This is not to say there's never a dull moment. There are probably thousands of them, but as a whole, there is an excitement that comes from the basic exercise of launching an investigation that can be very fulfilling.

PROFESSIONAL PROFILE
Avg. starting salary: $25,000
Avg. salary after 5 years: $39,800
Avg. salary 10 to 15 years: $77,500

JARGON
Authenticate Proving that a document is not a forgery
Vital records Birth, marriage, and death records

ARE YOU INTERESTED IN?
Law enforcement, research, intelligence

RELATED COLLEGE MAJORS
Criminal justice, criminology, business administration

FOR MORE INFORMATION
PI Magazine:
www.pimagazine.com
Private Investigator, Private Detectives, and Law Enforcement Resources:
www.einvestigator.com
World Association of Private Investigators:
www.wapi.com

RACE CAR DRIVER

A (Relatively) Typical Day in the Life

Burning rubber, squealing tires, and logo-covered vehicles are among the sights, smells, and sounds race car driving brings to mind, but the business behind the races can be just as consuming as the adrenaline rush that comes when you're behind the wheel. Just ask Ricky Bobby. Motor sports are big business in America with companies shelling out millions of dollars in advertising, promotional products, and driver endorsements. Even such unlikely products as an Elizabeth Arden Fragrance for Men have turned up at NASCAR events. Some race weekends pull in major bucks with hundreds of fans shelling out as much as $650 per person for three-day tickets to exclusive race track clubs.

Aspiring race car drivers must understand the business side of racing if they are to make a career where others have crashed and burned. On a race day, you may have to parade around in outfits bearing your sponsor's logo, meet with the companies' current and potential clients, pose for pictures, sign autographs, mingle with fans, and have media interviews before you even set foot in your car for the race. And you must do all this with a smile because winning fans and sponsors is nearly as important as winning races in this business.

When behind the wheel, the job takes a different turn and your concentration and driving skills come to the fore. Your sole focus is on executing the race strategy that you discussed with engineers and crewmembers prior to the race. Driving at extraordinary speeds may feel like an out-of-body experience, but you are in control behind the wheel and that has an adrenaline rush all its own.

An Extreme Day in the Life

Jason Jarrett is a third-generation race car driver who loves the calm that comes behind the wheel. "The best part is when you sit down on the seat and strap in and you know you're going to be in there for two hours. Everything you did earlier in the week was preparing for this. You just get a different peace of mind. You don't have anything else to worry about. You're just worried about winning that particular race."

Jason raced bi-weekly for several years in events from North Carolina to Kansas in the ARCA RE/MAX Series before becoming a spokesman for Dale Jarrett Racing Adventure. "While I was in that series, one of the hardest but most rewarding experiences was a stretch of nine days that we had three races in. There was a lot of traveling involved and three different types of racetracks—a short track, a one-mile dirt track, and a 1.5 mile super speedway. It was fun but stressful because you have to have a couple of different types of cars with you and it takes more logistically to get the right car at the right track. It might take a few more part-time employees. And then you're together with your crew nonstop for 9 or ten straight days and depending on how the week goes that can be kind of stressful too. If you're having a bad week, everyone gets stressed out quicker. The rewarding thing out of the series was winning the Bill France Triple Crown award for getting the most points in those three races. Although we didn't win the overall championship, it was rewarding for the whole team to get the most points."

Winning fans and sponsors is nearly as important as winning races in this business.

Prepare for Success

Aspiring race car drivers must become students of the sport and read everything they can to learn the ins and outs of the profession. You also need to be attentive to safety if you want a shot at going to the top. Some drivers say that knowing that you have the safest uniform, helmet, head and neck restraints, and other equipment gives you the confidence to go faster. You may also need to enroll in a reputable driving school and take a course that is at least three days long to learn the fundamentals of race car driving and begin building relationships with racers, coaches, and instructors. Participate in driving days hosted by regional car clubs and racing school events to network and test your skills. You'll also need to polish your public speaking and other communication skills to attract fans and potential sponsors.

Getting Your Foot in the Door

This is a relationship business so you'll need to spend lots of times hanging around racetracks and meeting drivers and crews. Soak up as much information as possible by observing everything they do and striking up conversations. Volunteer to sell tickets, be a race track usher, run errands, or wash cars if you have to. You'll also need to present yourself to sponsors in a professional manner as early as possible because you'll need a steady stream of financing to be competitive in this field. Some sports teams are already scouting the 14- and 15-year-olds who will be the next generation of drivers.

Biggest Challenges and Best Perks

Finding the sponsorship dollars to support your racing year after year is a major challenge in this industry. Once you have sponsorship, your payment as a driver will be tied to your performance, adding new pressures to win. You must rank high in order to keep the money coming in. And don't forget: collisions happen. One bad spill and you may be out of the race for weeks recovering from neck injuries, fractured bones, and other ailments. This hurts your body and your wallet.

There may be no more rewarding job if you love to drive. You could experience the thrill of racing past the competition to victory or crashing your car and walking away from the wreckage unharmed. You may become a celebrity among racing fans across the country, take pictures, give speeches, and sign autographs. If you've got the guts, this field has the potential for tremendous glory.

PROFESSIONAL PROFILE
Avg. starting salary: Varies considerably, based on experience, success rate, and sponsorship

JARGON
Sprint Cars Small, high-powered race cars designed primarily for racing on short dirt or paved tracks.

Rallying Form of automobile racing that takes place on public roads with modified or custom-built road cars.

ARE YOU INTERESTED IN?
Driving, racing

RELATED COLLEGE MAJORS
Automotive training, automotive engineering, business management

FOR MORE INFORMATION
NASCAR:
www.NASCAR.com

Vintage Sports Car Racing:
www.VSCDA.org

National Electric Drag Racing Association:
www.NEDRA.com

STUNT/BODY DOUBLE

A (Relatively) Typical Day in the Life

A stunt double is hired as an actor by a film crew to fill in for scenes that may be dangerous or have the potential to cause injury. He or she may have to fall out of cars, jump buildings, or act out a sophisticated fight sequence. But make no mistake: Stunt doubling isn't just a bunch of reckless fun. It takes a lot of time and hard work to hone the skills needed to become a successful stunt double. Timing, ingenuity, and experience are all important factors, not to mention endurance. This is because a typical day on the set might include long periods of time spent holding an uncomfortable position—suspended mid-air or underwater, for example—while the director and film crew struggle to get the right angle for the perfect shot.

Most stunt doubles specialize in a certain action, such as combat fighting, falling, driving, crashing, piloting, etc. A stunt double can expect to travel on location with the rest of the film production crew. Each scene can take several days to perfect, and directors and stunt coordinators will spend hours on set going over the most minute details of each sequence. The hours are long: Like actors, stunt doubles may have to report for hair and makeup as early as 4:30 A.M. and may not wrap for the day until 18 hours later. The time in between is spent warming up and stretching, checking and re-checking safety equipment, and going over the action sequence.

Of course, stunt people are not just hired for their skills alone. They also have to resemble the actors for whom they're filling in, which may entail copying their mannerisms and movements. Some stunt doubles become so adept at this impersonation that they become permanent members of an actor's contractual "support crew." While there is usually time to practice the stunts ahead of time, stunts that involve explosions and burning are only attempted

An Extreme Day in the Life

Almost every day on the set is an "extreme" day in the life of a stunt double, but some days are more extreme than others. Mike Massa, stunt double for David Boreanz on the set of the hit show Angel, describes one of his favorite (and most extreme) moments: "It was one of those things where I had just started working on the show and I was talking to the coordinator and the director and we wanted to make sure this show looks good. I mean, we've got some serious action going on and they gave me the opportunity. 'Well, you can go fly across this room and land your head up and just slam the wall and slide down to your feet or you can go inverted and slam it upside down and crash your head.' I sat there and looked at it and I just opted, 'well let's do the big gnarly looking, upside-down one.' . . . I had to hit it sideways, my back flat to the wall and kind of skip into it, but it just drove me right to the ground."

"It was just one of my many favorites to remember because the director (Jim Contner) came out there . . . and he was just ecstatic. He thought that was the best stunt he'd ever seen. He was jumping up and down. Everybody was checking me out. I was fine, but it looked so gnarly and so scary and he was just the happiest guy in the world."

Source: http://www.cityofangel.com/behindTheScenes/bts/massa1.html

Stunt doubles feel enormous pressure to deliver the perfect
shot—there are no second takes.

once. In these scenarios, stunt doubles feel enormous pressure to deliver the perfect shot—there are no second takes.

PREPARE FOR SUCCESS

There are no specific educational requirements for entering a career as a stunt double, but almost all have a strong set of skills that production coordinators will seek out. A background in gymnastics, martial arts, race-car driving and/or motorbike racing, and extreme outdoor sports are all particularly helpful. Those who are serious about pursuing a professional career in stunt doubling may choose to attend stunt schools that offer specialties in a variety of sports, including horseback riding, scuba diving, parachuting, and combat fighting. Most stunt doubles specialize in one or two areas and have experience in a broad range of other activities. All stunt doubles should be experts at first aid.

GETTING YOUR FOOT IN THE DOOR

Stunt doubles often start out as extras on a set. These low-paying roles help them build their production experience and give them the opportunity to network with the actors, directors, agents, and producers who can advance their careers. Getting to know stunt coordinators is important, and aspiring stunt doubles may eventually earn a job as an assistant to a stunt coordinator. These positions are far from glamorous, but they provide an excellent opportunity for aspirants to absorb on-the-set stunt knowledge. Eventually, the hard work will pay off, and they'll find themselves jumping out of cars and fighting off bad guys in no time.

BIGGEST CHALLENGES AND BEST PERKS

One of the biggest challenges of life as a stunt double is building enough experience and enough contacts to gain membership to the Screen Actor's Guild. Membership in this union gives stunt doubles access to better, higher-paying jobs, and affords them the opportunity to specialize in one area rather than filling in as extra on a variety of different stunt jobs. The life of a stunt double is physically grueling, and after 10 years in the business most transition into roles as stunt coordinators. Negotiating this period of transition, which comes quickly, is another challenge for people interested in pursuing this career path.

Stunt doubles with the right networking skills can land a gig as a permanent member of an actor's support crew, and travel from set to set with the cooks, trainers, and personal assistants whom the actor employs. Certainly the glamour of life in Hollywood is one of the best perks of becoming a stunt double. Access to famous stars, great parties, and more and more often, the opportunity to become stars in their own right, are a few of the reasons people choose this career.

PROFESSIONAL PROFILE
Avg. starting salary: $15,000
Avg. salary after 5 years: $45,500
Avg. salary 10 to 15 years: $100,000

JARGON
Honeywagon A trailer outfitted for and used as the dressing room for actors when on location

ARE YOU INTERESTED IN?
Gymnastics, martial arts, race car driving, horseback riding, acting

RELATED COLLEGE MAJORS
Acting, equestrian studies, automotive training

FOR MORE INFORMATION
Screen Actor's Guild:
www.sag.org

Stuntwomen's Association of Motion Pictures:
www.stuntwomen.com

United Stuntmen's Association:
www.stuntschool.com

ARTISTIC TALENT

ACROBAT

A (Relatively) Typical Day in the Life

If you spent your childhood listening to your mom tell you to stop swinging on the jungle gym like a monkey, we have some good news for you: You can actually make a living bending your body and flying through the air. Your mother might not agree, but those hours were well spent if you're thinking of becoming a professional acrobat.

Acrobatics—performing difficult feats of balance, agility, and coordination—requires grace, athleticism, flexibility, strength, and impressive muscle control. Even more, it calls for great discipline and concentration in making the human body an art form. Becoming an acrobat takes hard work and many years of long hours of practice so you can master great poise and develop technique. Today's most popular acrobatic shows blend avant-garde visual theatrics with traditional circus acts. Shows usually include dancing, juggling, clowns, singing, wild animal acts, horseback riding, balancing acts, fire-eating, bicycling, trampolining, high-wire acts, contortionists, and aerial choreography. Acrobats must continually learn new tricks to keep current with the latest performance trends.

Most acrobats work for a circus or other type of traveling show where their days are filled with practicing new moves or routines, working out, rehearsing their acts, setting up their props, getting into costume, performing in the shows, and, whenever there's time leftover, eating, sleeping, and trying to piece together some semblance of a personal life. Some touring shows spend several months in one city before moving on, while others spend only one night. Touring acrobats rehearse every day and spend a lot of time perfecting the timing and technical aspects of their routines. At night, accommodations may range from a circus trailer to luxurious hotels, depending on the

An Extreme Day in the Life

Just 22 years old, Marcello Balestracci has been on the go since the age of 4. That's when he started taking dance classes in jazz, ballet, modern, and hip-hop in addition to his competitive gymnastics training. When Marcello tore both shoulders two weeks before the Junior Olympics, he was forced to find something that could fulfill his passion for gymnastics but be less strenuous on his upper body. These days he's in Cirque Production's Atlantic City show Cirque Dreams Jungle Fantasy—a job that also keeps him moving on the road. When traveling and performing combine, days are bound to get extreme: "You get up at 4:00 A.M., get on a bus, and travel for 10, even 15 hours. When we get to our next stop, we set up the stage and run through a quick rehearsal. Then we have a little time to practice, warm up, stretch, and get something to eat before we go into makeup and prepare to do the show. Afterward, we break down the set, shower, eat, and go to bed. Then we get up at 4:00 A.M. and do it all over again!" Most days are packed with two performances, plus rehearsals, workouts, eating, and resting—an important component for the muscles and mind. Marcello explains, "It's one of the best jobs a kid my age could have, and for me it's a dream job. You have to love doing it and you have to want it, which I do. For our last show, we traveled to 20 states, doing almost a state a day. But I'm with a bunch of my friends and it's like they say, the circus is family."

You can actually make a living bending your body and flying through the air.

touring company. Acrobats learn to live life on the road, often developing family-like bonds with those in their troupe. Years spent building up trust among the people in their company enables acrobats to leap from a pole-top platform or do a triple somersault in midair and know that a strong pair of hands will be on the other side to catch them.

Prepare for Success

Most professional acrobats take rigorous gymnastics classes long before they reach their double digits. A background in competitive gymnastics and dance (especially ballet) is almost essential, but highly motivated and athletic late bloomers can still break into the profession by working hard at circus schools. There are several circus schools in California, Florida, and a few other U.S. locales. Florida State University has its own Flying High Circus on the school's campus that is open to any FSU student who wants to join.

Getting Your Foot in the Door

Talent and desire will propel you to significant heights when it comes to landing an acrobatic job. Circus organizations of all sizes recruit new acrobats and are frequently open to meeting those who approach them with a great act on video or in person. The road to a career as an acrobat may take some creative finagling. This means a willingness to relocate for a job, travel extensively while on tour, or take a position behind the scenes of a show until you're able to prove yourself.

Biggest Challenges and Best Perks

Life on the road can take its toll on anyone who craves stability. Acrobats have to put up with crammed quarters, noisy bunkmates, and constantly changing scenery. There are days when the audience will be few in number or slow to respond and acrobats need to paste smiles on their faces and put on stellar shows anyway. Flying above the earth in contortionist poses is obviously dangerous work. Injuries are common and when you're injured, you don't work. Pay is low, but there's not much time for shopping anyway, since you're working nights, weekends, and holidays. On the contrary, seeing a child's eyes light up in awe is all it takes to redeem a tough week sometimes. Acrobats get to enjoy audience members' delight and surprise at their amazing feats. Moreover, they get to see the world, make people happy, stay in top physical condition, and work with a group that feels like an extension of their own families.

PROFESSIONAL PROFILE
Avg. starting salary: $19,000

Avg. salary after 5 years:
$21,000 to $30,000

Avg. salary 10 to 15 years:
$31,000 to $47,000

JARGON
Aerial tissue Performing acrobatics while suspended by silk or other fabric

Contact juggling The art of juggling without letting the balls leave contact with one's body. Instead, they are rolled around one another (palm spinning) or along the arms and body (body rolling).

Enterology The practice of squeezing one's body into small, knee-high box, which appears to be much too small to accommodate a person, usually while seated cross-legged with the head between the knees

ARE YOU INTERESTED IN?
Ballet, gymnastics

RELATED COLLEGE MAJORS
Dance, fine arts, theater

FOR MORE INFORMATION
Performing Jobs:
www.performingjobs.com/acrobats.cfm

American Youth Circus Organization:
www.americanyouthcircus.org

Circus Maniacs School of Circus Arts:
www.circusmaniacs.com/en/index.php

ACTOR

A (Relatively) Typical Day in the Life

When you hear the word actor you probably think of Hollywood stars—the ones who work in film, network television, or theater in New York or Los Angeles. However, far more professional actors are found scattered in local or regional television studios, theaters, or film production companies, working in advertising, public relations, or independent, small-scale movie productions.

Your satisfaction with an acting career depends largely upon your expectations. Few people are able to survive on their acting paychecks alone. The average Actors' Equity Association (AEA) member earns less than $7,000 a year from his or her acting jobs. The big bucks are in Hollywood and are reserved for an elite group who will tell you that, although they have talent, they've also gotten a few lucky breaks along the way.

A hypothetical day in the life of a typical actor might begin to the sound of roommates fighting; after all, rent in Los Angeles and New York is expensive, and actors will likely not afford an apartment on their own. The actor probably checks e-mail and voicemail before beginning a day filled with auditions. The actor might then have a session with an acting coach and a meeting with an agent. All the while, he or she is probably checking voicemail periodically in the hopes of receiving a call-back for last week's auditions. Unfortunately, the actor has to report to work at a restaurant waiting tables until after midnight. Hopefully, the job also lets said actor network and meet at least three people during who say they know someone the actor should meet. Finally, the actor goes home, flops into bed after browsing the Internet for upcoming auditions and open calls for extras, and proceeds to engage in self-doubt.

When actors are working, the world is rosy. When they're not, they're desperately searching for roles and experiencing much self-doubt—especially when they're working at other jobs to pay the bills. Expect plenty of rejection before scoring the big break. Head shots, acting classes, voice lessons, teeth whitening, hairdos, manicures, and a stylish wardrobe are all part of the expensive self-packaging actors must undergo just to compete with the big dogs. Actors who are hired for union productions can apply for membership to the Screen Actors Guild (SAG) and Actors'

An Extreme Day in the Life

Lucia Brawley received her BA from Harvard and an MFA from the Yale School of Drama. She has appeared in numerous plays in New York; TV shows for NBC, CBS, FOX, and PBS; as well as Oliver Stone's *World Trade Center* and a Hungarian film titled *Blind Love*. She and her husband, Emmy award–winner Peter Macon, live in Hollywood, California—that is, when they're not traveling for work. "On the film I'm shooting now, I had to run out onto the street, barefoot, in only a man's shirt, under a crane that controls a rain machine. . . . Before each shot, I had to stand on the street and get hosed down by the wardrobe ladies, so that I would be sufficiently drenched, before the rain machine even started. By the end of the second night, shivering and covered in fake blood, I didn't even have to get into character to sob uncontrollably." Brawley says that during scenes like this, she has to keep reminding herself: "I am in beautiful Budapest doing what I love to do. The challenge of it will only make me a stronger artist and person."

You're only as good as your last film.

Equity—two unions that demand higher wages and are able to offer members health insurance discounts.

Prepare for Success

There's no formal training required in this field, so feel free to carve out your own path and don't be discouraged if you start out later than some. Nick Nolte got his first role in TV at age 35. Few actors who were not born into Hollywood families get by without some acting classes, if not a bachelor's and possibly a master's degree in theater from a college that's known for churning out stars. Most actors who work their way up from the bottom take any work they can get.

Getting Your Foot in the Door

Actors who find success have prepared for years and are more than ready for it. Continue to hone any special skills that might set you apart from the next actor for a part—stunts, martial arts, singing, dancing, horseback riding, surfing, a foreign language, you name it. An agent—if you can get a good one—will scout for parts that might be good fits for you. Play the who-you-know game and make as many connections as you can. Once you're getting paid to act, you'll know you're making progress. Success can be fleeting and even well-known actors feel compelled to keep proving themselves, living by the old creed: "You're only as good as your last film."

Biggest Challenges and Best Perks

Acting presents at least a million challenges. If you're not struggling to land a role between long stretches of unemployment, you're struggling to break out of the typecast role in which you're stuck. Steering clear of the unhealthy temptations of Hollywood, having confidence despite rejection and criticism, and supporting yourself until solid work comes along are just a few of the many challenges you will face in this profession. Despite the profession's intense lifestyle, there are many perks to becoming an actor. Theatrical people know how to have a good time, and if you're doing what you love surrounded by people who feel the same, the tough days working your way in and up should be balanced out by the days you're on top of the world. If you get anywhere in this business, you got farther than most. And if you're one of the lucky few to find fame and fortune—well, that possibility alone is enough to motivate most aspiring actors.

PROFESSIONAL PROFILE
Avg. starting salary: $15,000
Avg. salary after 5 years: $23,000
Avg. salary 10 to 15 years: $53,000

JARGON
Cheating When an actor takes on a physical position that would not be natural in real life—often necessary to get the right effect or perspective on film

Pickup A director's term to indicate that he or she wants to redo a small part of the scene

RELATED COLLEGE MAJORS
Theater, fine arts

FOR MORE INFORMATION
Actors' Equity Association:
www.actorsequity.org

Screen Actors Guild: www.sag.org

The Hollywood Reporter:
www.hollywoodreporter.com

ARTIST

A (Relatively) Typical Day in the Life

Artists are used to seeing the world a little differently from other people; no matter what fans or critics may say about their work, they continue to create. The drive and the physical process of making something that no one else has ever made before draws people to the profession. Painting, sculpture, drawing, photography, and mixed media are popular forms, but collage, found objects, silk screening, ceramics, jewelry and other wearable art, graffiti, and even performance art all have their own place in the art world. Artists are either creating or thinking about creating at all times. Their experiences and perceptions shape their work, so they are constantly inspired to create when the mood strikes. Some artists find ideas all around them but also go through tedious slumps.

For those fortunate enough to be able to make art their full-time job, it tends to be a very solitary process. Art involves research, buying new materials, cleaning up supplies, and planning new works. Artists also support fellow artists by attending their shows. Many artists take classes and market themselves by compiling portfolios and sending them to galleries, meeting with potential clients, submitting applications for juried shows or art festivals, and looking for new outlets where they can display and sell their work.

Many artists dream of receiving a commitment from a gallery or dealer that exclusively markets and sells their work in exchange for a percentage of the profits. Arrangements such as these free artists to devote all of their efforts to producing new work. Regrettably, most artists don't earn enough from their art to make rent; therefore, many flock to the creative fields as commercial artists; graphic designers; art directors; illustrators; various jobs in advertising, promotion, and product design; and even jobs as costume designers, makeup artists, set designers, or art teachers. While some artists find it tough to generate interest in their work and keep reinventing themselves, others enjoy the chance to evolve and essentially be someone new with each new work.

An Extreme Day in the Life

A successful commercial photographer who has done celebrity portraits, architecture, and fashion, David Blank also devotes time and energy to his fine art photography, which has been shown in galleries and bought by private collectors. He describes his artistic photography as a break from his extreme days on commercial shoots. "I make the cameras, and I make the lenses that I use. What I do is old-school, black-and-white photography that has to be processed in the field when I shoot it. Each shot is a visual study that is unique to my eyes—whether it's architecture, landscape, or nature. It's very meditative. The way I make the cameras, I look through one lens and shoot through another. So I never know what I'm going to get, which is exciting. I take the control away and leave it up to serendipity. I focus only on my aesthetic sensibilities and it feels pure. If I do that for a couple of days, I am rejuvenated and I feel better when I go back to my commercial work. . . . It calms me. And I find it is a good break from the extreme."

If you want to be an artist full-time, self-promotion is part of the business.

Prepare for Success

There are a great number of self-taught artists, many of whom are beyond famous. With no formal educational training, these pioneers possessed the sheer artistic genius to pick up a brush and paint masterpieces. Unfortunately, this is rare nowadays. Most modern artists understand that an academic background provides them with the necessary skills to assist them in their creative work. Many earn BFAs in graphic design, painting, sculpture, metalwork, photography, ceramics, printmaking, or art history. Some even earn graduate degrees—primarily MFAs—because it facilitates teaching art at the secondary level or above. Urban areas attract artistic types due to the plethora of museums, galleries, and other artists. Large cities also offer more opportunities for unknown artists to show and sell their work and carve out a niche.

Getting Your Foot in the Door

Being savvy at marketing yourself and your work can feel like it detracts from the process of creation, but if you want to be an artist full-time, self-promotion is part of the business. If you are lucky and find a gallery to show your work, then they will normally throw an opening reception and advertise the show. There you'll rub elbows with potential clients who may like what they see. Having a good relationship with a gallery is important, as is networking with dealers and critics in the art community. Taking your art to fairs and festivals or selling it on the street may increase exposure. Maintain a website, even if it's a simple one, so interested parties can view your work and contact you.

Biggest Challenges and Best Perks

Starving artists know that the biggest challenge of this career involves earning enough for food, shelter, and other necessities. Living frugally (or working other jobs) is common. It is not only tough to sell work, but also expensive to produce, unless you make sculptures from treasures you found in the trash. Some artists feel misunderstood and unable to relate to society at large, and when their work is displayed, it's open to intense critique.

Seeing the world through a different set of eyes and becoming part of a community that does the same is an artist's privilege. Those who create do so their whole lives. Even those who decide to pursue careers in other fields often practice their art after work and on weekends; some even enjoy commercial success. There are days when being an artist may feel like a burden or curse, but most artists relish their vision and ability to harness it to make something beautiful.

Professional Profile
Avg. starting salary: $24,000

Avg. salary after 5 years: $35,000

Avg. salary 10 to 15 years: $48,000

Jargon
Painted edges Refers to when artists paint over the edges and sides of the canvas because they don't intend the painting to be framed; it also creates a 3-D effect

Are you Interested In?
Sketching, sculpting, sketching, painting

Related College Majors
Art, art history, fine arts, graphic design

For More Information
American Design and Drafting Association:
www.adda.org

Art Niche New York:
www.anny.org

The Independent Artist's Resource:
www.artistsresources.org

CLOWN/MAGICIAN

A (RELATIVELY) TYPICAL DAY IN THE LIFE

Those who enter into fields of clowning and magic believe in the powers of awe, wonder, surprise, and laughter. Many have been performing for family and friends since they could walk and had a feeling since grade school that a regular job would never suit them. However, before clowns can even begin entertaining, they need to develop their characters and put together the appropriate costumes, makeup, and acts to match their personas. The rainbow wig clown is just one version in a coterie of mimes, jesters, tramps, baby, and fat lady clowns. Just developing your clown is a job in itself. An act might incorporate magic tricks, games, songs, balloon art, crafts, stunts, skits, acrobatics, jokes, face painting, unicycle riding, stilt walking, juggling, physical comedy, miming, and any other specialties that appeal to the performer.

Magicians have long amazed audiences with their never-ending scarves and disappearing coins. These kinds of magicians still exist. However, sophisticated magic tricks, feats of endurance, seemingly life-threatening stunts, and the art of illusion have attracted an increasing adult fan base in recent years.

More time is invested in practicing tricks or routines and developing new ones than in actually performing. Maintaining equipment and packing/unpacking for shows also eat up plenty of time. Self-employed entertainers have to drum up new business through contacts and advertising. Clowns and magicians perform shows at amusement parks, carnivals, toy stores, theme restaurants, hotels, birthday parties, fund-raisers, hospitals, schools, day camps, senior centers, and even the occasional used-car lot.

Clowns and magicians carry a suitcase full of confidence, brilliant hand-eye coordination, and an innate sense of timing. They adapt easily to new situations and enjoy interacting with people of all ages and from all walks of life. In addition to being in good physical condition, these entertainers must understand the health and safety aspects of performing—both their own and their audience's. When an act isn't having the desired effect, they should

An Extreme Day in the Life

Hanna Banana, AKA Karen Koziol, has been a full-time jester clown for 26 years and now teaches at her school for would-be clowns. Her three-day school is located at the famous Circus Hotel & Casino in Las Vegas, Nevada. In addition to working at parties and events, she volunteers her time at the YMCA and the Boys and Girls Club. A Christmas show at the YMCA several years ago took her by surprise. "I went up to the mike and looked at all of the children with smiles on their faces. I looked to the right and saw my friend who was dressed as Santa Claus as part of the show, and to the left at my friend dressed as Spiderman as another part, then out at the children smiling again. There was so much love in that room—between the love the kids had for us and the love we had for them—that I just started crying! Then the parents of the kids started crying too. The kids, they just smiled. They felt it like we did. That's what my work is all about. The newspaper ended up doing a story on the show and I was known as 'the crying clown.' Everyone agreed it was the most miraculous Christmas moment and everyone shared it together."

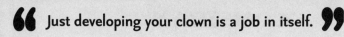
Just developing your clown is a job in itself.

be able to switch it up in a hurry. Those who choose a career based on delighting, astonishing, and humoring others cannot come to the job exhausted or distracted. In this line of work, there is no such thing as not feeling in the mood to perform—the show simply must go on.

Prepare for Success

Young clowns and magicians should test out their own natural talents. Entering a talent competition or amateur night is one option, but most of them start by volunteering their services at birthday parties, nursing homes, hospitals, or nonprofit events. Volunteering is a great way to try out new material, stay sharp between paid gigs, and build a list of references. Beyond general movement and acting classes, there are several specialized programs geared toward the aspiring clown or magician. Formal training offers a safe environment for critique by peers and instructors. In addition, it helps them to build confidence, develop skills, provide know-how for tapping into business opportunities, and possibly aid in a job search if full-time work is desired.

Getting Your Foot in the Door

Aspiring clowns and magicians should focus on building a wide client base and generating new business. Industry conferences and associations are one place to get new contacts. Advertising, having a great website and business cards, and teaming up with local businesses for referrals are others. Clowns and magicians increase their marketability when they expand their repertoire to include full party planning services, classes for children, or an array of different characters.

Biggest Challenges and Best Perks

Clowns and magicians work plenty of nights and weekends. Audiences—especially children—can be finicky and are not shy about showing disapproval. Some stunts, like juggling fire, can be dangerous. During busy times, these entertainers do a lot of driving and performances without rest. Demand can be limited and work can be sporadic. Even those who have steady gigs are unlikely to be raking in the big bucks.

On the contrary, living a life in costume is the best kind of work most clowns can imagine and magicians couldn't live without a venue for performing tricks that delight and amaze. Most in this field feel a special connection with children and cherish the opportunity to be able to work with them so often. Having a creative outlet, meeting new people, and the bonuses of smiles and applause are their own reward, not to mention the opportunity to land larger, more prestigious gigs with a chance for media exposure and notoriety.

Professional Profile
Avg. starting salary: $13,000
Avg. salary after 5 years: $18,000
Avg. salary 10 to 15 years: $32,000

Jargon
Plant For a magician, a person in the audience who knows how an illusion is done, used mostly in disappearing boxes

Are you Interested In?
Clowning, comedy, acting, dancing

Related College Majors
Theater, experimental performance

For More Information
International Brotherhood of Magicians:
www.magician.org

Clown-Ministry.Com:
www.clown-ministry.com

Clowns for Hire:
www.clownsforhire.com/clown-schools.html

COMEDIAN

A (RELATIVELY) TYPICAL DAY IN THE LIFE

Comedians get a thrill out of making people laugh. They develop unique styles, skills, and bodies of work as entertainers. Most non-comedians are familiar with only comic superstars such as Steve Martin, Whoopi Goldberg, and Jerry Seinfeld. While these success stories are certainly inspiring, most comedians work long hours for little (if any) pay and endure enormous uncertainty, never knowing from where the next paycheck will come. The average stand-up comedian earns around $50 for two 20-minute sets at a comedy club. While this translates into a solid hourly wage, a new comedian may do four sets per week, with the rest of the time spent writing material, watching other comedians, and working at another job to pay the rent. Successful comedians must have quick wits, think on their feet, be dedicated, and have a lot of luck. A great deal of self-confidence is required if a comedian is to last in this profession, since failure, disappointment, and rejection are standard. Many comedians join comedy troupes and help develop, perform, and publicize the troupe's material. Because attendees will not return to see the same material, it is a highly pressured large output environment. A troupe comedian must adapt to peers' comments and take criticism well. The ability to work with others is critical to success in comedy groups. The troupes are often formed in major urban centers due to the larger opportunity for work. Solo comedians perform on club circuits around the country, usually one after another on a given night, creating a very competitive atmosphere. Being a solo comedian can be an "if-you-win-I-lose" type of career.

An Extreme Day in the Life

As a writer and performer, Chris Kula knows comedy isn't just all about the timing; it's also about making the most of your time. Since arriving in New York five years ago, he's managed to carve out a successful career, most recently writing for a humor website. His days tend to unfold at a hectic pace: "I get to the office at 9:00 A.M. (about three hours earlier than I'd prefer), read the morning headlines, and plan out the 'timely' and 'topical' content I'm going to publish on the website for that day. That publishing cycle would continue till about 5:30 P.M., as I cranked out about one or two short satirical pieces per hour. In whatever downtime I could find I'd be selecting possible photos for a weekly photo gallery that would run on the site the next day. Once my writing cycle was done around 5:30 P.M., I'd get to work on coming up with (hopefully humorous) captions for said photo gallery. Once that was done, I'd spend another couple hours putting together the first pieces of content that would be running on the site the next morning. At about 10:30 P.M. I would head downtown to catch a performance by a sketch group I've been directing. We'd go over some ideas after the show before I finally headed home (around midnight)." Even after a 15-hour day, Kula says there's always more to do. "One opportunity leads to another, so it always feels like you need to be hustling for the next gig. Even when I'm being productive with my time, there's always a perpetual nagging in the back of my head that I should be doing more. Balancing the desire for professional success and the desire to actually have a life is a tough one."

> **All I've ever wanted was an honest week's pay for an honest day's work.** —Steve Martin

Prepare for Success

No academic requirements exist, but many performers get their start in college, either acting or joining comedy troupes, thereby gaining some exposure to large audiences. Many aspiring comedians also sign up for workshops where they get to critique one another's performances. Studying fellow performers' material, style, delivery, and presence are facets of the aspiring comedian's life. Comedians should develop 30 minutes of strong material and get significant stage experience before attempting to hit the club circuit. Most important, an aspiring comedian should have a steady source of income before striking out, since it takes a while to get enough steady gigs to pay the bills.

Getting Your Foot in the Door

Comics who are just developing their comedic personas need to get their feet wet on the comedy circuit. Aspiring comedians should start writing material and experimenting with different styles. Open mic nights are great for trying out new material, and you get to know the clubs and make contacts with other comics. Newcomers will be lucky to get a few gigs; getting to know bookers is key to getting exposure and building your resume. Finding a gig as an emcee or a feature is a great way to hone your skills while also bringing in some money. Above all you need persistence and confidence.

Biggest Challenges and Best Perks

The life of a comedian is not easy. It's certainly not funny. Solo stand-up comics face a significant level of isolation and have a more uncertain road than troupe comedians, going from club to club hoping for a big break. It is not unusual for an aspiring stand-up comic to log more than 200 days per year away from home. Dingy nightclubs, crappy audiences, and unpaid stand-up sets are part of the aspiring comedian's dues. On the upside, veteran performers who develop a following may enjoy many opportunities to show their work, possibly including TV specials and/or privately commissioned performances by political associations, for example. In addition, the skills associated with comedy—the ability to make others laugh, defuse tense situations with a well-timed remark, and think on one's feet—are invaluable assets in any other career, and many comedians make successful transitions to careers in advertising, teaching, writing, and even law enforcement. More than 30 percent of exiting comedians slide smoothly into acting, where they face much the same odds of success, but where the financial rewards can be significant for those lucky few people who make it.

PROFESSIONAL PROFILE
Avg. starting salary: $50 per gig
Avg. salary after 5 years: Varies
Avg. salary 10 to 15 years: Varies

JARGON
Rim shot The drum/cymbal combination that follows an extremely corny joke or pun

Saver A line used by a comedian to get a laugh after a previously delivered joke bombs

Working blue When a comic performs R-rated material

ARE YOU INTERESTED IN?
Acting, comedy

RELATED COLLEGE MAJORS
Theater, voice, rhetoric

FOR MORE INFORMATION
Second City Comedy:
www.secondcity.com

American Federation of Television and Radio Artists:
www.aftra.org

American Guild of Variety Artists:
http://americanguildofvarietyartistsag-va.visualnet.com

COMIC BOOK WRITER/ARTIST

A (Relatively) Typical Day in the Life

Whether you're a writer or an artist, there's a good chance that your desire to become involved in comic book/graphic novel production was sparked by an early love of this truly unique medium. Words and pictures work together to support a story—a narrative that employs language as colorful as the panels that help tell it. It's no secret why comics are popular with children and adolescents. There are some people who believe that once comic book fans get older, they grow out of their passion or should, anyway—but nothing could be a greater misconception. People who buy into the notion that grown-ups don't or shouldn't enjoy comic books have probably never opened a comic. But this profile isn't for them. This profile is for you: the lifelong comic fan who's trying to figure out how to break into the business.

Making comics is a collaborative effort between writers and illustrators. While outsiders often overlook the writing half of the art form, you can't have a good comic without a compelling story. The writer comes up with the arc and text of the narrative and works together with the illustrator to determine the best way to tell the story visually. While writing may not chain you to a desk, per se—that is, you don't have to work at a desk—you are going to spend a lot of time writing. It's a full-time job. Where you spend that time is up to you. Illustrators have a little less leeway. Traditional illustrators tend to work at a drafting table, which is like a desk, only slantier. However, there are some newfangled graphic illustrators who do all of their drawing on computer.

An Extreme Day in the Life

Comic book writer Drew Melbourne had his first script published by Dark Horse Comics in 2006 for a series called *ArchEnemies*. Drew broke into the business the way so many people do: He had a good idea, and pounced on the opportunity to get it out there. "Back in 2004, a studio called Top Cow Comics sponsored a contest to find new comic book writers. Somewhere around 10,000 people pitched stories to them, and they liked mine best. Top Cow bought the rights to a property I created, called *Heroes of Tomorrow*, which has been working it's way through their production process ever since," and should be out in 2007. Not long after he sold Top Cow on his idea for *Heroes of Tomorrow*, Dark Horse picked up *ArchEnemies*. Although he's still relatively new to the business, Drew's been pretty busy the last few years. Now that his work has been in print for some time, Drew has had to make the adjustment from fan and aspiring writer to professional comic book creator who has his own fans—with some of whom he came face-to-face at the 2006 Comic-Con International in San Diego. "This past year's con was my first as a big-shot pro with a comic on the stands. The folks at Dark Horse organized a signing for me, and I met a bunch of my fans, including a teenage girl who had just started reading comics with *ArchEnemies #1*. That just blew my mind. I was the one who'd hooked her on comics. That was the first time I really understood that not only can people enjoy my work—it can be genuinely important to them."

It's not just about the artist's vision. It's also about the people the artist cannot see.

Prepare for Success

The first prerequisite is simply that you have to love comics. That love is the foundation on which all the other stuff is built. Many people who go on to become comic book writers or artists are, in large part, self-taught. It's not a bad idea to consider at least an undergraduate education. Writers should think about pursuing a liberal arts education with an emphasis in creative writing; aspiring artists would be wise to consider art school. A word of warning, though: When it comes to drawing, not all art schools are created equal. Look for places that have more traditional drawing programs; many art schools place traditional drawing within their illustration programs.

Getting Your Foot in the Door

Publishing and art are not easy fields to break into. Comic book creation encompasses both. However, just because something is difficult doesn't mean it's not worth the effort. Many people take the self-publishing path. Unlike traditional novelists or artists, there's a respected tradition of the independently produced, self-promoted, underground comic book creator. If you want to get paid as a comic book writer or artist, your best chance may be producing and distributing a book on your own. The worst-case scenario is that you create a comic book of which you can be proud and show to people as part of your portfolio. Best case? It becomes a cult classic.

Biggest Challenges and Best Perks

This is not an easy field in which to succeed. There are many more people aspiring to become comic book creators than there are publishing deals to be had. Even if you are published, one success does not make a career. It's tough. It's not impossible, though. If you do get a foothold in the industry—whether at one of the giants, one of the many up-and-coming publishing houses, or in the underground market—the greatest reward comes from seeing your vision go from idea, to sketch, to final product, to production, and then to distribution. As Drew Melbourne reminds us, it's not just about the artist's vision. It's also about the people the artist cannot see: the people at home, who discover comics for the very first time by opening your book.

Professional Profile

Artists get paid more than writers; however, writers usually end up making more money than artists for the simple reason that it does not take as long to write as it does to illustrate.

WRITER
Avg. starting salary: $80 to 150/page

ARTIST
Avg. starting salary: $100 to 180/page

Jargon
In-betweener An artist who draws the minute movements between the larger ones

Are you Interested In?
Illustrating, drawing, creative writing

Related College Majors
Creative writing, art, drawing, graphic design

For More Information
Marvel Comics:
www.marvel.com

DC Comics:
www.dccomics.com

Comic-Con International:
www.comic-con.org

DANCER

A (Relatively) Typical Day in the Life

Often prepped from youth for a career in which the average retirement age is in the late 30s, dancers are hardworking, dedicated, patient, and—you guessed it—physically fit. Dancers appear in such diverse settings as operas, musical theater, television, and commercials. They perform most often in the evenings, with their days spent in long rehearsals. Traveling is also common for anyone pursuing a career as a dancer. Whether working with a dance company, in a musical production, at a school, or on a cruise ship, dancers can expect to spend a lot of time on the road, working very long and late hours. People who are attracted to dance because of the grace of the art form or the apparent effortlessness with which the professionals move may want to reflect on this observation by Martha Graham, one of the twentieth century's greatest choreographers: "Dancing appears glamorous, easy, delightful. But the path to the paradise of achievement is not easier than any other. There is fatigue so great that the body cries, even in its sleep. There are times of complete frustration; there are daily small deaths."

Despite all of its hardships, many people are attracted to the profession by the opportunity to participate in something new and creative—and to work on projects that change frequently. Many dancers work with choreographers to create new dances or reinterpret existing ones. The ability to work with others is essential, as most dancers— contrary to what many believe about the profession—spend their careers performing as part of a large group.

An Extreme Day in the Life

Elizabeth C. Sanchez, a professional dancer, was introduced to the possibilities of a professional career in the arts by her mother. "She traveled the world dancing in various companies, including the Ringling Bros Circus. So I began studying all various techniques of dance such as ballet, jazz, modern, tap, African, salsa, merengue, and my favorite, hip-hop. Before long, I started performing onstage and winning dance contests." Elizabeth furthered her dance study by attending New York City's prestigious Professional Performing Arts School. "That's where I discovered the depth of my passion and I knew this would be my career choice in life." A career as a professional dancer is full of extreme moments, both on and offstage. Elizabeth recalls one of her favorites: "I did a show with Def Leppard for VH1's 'Best of 2005.' It was the best and most inspirational experience ever. First, it's not often that you get to dance for legendary bands like Def Leppard, and secondly it was so amazing to meet a band that has survived all the changes of the world let alone the band. The thing that touched me most was not only that the band members were extremely nice and respectful, but the drummer completely amazed me. He only had one arm yet he played the drums like there was no tomorrow! They had to rig his drum set so his free foot could take the place of his missing left arm. Talk about coordination! He taught me, without even saying a word, that if you want something bad enough, nothing will stand in your way of getting it." Elizabeth has this advice for aspiring artists: "Stick to it!! It's not an easy business, so if you don't have thick skin you better get it! And if you are not ready to live, eat, and sleep dance, then you're in the wrong business, because you got to love it, breathe it, and need it to survive."

"If you are not ready to live, eat, and sleep dance, then you're in the wrong business, because you got to love it, breathe it, and need it to survive."

Prepare for Success

Industry professionals look favorably upon a general education in the arts because they believe such a background contributes to a dancer's ability to interpret a piece. While many dancers pursue a degree to prepare them for a career after dance, many others forgo a formal education to devote more time to practicing and performing. All successful dancers have patience, drive, and above all, a devotion to dance. The venerable Ms. Graham says, "Great dancers are not great because of their technique; they are great because of their passion." While training depends largely on the form of dance in which one specializes, many instructors and dancers agree that a foundation in classical dance is essential. Women typically begin their training around age 8, whereas men often begin between the ages of 10 and 15. Training is demanding, requiring around eight physically intense hours every day, and continues to be a necessary part of dancers' lives throughout their careers.

Getting Your Foot in the Door

Breaking into the dance profession requires tenaciousness, a thick skin, and a willingness to make sacrifices. New dancers should pursue opportunities to gain experience with well-known choreographers and make connections with other dancers. This means taking on many unpaid jobs at first. The attrition rate is high in this profession, and even many dancers who do stick with their art never see a reward commensurate with their early sacrifices. Those who do find work with a company can initially expect low pay, short-term contracts, and often a lot of traveling. Successful dancers tend to have made important connections, learned the industry, and, to some degree, established a fan base.

Biggest Challenges and Best Perks

The profession is not only highly competitive, but also very specialized. This creates a relative dearth of available jobs for the sizable and qualified applicant pool. Those who pursue dance will, undoubtedly, become accustomed to rather regular rejection when auditioning for work and will almost always face periodic bouts of unemployment. Advancement may be slow and depends largely on the reputation the dancer has built. It is a taxing profession, but dance can also be extremely rewarding for those who have the talent and drive to pursue it. A phenomenally fit physique, the respect and admiration of fans, and the opportunity to make a living doing something you love are the best perks.

PROFESSIONAL PROFILE

Avg. starting salary: Typically falls in the range of between $14,570 and $34,660

Avg. salary after 5 years: Averages at about $35,600

Avg. salary after 10 to 15 years: Has the potential to exceed $53,350

JARGON

Dance notation The symbolic representation of dance movement

Leverage move When one partner counterbalances the other so as to keep him or her from falling

Popper A break-dancer who uses "pop and lock" moves

ARE YOU INTERESTED IN?

Dancing, choreographing, performing

RELATED COLLEGE MAJORS

Dance, fine arts, musical theater

FOR MORE INFORMATION

Dance/USA:
www.danceusa.org

National Association of Schools of Dance:
http://nasd.arts-accredit.org

National Dance Association:
www.aahperd.org/nda

FASHION DESIGNER

A (Relatively) Typical Day in the Life

For all you *Project Runway* fans: If it's a career as a fashion designer that you're after, be ready to make it work. Designing clothing and accessories is the fashion world's equivalent of wanting to be an actor, a model, or a fiction writer. It's fairly easy to do on a small scale and nearly impossible be the next Robert DeNiro, Iman, or J. K. Rowling.

Don't let this discourage you. About 15,000 people in the United States identify themselves as fashion designers, and many thousands more enjoy careers in the fashion industry, working as textile designers, buyers for clothing stores, and various positions in clothing production. Certainly the fashion designer title sounds glamorous, but few people know what a rough business it can be.

Designers take society's mood, combine it with popular opinion on what's hot and what's not, bounce it off everything that's been done before, and try to come up with something new that will amaze and delight fashionistas. The most clever, creative, talented up-and-comers won't get the attention they deserve for their innovative ideas unless they know someone who can push them to the forefront. Those who follow fashion know that people are fickle, trends change like the wind, and the ability to capitalize on public opinion is rare. As Heidi Klum is so fond of saying: "You're either in or you're out."

Those with talent, vision, determination, and ambition can succeed in this highly competitive industry. Fashion designers are involved in every phase of designing, showing, and producing all types of clothing, from pajamas to evening gowns. Day to day, they sketch new designs; check production, distribution, and sales; choose textiles for new lines; and market themselves. A designer attends fashion shows and reads fashion magazines to get the low-down on current trends (especially celebrity wardrobes), and stays abreast of style trends in other countries. Designers should be able to communicate their philosophy and vision clearly and demonstrate what sets them apart. No matter what their personal styles, designers must produce creative, exciting, profitable product lines. While most designers would love to be the next Coco Chanel, most never get the chance to produce their own collections and end up working for larger design houses. Hours are long, and pay is paltry at first—definitely not enough to dress like a runway model.

An Extreme Day in the Life

Sheila Walker is the designer of She She New York Swimwear and the owner of Sheila Walker Studio, which, among other things, offers fashion labs and sewing classes in New York City. She is one busy lady. "It's true, I'm a fashion designer, but more important, I'm a business owner. Designing cute swimwear is a very tiny portion of my job. Since I produce all of my suits 'in house,' the first thing I do every morning is check in with the seamstresses and production manager. We review what will be made that day and review the timeline for completion." The rest of the day is a whirlwind of messages and e-mails ranging from lending swimsuits to fashion magazines and dealing with a late shipment of fabric to making reservations to the Swimwear Fabric Show in Cannes. "Before the day ends, we review production again so we are prepared for the next day when we start all over again!"

> **Designing clothing and accessories is the fashion world's equivalent of wanting to be an actor, a model, or a fiction writer.**

PREPARE FOR SUCCESS

Beyond an eye for color, style, and shape, and an ability to sketch fresh ideas, formal training in design is almost essential. A two- or four-year degree in fashion design not only arms you with knowledge of textiles, quirks inherent to a variety of fabrics, and a sense of the business and marketing side of the industry, but also helps you put together an excellent portfolio and possibly get an internship or apprenticeship under your belt before you graduate. Beginners often work as assistants, if they're lucky, and the duties are often administrative. Learn as much as you can, network fervently, and accept that you might need a second job to pay the rent.

GETTING YOUR FOOT IN THE DOOR

Websites featuring items by independent designers are a good place to start. Smart budding designers will have their own websites, too. It can be maddening to put in your time as a fashion underling only to find, five years later, you haven't moved up the ladder, while your boss is in *Women's Wear Daily* ad nauseam. No one said this was going to be easy. Many leave the profession when they don't go places fast enough. Those who stick with it may need to take some big risks to get noticed, or they'll need to settle for working for someone else. People who have years of experience have often developed a specialty, from shepherding designs through the production process, scheduling lines based on season and available fabrics, or overseeing young designers and scouting for talent. Look to them for advice and guidance; they know the business and many people in it. Those who can keep reinventing and proving themselves in the ever-changing fashion world may have a shot at greatness.

BIGGEST CHALLENGES AND BEST PERKS

This can be one catty industry. Some designers need to suit up in a coat of armor to shield themselves from the diva behavior and outrageous attitudes that may fly around the workplace each day. Until you're Michael Kors or Vera Wang, expect low pay, long hours, and a slim chance for advancement. Of course, there are perks too. You'll have lots to wear and plenty of places to go to if you get in with a social crowd. You'll be able to whip up an outfit in a pinch and alter existing designs if you don't like the fit or want to add your own touches. You'll be working in a globally influential industry that interests you, even if you don't like the grunt work at the beginning.

PROFESSIONAL PROFILE

Avg. starting salary: $35,550

Avg. salary after 5 years: $51,290

Avg. salary 10 to 15 years: $75,970

JARGON

Haute couture Refers to exclusive custom-fitted and often trendsetting fashions for women

Sourcing Researching, finding, and obtaining materials

Toile A mock-up model of a garment, sometimes done in a cheap fabric

ARE YOU INTERESTED IN?

Fashion, sewing, sketching

RELATED COLLEGE MAJORS

Fashion design, fashion merchandising, fiber textiles, weaving arts

FOR MORE INFORMATION

Fashion Group International: www.fgi.org

FREELANCER

A (Relatively) Typical Day in the Life

While a freelancer can work in a variety of different specialties and areas, there are a number of attributes nearly all freelancers share. First and foremost, there is freedom and flexibility. They're called independent contractors for a reason, and that independence shows itself in a freelancer's ability to determine which jobs to take and when to work on them. Depending on your field and whether it requires you to work outside the home, even freelancers with fairly regular nine-to-five gigs have much more say in terms of what they work on and when they do their work than the conventional employee. This authority comes not only from the fact that independent contractors are essentially self-employed, but also because the services they provide often require specific talents that many don't have.

The creative nature of many freelance positions procures good freelance gigs, which are highly sought after by people who want to devote time to the artistic aspirations that don't always pay the bills. It's difficult enough to write a novel even when you can devote all of your time to it, and doing it when you've got a conventional job is nearly impossible. That's why most would-be novelists jump at the opportunity to write freelance copy for, say, a travel guide, if it means they are freeing up time and energy that is sapped by the typical nine-to-five job.

An Extreme Day in the Life

Freelance writing may have started out as a hobby for Maya Payne Smart back in 2003, but after three years of putting her pen to paper (or, rather, her fingers to the keyboard), she made the leap to full-time freelancer. It's a good thing she gets to work in her sweatpants because her days can give her more of a workout than the gym: "If you're serious about making a great living, you have to hustle. I'm constantly thinking up article topics, pitching ideas to editors, and promoting myself face-to-face, over the phone, via e-mail, and online. This takes up an extraordinary amount of time and energy, but doesn't pay the bills directly—I still have to write the stories. The crazy days are when assignments pile up due to no fault of your own. I've had times when I'd be on pace to complete a few projects ahead of schedule, when another editor would call and suddenly need revisions to a piece I turned in weeks earlier, or worse, had decided that the story needed to go in another direction, requiring additional reporting and interviews. Now you have four imminent deadlines on totally unrelated topics, and you can't let any of the editors down because you need them for future assignments. And of course, other mini-disasters crop up to complicate matters further—maybe a key source is MIA for an interview, or your carpal tunnel syndrome flares up, making typing a real pain. Then there's the money factor. You're working at a grueling pace to finish all these projects and you can't even look forward to a big payday anytime soon because half of your clients pay upon publication and checks for the work you're doing that day may not arrive for months. You really learn what you're made of as a freelancer—how well you handle rejection, how fast you can write, how many things you can work on at once. I wouldn't trade the adrenaline rush or self-discovery for the world—or a steady paycheck."

If you're serious about making a great living, you have to hustle.

Of course, it's not all tickles and giggles. If you're working full-time for a single employer, then you probably rely on the basic belief that the job will still be there for you in a week, and salaried employees typically enjoy the benefit of, well, benefits. Freelancers don't have the luxury of loyal employers. They have clients who, regardless of performance and loyalty, may call on them for only one job. Freelancers must therefore have a number of regular clients on whom they can rely for continuous business.

Prepare for Success

Depending on the services that you plan to provide, freelancing doesn't necessarily require a specific educational background. This is not to say that pursuing a degree in the area in which you plan to freelance would not make things easier on you. Freelancers have to know their stuff—indeed, the whole point of being an independent contractor is that you possess skills uncommon for most of the population. A background that includes formal training and a certificate or bachelor's degree, especially for those working in creative or technical fields, is usually par for the course. Freelance opportunities typically grow in number as companies downsize and seek to outsource specialized labor, so keeping your eye on the playing field can work wonders for employment opportunities.

Getting Your Foot in the Door

Since most freelance opportunities are in creative fields, many people who find it too daunting a task to make their living as artists or writers may start out as freelancers until they reach a point of stability, and then ultimately move into their chosen vocation full-time. More so than most steady day jobs, freelancing gigs are often obtained through word of mouth, so keep your ears open for any possibilities. A business card and accessibility are two of the most valuable assets a freelancer can have.

Biggest Challenges and Best Perks

The independence that looks so attractive carries with it a very real drawback when it comes to the topic of job security: Freelancing provides very little of it. Still, even the most successful freelancers will have occasional lulls of little or no work, especially early in their careers. Freelancers at the two-year mark typically still have to take on projects that may not be of particular interest to them so they can pay the bills, and they may experience relatively frequent ebbs in workflow. After several years in the business, professional, full-time freelancers are likely to have established a steady client base, enjoy their freedom more, and probably worry less about money. Freelancers who stay in their industries for many years enjoy solid salaries and choice jobs.

PROFESSIONAL PROFILE
Avg. salary: Varies

JARGON
Body copy Your main text as opposed to display matter, captions, headers, and so on

ARE YOU INTERESTED IN?
Creative arts

RELATED COLLEGE MAJORS
English, journalism, communications, business, art

FOR MORE INFORMATION
The Editorial Freelancers Association:
www.the-efa.org
Working Today:
www.workingtoday.org

INDEPENDENT FILMMAKER

A (Relatively) Typical Day in the Life

Lights . . . camera . . . action! These words are so ingrained into our collective consciousness that it's easy to forget just how recently the moving image came onto the scene and in how short a time filmmaking became the preeminent art form of the human experience. It's virtually impossible to escape moving pictures. No longer content to be contained in theater houses—or even private homes—movies are becoming increasingly portable and people are literally beginning to carry multiple, playable, feature-length movies in devices that fit in their pockets. While it's certainly true that the pictures have gotten smaller, the efforts required to put them together are still expansive and expensive productions that involve a whole team of specialists. At the head of every film production you'll find two people: The director who oversees most of the creative aspects of the production, and the director of photography (DP/cinematographer) who oversees the technical aspects of filming and is largely responsible for the overall look of the film.

Production schedules involve far more than what occurs between action and cut. A typical day shoot begins early: You may need to be up by no later than four in the morning, at the production office by five, and at the shoot by seven. Once on location, there are at least a couple of hours of planning and set up before cameras roll on the first shot. The day's pace depends on the type and budget of production, and a 10-second shot may take several hours to film. Once the first shot is complete, the process of planning and setting up the next shot begins. When shooting wraps at the end of the day, the crew packs up, and the film is packed, labeled, and sent to the lab.

An Extreme Day in the Life

Fred Schroeder didn't dream of becoming a director of photography when he was growing up. "I was always interested in film, but it was only in film school that I discovered cinematography." He entered the field 12 years ago and took the unusual route of the cinematographer. "One traditionally works one's way up from camera trainee, to loader, to second assistant camera, to first assistant to camera operator, and finally to director of photography." It's a process that may take many years. "I never took the route of working as an assistant and moving up the ranks to DP. I always wanted to be a shooter and took jobs where I could work on my craft as a DP and shot as many things as possible some times for little or no money so I could put a great reel together." One of Fred's first low-paying gigs got him up close and personal with a side of shooting one might not expect—as a crime scene photographer. It took him about four years to get to where he is today: An independent cinematographer living in Los Angeles who works all over the country on various projects ranging from television commercials to feature films.

To succeed as a filmmaker, you really need to be devoted to **the art form.**

Prepare for Success

Regardless of what role you want to play in the process of making motion pictures, it's probably a good idea to consider film school. Cinematography is a very technical field, and you really need a firm understanding of all aspects of photography and a deep understanding of the principles and physics of optics; additionally, as with any visual medium, a strong background in art history and aesthetics is essential. All of these are principles that can be addressed in the classroom, but to succeed as a filmmaker, you really need to be devoted to the art form.

Getting Your Foot in the Door

Where you live definitely makes a difference. There are only so many cities with thriving film communities. If you're not living in one of those places already, your first step is clear: Move. It's tough enough to become a filmmaker without allowing geography to be an obstacle. Once you've made that leap, all you've done is made the possibility of becoming a filmmaker only slightly more plausible. To get your foot in the door, look into internships and entry-level positions. Some people say you should show up to sets and hang out until they give you something to do. Stranger things have happened, but again, the important thing is that you continue to explore the craft in any way that's available to you. Once you do get on a set, you're going to have to appear like you know what you're doing.

Biggest Challenges and Best Perks

Did we mention that it's difficult to make it in the film industry? Well, it bears repeating. It's difficult—really, really difficult. In the United States, there are only about 400 movies made annually. At most, that makes 400 directors and 400 directors of photography. There are many more television commercials and music videos that get made, but still, the number of aspiring filmmakers outnumbers the number of working filmmakers by a discouraging margin. If you find some work, it can be very difficult finding anybody to look at your work, see your promise, and offer you more work. Even then, the schedule is intense, and you're always working against logistical forces like money and time. All of that notwithstanding, every production is a team effort, and on the set you're surrounded by a group of talented and serious people working together toward a common goal, and the fruits of that labor are clear when you see the final product.

Professional Profile
Avg. salary: Varies

Jargon
PA Production assistant

Are you Interested In?
Photography, movies, screenwriting, art

Related College Majors
Cinematography and film/video production, film, special effects, photography, art history

For More Information
Independent Filmmakers Alliance:
www.ifilmalliance.com

Independent Feature Project:
www.ifp.org

Filmmaker Magazine:
www.filmmakermagazine.com

JEWELER/JEWELRY DESIGNER

A (Relatively) Typical Day in the Life

Diamonds may be a girl's best friend, but diamonds are also good friends to jewelers. A jeweler—whether in a small-town, mom-and-pop jewelry store or at the landmark Fifth Avenue location of Tiffany & Co. in New York City—spends most days surrounded by sparkling stones worth thousands, possibly millions, of dollars. How's that for swanky office decor?

For those who couldn't get enough of making those macaroni necklaces in preschool, imagine what you'll be capable of with access to silver, gold, and platinum, or trendy new metals like stainless steel and titanium. Jewelry designers have an artistic role in the jewelry industry, researching, sketching, making models, and finalizing designs. They are part of a larger process that encompasses goldsmiths, stone-setters, appraisers, repair people, and of course, your neighborhood jeweler.

Jewelers have specialized knowledge of jewelry and the business behind it. They own, manage, or work in a jewelry shop and may be charged with cleaning, repairing, engraving, and resizing jewelry; ordering merchandise for the store; and providing customer service to each discerning buyer, especially for those once-in-a-lifetime purchases. Some jewelers are jewelry designers as well and have their own collections of wearable art.

Jewelry designers spend their time designing, casting, making, marketing, and selling their pieces. Many say they enjoy designing most—where science and art come together. One designer might prefer sketching freehand while another uses computer-aided software. Designers work with semiprecious materials (silver, turquoise, pearls, and onyx), while many others prefer big-ticket materials (gold, platinum, diamonds, sapphires, and rubies). If they are self-employed—which 30 to 40 percent are—designers also need to have business savvy, since it is not an easy field to break into. They must be motivated and willing to spend long hours working alone. Most jewelers dream of a day when they can create designs for a private client base.

Prepare for Success

For both jewelers and designers, manual dexterity and an enjoyment in working with one's hands are desirable, though lasers are used increasingly to make flawless repairs. Both will find the going a bit easier with some formal training—including having knowledge of metals, gems, techniques, grades of quality, design work, and customer service. Learning on-the-job is common for jewelers, but designers often get started by going through a college program

An Extreme Day in the Life

Annick Ebersole is a former photographer turned self-employed jewelry designer. She sells her designs online and at craft shows, art fairs, and music festivals, where she has had her share of bum days. Since many of these events are held outside, weather conditions are essential to a good sell day. Ebersole spends much of her time traveling—away from her family—and many weekends working shows. "Even though I struggle with competition, theft, and Mother Nature, seeing my work on other people can be very gratifying. It feels good to know that [customers] get excited to buy a new piece from me every year. There's no guarantee of how much money I'll make, but I'm being paid to be creative. Sometimes it only takes one customer to make the show worthwhile."

Jewelry designers spend their time designing, casting, making, marketing, and selling their pieces.

or going to trade school. More than 40 colleges and universities offer full-time, four-year programs related to the jewelry/metalworking field. Look for a program that covers casting, forging, and raising and how to enamel and set stones. These programs should also introduce budding designers to equipment such as ultrasonic cleaners, buffing machines, ring sizers, sandblasters, enameling kilns, and rolling mills. Most programs fall under a college's school of art, so fine arts and art history will be explored. College programs tend to focus on the artistic design process, while a trade school puts more emphasis on the technical side of metalwork and business fundamentals.

GETTING YOUR FOOT IN THE DOOR

Many designers start making jewelry as a hobby, gifting their creations to family and friends and wearing them. Soon they get into arts and crafts fairs or local boutiques and try to develop a modest following. Of course, making jewelry isn't cheap—the materials they can afford may limit designers' early work. The Internet gives novice designers a virtual storefront for their wares. Apprenticeships and internships with other jewelers are another good way to break in. Designers who don't mind working for someone else can move up the ranks at better and more widely known companies. Those staking it out on their own should be savvy about self-promotion through public relations and marketing. Ongoing training—from specialized classes in jewelry design, computer-aided design, or gemology to getting an MBA—could prove valuable as well.

BIGGEST CHALLENGES AND BEST PERKS

Keeping up with trends—or better yet, setting them with new designs—can place designers under pressure. On a purely physical note, jewelry creation requires hot materials, dangerous tools, and precise hand-eye coordination. For technical jobs in the industry, the work can be repetitive. Design jobs can be expensive and building a business and a name people recognize can be cutthroat. If a designer wants out, finding a new career could be tricky since their skills and experience is so specific to the jewelry-making field.

On the upside, in this field, you'll get up and close and personal with a whole lot of bling. If you working in a jewelry shop, you might get a nice discount, and if you work behind the counter you might have the privilege of modeling the merchandise during business hours. Self-employed designers will want to wear their own designs and will know exactly what to give loved ones whenever there's a birthday or special holiday. Beyond the glitz, those in this field derive deep pleasure from working with their hands and manipulating raw materials into beautifully detailed jewelry pieces that people will wear, cherish, and pass down through the generations.

MUSIC VIDEO DIRECTOR

A (Relatively) Typical Day in the Life

Anyone who is interested in both cinematography and music might want to consider the world of music video directing. As you might expect, a music video director is the mastermind behind those four- to five-minute videos you see on channels such as MTV, VH1, BET, and CMT. During big shoots, music video directors get to rub elbows with all sorts of creative types, ranging from high-profile musicians to behind-the-scenes makeup artists. The director tells the cameras when to roll, the dancers when to dance, and the actors when to act. When filming is complete, the director goes into the editing studio to create a product that aims to win over the musicians and executives at the music label.

The daily life of a music video director is not all filming and fun—particularly early on. A director may come up with 10, 20, or even 50 fully conceived ideas for a video before a client actually bites. Therefore, a lot of work goes into coming up with ideas, getting together with a creative team to develop those ideas, and landing face time with musicians or representatives to pitch them. In a way, it's very similar to when a marketing firm meets with a client to sell an idea for a television commercial. Once music video directors are hired, they must begin working on preproduction, which includes budgeting; casting; selecting locations; creating shot lists; acquiring equipment and props; and hiring actors, choreographers, dancers, makeup artists, and anyone else who may need to be on hand. Music video directors also need to have everyone rehearse as many times as it takes to get things right. There is the additional pressure of racing against the clock, since often all the preproduction has to be completed in a condensed period of time.

So what's the catch? The catch is that your odds of hitting it big as a music video director are akin to the odds that you'll win that sweepstakes into which you were automatically entered at the gas station. OK, maybe that's a slight exaggeration, but the point is that this is a cutthroat business, and those who survive will be those who—early on, at least—are not willing to take no for an answer.

An Extreme Day in the Life

When he was just nine years old, Ethan Lader decided that he wanted to be a director. He used to lug around his parents' hefty VHS camcorder, taking shots of whatever turned up in the viewfinder. Ten years later, after graduating from college in Boston, he moved to LA and started Oneworld Films, which was headquartered in his one-bedroom apartment. Now 26 and an up-and-coming music video director, he continues to run Oneworld and is a contributing director at Oil Factory, a Beverly Hills studio. "One of the really big stepping stones for me was when we shot a video for an artist named Angel," he says. "We shut down the Colorado Street Bridge [in Pasadena] for the day and created a traffic jam. We needed police cars and school buses and cheerleaders and punk kids . . . it was massive." After making it through the day, he thought, "Whatever's gonna come next, we can handle it."

The first time you turn on MTV or BET and see one of your
videos . . . you'll feel a rush of satisfaction.

PREPARE FOR SUCCESS

Majoring in film is a good idea, but it's neither necessary nor a guarantee of future success. If you do study film in college, take advantage of the opportunity to practice as many techniques as possible, to build a network with other filmmakers on and off campus, and to put together a complete project—music video or otherwise—that you'll be able to show to potential employers or clients. However, if you really want to increase your chances of success, then sign up for internships whenever possible. You might not get paid in cash for the hours you work—yes, you may have to plead your way into a free internship—but the future benefits will be great.

GETTING YOUR FOOT IN THE DOOR

For some people, music video directing is the apex. For others, it's a stepping-stone to lengthier film projects, such as motion pictures. The directing business—particularly in towns like LA and New York—can be very difficult to break into, no matter what your goals. Therefore, you need to start at the bottom of the totem pole. Make sure to get your foot in the door and impress people. If you show them that you're a hard worker and that you know your stuff, then you can expect to advance. Be sure to also build your network of associates as you cross paths with new people. Don't forget to work on your own creative projects on the side. Keep yourself fresh. You may even decide, as Ethan Lader did, to start your own production company.

BIGGEST CHALLENGES AND BEST PERKS

There are no guarantees in this business, so you have to be able to throw caution to the wind and focus on achieving your goals. Early on, if the work is sporadic, you may find yourself frantic and desperate for clients. Basically, you need to be comfortable with risk. Just ask those who persist and continue to develop their artistic abilities: Taking a risk can pay off quite mightily. You get to spend your days with other people who are wildly creative, wildly talented, and sometimes just plain wild. The first time you turn on MTV or BET and see one of your videos—a video whose conception, preproduction, production, and postproduction were all your responsibility—you'll feel a rush of satisfaction. It's probably the greatest perk of all.

MUSICIAN

A (Relatively) Typical Day in the Life

All things considered, being a musician is not difficult. Any seven-year-old who sits down at a shiny baby grand for a first piano recital is a musician. Becoming a professional musician is very possible as long as you're not hoping to be rich, famous, or even mildly successful. However, if you are hoping to be rich, famous, or at least mildly successful, then that's a very different story. Whether you're playing Bach or Led Zeppelin, being a full-time, self-supporting musician is not an easy gig.

Musicians have a few things in common with artists, chefs, and actors. They are driven and obsessed by what they do and usually cannot picture another career they would rather pursue. This kind of fanatic enthusiasm is important in a career that tests you with criticism, rejection, vicious competition, and the anticipation of whether you will make it big and get to enjoy paid bookings, good press, and genuinely appreciative fans.

Musicians come in all shapes and sizes: rock bands, folk bands, jazz saxophonists, classical violinists, and anyone who creates and performs music. Career musicians compose, rehearse, tune and care for their instruments, perform, possibly record, and definitely promote themselves to drum up more work. Those who have "day jobs" to support themselves while pursuing their music careers have to manage all the responsibilities that come with being a musician around their work schedules.

Musicians have to sacrifice a lot to become full-fledged musical sensations, even on a small scale. Leisure time is usually devoted to improving any weak areas they might have. Even musicians who are dizzyingly talented may not earn enough to do it full-time. Some lucky musicians make a very good living, usually through regular work (playing at the same club several nights a week, for example) mixed with independent gigs and special events bookings. They might sell a few CDs, play at weddings, or go on tour opening for larger acts. Many musicians give private lessons as well. Very few become rich and famous; most are happy to make music and play as often as they can. On the commercial side, musicians can play and compose for the television, motion picture, and advertising industries.

An Extreme Day in the Life

Pianist/singer Gary Negbaur has released two CDs; toured in the United States, Europe, and Australia; and composed music for theater, film, and dance. For him, a musician's greatest reward is to know your music impacted others. During his tour of the country to promote an original CD, one of his stops was at a radio station in Little Rock, Arkansas. "After the interview, the station manager ran up to me and asked if I had any CDs in my car because someone was driving over to buy one. Sure enough, in moments a woman pulled up to the station. She had just been to a family funeral and was driving through Arkansas on her way back home to Texas. She heard my music and was really touched by it. For years, whenever I would come to her town in Texas to perform, she would come to my shows. It is this kind of unique communication between a performer and an audience that makes being a musician something special."

Talent is essential, but offers no guarantees in the music business.

Prepare for Success

Most musicians start young. They start taking private lessons when they are children. They receive formal training from reputable mentors and spend endless hours practicing, often enrolling in a college program to get a degree in music or something related to it. Musicians who are just starting out can and should play anywhere for the experience: from community concerts and birthday parties to bars, restaurants, and weddings. Musicians with the busiest schedules are often the best self-promoters, not necessarily the most talented sounds in town. The more gigs and exposure you can get, the better your chances for increased compensation and new opportunities.

Getting Your Foot in the Door

Talent is essential but offers no guarantees in the music business. Sometimes the entertainment industry rewards those who are in the right place at the right time. A passion for making music, performing, and being around others who enjoy making music keeps long-term musicians going. Music is a way of life and success is largely secondary. Developing your own music style, letting it evolve, and learning to be happy with wherever that takes you may end up being a career in itself, even if something else is paying the bills. Those who are in high demand usually hire agents or managers to help them get work and handle their careers. Musicians must have self-discipline, passion, and confidence.

Biggest Challenges and Best Perks

Many musicians who become successful enough to play full-time encounter as many challenges as they had when they were scrambling to find work, albeit of a different nature. Mastering the convoluted relationships among agents, managers, lawyers, and other pros attached to the profession is a job in itself. Being on the road can be exhausting.

On the contrary, most musicians can find joy and comfort in playing just about anywhere. Even those who never take their show on the road, manage to get in front of an audience whenever and wherever they can (see Street Performer for more info on that). Doing what they love the most and meeting adoring fans are a musician's biggest perks. Anything above that—awards, press, fame—is just extra.

PROFESSIONAL PROFILE
Avg. starting salary: $18,660
Avg. salary after 5 years: $36,290
Avg. salary 10 to 15 years: $59,970

JARGON
Idiot check After a performance, a final check of the immediate staging area to make sure no equipment or belongings have been left behind.

ARE YOU INTERESTED IN?
Music

RELATED COLLEGE MAJORS
Music, music education, piano, jazz studies, composition and theory

FOR MORE INFORMATION
American Federation of Musicians:
www.afm.org
American Guild of Musical Artists:
www.musicalartists.org
Musicians Foundation:
www.musiciansfoundation.org

PHOTOGRAPHER

A (Relatively) Typical Day in the Life

Photography seeps into many fields. Photographers may be on assignments for newspapers, magazines, or book publishers. They may be hired to capture appealing shots of a new car or shampoo for an advertising or public relations firm. Photographers specializing in portraits to commemorate first birthdays, graduations, weddings, and anniversaries shoot in a studio or may travel for on-location celebrity shoots for magazines, album covers, or promotional material. Some photographers pursue the art of photography with an inner drive to complete an artistic vision and share their work with the world. Forensic photographers travel with police to crime scenes to document evidence, archaeological photographers visit excavation sites to capture the dig and finds, and scientific photographers provide images for science publications, research reports, and textbooks. No matter what their specialty, photographers aim to capture and evoke a mood or feeling surrounding a particular subject—whether it's people, products, or events. Photographers rely on their own perspectives combined with artistic and technical finesse to meet their clients' needs.

It takes years of practice to learn the intricacies of lenses, film, filters, lighting, exposure, and processing and developing. They must also learn how to apply all this knowledge creatively every day on the job. Some photographers—especially art photographers—do their own developing and printing, but many rely on a commercial lab to process their film. Other photographers prefer the cost and convenience associated with digital shoots. Plenty of photographers are prepared to process film in an old-fashioned darkroom even though they are also skilled digital photographers. Photographers work long and irregular hours and sometimes have to be available on short notice. Tight deadlines and a constant pressure to produce stunning images are a daily part of the job.

Prepare for Success

For news photographers, a college degree in photography or photojournalism is a great start, as is getting newsroom internships that may lead to full-time jobs. Other photographers can benefit most from a photography degree through a college's fine arts department. Whether you have a photography degree or not, practice is key. Get

An Extreme Day in the Life

The excitement and challenges on the job are directly related to the avenue of photography they choose to pursue. Tobi Bratcher of Tobi Rose Photography specializes in "key life moments," namely weddings, pregnancy, and children's photography. "I use my camera the way an artist uses a brush, as a tool to capture unique perspectives of the world around me," she says. Due to her line of work, her world can get a little crazy at times, especially when shooting an outdoor wedding where the couple's dog is a ring bearer and a meandering cat interrupts the ceremony. After chasing Fido and making sure the rings were still attached to his jeweled collar, she was able to laugh ruefully; she says: "The moral of the story is this [to] always be prepared. In this job, you never know what's going to happen. It was only hilarious after Fido was found and he still had his collar on. Whew! The wedding still took place, of course, just a little later than expected." The photos turned out great.

> **Photographers rely on their own perspectives combined with artistic and technical finesse to meet their clients' needs.**

out the camera and shoot even when you're not at work or being paid. Read everything you can about the latest trends and technology. Having a specialization—portraits, nature, sports, or architecture—helps you to build expertise as well as an impressive portfolio. Throw in a few diverse shots to show you can handle a variety.

Getting Your Foot in the Door

Many photographers, particularly those who work in large production specialties such as fashion photography, magazine editorials, or commercial photography, start out as assistants to well-established photographers. The job pays either nothing or very little and is valuable purely for the experience and knowledge you may gain by watching a successful photographer at work. As an assistant you will be doing the grunt work: holding reflectors, lugging equipment, and setting up shots. However, assistants who learn the tricks soon start taking on their own assignments. The self-employed photographer will discover it takes time to build a reputation and client base; getting work published is a big step toward both. Networking, building a website that showcases a virtual portfolio, signing with stock photo agencies, and advertising helps get your name out there.

Biggest Challenges and Best Perks

Photography is expensive to pursue as a hobby and even more so as a profession. Photographers in all genres need multiple cameras and lenses, film, printing supplies (or an arrangement with someone to print their photos), lighting equipment—the list goes on. Long hours, strict deadlines, fussy clients, and a feast-or-famine workflow are some of the other challenges. Dealing with sticky situations might be a fact of life: What do you do if two of your clients want you to shoot on the same day and at the same time? It's now or never and turning down work can be painful mentally and financially. Photographers need to be creative and efficient on every assignment. Photojournalists have the added challenge of putting themselves in life-or-death situations when they capture newsworthy events, people, places, and things for newspapers, journals, and magazines.

Photographers are lucky because at the end of the day they have a finished product. Tangible results are one of the best perks of the job, as are recognition from peers, clients, and the media. There have been plenty of famous shutterbugs since cameras were invented, but many photographers derive their joy simply from capturing a moment in time; from working with people, nature, or other subjects; and from having a livelihood that they can take with them wherever they go. Depending on who employs them, photographers don't have to pay for their travel expenses. At some levels, photography can be quite lucrative—even after shelling out money to get the proper tools of the trade.

Professional Profile
Avg. starting salary: $17,740
Avg. salary after 5 years: $24,040
Avg. salary 10 to 15 years: $34,910

Jargon
Burning Using an image-editing program to darken parts of a photo

Gray scale An image made up of varying black and white tones

Saturation The richness of the colors in a photo

Are you Interested In?
Photography

Related College Majors
Photography, photojournalism, fine arts

For More Information
American Society of Media Photographers:
www.asmp.org

Professional Photographers of America:
www.ppa.com

Professional Photographer Magazine:
www.ppmag.com

SCREENWRITER

A (Relatively) Typical Day in the Life

What do bank heists, courtroom dramas, love stories, and puppet adventures all have in common? They're things about which a screenwriter might write at any point. A screenwriter creates scripts for all sorts of television, movie, and stage productions. Sometimes screenwriters work with original ideas, while other times they adapt a book or a play to a new media. The job takes a different route for each screenwriter, since it can take years to have your first script bought by a company or broadcast, and can involve months spent working on the writing and then subsequent revision of a single script.

A typical day for a new screenwriter will usually involve going to a day job of some sort to pay the bills. This may seem disheartening, but many screenwriters say that each experience provides fodder for new stories. Since a script doesn't generate any income until someone buys it, and often not for months after that, many screenwriters choose to work in other capacities in the television or movie industry to make contacts, familiarize themselves with the field, and wait for the chance to get their scripts into the right hands. The real work of a screenwriter usually happens at home in front of a computer, typewriter, or notebook, writing out scripts. However, the job isn't just about writing. If your work has been bought or one of your scripts has generated some buzz, you could spend a typical day meeting

An Extreme Day in the Life

A screenwriter we interviewed, who prefers to remain anonymous, has been working in film one way or another for the past six years. "I work mostly as a post-production editor. About a year and a half ago someone I knew from college put me in touch with a producer who was looking to tap into an undiscovered niche of writing talent. That was the beginning of an on and off collaboration that has been ongoing." The process of collaboration was its own extended extreme moment, according to the screenwriter. "We were adapting an unpublished novella. What's been a learning experience for me is the amount of attention that went into it. It was more exacting and arduous than I'd imagined. We worked on it for [more than] a year—I wasn't getting any money for it and there was a lot of back and forth and sporadic stops." It's probably not uncommon for a script to unfold this way. The screenwriter adds, "I know of screenwriting teams who will sit in a room for a month until the work is finished." Whether the deadlines are short or long, one thing all screenwriters enjoy is the opportunity to meet other artists whose vision they admire: "The first full-blooded producer I ever worked with didn't live up to the stereotypes. He was as much of a writer as anything, smart—not manipulative, as you might expect. Another friend of mine whose done screenwriting work for years is a very insightful person who can get you to look at problems that arise in the writing process in a new way." The screenwriter offers this advice for people who are considering screenwriting as a profession: "Just be aware of the realities. Very few spec scripts get looked at, let alone turned into movies. You shouldn't be doing it if you don't love writing—it can be so frustrating . . . you need to enjoy the process and get something out of that."

> The script you consider your life's best work may never be picked up, but along the way you could sell a dozen others.

with your agent; attending meetings with the producer, director, and cast of a television show or movie; and making extensive edits to your script to fit the creative ideas of the group of people with whom you're working.

Prepare for Success

A college degree isn't required to become a screenwriter, and many have achieved success in their field by knowing the right people and aggressively shopping their work in the industry until someone bites. An MFA in screenwriting, however, can provide invaluable information about how to write a successful script, choose the right agent, and get your script into the right hands. Be prepared to support yourself by some other means until your career gets going, and don't underestimate the importance of constant networking. Above all, write constantly, whether it's revising your previous work, or generating new scripts. The script you consider your life's best work may never be picked up, but along the way you could sell a dozen others and put yourself in a position to call the shots down the line.

Getting Your Foot in the Door

Aspiring screenwriters should consider attending seminars, classes, or even getting a degree in screenwriting to build up their credentials and bolster skills. The Screenwriters Federation of America provides a network for screenwriters to gain information about the industry, make contacts with fellow writers, and access a marketplace for selling their work. Set up a website that includes summaries of your scripts and some information about yourself. A great way to break into the industry is to take on a full- or part-time job in the field and meet people who can read or forward your work to others. An agent might be hard to find without some solid previous work, but it's a good idea to retain one as you start out.

Biggest Challenges and Best Perks

The biggest challenge is getting to the point where you are living off your writing and have a choice in what you write. Many screenwriters develop their craft for years while holding down other assignments to pay the bills. The toughest challenge, however, seems to be letting go: Many screenwriters find it difficult to edit and revise scripts they've already spent so much time perfecting, to make it fit a TV show or movie director's vision.

On the upside, seeing your name in the credits of a successful production is the biggest perk of this profession. A successful screenwriter can command a large advance on future work and is often requested for revisions and adaptations. Location can be another bonus: You might be asked to travel with a movie or TV show cast and crew to provide daily edits and rewrites to the script.

Professional Profile
Avg. salary: Varies

Jargon
Auction/bidding war When a script is presented to several studios, all of which want to buy the work

Reader The person who reads scripts and writes down a synopsis of the plotline with commentary, which assists studio execs in determining if any of the scripts are worthwhile

Are you Interested In?
Creative writing, media

Related College Majors
Screenwriting, creative writing, film

For More Information
American Screenwriters Association:
www.asascreenwriters.com

National Writers Union:
www.nwu.org

Screenwriters Federation:
www.screenwritersfederation.org

SET DESIGNER

A (RELATIVELY) TYPICAL DAY IN THE LIFE

The importance of a set designer to a play, musical, or movie is paramount. From grade school plays to multimillion-dollar movies, the set is like a silent supporting actor. Moods, meaning, and media are all affected by the set design. Any flaw, such as a misplaced building or an uncomplimentary color scheme, can ruin the authenticity of any production.

Set designers are involved in all aspects of creating the scene, from stage construction to costume creation to the use of props. They research, design, and supervise construction of the visual aids required in stage, film, and television productions. Set designers have above average artistic ability. They are the drawers, painters, sculptors, sewers, and carpenters of the set. Set designers usually start with freehand sketches before creating scale models; they work in tandem with directors, production managers, and writers. Once their plans are finalized, the set designer supervises the construction workers who build the sets and works with people in charge of lighting and sound to create the proper mood.

Lately, as the trend toward using computer-generated sets grows, specially trained set designers are called on to create fantastic worlds using their mighty laptops. The set designer has to take into consideration a production's

An Extreme Day in the Life

Eric Southern is a production manager at the Atlantic Theater Company Second Stage in New York City. He was kind to briefly break from his duties of coordinating the theater's latest show, to rehash one of his more extreme days on the job: "We just finished the details of the construction on a new theater, and I'm the lighting and set designer for the first full-length show. I went to the theater for our first day of loading in the set and was greeted by the building's VP. A fire hydrant on the street above burst in the night, and there was major water damage. A year of hard work, and there was water dripping on my head."

He continued, "Cut to a week later, opening night . . . We cleaned up the lobby, but one piece of furniture hadn't been delivered, and it was a big deal, because the show only had four furniture pieces total. The trucking company had assured me (for the umpteenth time) that it would be delivered, and put me in contact with the driver, who said he could get the package to me in half an hour. In the meantime, I was scheduled to be on a conference call about the damages from the week before. I managed to notify my assistant, who went to get the package. Instead of delivering our beautiful ottoman, they accidentally gave us twenty boxes of light bulbs.

"[With] two hours to showtime and counting, I badger the driver into coming back. The audience was arriving, the actors were preparing, and finally, I saw the truck turn the corner. I grabbed the box and rushed into the theater to show the stagehands the new piece. Of course, it needed to be modified so no one got injured during the fight sequence. I rushed to the scene shop, then rushed backstage; the actors ran through the blocking in the dressing room, the director approved it, and we carried it ourselves to its preshow location. The lights dimmed, we rushed to our seats, and watched the show open without a hitch."

The set is like a silent supporting actor. Moods, meaning, and media are all affected by the set design.

budget when building sets. If the budget is small, then set designers have to be really creative to build worlds that entrance audiences without spending a fortune. Set designers work mostly in large production theaters and movie studios; they work long hours, often up to the night of the first performance.

Prepare for Success

Set designers usually attend specialized design institutes or artistic academies. However, you can also learn how to build a set with on-the-job training. Most set designers study specific courses and get degrees in theater; they must have a strong understanding of theatrical rigging and safety. Good set designers have an artistic ability that can translate into many other mediums, including painting, sculpting, and carpentry. Set designers are required to attend interviews or auditions and must bring with them a portfolio of past design or artwork. While some people can squeak by with less experience, the quality of their previous work has to be above par.

Getting Your Foot in the Door

Set designers start out their careers in small church or grade school productions and work their way up to college productions. Broadway is a long shot; but with a ton of talent and determination, it's not impossible. Some set designers work under the tutelage of more experienced set designers, and the connections made during these apprenticeships can lead to more frequent or even permanent jobs. High profile, high-paying jobs require an outstanding ability and artistic flair, so the development of an individual style can sometimes take you just as far as any technical abilities.

Biggest Challenges and Best Perks

With the industry's current predilection for digital shots, more set designers are finding themselves in front of computer screens, developing sets that exist only in cyberspace. Demand for more traditional set designers is linked to the number of films, television programs, and stage shows under production at a given time and the level of funding available. Though work has remained relatively constant through the years, the entertainment industry can be cruel.

While stress levels peak in the earlier years, a seasoned set designer is invaluable to a producer and director, and the pay and level of respect reflect as much. If your reputation as a set designer grows, then the possibilities of working in larger productions increase. Who knows? Someday you might find yourself in front of an audience of your peers, thanking your parents and the producers, crew, and everyone else with whom you've worked for a lucrative statuette.

PROFESSIONAL PROFILE
Avg. starting salary: $24,780
Avg. salary 5 years: $33,870
Avg. salary 10 to 15 years: $46,350

JARGON
Presentational set Individually styled sets used for newscast, sports interviews, and talk shows

Representational set A set meant to look like something from real life, such as a living room, back porch, or hotel room

ARE YOU INTERESTED IN?
Architecture, construction, design, sketching

RELATED COLLEGE MAJORS
Set design, technical theater, computer graphics

FOR MORE INFORMATION
Art Directors Guild:
www.artdirectors.org

United Scenic Artists Local 829:
www.usa829.org

SONGWRITER

A (Relatively) Typical Day in the Life

While some songwriters try to sell their songs to production companies, corporations, and singers, others are singer-songwriters who perform their own music. What all songwriters have in common, however, is the ability to express their thoughts in a way that grabs listeners and makes them want to hear more. While this career may seem easy (many of us have heard some popular song and thought: "I can do better than that!"), it requires intense discipline and dedication.

Songwriters usually look over notes and ideas they've previously jotted down for a good song, write down lines they've been hammering out in their heads, and try to get fresh takes on songs on which they've been working. Songwriters also need to check in with their music publishers to get updates on songs they've sold or payments that are due, or research courses they might take or contests they might enter. Songwriters who perform their own music might spend part of their days confirming shows or cold-calling venues to book new gigs. A typical day should

An Extreme Day in the Life

Dave Mendelsohn is a New York–based professional songwriter whose career in music began back in high school. "It took me a while to develop my talents. I was in a pretty horrendous band in high school and only started writing music in college." While the two go hand in hand, "you can't be a storyteller without life experience. Songwriting is a skill you develop through trial and error." Not to mention sacrifice. "As a songwriter, there aren't that many outlets to make money so you have to do other things to get by. I waited tables—something a lot of creative people do." After college, Dave reconnected with his high school bandmate, Michael Moshan, and together they came up with the idea for Rock the SAT, a study guide that uses songs to help students memorize SAT vocabulary. "Mike first got the idea for the book in high school when he was studying for the SAT. His mom bought him some audiotapes of a guy reading the vocabulary. Right then and there Mike had the idea to use music to help students study. For years he sat on it. After rehearsal one day he told me his idea and I went home and wrote the book's first song." But taking this idea from concept to creation proved to be difficult. "One of the challenges with Rock the SAT was its really specific parameters. We had to write songs that used SAT vocabulary, defined the words in context, and also used subject matter that appealed to students. At first we tried to market it ourselves, but that was a lot of work. . . . So we decided to try to hook up with a company with a little more experience." Eventually Dave and his partner found a publisher who shared their vision. "Basically Rock the SAT was an idea that needed to find the right home at the right time. It ultimately belonged on shelves at bookstores. The publishing industry needed time to catch up with edutainment concept, but hopefully now they really embrace that." For Dave, Rock the SAT is an example of some of the more creative ways professional songwriters can make a living. Dave, whose songs have been played on television shows, at football stadiums, and even some local malls, says that while his career choice is definitely "nontraditional," the ability to "be [his] own boss" and "make [his] own schedule" makes it worth it.

You can't be a storyteller without life experience. Songwriting is a skill you develop through trial and error.

include a lot of writing, even if it's not songs. Most songwriters advise that you write every day for practice. While you might not write a whole song in one day, you can certainly tweak an existing one, write a letter or journal entry, or just keep yourself in the habit of writing. Be advised, if you're just starting out as a songwriter, a typical day could involve having another job. As with many creative careers, songwriters often have to work at jobs that provide steadier sources of income.

Prepare for Success

Preparation for being a songwriter depends on the area of interest and how personal the material is to the person. Songwriters overwhelmingly stress the importance of staying busy and engaged, or of "feeding your mind." You can't write if you haven't lived and read a lot! The next practical step is getting in the habit of writing every day. Useful college degrees include literature, music, and English, which give you some basis in music theory, writing, and poetry. Once you've gotten started, it's useful to join the American Society of Composers, Authors and Publishers, a membership association that "protect[s] the rights of its members by licensing and distributing royalties for the non-dramatic public performances of their copyrighted works."

Getting Your Foot in the Door

Start writing! Seriously, there'll be no getting your foot in the door if you have no material. Join a community or membership association such as ASCAP to get tips, network, and hear about workshops and classes. Create a website for your work, or create a page or profile on a music-friendly site. Also, consider copyrighting your work. If you perform, send out e-mails to your contacts with samples of your recent work and invite everyone you know to your shows. The best buzz is often created by word of mouth.

Biggest Challenges and Best Perks

The biggest challenges may lie in overcoming shyness and maintaining self-discipline. No one will hound you for your next song, so it's important to stay focused and work every day, even when you feel distracted. Many songwriters who perform find that it takes a lot of time and practice to get used to sharing songs that came out of intense personal feelings and experiences with a room [or auditorium] full of strangers.

Some of the best perks of this job are hearing a song you wrote playing on the radio or bowing to thunderous applause. For people who crave celebrity and fame, the music industry is a place where being successful also means becoming a star. Watching others respond to the words of a song you wrote can be immensely satisfying. Working from home and at your own pace makes for an ideal lifestyle. Of course, receiving those royalty checks doesn't hurt either!

PROFESSIONAL PROFILE
Avg. salary: Varies

JARGON

Mechanical royalty Money paid by the record company to the songwriter and publishers of the songs appearing on each record, tape, or CD that they manufacture and distribute. These royalties must be paid even if a record, tape, or CD is given away free.

On hold When someone indicates their intent to use the song and requests you temporarily refrain from pitching the song to other clients

ARE YOU INTERESTED IN?
Music, creative writing, singing

RELATED COLLEGE MAJORS
English, music, music theater, voice

FOR MORE INFORMATION
American Society of Composers, Authors and Publishers:
www.ascap.com

American Songwriter Magazine:
www.americansongwriter.com

BMI:
www.bmi.com

STREET PERFORMER

A (Relatively) Typical Day in the Life

There is something very salt-of-the-earth about street performers. With cups, hats, or open guitar cases at their feet, they seem content to have a few grateful audience members at a time leave behind some crumpled bills and a smattering of coins. However, first glances can be deceiving. Many street performers also get paid to work on more traditional stages as well—and do quite well at it. They simply enjoy the unpredictable nature of street performances.

A plethora of entertainers use empty sidewalk corners, parks, or subway stations as their stage. Musicians, mimes, singers, and break-dancers have done it, as have orators, jugglers, poets, living statues, bucket drummers, magicians, puppeteers, acrobats, comedians, and painters. On any given day, street performers must brace themselves for applause, laughter, compliments, personal questions, flirtation, general conversations, as well as jeers, criticisms, and even hostility from complete strangers. Ouch.

Street performers set up at their regular spots (where fans know them), at one of a handful of their favorite spots, or at a completely new spot where they have never worked. Location and time of day affects foot traffic as well as potential income they may receive from passersby. Musicians and singers often self-produce CDs and make them available for sale at the spots where they perform. Business-minded performers like to post signs or pass out business cards to boost interest, fan interaction, and get bookings.

An Extreme Day in the Life

When Natalia Paruz was hit by a taxicab and could no longer continue her dance career, she found a new calling: the saw. After 10 years of playing the musical saw—beginning as a street performer in New York City—the Saw Lady, as she is affectionately known, has since performed on *Good Morning America*, *Live with Regis & Kathy Lee*, in movies, on radio shows such as *A Prairie Home Companion*, and at some of the world's greatest concert halls and clubs. She even has her own CDs, but she still plays on the street. "People have a misconception that street performers cannot get work elsewhere. But many choose to perform on the street. They like it and they crave that kind of interaction. It's an art form all its own, and it is a great community. If you feel lost in a foreign city, just find a spot and start playing. Immediately you will have friends and feel welcome."

Natalia says it is tough to describe an extreme day because of the intense nature of the work. "You've got to really love people. On the street, the audience is right there, in your face." Natalia says she loves every day of her work. "My father says, 'The New York City subway is Natalia's office', and it's true. Today I had an audition for an opera I'm working on and afterward I went to play on the street. Last week I had an audition for Spike TV and afterward, same thing. It's not something I do in-between or until my career picks up. Even when I was a dancer with the Martha Graham Company, I would take a board and tap dance on the street. I love the freedom and I love meeting people." Natalia says that talent, courage, optimism, and a love of people get street performers through the worst of times. "If they tell you you're horrible, it doesn't mean you're horrible. You have to just brush it off. It takes a lot of energy, but you get that back tenfold."

Many street performers also get paid to work on more traditional stages as well—and do quite well at it. They simply enjoy the unpredictable nature of street performances.

Prepare for Success

Wanting to get discovered by a Hollywood agent or major record label is an unrealistic ambition when you are a street performer—though, of course, it is not impossible. Simon & Garfunkel, Bob Dylan, Joni Mitchell, Joan Baez, and the Blue Man Group got their starts performing on the street. The ability to increase exposure, develop a modest fan base, and build the experience, connections, and confidence to secure paid gigs around town is completely within reach for street performers who have raw talent and persistent natures. Success comes for those who prepare themselves before they hit the streets. Popular street performers may receive invitations to perform at events around the cities in which they live and perform, county fairs, and private parties, especially if word gets out that they are available.

Getting Your Foot in the Door

Some street performers believe that they may as well entertain people in the process of practicing their skills. As we said, to get your foot in the door you really just need to have a mobile act and take it to the right place at the right time. Bring materials for networking, along with plenty of water and food. Knowing of a good spot for a bathroom break isn't a bad idea either. Some areas may forbid street performers or require you to have a permit—be sure to check before you set up.

Biggest Challenges and Best Perks

Did we mention the importance of being able to maintain your composure, no matter what the general public might throw at you (literally)? Thieves have been known to target performers for their earnings or props. Unpredictable income, fluctuating audience sizes and interest, and a wide range of good and bad days are some of the greatest challenges. Weather can also literally dampen spirits and close a show prematurely.

For all of the hecklers and grumps who street performers run into, there are even more supportive and appreciative audience members; the nice audience members far outweigh losers who want to take their anger out on the first available target. Meeting fans who admire what you're trying to do will enhance your love of performing.

PROFESSIONAL PROFILE
Avg. salary: Varies

JARGON
Busker A person who performs an art in public places for monetary donations

ARE YOU INTERESTED IN?
Music, acting, dancing

RELATED COLLEGE MAJORS
Performance arts, theater, dance, music

FOR MORE INFORMATION
Busker Central:
www.buskercentral.com

The Performers Network:
www.performers.net

Professional Street Performers Association:
www.cafepress.com

TATTOO ARTIST/BODY PIERCER

A (Relatively) Typical Day in the Life

Tattoo artists use skin as their canvas. They are often open-minded, wonderfully artistic individuals whose success stems from raw talent combined with years of hard work and dedication to the craft. Body piercers share an equal passion for their job. Both professionals see body modification as a form of self-expression for people of all ages and walks of life. Because of the strong overlap of clientele, some tattoo artists are also skilled at body piercing.

Most tattoo artists work in small studios with a handful of other artists. A clean, safe work environment is essential to attracting clients. Each artist must know how to set up and operate a tattoo machine (also called a tattoo gun) and be familiar with inks, medical supplies, and sanitation equipment. Artists showcase their specialties in portfolios so others can look at their best work.

Sitting in the same position for hours is all in a day's work for tattoo artists. Piercers have it a little easier, since nose and eyebrow piercings take only a few minutes. Tattoo artists have to create work of arts under pressure, which may include clients who are screaming, crying, and squirming or have brought their friends to watch, comment, or tease. Focus, patience, and an ability to communicate with different types of people are essential. There may be lulls

An Extreme Day in the Life

Jon Lane, who is known as Jon Jon, is a 25-year-old tattoo artist from England, who works at Cutting Edge studio in New York City. He has succeeded through hard work and extreme days. He says, "In 2004, I worked my first tattoo convention in Woodstock, New York. It was intimidating because there were artists from all over the country. On Friday, we set up our booth and started work right away. I brought my friend Rob Huller from New York and together we designed a tattoo for his thigh—a huge skull with an open mouth blowing smoke all around his leg. The tattoo was so big that I had to special order a box of needles I had never used before, which basically look like half-inch chisels. Within minutes, the tattoo was already taking great shape. It wasn't long before we had a crowd around the table and I could hear people saying, 'What's that needle he's using?' and, 'Wow, look at that crazy skull, man. That's cool!' I felt great. We were doing this amazing tattoo really fast with this crazy needle that I never used before and people were loving it. That night, hanging out with other tattoo artists, people kept stopping to compliment my wife Holly's tattoo, which I had done earlier that year. One was a tattoo artist named James Kern, whose work is truly amazing. To get a compliment from him was an honor. On Saturday, Holly and Rob went to enter the contests. Holly entered her flower for small color and Rob entered for best in show. On Sunday, I had a couple small tattoos to do before we left. I had just started my second one when Holly came rushing over with a big smile on her face. She had won second place for small color and Rob took third place best in show. I couldn't believe it: My first convention and I received not one, but two awards. Since then, I've done conventions all over the East Coast. I've continued to win awards for my work, get recognition from other tattoo artists, and make friends along the way."

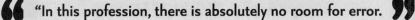
"In this profession, there is absolutely no room for error.

in the day when no one walks through the door. Artists use this time to hone their skills, read industry magazines, and socialize. Some shops take on a lounge-like feel, with clients dropping in to chat and see one another's latest tatt or piercing.

Prepare for Success

Industry pros agree that the wrong way to learn is by buying a kit and attempting to teach yourself. It's simply too dangerous. While there is no formal education or required training for tattoo designer artists, classes or a college degree in fine arts could prove valuable. Most people break into the business through personal connections and networking. In fact, people who want to become tattoo artists start out by being good customers at great studios, where they can build strong relationships and study firsthand. Eventually, they apprentice under experienced artists. Some apprenticeships are free, but others cost thousands of dollars. Find a good mentor who is not out to make some quick cash. A good mentor will teach you not only about tattooing, but also sterilization, safety, business management, and licensing (if required by state law). Practice is very important, as is building an impressive portfolio.

Getting Your Foot in the Door

Safety is the top concern for studios—the safety of each artist and client. Beyond that, artists must be prepared to keep up with trends, styles, and techniques by attending conventions and networking. Even successful artists practice often and strive to be featured in specialty publications. Celebrity clients are another boon to portfolios. With experience, artists and piercers become faster, more efficient, and more consistent. They also develop the business savvy to open up their own shops.

Biggest Challenges and Best Perks

Much of the challenge of becoming a tattoo artist of body piercer involves getting started. Creating the right opportunities to become work full-time takes time, drive, and commitment. In this profession, there is absolutely no room for error. Everyone has seen a less-than-stellar tattoo or piercing—it's tragic. The art of tattooing takes a long time to master and can be very costly to pursue. Unhappy clients and long stretches of little or no business are other hurdles that you have to overcome in this career.

It's a great compliment for an artist to have his or her work displayed on someone else's body—possibly forever! Tattoo artists can be almost completely sure that their work will live on. Tattoo artists and body piercers meet a constant stream of interesting clients.

TV ANCHOR/HOST

A (Relatively) Typical Day in the Life

Actor meets broadcast journalist in a TV anchor/host. TV anchors play themselves on television and their job is to keep the emphasis on the news or human-interest stories they present. Their job is usually one in which they can grow and develop over a long period of time.

People break into the career through many means. Conan O'Brien spent eight years as a writer for television shows such as *Saturday Night Live* and *The Simpsons*. He also did occasional improv comedy before starting his career as a host on *Late Night with Conan O'Brien* in 1993. David Letterman worked as a radio talk show host and on an Indianapolis television station as a local anchor and weatherman. Both longed for a brighter spotlight and went all out to get it.

On any given day, a TV anchor may be called upon to write, report, and package a news story and to improvise witty banter at the beginning of a show, interview guests, and travel far and wide to get a story. Their personalities need to be charismatic, inquisitive, and assertive. They should be flexible and cooperative because they will have to work with producers, crew, hair and makeup artists, other hosts, guests, and fans. They must be articulate public speakers who can talk to anyone about anything, including controversial or taboo topics. It's important for TV anchors to remain professional while still retaining their trademark personalities. TV anchors can't have stars in their eyes when they meet Johnny Depp or hem and haw about asking Jennifer Anniston whether she's planning to have a baby.

To be successful, you need to be able to focus on the big picture and pay attention to detail. You must sharpen your skills while building a name for your employer and yourself. When you are on the air, you'll need to avoid clichés and be memorable, accurate, and ethical. Review tapes of your shows for ways to improve your overall presentation and trademark style.

An Extreme Day in the Life

For nine years, Stacey Gualandi hosted the syndicated newsmagazine show *Inside Edition*. She studied journalism at Miami University and when the movie *Fresh Horses* filmed in Cincinnati where she was living, she jumped at the chance to be Molly Ringwald's stand-in. With that brief taste of life on the set, Stacey moved to LA and found work as a writer and producer before eventually becoming an I.O. host. (This is all from a girl who remembers freezing up in a speech class she took in college.) "In this business, you have to be able to switch on a dime. Every day was different. Even if you thought you knew what you were going to do that day, you could get a call at 5:00 A.M. telling you to get on a plane to Vegas and go cover a story. You might do a . . . story one day about a cop's dog getting shot in the line of duty and the next day you're reporting from the Super Bowl or covering the Grammy [awards]. Often you're strapped for support staff and competing with six other shows just like yours to get the scoop, all while trying to look good. I look back and it was an amazing experience and I'm proud of what I did. But at the time, my head was about to explode."

Pressure to get the scoop and deliver it in the most entertaining way possible is intense.

Prepare for Success

A degree in communications or broadcast journalism gets you off to a good start. While in college, secure a position at the school's radio or television station and possibly on the campus newspaper as a reporter. Consider taking an acting classes to help give you poise. Joining an improv group can help you think on your feet, an essential skill in this profession. Looking like a million bucks helps, especially if you're moving to Los Angeles where most of the jobs are.

Getting Your Foot in the Door

At least one internship or part-time job in radio or TV will provide insight into the business, give you some hands-on experience, and a handful of professional contacts. The bigger and more well-known the station the better. Good references may be more valuable than an outstanding resume or audition tape. It's a tough arena in which to land a good first job without a personal connection. In the process of building your career, you must distinguish yourself from the crowd. Never be shy about self-promotion.

Biggest Challenges and Best Perks

The entertainment industry can be an amazing or a terrible place to work, depending on the day. Mostly, it is amazing. Even your greatest challenges—interviewing celebrities, looking fabulous on and off camera, flying from city to city to follow the news—have a glamorous vibe. On tough days, pressure to get the scoop and deliver it in the most entertaining way possible is intense. You won't find much downtime or alone time. Deadlines may seem unreasonable, hours are long, and competition is so fierce that even when you have a good position, people may try to steal it out from under you. It takes guts, confidence, talent, and determination to keep your chin up. Many TV anchors get to enjoy parties, travel, meet people, and have varying levels of fame. The long hours and hectic schedules pay off for people who love a steady job in the limelight. Pay and opportunities increase with experience.

PROFESSIONAL PROFILE

Avg. starting salary: $22,350

Avg. salary after 5 years: $30,510

Avg. salary 10 to 15 years: $47,170

Salary also varies based on the size of the market, network, and popularity of the host.

JARGON

The call Directions that begin a take (e.g., roll sound or roll camera)

Eye line The direction in which an interviewee should look offscreen so it matches the shot's point of view

M&E Stands for music and effects

ARE YOU INTERESTED IN?

Media and entertainment, news

RELATED COLLEGE MAJORS

Broadcast journalism, communications, journalism

FOR MORE INFORMATION

Broadcast Education Association:
www.beaweb.org

National Association of Broadcasters:
www.nab.org

Radio-Television News Directors Association:
www.rtnda.com

BONUS INTERVIEW SECTION

Many of the jobs in the book involve some element of entrepreneurial work, which can cover everything from writing to political organizing to conflict mediation. For that reason, we thought it might be helpful to hear from some other folks about what it takes to make a comfortable living as a permanent work-for-hire. These testimonials are sure to give you further insights into life as your own boss, and more than a little bit of inspiration.

FICTION WRITER

Barbara Moss, author of *Little Edens* says: "The standard advice for aspiring writers is this: Don't write unless you have to, but if you have to, do it with your whole heart. In other words, persevere. This is a difficult and uncertain profession, and success rarely comes right away. Be prepared to write through dry patches and inevitable rejection, always with the goal of perfecting your work, of bringing the words on the page closer to the vision in your head. No matter how crowded your schedule, try to carve out time to write each day. And when you're not writing, read. The writers you admire will be your best teachers. Read first to absorb the story, and then to analyze how the writer achieved the effects that drew you in. Don't worry about being overly influenced. If your talent is real, you will find your own voice." According to Barbara, camaraderie is also very important for writers: "Because writing is a solitary profession, it's important to seek out others to share your work with and to give you honest feedback: a friend, a teacher, a writers' group, a class. The ideal reader will have some receptivity to your writing, but will also be able to view it with cool objectivity. In return, be open to what is offered, and learn to evaluate it, to sift through both praise and criticism for the gold that will enrich your work. Eventually you may want to consider an extended workshop or a post-graduate MFA program; these are competitive and costly, but they provide a community of serious writers and a wide network of contacts. Non-writers sometimes think that producing fiction is a simple process akin to automatic writing: Get an idea, record it, and voila! a book. They have no idea of the skill and effort and time it takes to create something that lives on the page. For most writers, revision is a constant process. There's some truth to the writer's cliché, 'It's all a draft till you die.' And often this work is done with no promise of remuneration: you won't be getting a stipend while you go through the long labor of mastering your art. Another misconception is that publication guarantees instant fame and fortune. The literary journals that publish most emerging writers' stories have small circulations and smaller budgets; many don't pay at all, and even the most established don't pay much. Of course, the exposure is valuable in itself: when your work is in the world, things can happen. Occasionally a literary novel will reap both critical acclaim and popular success, but in this culture, that combination is a rarity. Very few writers of literary fiction expect that their work will make them rich. Money, when it comes, is an unexpected gift."

According to Barbara, "The best aspect of writing fiction is the sheer exhilaration of creating a world out of your imagination. The characters take on a life that seems to be independent of you, and yet you've made them. Things float up out of your subconscious that you had no idea were there. And the shaping process is very exciting—-taking this raw material and rendering it in words. It's the ultimate high, and I never let myself forget what a privilege it is to do this work.

The worst aspects are the isolation and the constant self-editing and self-criticism—the vision of perfection and the falling-short. In this precarious profession there are very few plateaus. Each new project, each day's work, is a challenge, but the moments of triumph are sweeter because of that.

And then, once the book comes out, there's the marketing process—a whole other subject. These days, writers have to work hard to publicize their own work. The transition from producing the work in private, in this most introverted of professions, to hawking it in public can be a difficult one."

TRAVEL WRITER

Bill Hinchberger, founder and chief editor of the highly praised "Hip Gringo's Guide to Brazil," got his start freelance writing in the 1980s: "I got into freelance writing because I didn't want a job but needed to work. When I started, we thought things were bad. Unfortunately, I have to say that they've gotten progressively worse. The publishing industry has become somewhat dysfunctional. I would like to be more encouraging, but frankly I wouldn't easily encourage anyone to begin a career as a freelancer today. Indeed I'm becoming more of an entrepreneur than a pure freelancer with BrazilMax.com. Despite my warnings, some people will still enthusiastically enter the field. Here are some suggestions: Get a specialty (business, health, etc, or a geographic focus if you want to work abroad), and mine your personal contacts to find sympathetic editors. When you know the editor, or are referred by a trusted friend or colleague, everything goes more smoothly. Otherwise your queries usually end up in the slush pile. You must be self-motivated, thick-skinned, and able to not take rejection personally. Most of your proposals will be rejected, no matter how good you are and how great your ideas are." As for the best and worst aspects of freelancing, according to Bill, the answer is people, people, people. "People pay me to learn, experience things, and explain them to others. I've done and seen some amazing things. Worst: Responses from editors like this one I got recently: 'This is a fantastic story. Sadly, we are not allowed to buy any freelance the rest of the year.' Two, falling payment rates, increasingly obnoxious contracts and working with overburdened editors who are often inexperienced and low paid."

"However, many interesting things have happened to me on the job. I've ridden through the streets of Salvador atop a 'trio elétrico' (the sound trucks that Carnival bands use to roll through the streets), and I've danced in the winning Samba School of Rio's Carnival parade. I've slugged through the Amazonian mud and crouched in canoes with native fishermen after the pirarucu, the world's largest freshwater fish. I've chased down the last remaining speakers of dying Amazon languages. I've toured the mega-dam Itaipú with company officials and flown over nearby Iguaçu Falls in a military plane. I've ridden on horseback through the plains of Rio Grande do Sul. I've witnessed the São João mid-winter extravaganza in Caruaru and the post-Christmas Wise Men Festival in Minas Gerais. I've surfed the primo waves of Santa Catarina. I've hung out in the shantytowns of São Paulo, Rio de Janeiro and Salvador. I've flown over São Paulo in a helicopter courtesy of a bank executive. I've interviewed everyone from the late author Jorge Amado to President Lula. Not only that, but I practice the Brazilian martial art capoeira twice a week."

INDEPENDENT PRODUCER

Daniela Ryan, producer at Basra Entertainment, acknowledges that there is no "easy" way to break into production. "It is not an easy field to get into at any level by anyone. Even Stephen Spielberg, in the studio that he created, gets 'nos'. Here is the first thing, if you can possibly think of anything else you would like to do then go do that. At *most* levels in the entertainment industry there is not very much money, glamour or appreciation. It can be long hours and tedious work, and many, many highly-talented and creative people have gone years without a shred of success. My best advice is to get your emotional self in order as soon and as thoroughly as possible before you step foot in Hollywood, or New York. You will be rejected often in small and large ways. Once that is done try to hone in on what aspect of the business you think you'd like to be in. If you are not sure take the first job in the industry you are offered—no one will bat an eye if you quit in 6 months and move on to something better. Be persistent. A 'no' sucks, it can hurt, it can send you reeling (no pun intended) but, as a very wise and talented producer once said to me, it only takes one 'yes'. Then get yourself ready to deliver the most brilliant work you can muster... and then start the process all over again."

What's worse than a world of no's? Daniela feels it's the excruciatingly slow pace of production. "The worst part of the job is not the many 'nos' as one would immediately think, but how glacial the whole process of getting a movie made is. If you are producing for a local television station or a show, where they are in constant need of shows to fill their schedule, you get your marching orders, you produce the show and you may or may not like it. But if you are an independent producer—which everyone of them is until they have a show on the air and then once it's off they are independent again—it can take years to get a film off the ground. If you are producing TV shows then you can come up with your best idea ever, share it with all your friends at dinner who *love* it, shop it to all the networks and cable channels and they can all say 'no', and it is effectively dead, without possibility of resurrection. Then next year, the exact same idea can be the season's biggest hit. There is no way to tell what will be hot and what will suck, it is how the cookie crumbles. It is sort of like being a kid and learning the hard knocks of life over and over and over. Sometimes the reasons are just not ascertainable. The best part of my job is that it is extremely fun when you are working on a production. Long hours, lots of work, but if you are a creative person and you like problem solving it can be exciting and rewarding. There is nothing like seeing your first credit roll by.

For Daniela, the most interesting aspect of the job is the people she meets: "Meeting other creative people and having that meeting come around to be mutually beneficial in work is great. It is a small world and you just never know who will have the next great show, or if your turn is next. If you want predictable, this is not the business for you. It is the constant possibility dangling in front of you that makes the business fascinating."

RADIO PRODUCER

Ben Manilla, founder of Ben Manilla Productions, has extensive experience in radio production, and recommends that radio production hopefuls be ready and willing to do whatever is necessary to catch their break: "Be willing to do anything to get in the door. Most operations will allow team members to contribute. So even if you don't have the dream job, if you're fun to be around, excited about what's happening, and offer ideas at appropriate times—you will be noticed and before long, find your proper niche. Also, read the trades—Current, Association of Independents in Radio, Radio and Records, All Access—some of it will be in jargon and may hard to follow, but if you are up on what's happening people will want to confide in you. The best thing about my job is that radio is an incredibly creative medium. Whenever I'm allowed the freedom to be creative, I get tremendous job satisfaction. On the other hand, the worst aspect is being forced into the position to pay people small amounts of money for large amounts of work. Also having to dun people into paying me for work they've contracted and I've delivered."

What's most interesting about Ben's job? "Because I have chosen to be a generalist, I have learned about fascinating things: Children's literature, philosophy, Olympic sports, gay travel... things I might never have pursued if left to my own devices. Truly, the best thing about my job is the opportunity it offers to meet interesting people, ask them probing questions, and be paid for it."

APPENDICES

APPENDIX I:
CRASH COURSE IN NETWORKING

Everywhere you go is a new opportunity to meet people.

But meeting them is just one part of the important equation of networking. It looks something like this: Meeting people + making meaningful connections + forming a valuable relationship with potential future benefits for both parties = networking.

Books have been written on the topic. (And Hollywood couldn't function without it!) The authors might call it schmoozing or building business relationships or something else entirely. But its fairly straightforward formula is one of the most important tools not only in job hunting and advancing your career but also in life. Knowing how to network can give you a leg up in finding an apartment, buying a car, or putting together a dream vacation. Here, though, we're going to focus on the aspects of networking which relate to your job prospects.

You've probably already been engaging in your own form of networking. Scoring an invite to the best New Year's Eve party, getting a new friend to let you borrow his new snowboard, finding out about a lead on a great summer job or a simple head's up about a great sale at your favorite store. You've met people (maybe in person, maybe on Myspace.com), bonded over a common interest, kept in touch, and reaped the benefits of a good schmooze. Sometimes these acquaintances turn into true friends. Sometimes they remain contacts on the amicable fringes of your social circle. Either way, take note of our how-to tips below. Honing the skills that will enable you to form a support network of mutually positive relationships will prove priceless from here on out.

- **Get a professional sounding e-mail address, and check it often.** Use an e-mail "signature" at the bottom with your name, address, and phone number for easy reference. Use this account for all networking opportunities. We don't need to tell you to leave the colored fonts and backgrounds and emoticons for e-mails to friends.

- **Get simple business cards made.** It's an easy, fast, economical way of doing business and makes it look like you know what you're doing. You don't need to have a title or even a job to have personal business cards printed. It looks better than scribbling your info on an old receipt or a bulky java jacket.

- **Become an expert in the art of conversation.** The content and quality of your conversations matter. Pay attention to styles you like and dislike and adapt your own.

- **Follow up.** The best networkers—and the people at the top of their fields—know how to dash off a quick e-mail after they have met someone reaffirming it was good to make their acquaintance. They are also pros at writing thank-you notes to anyone who has gone out of their way even the slightest bit to help them out. And when someone asks for a favor from them, they do it quickly and gladly. They are impression-makers who know that little gestures mean a lot in the networking world. They plant networking seeds and when people hear of something that might be a good fit for them, they are first on their list of good candidates to call.

- **Put yourself out there.** Get involved in at least one high-profile professional or community organization. Look for groups with whom you share a common background, trait, or career goal. Groups that share your ethnicity, religion, and/or personal hobbies are good places to start.

- **Attend events.** Colleges and even some high schools hold networking events, job fairs, and resume and interviewing workshops. Take advantage of these resources.

- **Keep in touch.** Be that person who calls, e-mails, or checks in with people you know once in a while for a quick "Hi, how are things?" or "Did you catch the game on Saturday?" or "Want to grab lunch next week?" No one appreciates the networking wannabe who only gets in touch when they need a favor or some insider information.

- **The Internet makes it easy.** Take advantage of the message boards you frequent and the forums you belong to. This can be a good starting point for meeting people in your field of interest.

- **But don't be afraid of the phone.** When you call, always ask someone "Do you have a moment?" or, "Have I caught you at a good time?" Keep it brief during business hours and stay on topic.

- **Put other people together when it is mutually beneficial to them.** Helping other people connect over a common interest or need increases your network and boosts your reputation on the schmooze circuit.

- **Family, friends, and everyone else.** Don't be afraid to use every connection you have. Networking is no longer just accepted, it's expected. If you know, for example, that you're capable of doing a certain job, there's no harm in making a call to someone you know at the company and using your connection to get your resume in front of the right person. Look polished and professional at the interview, and make all the right moves that any candidate without an inside connection would. Don't assume you'll get the job, even though you have a personal connection. The applicant pool is filled with great choices. If you do get it, do your very best, remembering that your work ethic, appearance, and quality will reflect on the person who was kind enough to recommend you.

- **Yes, your parents are part of your network.** Here are two adults with years of experience in the workplace and in life. They not only have words of advice on the best ways to meet, greet, and mingle, but they also know an entire circle of other adults. If they know someone who can help you, all the better. Some day when you're established, you can do the same for your own children.

- **Don't let anyone accuse you of being a brown-noser.** Networking is an adult way of life and has nothing to do with being teacher's pet. If you are savvy in making connections and building a network, others may be jealous. Whatever!

APPENDIX II:
RESUMES FOR CREATIVE PEOPLE

Many of the jobs profiled in this book are in creative fields. This entry-level resume belongs to a fictional journalism grad who combined a summer internship during college, experience on high school and college newspapers, volunteer work, and a few awards to create a substantial and professional resume ready to secure an entry-level job in journalism. While this resume aims to land a writing job, the theories and tactics we used to create it can be applied to any number of desk and non-desk jobs in creative fields.

Here is a list of the resume's key features, and a brief explanation of why they work well. See each of these features labeled on the resume below.

KEY FEATURES:

1. Contact information is concise, with only one phone number and one, professional-sounding e-mail address.

2. Headline font (Century Gothic) is slightly unusual but easy to read. Used in moderation.

3. Body text font is standard and one employers have seen before (Times New Roman).

4. Two-column format is different but works for this person who is looking for a job in newspapers.

5. An objective helps to quickly explain the kind of job you are looking for.

6. Experience is grouped by type and then chronologically within that category. This helps employers see that experience is varied rather than jumping around chronologically through different types of experience.

7. Rather than announce an internship, play up the field and the experience.

8. High school experience was added because it was significant and career-related.

9. Results of efforts add weight to the experience.

10. Volunteer work counts, too. Use it to round out your resume and develop new skills.

11. Make efforts to take on a summer or part-time job that is relevant to your career; make sure it appears on your resume.

12. When your experience is limited, awards and accomplishments can boost your background and show potential.

13. Include all computer skills, especially if mentioned in the job description for jobs to which you're applying.

A final point: You'll note that there was no mention of references on the resume. An employer will ask for them if needed. Have them ready to send out.

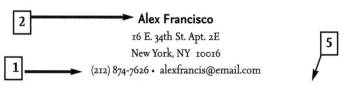

Alex Francisco

16 E. 34th St. Apt. 2E
New York, NY 10016
(212) 874-7626 • alexfrancis@email.com

A diverse background in writing, editing, and online content development has honed strong written and verbal communication skills, a sense of teamwork, and the ability to convey information to varied audiences with creativity and innovation. Seeking an entry-level journalism position in a deadline-driven environment.

Book publishing

The Princeton Review, Editorial Intern, 5/06-9/06.
Assisted editors with research, copy editing/proofreading, and administrative tasks for education and career books published in conjunction with Random House. Managed mass mailings of survey materials and updated database of college majors. Wrote a weekly blog on finding the right career from the eyes of a college student. Developed a spreadsheet system to track survey responses. Participated in editorial meetings with creative initiatives.

News writing

West Side Daily, Managing Editor, NYC, NY. 9/04-1/07.
Three years experience on staff at West Side University's daily newspaper. Covered the city beat as a staff reporter and earned the Managing Editor position by senior year. Responsible for overseeing paper's budget, assigning and editing stories, and working with production staff on layout.

What's News? Staff Writer, Copper Canyon, CA, 02/04-1/06.
Covered sports and after-school activities for monthly newspaper of Copper Canyon High School. Took photos to accompany stories, proofed paper before it went to press. Pitched and wrote feature stories, including an expose on the politics of the school's soccer try-outs, which was picked up and reprinted by the Copper Canyon weekly paper, *The Canyon Gazette*.

Website content

ChildrensDiscoveryCamp.com, Content Developer, NYC, 1/06-present.
Worked with senior coordinator of nonprofit camp for inner-city youth to launch website. Developed, organized, and wrote content to create a dynamic, up-to-date website with distinct sections for campers, parents, educators, and philanthropists. Camp experienced a record 30 percent jump in fundraising efforts in the year following website's launch.

Administrative and proofreading

The Canyon Gazette, Administrative assistant and proofreader, Summers 2005 and 2006.
Learned newspaper business firsthand at hometown weekly newspaper. First summer compiled calendar listings and classifieds while managing the front desk. Summer 2006 was given additional pre-press proofreading and fact-checking duties for all sections.

Education

West Side University, New York, NY. 9/03-6/07.
Magna Cum Laude, Bachelor of Science in Journalism. Political science minor.

Awards and accomplishments

Student Journalist of the Year, 2006.
West Side University's award to one School of Journalism student each academic year, based upon a combination of grades, coursework, professor feedback, demonstrated talent, and dedication to the field.

Community Volunteer Corps, Secretary, 9/05-6/07.
Leadership position for on-campus volunteer organization involved publishing meeting notes, updating website, and promoting events.

Philip Johnson Memorial Award Scholarship, 2005.
Awarded to one West Side University student each year for excellence in in-depth news reporting. Story on New York City's police department's involvement with the school to combat campus crime earned this award.

Computer skills

Word processing expertise with MAC/PC.
Spreadsheet experience with Excel.
Page layout experience with Quark Xpress.
Also proficient in: HTML, Photoshop, and PowerPoint.

Other skills

Spanish. Fluent in speaking and writing.

APPENDIX III:
POWER JARGON

"POWER JARGON": LEARNING TO TALK THE TALK

Whenever you enter a new industry or company, you'll quickly find that each one has its own unique vernacular you must understand—and eventually adopt. Paying attention to the language insiders use to describe their industry and their specific roles should be part of your job-search preparation. If used subtly and judiciously, incorporating "power jargon" into your resume, cover letter, and interview can help influence the decision-maker in your favor; if you speak someone's language, they'll probably—perhaps subconsciously—consider you one of their own.

Interestingly, the purpose of power jargon is slightly different depending on the stage of the job-search process you're in when you use it. In the context of a resume, the purpose of industry jargon is getting your resume noticed—either by the human being who has the unenviable task of screening through thousands of resumes and deciding which ones make the first cut, or by the non-human resume scanner whose job it is to do basically the same thing by identifying and counting specific key words in resumes. In the context of a cover letter or an interview, the purpose is less to get noticed than, ironically enough, to blend in. And once you arrive for your first day of work, the purpose of power jargon is knowing what the heck you're supposed to be doing.

To illustrate the importance of understanding jargon before your first day on the job, consider the experience endured by Monica—now a 30-year old associate editor—on her first day of freelance proofreading at a food and wine magazine. "I had no idea that in the magazine biz, the term 'hot' means that something is extremely urgent," she says. "So someone came up to my desk and asked me if I'd finished proofreading a particular story. When I said that I hadn't, she politely reminded me that it was 'pretty hot.' Not knowing what she meant—that I needed to get it done ASAP—I thought to myself, 'What's she making such a big deal about? The story's about *coleslaw* for God's sake—what's so trendy about that?'"

This is why it's important to do your homework early on in the process—preferably before you make contact with a company about a job.

Understanding the importance of key words, however, doesn't give you license to use them recklessly. Power jargon can be, and often is, overused in resumes, obscuring the very credentials the candidate was hoping to highlight in the first place. And if you use jargon without understanding what it means, you may use it in the wrong context and sound uninformed when you intended to sound savvy. Our advice for avoiding potential power-jargon pitfalls? Have someone who's in the know take a look at your resume and cover letter to alert you to any egregious misuses of industry or company terminology. And in the interview, play it safe—your goal is to use power jargon to blend in, not stand out. Overusing jargon (or using it in a forced, contrived way) won't win you any points, especially with hiring managers who've logged countless hours interviewing candidates. Not only will experienced interviewers see right through your attempt to sound like an expert, but they'll often go to great lengths to put you back in your place.

"That happened to me once," says Thomas, an assistant editor for an academic journal. "I was interviewing for my first editorial job, and I mentioned that I was familiar with the *Chicago Manual of Style*. My interviewer said, 'Oh really? Which edition do you normally use?' I was completely stumped. I had no idea which edition it was—I had to look at my copy when I got home (it was 11, incidentally). Even though I had to admit that I didn't know, I got the job anyway. After a few months in the office, I eventually found out that none of the copyeditors knew exactly which version they were using, either. The interviewer had just been doing that to rattle my cage, I guess, and figure out whether I was bluffing."

Even though this story has a happy ending, it still offers a valuable lesson: don't use terminology you don't understand, and if you are asked a question you don't know the answer to, just say that you don't know. If your interviewer calls your bluff, you've not only lost face, but you've potentially lost a job. It's not worth the risk.

WHAT'S THE MAGIC WORD?

In the 1991 remake of the film *Father of the Bride*, Steve Martin's character, George, snoops through the home of his future son-in-law's parents, only to be confronted by a pair of growling, snarling Rottweilers who seem poised to eat him alive. He knows there's a one-word command that will make them go away, but he can't quite remember what it is—only that it begins with "re." He tries a few: "Relent. Re-Recoil . . . Reverse," but they only make the dogs angrier. (The word he was looking for was release). As George found out with the attack dogs, using correct keywords is important. For him, it meant he wouldn't get devoured; for you, it means your resume won't get discarded because you appear not to have experience relevant to a particular job.

Keywords are almost always nouns or short phrases. They name the characteristics, skills, tools, training, and experience of a successful candidate for a particular job. As you may already know, many organizations use resume scanning software to identify qualified candidates among a sea of online applications; by scanning resumes for certain words and phrases, scanning software is intended to streamline the resume review process for time-starved recruiters, who may receive literally thousands of applications for a single job posting. If your target company uses this type of software as a preliminary screening tool, you'll want to be sure your resume includes the relevant key words. The number of "hits" (times the key words appear in any given resume) will often determine which resumes are actually read by a human being.

How do you know which keywords to include? Well, writing a resume in a scanner-friendly way is definitely more an art than a science—and it requires common sense, good judgment, and a little bit of research. Before you submit a resume online, visit the company's website and pay attention to the language used to describe what the company does, what it's looking for in potential employees, and the job requirements it lists for specific positions; the job description and the list of qualifications associated with the position are also great resources when tailoring and tweaking the version of the resume you use.

As is the case with any job-search advice we provide in this guide, it's best to temper your enthusiasm for power jargon with a healthy dose of good judgment. Particularly if you're applying for a position through an on-campus recruiting process or through an internal referral that forwards your correspondence directly to the hiring manager, your resume may be initially reviewed by a human being—not a scanner.

A ROSE BY ANY OTHER NAME . . . MIGHT BE SOMETHING ELSE ENTIRELY

To make matters even more complicated, there are a couple of different levels of jargon you'll need to weed through to use it effectively. There's both industry jargon and company-specific jargon. At the industry level, seemingly identical processes or functions will be described differently depending on the industry in question. For example, book publishing uses different terminology than magazine publishing, and academic and financial publishing each use a different lexicon entirely. If you looked at a "blueline" (the last version of a publication editors have a chance to review before it goes to print) at a magazine publisher, you'd be looking at the "blues," but if you looked at one at an investment bank, you'd probably be looking at a "red." And if you say "blackline" instead of "blueline" because you worked at a law firm one summer and you're still in the habit of saying it, you're going to look pretty silly in your magazine-publishing interview.

At the organizational level, power jargon might include something as seemingly insignificant as the use of acronyms and abbreviations (and it seems the larger the organization, the more acronyms there are to remember). The names of groups, functions, even job titles may be abbreviated so widely within an organization that you'll stand out if you don't use them when you communicate with your potential employer.

Is your head spinning yet? Don't worry. When it comes to power jargon, there are plenty of ways to pick it up so you're at least conversational by the time you apply for a job. When you speak with industry insiders in the context of networking or conducting informational interviews, pay attention to the terminology they use to describe what they do and where they work. (In fact, the ability to pick up on power jargon is one of the many good reasons you should be focused on listening rather than talking when it comes to informational interviews). If your industry insider uses a term you're not familiar with, don't just nod as though you are—ask what it means! Remember, you're not being evaluated during your informational interviews or networking conversations; you're there to learn and ask questions. And if stopping to ask what something means during one of these conversations means you actually know what it means when it comes up later in a job interview, then asking was a worthwhile investment. In addition to one-on-one conversations with insiders, you can pick up power jargon by paying attention to the lingo used in trade publications, on industry-specific websites, and in job listings for similar positions at other companies in the industry.

When it comes time to interview with a specific company, your understanding of that organization's terminology is just as important as your fluency in industry lingo. Before you walk out the door to meet with your prospective employer, you should understand the jargon the company uses in the following contexts:

- **Its name—** Know when a company goes by its initials and when it's abbreviated some other way when its own employees refer to it. We'll illustrate our point using an example from the financial services world: If you were working on Wall Street, you would never call Goldman Sachs or Merrill Lynch "GS" or "ML." If you were an employee—or an industry insider—you'd refer to them as "Goldman" and "Merrill," respectively. However, you would refer to Credit Suisse First Boston as "CSFB."

- **Its job titles—**If everyone at a particular firm always says "RA" instead of "Research Associate," it will ever so subtly work in your favor if you refer to the job that way, too (even though it still might mean "Resident Advisor" to you). The same goes for support roles—sometimes, assistants are just that: assistants. At other organizations, they're called "admins" or "PAs." If you're applying for one of those jobs, know what you'll be called (how else will you know when someone's talking to you?)

- **Its organizational structure and hierarchy—**It sounds almost silly, but pay attention to how employees and insiders refer to the specific department with which you're interviewing. Is the custom publishing department referred to as "custom pub?" Is the book publishing division referred to as "BPD" or simply "books"? Even more importantly, how are roles and job titles described? At some companies, "analyst" is a more senior role than "associate," for example, while at others, the exact opposite is true. Know which level and job title would apply to you; if you don't, your ignorance might be misinterpreted as an inflated ego.

INDEXES

ALPHABETICAL INDEX

Index by Category

Mobile Office

Schmoozing

Travel

Roll Up Your Sleeves

NOTES

NOTES

NOTES

NOTES

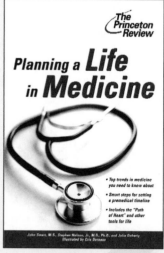